# TREATING
# EATING DISORDERS

# THE JOSSEY-BASS LIBRARY OF CURRENT CLINICAL TECHNIQUE

Irvin D. Yalom, General Editor

NOW AVAILABLE

*Treating Alcoholism*
Stephanie Brown, Editor

*Treating Schizophrenia*
Sophia Vinogradov, Editor

*Treating Women Molested in Childhood*
Catherine Classen, Editor

*Treating Depression*
Ira D. Glick, Editor

*Treating Eating Disorders*
Joellen Werne, Editor

*Treating Dissociative Identity Disorder*
James L. Spira, Editor

FORTHCOMING

*Treating Adolescents*
Hans Steiner, Editor

*Treating the Elderly*
Javaid I. Sheikh, Editor

*Treating Posttraumatic Stress Disorder*
Charles R. Marmar, Editor

*Treating Anxiety Disorders*
Walton T. Roth, Editor

*Treating Couples*
Hilda Kessler, Editor

*Treating Difficult Personality Disorders*
Michael Rosenbluth, Editor

# TREATING
# EATING DISORDERS

**A VOLUME IN THE JOSSEY-BASS
LIBRARY OF CURRENT CLINICAL TECHNIQUE**

**Joellen Werne,** EDITOR
**Irvin D. Yalom,** GENERAL EDITOR

Jossey-Bass Publishers • San Francisco

# Coventry University

Substantial discounts on bulk quantities of Jossey-Bass books are available to corporations, professional associations, and other organizations. For details and discount information, contact the special sales department at Jossey-Bass Inc., Publishers. (415) 433–1740; Fax (800) 605–2665.

For sales outside the United States, please contact your local Simon & Schuster International Office.

 Manufactured in the United States of America on Lyons Falls Pathfinder Tradebook. This paper is acid-free and 100 percent totally chlorine-free.

## Library of Congress Cataloging-in-Publication Data

Treating eating disorders/edited by Joellen Werne.
   p.   cm.—(A volume in the Jossey-Bass library of current clinical technique)
   Includes index.
   ISBN 0-7879-0159-8 (alk. paper)
   1. Eating disorders—Treatment. 2. Eating disorders—Treatment—Case studies. I. Werne, Joellen, date–. II. Series: Jossey-Bass library of current clinical technique.
RC552. E18T74 1996
616.85'2606—dc20
                                        95-35007
                                            CIP

FIRST EDITION
*HB Printing* 10 9 8 7 6 5 4 3 2 1

PG. 971

25/6/97

# CONTENTS

# FOREWORD

At a recent meeting of clinical practitioners, a senior practitioner declared that more change had occurred in his practice of psychotherapy in the past year than in the twenty preceding years. Nodding assent, the others all agreed.

And was that a good thing for their practice? A resounding "No!" Again, unanimous concurrence—too much interference from managed care; too much bureaucracy; too much paper work; too many limits set on fees, length, and format of therapy; too much competition from new psychotherapy professions.

Were these changes a good or a bad thing for the general public? Less unanimity on this question. Some pointed to recent positive developments. Psychotherapy was becoming more mainstream, more available, and more acceptable to larger segments of the American public. It was being subjected to closer scrutiny and accountability—uncomfortable for the practitioner but, if done properly, of potential benefit to the quality and efficiency of behavioral health care delivery.

But without dissent this discussion group agreed—and every aggregate of therapists would concur—that astounding changes are looming for our profession: changes in the reasons that clients request therapy; changes in the perception and practice of mental health care; changes in therapeutic theory and technique; and changes in the training, certification, and supervision of professional therapists.

From the perspective of the clientele, several important currents are apparent. A major development is the de-stigmatization of psychotherapy. No longer is psychotherapy invariably a hush-hush affair, laced with shame and conducted in offices with separate entrance and exit doors to prevent the uncomfortable possibility of clients meeting one another.

Today such shame and secrecy have been exploded. Television talk shows—Oprah, Geraldo, Donahue—have normalized psychopathology and psychotherapy by presenting a continuous public parade of dysfunctional human situations: hardly a day passes without television fare of confessions and audience inter-actions with dead-beat fathers, sex addicts, adult children of alco-holics, battering husbands and abused wives, drug dealers and substance abusers, food bingers and purgers, thieving children, abusing parents, victimized children suing parents.

The implications of such de-stigmatization have not been lost on professionals who no longer concentrate their efforts on the increasingly elusive analytically suitable neurotic patient. Clin-ics everywhere are dealing with a far broader spectrum of prob-lem areas and must be prepared to offer help to substance abusers and their families, to patients with a wide variety of eat-ing disorders, adult survivors of incest, victims and perpetrators of domestic abuse. No longer do trauma victims or substance abusers furtively seek counseling. Public awareness of the nox-ious long-term effects of trauma has been so sensitized that there is an increasing call for public counseling facilities and a grow-ing demand, as well, for adequate counseling provisions in health care plans.

The mental health profession is changing as well. No longer is there such automatic adoration of lengthy "depth" psy-chotherapy where "deep" or "profound" is equated with a focus on the earliest years of the patient's life. The contemporary field is more pluralistic: many diverse approaches have proven thera-peutically effective and the therapist of today is more apt to tai-lor the therapy to fit the particular clinical needs of each patient.

In past years there was an unproductive emphasis on territo-riality and on the maintaining of hierarchy and status—with the more prestigious professions like psychiatry and doctoral-level psychologists expending considerable energy toward excluding master's level therapists. But those battles belong more to the psychotherapists of yesterday; today there is a significant shift toward a more collaborative interdisciplinary climate.

Managed care and cost containment is driving some of these changes. The role of the psychiatrist has been particularly affected as cost efficiency has decreed that psychiatrists will less frequently deliver psychotherapy personally but, instead, limit their activities to supervision and to psychopharmacological treatment.

In its efforts to contain costs, managed care has asked therapists to deliver a briefer, focused therapy. But gradually managed care is realizing that the bulk of mental health treatment cost is consumed by inpatient care and that outpatient treatment, even long-term therapy, is not only salubrious for the patient but far less costly. Another looming change is that the field is turning more frequently toward the group therapies. How much longer can we ignore the many comparative research studies demonstrating that the group therapy format is equally or more effective than higher cost individual therapies?

Some of these cost-driven edicts may prove to be good for the patients; but many of the changes that issue from medical model mimicry—for example, efforts at extreme brevity and overly precise treatment plans and goals that are inappropriate to the therapy endeavor and provide only the illusion of efficiency—can hamper the therapeutic work. Consequently, it is of paramount importance that therapists gain control of their field and that managed care administrators not be permitted to dictate how psychotherapy or, for that matter, any other form of health care be conducted. That is one of the goals of this series of texts: to provide mental health professionals with such a deep grounding in theory and such a clear vision of effective therapeutic technique that they will be empowered to fight confidently for the highest standards of patient care.

The Jossey-Bass Library of Current Clinical Technique is directed and dedicated to the frontline therapist—to master's and doctoral-level clinicians who personally provide the great bulk of mental health care. The purpose of this entire series is to offer state-of-the-art instruction in treatment techniques for the most commonly encountered clinical conditions. Each volume offers a focused theoretical background as a foundation for practice and then dedicates itself to the practical task of what to do for the patient—how to assess, diagnose, and treat.

I have selected volume editors who are either nationally recognized experts or are rising young stars. In either case, they possess a comprehensive view of their specialty field and have selected leading therapists of a variety of persuasions to describe their therapeutic approaches.

Although all the contributors have incorporated the most recent and relevant clinical research in their chapters, the emphasis in these volumes is the practical technique of therapy. We shall offer specific therapeutic guidelines, and augment concrete suggestions with the liberal use of clinical vignettes and detailed case histories. Our intention is not to impress or to awe the reader, and not to add footnotes to arcane academic debates. Instead, each chapter is designed to communicate guidelines of immediate pragmatic value to the practicing clinician. In fact, the general editor, the volume editors, and the chapter contributors have all accepted our assignments for that very reason: a rare opportunity to make a significant, immediate, and concrete contribution to the lives of our patients.

Irvin D. Yalom, M.D.
*Professor Emeritus of Psychiatry*
*Stanford University School of Medicine*

# INTRODUCTION

## Joellen Werne

One of my earliest teachers in psychiatry was a professor known for his clinical wisdom, crustiness, and certain minor oddities of behavior. A colleague and I met with him weekly for supervision—reading, in turn, the "process notes" of our most recent therapy session and awaiting, somewhat anxiously, his comments.

Invariably, our professor seemed to drift off to some far distant place as we faithfully reported our patients' distressed meanderings. From time to time, however, he would sit bolt upright, murmuring quizzically, "For example?" Usually we had none, for we had not stopped to inquire of the patient what specifically she or he had in mind about the feeling or concern under scrutiny. More and more often, in the course of our supervision, I found myself asking that same question during my meetings with patients. Almost always, it was illuminating—for both of us—whether there was a concrete answer or not.

In the pedagogic spirit of my old professor, I have invited distinguished clinicians, all of whom are experts in the field of eating disorders, to share with us their approaches by presenting detailed examples of their work with patients. I have chosen therapists who represent diverse points of view and who practice different kinds of therapy. Many have made major contributions to theory and research. They hold in common an appreciation of the multifaceted nature of their patients' difficulties and a knowledgeable, creative therapeutic stance. I hope, as their stories unfold, you will find particularly useful the ways in which these experienced clinicians integrate concepts and techniques from several perspectives and effectively combine, as needed, more than one therapeutic modality into a coherent treatment approach.

Professional interest in the eating disorders has grown significantly within the past two decades, matching an increase in the prevalence of these problems. Between 4 and 6 percent of women in the Western (and Westernized) world now meet the criteria for a formal diagnosis. Many more, who may not fit all these conditions, are seriously troubled by disordered eating and self-critical attitudes toward their size and shape. *Anorexic* has even entered the vernacular, applied equally to the dieting teenager and the successful fashion model. *Bulimia nervosa*, the binge/purge syndrome, has become an open secret on most college campuses. It is also the hidden shame of a growing number of men and women from all walks of life. Those who struggle with *binge eating* often have an additional burden to bear: the social stigma of being overweight.

We now have a varied repertoire of treatments from which to choose: a range of individual, family, and group therapies—often a combination of several—that may be conducted in office or clinic, day hospital or inpatient settings. This was not the case when I began my training twenty-four years ago.

As a prelude to the tales told in this volume, I would like to share with you my first experience working with a patient who had anorexia nervosa—one that sparked my interest in the eating disorders and that has shaped, ever since, my own search for more effective modes of treatment.

## TWENTY YEARS AGO: A CASE HISTORY

Seventeen-year-old Anna was hospitalized on our ward because she had been losing weight steadily for several months and now, at five feet six inches tall, weighed about seventy-five pounds. The parents—mother, a college graduate and homemaker; father, successful in his chosen field—traced the onset of their daughter's troubles to nine months previously, when the family had relocated to a new city and Anna's younger sister had developed a relationship with a boyfriend. Another daughter, Margaret, already in college, had a history of depression and bouts of overeating and vomiting.

Anna differed only in details from the portrait that had been sketched since the first "modern" descriptions of eating disorders by French and English physicians Charles Lasegue and William Gull in 1873: an adolescent, almost always a girl, from an intact middle-class family, embarks on a project that is quite concrete—to lose a few pounds—often spurred on by some disappointment in friendship or a stressful life event. This idea of self-improvement soon becomes lost in the pursuit of thinness for its own sake. For many, Anna included, the fear of fatness predominates. Like some patients, Anna could not recall either a wish or a decision to diet, although she could later remember her loneliness and confusion before the weight loss began.

Anna's family was well educated and socially privileged. Today the canvas has enlarged to include more people of more varied backgrounds and ages, from poor to well-off, and including single-parent, Black, Hispanic, and immigrant families.

As a beginning therapist not yet attached to any psychiatric dogma, I learned a great deal from my patient—about the closeness that Anna shared with her sister and the pain she felt at her sibling's sometimes thoughtless attempts to separate from her; about life in this rather formal family that put feelings on the back burner, prided itself on the intellectual level of its dinnertime conversations, and gathered together beside a crackling fire each Christmas morning, as far back as Anna could remember, to listen to Father read excerpts from James Barrie's story of *Peter Pan.*

Over the course of our work together, Anna gradually trusted me with her innermost thoughts. She spoke of the "blankness" that had enveloped and comforted her during the period she was losing weight; of her outward compliance but inner resistance to the hospital's arbitrary refeeding schedule; and of her fury at the ward chief's kindly encouragement, "We're going to help you grow up!" She quoted me her family's favorite, Peter Pan himself: "O Wendy's mother, if I was to wake up and feel there was a beard! Keep back lady, no one is going to catch me and make me a man!" She told me of her fear of losing the ability *not* to eat—the only control she felt she had.

She shared with me her "sadness and the specific hurts that come from contacts with people, that you can never protect yourself from"; her beginning recognition that "whatever it is I'm protecting myself from, it isn't worth it, because the protection is horrible"; and finally, on the eve of discharge, and now within the normal weight range: "It's not easy being with people. . . . Slowly your pleasure builds itself, stacks itself up, and it can crash so easily. . . . I hate it that my hope is so fragile."

At the time Anna came for treatment, in the early 1970s, anorexia nervosa was still considered a rare condition. The prevailing psychodynamic viewpoint considered the self-starvation a severe form of neurotic conflict around sexuality. The treatment plan we offered her was a standard *medical model* for treating anorexia nervosa. It included tube feedings if a daily specified weight gain was not achieved, psychotherapy (that was to steer clear of weight and eating concerns—to circumvent "power struggles" and resistance to the "more important" issues), and family meetings led by a social worker who was also available to meet separately with the parents.

Family issues were recognized but not treated in-depth. For example, Anna, her parents, and siblings shared a perfectionist stance that had been noted to be a hallmark of many families with an anorexic child. In this family it was expressed as a commitment to the highest standards of academic and moral excellence. In addition, there were intimations of marital distress. Anna's parents appeared visibly tense and distant with each other despite their mutual assertions of affection and loyalty. But we never addressed their strain, either in the few separate parent meetings or during our joint sessions. In a letter she wrote months after her discharge, Anna painfully confided: "My father and mother don't love each other. He has only scorn for her.

That's the worst. And that's what I wouldn't speak, not even in my mind."

Anna left the hospital, having gained back to within five pounds of her previous (and normal) weight. This goal had been reached through a combination of tube feedings (in the early weeks) and, later, compliance with the weight-gain regimen. At the time of discharge she was referred to a psychiatrist in her hometown some distance from our medical center. My follow-up information eight months after our therapy ended, in the form of a letter she wrote me, was discouraging. Although she had lost only a few pounds, Anna remained preoccupied with her body and her eating, isolated from peers, and seriously depressed despite medication and continuing individual psychotherapy.

Were she hospitalized today, I would treat Anna very differently. I would use skilled nursing care and a variety of behavioral techniques to enlist her collaboration and to support her weight gain, obviating the need for tube feeding unless there were a medical crisis. Consultation with a nutritionist would be a valued part of the program. Participation in groups that foster interpersonal skills and address concerns about eating and body image might strengthen Anna's fragile wish to change.

Family therapy, guided by conceptual frameworks that did not simply blame the parents, would help the couple be more effective in their parenting, disentangle their disappointment with each other from their daughter's symptom, and thus relieve Anna and her siblings from bearing wordlessly the marital unhappiness. Finally, I would broaden her individual psychotherapy by speaking to her fears of eating and weight gain.

## CONTEMPORARY PERSPECTIVE

The change in my approach reflects major shifts in knowledge, in theory, and in practice. Looking back on Anna's therapy and the professional climate in which her eating disorder was understood, I am struck by how much we know now that we did not know then. Bearing in mind Donald Spence's caveat that "knowledge is lost if we leap too quickly at explanation," I'd like to highlight a few recent findings from clinical research and then discuss the theoretical models that inform current practice.

### New Considerations

There are ongoing efforts to make the diagnostic categories more accurate and clinically relevant. My patient Anna, for example, would now be given the diagnosis *anorexia nervosa, restricting subtype* because she did not overeat and vomit, in which case we would have placed her in the *bingeing/purging subtype*. Anna's normal-weight older sister, Margaret, whose frequent episodes of gorging and vomiting were at the time considered incidental to her depression, would today be diagnosed with *bulimia nervosa*, first identified as a separate syndrome in 1980 and officially a diagnostic entity since 1986, although it had long been mentioned as a variant of anorexia nervosa. *Binge-eating disorder* has been included in *eating disorders not otherwise specified* and delineated as a proposed new category in Appendix B of the fourth edition of the *Diagnostic and Statistical Manual of Mental Disorders (DSM-IV)*.

These categories have their limitations. For example, anorexics who binge and purge often have more in common, in personality characteristics and treatment needs, with bulimic patients than with other restricting anorexics. To further complicate the picture, individuals may have more than one diagnosis during the course of their eating disorder. For example, Lisa, the young woman Judith Brisman presents in this volume, was anorexic for a brief period in high school, recovered, then developed a tenacious bulimia that resolved only with several years of intensive psychotherapy. Likewise, Andrew, Arthur Crisp's patient, went through a period of bingeing and purging for nearly a year after his successful treatment, at age fourteen, for anorexia nervosa.

## Associated Problems

Current research confirms our clinical experience that the presence of substance abuse, depression, or co-existing personality disorder makes treatment more problematic. In his chapter, Bruce Arnow addresses the limitations of a symptom-focused approach in working with patients who have serious interpersonal difficulties. For those individuals addicted to alcohol or other drugs, successful completion of a treatment program for chemical dependency is now often a prerequisite for acceptance into an eating disorder therapy group. Allan Kaplan and Harold Spivak's day treatment program, the setting for Sue's therapy, is a response to the special needs of patients with complex psychological and medical problems. H. Charles Fishman's structural family therapy is effective with Joy, who had been bulimic for twenty years and carried multiple diagnoses.

The relationship between depression and bulimia has been a particular focus of attention because the two disorders can share such symptoms as increased appetite, lethargy, and feelings of worthlessness. A significant number of patients have both diagnoses, although no direct link has been established. Interestingly, antidepressant medication has been found in controlled studies to successfully diminish the binge-purge symptoms of many patients—independent of its effect on mood. In this volume Sue's depression and binge eating responded to the antidepressant Zoloft (sertraline). Both Erin (Kathryn Zerbe's patient) and Lisa found Prozac (fluoxetine) helpful at certain points during the course of their therapies.

Poor self-esteem, difficulties regulating affect and impulses, and issues around separation and individuation have long been associated with eating disorders. Problems in family functioning and family relationships are often very much in evidence as well. Clinical researchers are investigating predisposing risk factors. Recent studies link the personality traits of *emotional restraint* and *risk avoidance*, for example, with the restricting subtype of anorexia nervosa. Early puberty in girls and a tendency toward overweight in childhood also appear to contribute to a youngster's greater vulnerability to the pressures of adolescence in our society.

Sexual, physical, and psychological abuse in childhood, profound violations of body and soul, can often be found in our patients' histories. The extent and repercussions of these problems have only recently been acknowledged, yet studies already support the clinical observation that the victims of such abuse—who often cannot bear witness until many years later—are at higher risk for many psychological difficulties, including eating disorders. Brisman articulates a heightened awareness of these issues in her discussion of Lisa's case. In the treatment of the child Chloe, Rachel Bryant-Waugh and Bryan Lask's alertness to the presence of abuse enabled the adults in charge to intervene effectively, to protect the girl, and to prevent further damage. In the case of Sue, her therapists and the group members of her day treatment program responded with sensitivity to the revelation that she had been molested as a child by her mother's boyfriend. Our patients with these traumas often require modifications in the therapeutic approach. Understandably, they have more difficulty trusting others, including their therapists, and suffer from serious disturbances in self-esteem, with many fears about their bodily integrity.

### Body and Mind

The pursuit of thinness extracts a price on both body *and* mind. Anorexics are plagued by concentration and sleep problems, preoccupied with fantasies and thoughts of food and meal preparation, and absorbed in rituals of hoarding and eating. Studies have shown that these symptoms, once considered unique, are found in all persons who are severely food deprived: prisoners of war, psychological study subjects, and self-directed "hunger artists" like Ms. Q, whose long-term therapy with Paul Hamburg is illustrated.

Starvation, whether chosen or not, is truly the Great Masquerader, cloaking individual personalities and ways of being with others under a common, constricted mantle. We have consequently learned to assess only cautiously, at the outset, the psychological resources such an individual can bring to the treatment. Many strengths lie profoundly hidden. What we can be fairly sure about, from outcome studies now available, is that how long one has been starving has some bearing on how hard and how long the road to recovery is. The patients in this volume confirm the general observation.

Chloe, for example, entered treatment within a few months of beginning symptoms and in one year made a full recovery under the care (with her family) of Bryant-Waugh and Lask's multidisciplinary team. Sara's therapeutic journey represents the middle course. After four years of anorexia that had included two hospitalizations, she and her family began to work with Ivan Eisler in a creative mix of family and individual therapy that brought her, some two and one-half years later, to the point of living and studying independently, able to accept a weight within the normal range.

At the other extreme, the history of Hamburg's patient Ms. Q demonstrates poignantly the consequences of the chronic condition, lived in an emotional and physical wasteland. Cognizant that her diagnosis carried a mortality rate of 3 to 18 percent, her doctors, for long periods of time, defined success as merely keeping her alive!

Both biologically driven and psychologically laden, eating has proven to be more vulnerable and complex a behavior than we had once was thought. Current research shows that vigorous dieting, a commonplace activity in today's culture, may seriously disturb the delicate regulatory balance of the body's appetite control system even before significant weight loss occurs. Bingeing and purging can have a similar impact, disrupting and distorting the experience of hunger and fullness. Thus, physiological mechanisms often trigger or become active factors in perpetuating the eating disorders.

## The "Tyranny of Slenderness"

It may be said that our society suffers from a collective body image disturbance. And the age at which children begin to voice a concern about their size is dropping. In a 1993 survey of 3,175 Black and White boys and girls from the public and private middle schools of Charleston County, North Carolina, more than 40 percent of these healthy young students said they felt fat or wanted to lose weight! For decades, the inability to see their skinniness was accepted as a defining characteristic of those with anorexia nervosa. People who struggled with bulimia were thought to be more realistic despite their self-critical appraisals. We now know that both groups of patients vary greatly in their ability to perceive their size accurately. And it is the absolute preeminence of our patients' striving for a thinner and otherwise more perfect shape that distinguishes their body image concerns from those of many non-eating-disordered but weight-preoccupied men and women today—a difference in degree, rather than in kind.

Feminist thinkers and therapists have been pivotal in drawing our attention to the perils of what Kim Chernin has called "the tyranny of slenderness." It is not enough to acknowledge that such cultural norms and pressures exist and may contribute to the development of eating problems. In philosopher Susan Bordo's words, these factors "have a preeminent role in providing the necessary *ground* for the historical flourishing of the disorders." Feminists point out that the notion "a woman is only as good as her man" persists despite the increase of career opportunities for women over the past quarter century. Also, the most "desirable" as well as most marketable woman today is a good fifteen pounds lighter than her 1950s counterpart. I think, in this regard, of a very capable patient of mine, briefly derailed by anorexia, whose childhood was dominated by three ambitions: to be a success in the world like her father, to avoid the obesity of her grandmother, and to grow into the impossible contours of her beloved Barbie dolls. We could, in fact, ask a different question from the one usually posed—namely, What special strengths of character and family, what fortunate accidents of birth and circumstance, might protect some women against such pervasive, powerful, and contradictory pressures?

### Multiple Causes

I have noted some of the more recently elaborated biological, psychological, and sociocultural factors implicated in the development and perpetuation of an eating disorder. There is nearly universal agreement today that no single cause can be held accountable and that, in any given case, a number of forces converge. Paul Garfinkel has pioneered the application of this multiple risk factor model of illness to the field. In a book written with colleague David Garner, *Anorexia Nervosa: A Multidimensional Perspective*, he delineates potential *predisposing* and *precipitating* factors that, in complex interaction with one another, can lead to the final common pathway of an eating disorder. To add to the complexity, factors very different from those that set a disorder in motion may *perpetuate* it. This biopsychosocial paradigm provides a framework for combining diverse theoretical concepts and techniques into treatment approaches that can be responsive to patients' differing needs.

Despite our greater appreciation of the many possible etiological factors at work, we still cannot say with any degree of certainty which individual will escape an eating disorder, who will be only temporarily waylaid, and who will be held hostage for a lifetime. With each new patient, we must travel partially uncharted waters. I am reminded here of philosopher George Santayana's remark that "theory helps us bear our ignorance of fact." We owe a debt to those who have been able to offer us some direction.

## FROM THEORY TO PRACTICE

The conceptual underpinnings of most treatment efforts today are drawn from the domains of psychodynamic theory, learning theory, and general systems theory.

## Addressing the Individual

Analytic explanations of oedipal conflicts had informed the individual psychotherapy of eating disorders for nearly half a century when American psychiatrist Hilde Bruch first began work with her anorexic patients in the 1950s. Bruch turned her attention to the impact of failures in the early relationships of these individuals, emphasizing the importance of maternal responsiveness to *child-initiated* cues in ensuring healthy development. Inappropriate or indifferent responses to the baby's signals (cries of hunger, fatigue, or distress) led, she believed, to deficits in the growing child's awareness of bodily states and feelings. Compliant, "successful" functioning before the onset of symptoms masked a pervasive sense of ineffectiveness and lack of autonomy.

A new way of conducting the therapy emerged from this understanding of her patients' struggles for autonomy and identity. Bruch called it the "fact-finding approach"—a respectful, therapeutic collaboration that encouraged the patient to identify his or her "abilities, resources and inner capacities for judging and listening."

Her influence continues to be widely and deeply felt across our field, and interpersonal psychoanalysts like Judith Brisman are her most direct theoretical heirs. In her work with Lisa, Brisman expands Bruch's stance of "careful listening" to include attention to the therapeutic relationship and the evolving interplay of language between patient and therapist.

In England, during the same period, researcher and clinician Arthur Crisp began to publish the results of his extensive investigations. He considered anorexia nervosa, with its inevitable reversal of the pubertal process, a phobic avoidance of adolescence. He suggested that the impetus for this retreat lay both in the individual vulnerabilities (psychological and biological) of the patient and in developmental disturbances within the family that left it ill-equipped for their child's sexual and emotional maturation. His work with Andrew played a key role in the elaboration of these influential ideas.

Both Bruch and Crisp adapted the psychodynamic formulations they inherited to treat their starving patients more effectively. In recent years, further developments in psychoanalytic thinking have led many clinicians to adopt a more active, supportive, and empathic stance with their patients, and to consider the therapeutic relationship not simply as a vehicle for elucidating inner conflicts and past interactions, but as a powerful medium for restoration and growth. Object relations theory and self psychology have been particular beacons. Understandings drawn from these sources at times guide Hamburg in his treatment of Ms. Q.

### Addressing the Symptom

Alternatively, the frequent inability of psychodynamically based therapies to correct the medically dangerous emaciation of their patients tilted some clinicians toward very different terrain. Treatment that rested on the foundation of learning theory focused specifically on the problematic behaviors—gaining weight and achieving control over binge eating and vomiting. Working with the hypothesis that the majority of behaviors, including symptoms, are acquired and can be unlearned or modified with appropriate techniques, behavior therapy was initially used in the hospital treatment of patients with anorexia nervosa.

The multimodal inpatient treatment program for anorexia nervosa I directed at Stanford between 1975 and 1980, for example, applied a full-fledged, operant conditioning paradigm—with contingencies for weight gain, positive and negative reinforcers, and a written contract between patient and treatment team that detailed the plan of action and the mutually agreed-on target weight. In this consistent and supportive milieu, which addressed the individual's psychodynamic and family issues as well, our patients reached and maintained their weight goals without the need for tube feeding or other medical intervention.

The hospital programs illustrated in this volume provide a firm but nurturing setting in which, with the active involvement of a cohesive and skilled nursing staff, weight gain is achieved through bed rest and the use of a few select behavioral techniques, such as behavioral contracting (Crisp) and making activities contingent on weight gain (Bryant-Waugh and Lask; Crisp; and Garfinkel).

Important elements of the behavioral perspective also flourish today in cognitive-behavioral therapy (CBT). In addition to providing techniques for behavior change, CBT focuses on identifying and intervening in the thoughts and beliefs that underlie symptoms. Two treatments patterned on these principles are illustrated here: Carol Peterson and James Mitchell's group therapy of Ellen, and Bruce Arnow's individual therapy of Jane. Each therapy uses the tools of the trade somewhat differently. For example, the record keeping for self-monitoring, the search for cues and triggers, the introduction of alternative behaviors, and the discussions on changing thoughts all have different emphases and different flavors in Peterson and Mitchell's structured group environment and in Arnow's intimate, individual setting. Each offers unique advantages: in one, the benefits of peer support, encouragement, and validation; in the other, the opportunity to explore in greater depth the troublesome beliefs and feelings that sustain symptoms.

This way of working has an educative component. Both Jane and Ellen learned directly in the sessions, for example, about the repercussions of going all day without eating "to make up for a binge" and about the relevance to dietary efforts of the body's internal "set point." Arnow gently challenged Jane's belief that she lacked willpower, explaining in detail how her chronic caloric restriction contributed to her intense preoccupation with thoughts of food.

Many psychodynamic clinicians also include some behavioral or cognitive-behavioral techniques to help patients grapple with their symptoms. Brisman contracted with Lisa to structure her eating and to experiment with alternative activities, encouraging her patient to actively confront the urge to binge as well as to understand it. Within the empathic environment of her psychotherapy with Hamburg, Ms. Q was finally able to experience how much her starving impeded her ability to think and learn. Only then could she join her doctors in their efforts to help her toward physical and emotional well-being.

### Addressing the Family

Dissatisfaction with existing options also led to the introduction of a new way of thinking about families and their treatment. Frustrated by the constraints of their psychoanalytic heritage, Salvador Minuchin, at the Philadelphia Child Guidance Clinic, and Mara Selvini Palazzoli, with her Milan team, began independently during the late 1960s to consider their patients from the vantage point of a widened frame. They concluded that the problem resided, not in the individual sufferer—for example, the starving daughter—but within the context of the *family system*.

Minuchin and his colleagues identified particular characteristics of the "psychosomatic family," such as rigid boundaries and enmeshed subsystems, that left the family members more vulnerable to external stresses or developmental challenges (such as a child's leaving home) and more likely to become "stuck" in symptoms. The entire family, therefore, became the subject of treatment. The therapeutic task was now to mobilize the family's natural potential for growth by challenging the usual symptom-maintaining transactions in order to create the opportunity for change.

Their method of working with anorexic families often led to the dramatic and rapid resolution of symptoms, especially in youngsters who had not been starving for long. Controlled studies have now verified the particular effectiveness of family therapy for the young patient with anorexia of recent onset. Treating the chronic bulimic woman Joy and her family, Fishman takes the structural approach even further by extending the therapeutic focus beyond the immediate family group to the wider context of work, peers, and in this case, the world of martial arts instruction.

Like Minuchin, Palazzoli's team also considered the family an *open system* whose members mutually influenced one another through their reciprocal interactions. The team observed how each family member struggled to define the relationships within the family, the ways in which individuals blamed and disqualified one another. The Milan group developed a *circular* mode of inquiry, which, for example, through *triadic questions* (directed to one family member about the interaction between two others) and questions about the difference between individuals and relationships, sought to elicit information about and make therapeutic interventions in the many transactions guarding the family's rigid status quo. Eisler's work with Sara and her family incorporates elements of both the structural and the Milan approaches as well as further developments: the application of systemic thinking to individual therapy and a curiosity about the therapist's own participation in the system at hand.

Although the family systems approach has become, for many clinicians like Fishman and Eisler, the *principal* forum in which to address such problems as eating disorders, many more therapists today include *some* family intervention in their multimodal treatment. A range of family work is illustrated in several of the chapters: for Garfinkel's anorexic young mother, Mrs. L. R., couples therapy and the subsequent individual treatment for her husband were important to her recovery. In the case of Chloe, parental counseling and individual therapy marked the first stage of treatment. Family therapy followed to deal with emerging relationship issues and the impact of the parents' decision to separate.

Family involvement can be useful even when brief. Lisa's parents participated in family sessions only in the wake of a crisis, yet were able to make a dent in the patterns of interaction that limited their daughter's willingness and ability to become a more responsible, less symptomatic young adult. And, from his perspective thirty-five years later, Crisp, in a coda to his chapter, considers how he might have approached the initial treatment of Andrew's family today.

### *Addressing the Insurance Company*

A joint effort by therapist, patient, and parents was fashioned by Kathryn Zerbe to convince Erin's case manager of the urgent need to continue benefits for her patient's ongoing hospitalization and psychotherapy. This story of the forging of an effective relationship with managed care required collaboration on many fronts. Parents mobilized to make a difference for their daughter. The case manager, listening to therapist and patient, grew wiser about the demons they struggled with and applied his knowledge to "move mountains." And Erin, feeling the power of her voice, continued the work of recovery.

## INTEGRATING TREATMENTS

Contemporary treatment for the eating disorders moves in the direction of embracing multiple perspectives. Departing from the rigidly sectarian or dialectical stances so characteristic of earlier decades, clinicians have begun to appreciate more fully that different theories and therapeutic approaches speak to differing yet equally relevant dimensions of human experience. They acknowledge more freely that their own particular techniques may be more helpful with some individuals than with others. Given the considerable treatment challenge that many patients still present despite scientific and clinical advances, the increasing reliance on carefully thought-out approaches that integrate more than one modality and draw on more than one theoretical perspective is a most promising development.

Integration can take many shapes, and several important configurations are represented here. Garfinkel's approach to Mrs. L. R.'s treatment rests on a clear conceptual framework and is flexibly adapted to her needs, using inpatient and outpatient treatment with individual psychotherapy, couples therapy, and eventually therapy for the patient's daughter. A thorough understanding of the intrapsychic and interpersonal dynamics of the patient and the provision of a unified team effort are essential to its effective implementation.

Similarly, Bryant-Waugh and Lask's treatment of Chloe occurs in a comprehensive program, strictly for children and young adolescents, which offers outpatient, day treatment, and inpatient options. A multidisciplinary team carefully assesses and then places its young patients and their families in the appropriate mix of modalities: parental counseling, family therapy, and individual psychotherapy. Kaplan and Spivak's day treatment approach is a time-limited, structured alternative to hospitalization. Built around multiple group therapies, their program provides Sue with cognitive and behavioral techniques for her eating problem, an interpersonal framework for her relationship difficulties, and a psychodynamic understanding of her traumas, deprivations, and losses.

The *treatment team* occupies a central place in any multimodal therapy. It is a forum for the exchange of information, for conceptual integration, for the careful articulation of strategies, and for problem solving. The director of the program assumes leadership in some treatments; the individual therapist provides the unifying link in others. In this environment, clinicians can receive much-needed ongoing collegial support and consultation. Hamburg's treatment of Ms. Q is sustained within such a team setting. Here, four years of group therapy were part of the joint effort to make a difference in a life that had permitted no differences to be made for decades—to no seeming avail. The enduring individual work, however, leads finally to unexpected changes, including the patient's ability to make use of a partial hospitalization program.

We have examples, in addition, of multimodal integration by a single practitioner. Eisler, guided by his systemic perspective, engages Sara and her family in individual, sibling, parental, and family therapy. During her intensive hospital-based psychotherapy with Erin, psychoanalyst Zerbe expands the therapeutic frame to include both the parents and the case manager in charge of authorizing her patient's psychiatric benefits. Fishman integrates important figures—friend, boss—from his patient's "outside" life into the therapy and introduces new contexts—sessions with a martial artist—into his work with Joy's family.

Collaboration with consulting physicians and nutritionists is an essential aspect of an integrated treatment. This collaboration develops naturally in the context of an inpatient or day hospital program. Many of our outpatients also come to us with internists, gynecologists, or pediatricians already anxiously looking after them. If not, as with the bulimic who has managed to keep her symptoms under wraps or the anorexic who has been able to deny the extent of her wasting, effective therapy will often lead later to more medical involvement. The therapists represented in this volume make the connection with their medical colleagues more than nominal.

Our work with patients, whether multimodal or single modality—psychodynamic, systemic, or cognitive-behavioral—must always be appreciated within its interpersonal context: the patient-therapist relationship. The patients in these chapters acknowledge the healing nature of this human connection in varied ways: for example, Andrew's grateful recollection, as a middle-aged man, of the doctors who served him so well in his youth; Mrs. L. R.'s willingness, years past her successful treatment for anorexia nervosa, to contact her therapist for additional sessions when life's pressures became temporarily overwhelming. The clinicians also speak to the relevance of the therapeutic relationship. For some it is central to the treatment process. For others it is one ingredient in the larger recipe for change.

Many of our contributors fully expect that their commitment to their patients will endure beyond the initial course of treatment. Given that individuals who have had an eating disorder have a significant risk of further difficulties in living, the ongoing availability of a trusted therapist may in itself confer some protection.

The stories you are about to read encompass a spectrum of theory and practice—variations in therapeutic focus, structure, goals, and even beliefs about the outer limits of our capacity for change. I hope you will note and savor the distinctions as well as the commonalities, that you will be inspired to explore further some of these therapeutic possibilities.

Despite the reality of dwindling financial resources for treatment and the shadows of cost containment and managed care, these are exciting times. For while we have not yet achieved a common language, the dialogue is more collaborative and less defensive than at any point in the history of our field and will enrich our efforts to treat the patients who seek our help.

# ACKNOWLEDGMENTS

It is a privilege to be able to acknowledge in print those who have had a role in the making of this book. First, I'd like to thank my authors for their superb contributions and my many patients, who over the years have taught me so much.

I had the good fortune to learn from several truly great psychotherapists: Dr. Stephen Fleck at Yale University; Dr. Erich Lindemann, in his last years of "semiretirement" at Stanford University; and Dr. Hilde Bruch, at Baylor University, with whom I was able to share a patient, a university student, across half a continent.

My chairman of psychiatry while I was chief resident at Stanford, Dr. Albert J. Stunkard, gave me the benefit of his considerable expertise in eating disorders and the opportunity to participate in the development, with Dr. Stewart Agras and Dr. James Ferguson, of an innovative treatment program for our anorexic patients. I am grateful to Dr. Agras for introducing me to the principles of behavioral treatment and to the field of clinical research. I am indebted to Dr. George Gulevich, who, as Medical Director of Stanford's adult psychiatry inpatient unit, provided a sturdy and supportive milieu for our multimodal program for patients with anorexia nervosa and in addition was a vital member of the treatment team. I would like to acknowledge, as well, the influence of Mara Selvini Palazzoli and her original Milan colleagues: Guiliana Prata, Luigi Boscolo, and

Gianfranco Cecchin. They arrived at Stanford in the spring of 1977 and, in a memorable few days, left us with the systemic principles that have changed the shape of my enduring psychodynamic perspective.

I'd like to thank Dr. Irv Yalom for the invitation to edit a volume on treating eating disorders, Alan Rinzler, my editor at Jossey-Bass, for his guidance and extensive, incisive editorial involvement, and Rachel Anderson for her invaluable collaboration on the final text.

Friends and colleagues have supported this undertaking, encouraging my effort and graciously accepting my unavailability when editing duties intervened. I'd like to especially thank Dr. Norman Dishotsky, Dr. Carol Koplan, Dr. Lynn Gorodsky, Joan Haller, L.C.S.W, Dr. Paul Garfinkel, Dr. David Herzog, Dr. Joel Yager, Dr. Regina Casper, and Dr. Bruce Arnow for their enthusiastic response to the idea of this book. Dr. Arnow also provided helpful comments on my chapter and was throughout a valued resource.

Finally, I want to express my appreciation to my family for their sustenance and joyful presence in my life. I am deeply grateful to my mother, Dr. Irene Garrow Werne, who believed, without a hesitation or doubt, that her children, two of whom were daughters growing up in the 1950s, would find satisfaction in a profession of their choice. I would like to thank my husband, Dr. John S. Smolowe, for his patience with my extra preoccupations during the past year, his thoughtful readings of my chapter and his invaluable editorial suggestions, and his encouragement, now and always, of my own voice. I would like to thank my daughter, Laura, for her wise commentaries and interest in her mother's project, and my son, Jacob, for treating my periodic absences from family life with just the right mixture of resentment, humor, and tolerance.

# NOTES

P. xviii, *Donald Spence's caveat:* Spence, D. (1987). *The Freudian metaphor: Toward paradigm change in psychoanalysis.* New York: W. W. Norton, p. 207.

P. xviii, *These categories have their limitations:* DaCosta, M., & Halmi, K. A. (1992). Classification of anorexia nervosa: Question of subtypes. *International Journal of Eating Disorders, 11*(4), 305–313; Garfinkel, P. (1992). Classification and diagnosis. In K. Halmi (Ed.), *Psychobiology and treatment of anorexia nervosa and bulimia nervosa* (pp. 37–60). Washington, DC: American Psychiatric Press.

P. xix, *Current research confirms:* Three excellent chapters provide summaries of much of the recent research: Edelstein, C., & Yager, J. (1992). Eating disorders and affective disorders. In J. Yager, H. E. Gwirtsman, & C. K. Edelstein (Eds.), *Special problems in managing eating disorders* (pp. 15–50). Washington, DC: American Psychiatric Press; Mitchell, J., Pyle, R., Specker, S., & Hanson, K. (1992). Eating disorders and chemical dependency. In J. Yager, H. E. Gwirtsman, & C. K. Edelstein (Eds.), *Special problems in managing eating disorders* (pp. 1–14). Washington, DC: American Psychiatric Press; and Wonderlich, S., & Mitchell, J. (1992). Eating disorders and personality disorders. In J. Yager, H. E. Gwirtsman, & C. K. Edelstein (Eds.), (1992). *Special problems in managing eating disorders* (pp. 51–86). Washington, DC: American Psychiatric Press.

P. xix, *The relationship between depression and bulimia:* Levy, A. L., Dixon, K. N., & Stern, S. L. (1989). How are depression and bulimia related? *American Journal of Psychiatry, 146*(2), 162–169; and Strober, M., & Katz, J. (1988). Depression in the eating disorders: A review and analysis of descriptive, family, and biological findings. In D. Garner & P. Garfinkel (Eds.), *Diagnostic issues in anorexia nervosa and bulimia nervosa* (pp. 80–111). New York: Brunner/Mazel.

P. xix, *antidepressant medication has been found:* Agras, W. S., Rossiter, E. M., Arnow, B., Telch, C. F., Raeburn, S. D., Bruce, B., & Koran, L. M. (1994). One year follow up of psychosocial and pharmacological treatment for bulimia nervosa. *Journal of Clinical Psychiatry, 55*(5), 179–183. For a thorough review, see Mitchell, J. E., & de Zwaan, M. (1993). Pharmacological treatments of binge eating. In C. Fairburn & G. Wilson (Eds.), *Binge eating: Nature, assessment, and treatment* (pp. 250–269). New York: Guilford Press.

P. xix, *issues around separation and individuation:* See Bruch, H. (1973). *Eating disorders: Obesity, anorexia, and the person within.* New York: Basic Books; Bruch, H. (1978). *The golden cage.* Cambridge, MA: Harvard University Press; Crisp, A. (1980). *Anorexia nervosa: Let me be.* New York: Grune & Stratton; Garfinkel, P., & Garner, D. (1982). *Anorexia nervosa: A multidimensional perspective.* New York: Brunner/Mazel; Johnson, C., & Connors, M. E. (1987). *The etiology and treatment of bulimia nervosa: A biopsychosocial perspective.* New York: Basic Books.

P. xix, *Problems in family functioning:* In addition to the above cited works, see Minuchin, S. Rosman, B. L., & Baker, L. (1978). *Psychosomatic families: Anorexia nervosa in context.* Boston: Harvard University Press; Root, M., Fallon, P., & Friedrich, W. (1986). *Bulimia: A systems approach to treatment.* New York: W. W. Norton.

P. xix, *Recent studies link the personality traits:* Casper, R. C. (1990). Personality features of women with good outcome from restricting anorexia nervosa. *Psychosomatic Medicine, 52,* 156–170; Casper, R. C., Hedeker, D., & McClough, J. F. (1992). Personality dimensions in eating disorders and their relevance to subtyping. *Journal of the American Academy of Child and Adolescent Psychiatry, 31*(5), 830–840; Strober, M. (1990). Disorders of the self in anorexia nervosa: An organismic-developmental paradigm. In C. Johnson, (Ed.). *Psychodynamic theory and treatment for eating disorders* (pp. 354–373). New York: Guilford Press.

P. xx, *Early puberty:* Dubas, J., & Peterson, A. (1993). Female pubertal development. In M. Sugar (Ed.), *Female adolescent development* (pp. 3–26). New York: Brunner/Mazel; Striegel-Moore, R. (1994). Etiology of binge eating: A developmental perspective. In C. Fairburn & G. Wilson (Eds.), *Binge eating: Nature, assessment, and treatment* (pp. 144–172). New York: Guilford Press.

P. xx, *Sexual, physical, and psychological abuse in childhood:* Pribor, E., & Dinwiddie, M. (1992). Psychiatric correlates of incest in childhood. *American Journal of Psychiatry, 149*(1), 52–56; Rorty, M., Yager, J., & Rossotto, E. (1994a). Childhood sexual, physical, and psychological abuse and their relationship to comorbid psychopathology in bulimia nervosa. *International Journal of Eating Disorders, 16*(4), 317–334; Rorty, M., Yager, J., & Rossotto, E. (1994b). Childhood sexual, physical, and psychological abuse in bulimia nervosa. *American Journal of Psychiatry, 151*(8), 1122–1126; Gleaves, D. H., & Eberenz, K. P. (1994). Sexual abuse histories among treatment resistant bulimia nervosa patients. *International Journal of Eating Disorders, 15*(3), 227–231; Welch, S., & Fairburn, C. (1994). Sexual abuse and bulimia nervosa: Three integrated case control comparisons. *American Journal of Psychiatry, 151*(3), 402–407; Wooley, S. (1994). Sexual abuse and eating disorders: The concealed debate. In P. Fallon, M. A. Katzman, & S. C. Wooley (Eds.), *Feminist perspectives on eating disorders* (pp. 171–211). New York: Guilford Press; Everill, J. T., & Waller, G. (1995). Reported sexual abuse and eating psychopathology: A review of the evidence for a causal link. *International Journal of Eating Disorders, 18*(1), 1–11.

P. xx, *Our patients with these traumas:* Gutwill, S., & Gitter, A. (1994). Eating problems and sexual abuse: Treatment considerations. In C. Bloom, A. Gitter, S. Gutwill, L. Kogel, & L. Zaphiropoulos. *Eating problems: A feminist psychoanalytic treatment model* (pp. 205–226). New York: Basic Books; Herman, J. (1992). *Trauma and recovery*. New York: Basic Books; Kearney-Cooke, A., & Striegel-Moore, R. (1994). Treatment of childhood sexual abuse in anorexia nervosa and bulimia nervosa. *International Journal of Eating Disorders, 15*(4), 305–319; Wooley, S. (1991). Uses of countertransference in the treatment of eating disorders: A gender perspective. In C. Johnson (Ed.), *Psychodynamic treatment of anorexia and bulimia* (pp. 245–294). New York: Guilford Press.

P. xx, *Studies have shown that these symptoms:* Keys, A., Brozek, J., Henschel, A. J., Mickelsen, O., & Taylor, H. L. (1950). *The biology of human starvation*. Minneapolis: University of Minnesota Press; Pirke, K. M., & Ploog, D. (1987). Biology of human starvation. In P.J.V. Beumont, G. D. Burrows, & R. C. Casper (Eds.), *Handbook of eating disorders: Part 1. Anorexia and bulimia nervosa* (pp. 79–102). New York: Elsevier Science.

P. xxi, *from outcome studies now available:* See Anderson, A. (1992). Analysis of treatment experience and outcome from the Johns Hopkins Eating Disorders Program 1957–1990. In K. A. Halmi (Ed.), *Psychobiology and treatment of anorexia nervosa and bulimia nervosa* (pp. 93–124). Washington, DC: American Psychiatric Press; Hoffman, L., & Yager, J. (1992). Patients with chronic recalcitrant eating disorders. In J. Yager, H. E. Gwirtsman, & C. K. Edelstein (Eds.), *Special problems in managing eating disorders* (pp. 205–231). Washington, DC: American Psychiatric Press; Russell, G.F.M. (1992). The prognosis of eating disorders: A clinician's approach. In W. Herzog, H.-C. Deter, & W. Vandereycken (Eds.), *The course of eating disorders* (pp. 198–213). Berlin: Springer-Verlag.

P. xxi, *Current research shows that vigorous dieting:* See these two articles: Blundell, J. E., & Hill, A. J. (1993). Binge eating: Psychobiological mechanisms. In C. G. Fairburn & G. T. Wilson (Eds.), *Binge eating: Nature, assessment, and treatment* (pp. 206–224). New York: Guilford Press; and Polivy, J., & Herman, C. P. (1993). Binge eating: Psychological mechanisms. In C. G. Fairburn & G. T. Wilson (Eds.), *Binge eating: Nature, assessment, and treatment* (pp. 173–205). New York: Guilford Press.

P. xxii, *our society suffers from a collective body image disturbance:* Fallon, A. (1990). Culture in the mirror: Sociocultural determinants of body image. In T. F. Cash & T. Pruzinsky (Eds.), *Body images: Development, deviance, and change* (pp. 80–109). New York: Guilford Press; Seid, R. P. (1989). *Never too thin: Why women are at war with their bodies*. Englewood Cliffs, NJ: Prentice Hall.

P. xxii, *In a 1993 survey:* Childress, A. C., Braverton, T. D., Hodges, M. S. W., & Jarrell, M. K. (1993). The Kids' Eating Disorders Survey (KEDS): A study of middle school students. *Journal of the American Academy of Child and Adolescent Psychiatry, 32*(4), 843–850.

P. xxii, *both groups of patients vary greatly:* Hsu, L.K.G., & Sobkiewicz, T. A. (1991). Body image disturbance: Time to abandon the concept for eating disorders? *International Journal of Eating Disorders, 10*(1), 15–30; Sunday, S. R., Halmi, K. A., Werdann, L., & Levey. C. (1992). Comparison of body size estimation and eating disorder inventory scores in anorexia and bulimia patients with obese, and restrained and unrestrained controls. *International Journal of Eating Disorders, 11*(2), 133–149.

P. xxii, *And it is the absolute preeminence of our patients' striving:* Garner, D. M., Olmstead, M. P., Polivy, J., & Garfinkel, P. E. (1984). Comparison between weight preoccupied women and anorexia nervosa. *Psychosomatic Medicine, 46,* 255–266; Hadigan, C. M., & Walsh, B. T. (1991). Body shape concerns in bulimia nervosa. *International Journal of Eating Disorders, 10*(3), 323–331.

P. xxii, *Feminist thinkers and therapists:* Bordo, S. (1993). *Unbearable weight: Feminism, Western culture, and the body.* Berkeley: University of California Press; Chernin, K. (1981). *Obsession: Reflections on the tyranny of slenderness.* New York: Harper & Row; Fallon, P., Katzman, M., & Wooley, S. (Eds.). (1994). *Feminist perspectives on eating disorders.* New York: Guilford Press; Orbach, S. (1986). *Hunger strike: The anorectic's struggle as a metaphor for our age.* New York: W. W. Norton.

P. xxii, *"the tyranny of slenderness":* Chernin, K. (1981). *The obsession: Reflections on the tyranny of slenderness.* New York: Harper & Row.

P. xxii, *historical flourishing of the disorders:* Bordo, S. (1993). *Unbearable weight: Feminism, Western culture, and the body.* Berkeley: University of California Press, p. 52.

P. xxiii, *Paul Garfinkel has pioneered:* Garfinkel, P., & Garner, D. (1982). *Anorexia nervosa: A multidimensional perspective.* New York: Brunner/Mazel.

P. xxiv, *Bruch called it the "fact-finding approach":* Bruch, H. (1974). *Eating disorders.* New York: Basic Books, p. 336.

P. xxiv, *judging and listening:* Bruch, H. (1974). *Eating disorders.* New York: Basic Books, p. 338.

P. xxiv, *researcher and clinician Arthur Crisp:* See Crisp, A. H. (1980). *Anorexia nervosa: Let me be.* New York: Grune & Stratton.

P. xxv, *further developments in psychoanalytic thinking:* Casper, R. (1987). Psychotherapy in anorexia nervosa. In P.J.V. Beumont, G. D. Burrows, & R. C. Casper (Eds.), *Handbook of eating disorders: Part 1. Anorexia and bulimia nervosa* (pp. 255–270). Amsterdam: Elsevier; Geist, R. A. (1989). Self psychological reflections on the origins of eating disorders. In J. R. Bemporad & D. B. Herzog (Eds.), *Psychoanalysis and eating disorders* (pp. 5–27). New York: Guilford Press; Goodsitt, A. (1985). Self psychology and the treatment of anorexia nervosa. In D. M. Garner and P. E. Garfinkle (Eds.),

*Handbook of psychotherapy for anorexia nervosa and bulimia* (pp. 55–82). New York: Guilford Press. For a variety of recent writings on psychodynamic approaches to the eating disorders, see Johnson, C. (Ed.). (1991). *Psychodynamic treatment of anorexia nervosa and bulimia*. New York: Guilford Press.

P. xxv, *behavior therapy was initially used:* Agras, W. S., Barlow, D. H., Chapin, H. N., Abel, G. G., & Leitenberg, H. (1974). Behavior modification of anorexia nervosa. *Archives of General Psychiatry, 30,* 279–286; Agras, W. S., & Werne, J. (1977). Behavior modification in anorexia nervosa: Research foundations. In R. A. Vigersky (Ed.), *Anorexia nervosa: A monograph of the National Institute of Child Health and Human Development*. New York: Raven Press.

P. xxv, *The multimodal inpatient treatment program:* Agras, W. S., & Werne, J. (1978). Behavior therapy in anorexia nervosa: A data-based approach to the question. In J. P. Brady & H.K.H. Brodie (Eds.), *Controversy in psychiatry* (pp. 655–673). Philadelphia: Saunders.

P. xxvi, *Important elements of the behavioral perspective:* For an exegesis of the cognitive approach to anorexia nervosa, see Garner, D. M., & Bemis, K. M. (1985). Cognitive therapy for anorexia nervosa. In D. M. Garner & P. E. Garfinkel, *Handbook of psychotherapy for anorexia nervosa and bulimia* (pp. 107–146). New York: Guilford Press. For a thorough review, see Fairburn, C. G., & Cooper, Z. (1987). Behavioral and cognitive approaches to the treatment of anorexia nervosa and bulimia nervosa. In P.J.V. Beumont, G. D. Burrows, & R. C. Casper (Eds.), *Handbook of eating disorders: Part 1. Anorexia and bulimia* (pp. 271–298). Amsterdam: Elsevier.

P. xxvii, *Salvador Minuchin, at the Philadelphia Child Guidance Clinic:* Minuchin, S., Rosman, B. L., & Baker, L. (1978). *Psychosomatic families*. Cambridge, MA: Harvard University Press.

P. xxvii, *Mara Selvini Palazzoli, with her Milan team:* Palazzoli, M. S. (1974). *Self starvation*. London: Human Context Books; Selvini, M. (Ed.). (1988). *The work of Mara Selvini Palazzoli*. New York: Jason Aronson.

P. xxviii, *Controlled studies have now verified:* Russell, G.F.M., Dare, C., Eisler, I., & Le Grange, P.D.F. (1992). Controlled trials of family treatments in anorexia nervosa. In K. A. Halmi (Ed.), *Psychobiology and treatment of anorexia nervosa and bulimia nervosa* (pp. 237–261). Washington, DC: American Psychiatric Press.

P. xxviii, *some family intervention in their multimodal treatments:* See Woodside, D. B., & Shekter-Wolfson, L. (Eds.). (1991). *Family approaches in treatment of eating disorders*. Washington, DC: American Psychiatric Press; Woodside, D. B., Shekter-Wolfson, L. F., & Brandes, J. B. (Eds.). (1993). *Eating disorders and marriage: The couple in focus*. New York: Brunner/Mazel.

P. xxix, *the increasing reliance on carefully thought-out approaches:* See Anderson, A. E. (1985). *Practical comprehensive treatment of anorexia nervosa and bulimia.* Baltimore: Johns Hopkins University Press; Garfinkel, P. E., & Garner, D. M. (1982). *Anorexia nervosa: A multidimensional perspective.* New York: Brunner/Mazel; several chapters on multicomponent treatment programs in Garner, D. M., & Garfinkel, P. E. (1985). *Handbook of psychotherapy for anorexia nervosa and bulimia.* New York: Guilford Press; Herzog, D. B., Franco, D. L., & Brotman, A. W. (1989). Integrating treatments for bulimia nervosa. In J. R. Bemporad & D. Herzog, *Psychoanalysis and eating disorders* (pp. 141–150). New York: Guilford Press; Vanderlinden, J., Norre, J., & Vandereycken, W. (1992). *A practical guide to the treatment of bulimia nervosa.* New York: Brunner/Mazel.

P. xxxi, *Collaboration with consulting physicians:* Kaplan, A. S., & Garfinkel, P. E. (1993). *Medical issues and the eating disorders.* New York: Brunner/Mazel. An important resource for therapists, which describes in-depth the many medical complications of the eating disorders.

*To John and our children, Laura and Jacob,*
*and my parents*

# TREATING
# EATING DISORDERS

# I

# ANOREXIA NERVOSA IN A YOUNG MALE

## Arthur H. Crisp

Thirty-five years ago, I first found myself, as a liaison psychiatrist, with medical responsibility for a seriously ill anorectic. He was a fourteen-year-old boy, severely emaciated, admitted to a medical ward, and refusing to eat.

I had met anorectics previously, self-absorbed and avoidant in the inpatient setting, bent on doing their own thing and resistant to any significant intervention. They were clearly biding their time, doing just enough to encourage the bewildered and disempowered staff to consider discharging them sooner rather than later. My recent training had left me with both biological and social ways of attempting to understand psychopathology. I already held the view that relationship-based psychotherapy coupled with some degree of behavioral control over symptoms (within a therapeutic contract) was a powerful tool, possibly capable of changing the chemistry of the mind through its lasting effects on mental structure and function, brain maturation, and memory. Anorexia nervosa beckoned.

*Note:* The author wishes to express great gratitude (and that of Andrew) to Ross Kalucy—now Professor of Psychiatry in the Medical School, Flinders University, Adelaide, South Australia, and as identified in the chapter, the active psychotherapist with Andrew during his second and third postanorexic admissions.

I had been trained to take systematic histories from patients and their families, and my conviction that a substantial amount of time spent at the outset was essential proved especially possible in this instance and served me well. Andrew, and his parents to some extent, became my patient as we came to agree on the nature of the problem. We embarked on treatment.

## General Background

Anorexia nervosa can erupt at any age, but classically it arises in the mid to late teens. In women's cases, I often hear people say, "Fifteen percent of my cases have arisen within childhood," meaning before the onset of menstruation. This is a quaint idea akin to the tribal view of instant passage from childhood to adulthood. Puberty is a three- to four-year-long process, with menarche a late event. In my view, anorexia nervosa rarely if ever erupts before the onset of puberty. The onset of puberty is insidious and probably more experiential than tangible in the first instance: a mounting shyness, self-consciousness, and self-awareness; the beginnings of blushing; the first spot; and the emergence of new panic as escalating unasked-for and seemingly uncontrollable growth and new bodily sensations take over.

Boys, of course, start puberty somewhat later than girls. Andrew was probably in the first or second year of his puberty. He had been masturbating for several years (guiltily, as is described later); pubic hair was not much in evidence, but linear growth had accelerated recently and he was tall for his age.

I tackled the case of Andrew and his family with the confidence of a youthful professional. He recovered and was duly written up. I will return to the case later on, but let me share with you now that it profoundly awakened my interest in such apparently diverse matters as the psychobiology of pubertal maturation and growth, family systems, body temperature regulation and hence circadian rhythms and sleep, and the clinical area of empowering people to change.

I had treated Andrew (and his parents) psychotherapeutically, but also prescribed chlorpromazine in quite large doses, something I continued to do in the treatment of anorexia nervosa for some years and would still defend today, although I have rarely used drugs of any kind in its treatment for more than twenty years.

Andrew tolerated large doses of the drug for some weeks, and then, as his weight rose through pubertal levels once more, he became drowsy. I concluded that his initial high arousal had been a product of his hunger and predominantly calorie starvation. As his weight rose, his wet dreams and his tendency to bed-wetting also returned, and he became much troubled by this behavior. His panic about his continued weight gain escalated but was contained.

Some others argued that his tolerance of neuroleptics hinted at psychosis and that his early morning wakening was indicative of depression, but I persisted with the view that these were starvation-related phenomena.

### The Model

My views about the nature of anorexia nervosa were crystallized by my study of Andrew. Since then, I have perceived the disorder to be based in a phobic *avoidance* response, with the *feared and avoided object being normal adult body shape and hence weight.* Calorie restriction, crucially generating reversal of calorie/growth-dependent pubertal development, is the avoidant mechanism through its associated experiential relief. Anorexia nervosa is a refuge, sometimes defiantly denied as such. Statistically speaking, this threshold (biological, perceptual, and experiential), below which weight must be maintained to secure the stance of total avoidance, seems to be, from our own studies, neither 75 percent nor 85 percent but precisely 82 percent of mean matched population weight.

The fear of normal adult body weight may not be obvious or readily communicated, but it is exposed as powerful in any situation that requires weight gain to a fully normal level. It is often most covert in early-onset cases (in which an abortion of development and associated weight gain, rather than a retreat from mature adult body weight, is of the essence) and in chronic cases (in which it can be lost sight of after years of satisfactory maintenance of a pathologically low and subpubertal body weight).

This fear is, for me, a defining characteristic of anorexia nervosa but, of course, is driven by the particular conflict-laden meaning of normal body shape and weight for that individual. In Andrew's early-onset case, the panic was more about the escalation of growth he was experiencing.

The first level of necessary diagnosis is the behavioral syndrome borne of the biology of starvation, its unstable status in terms of weight regulation, and the defenses mustered to avoid ingestion or retention of ingested food in the presence of plenty. It is coupled with acknowledgment of the perception of being too fat. The second level of necessary diagnosis is the identification of the specific phobic avoidance stance, sometimes paradoxically not possible until significant weight gain occurs. The third level of necessary diagnosis is the identification of the underlying maturational problem. This problem can prove to be even more elusive of detection. The one protective effect of the anorexia nervosa has been to abolish it, whether it has been a simple fear of further development, differentiation and separation, shame or disgust over sexuality, gender doubt and pain, threatened disintegration of the family, exposure of alternative paternity, or whatever. Moreover, the maturational problem may never have been articulated even at the time when it was so powerfully operative, before the onset of the illness. With Andrew, the problems were recent and, to some extent, more explicit than is often the case. My first case was going to prove deceptively easy!

## Why Males?

No other disorder, apart from those based in the distinct male and female reproductive systems, presents such a skewed gender distribution. Some claim that as many as 5 to 10 percent of all cases of anorexia are male, but I believe that it is much rarer—closer to just 2 percent of all cases at the most. Some claim that it is becoming more common in males and that it is arising earlier—again, I doubt it as yet. It may be true that anorexia nervosa can lurk undetected in the male even more readily than in the female. After all, male clothing conceals skinniness more easily while the hallmark of secondary amenorrhoea is absent in the male. Yet, dietary restraint and preoccupation with undue thinness surely stand out more in the male. It is noteworthy that one of the first two cases ever identified as what was later to become known as anorexia nervosa was a male.

It is also often argued that both sexes are more driven these days, during adolescence, by a preoccupation with bodily appearance and control. Fashion is implicated as the driving force. Our own studies suggest that teenage females are no more concerned now with body shape and size than they were twenty years ago: 60 percent of seventeen-year-olds then reported feeling fat, wishing to be thinner, striving to lose weight then, and 60 percent report the same feelings, attitudes, and behaviors now; 15 percent then reported a desired weight of very low proportions (seemingly a subpubertal weight), and around the same proportion do so now. In my own practice, the numbers of new cases coming forward from a given catchment area have not changed in the past twenty-five years, nor has the mean age of onset.

In contrast with the females, only a small minority of adolescent males, recorded by others across the Western world, reported feeling too fat twenty to twenty-five years ago, and the same figures obtain more recently. Such males are likely to be actually overweight, growing rapidly, or transitionally or otherwise in a state of gender-identity doubt. Thus, in contrast with females, who are largely preoccupied with the amount of fat in their appearance, most males are more preoccupied with lean body mass: bodybuilding is the most common activity. Of course, in adolescence, both sexes may engage in excessive physical activity—for example, jogging, athletics, gymnastics—as a means of both weight control and the building up of lean body mass.

Claims that these biological gender-dependent behaviors are changing as male and female roles merge may have substance, but I believe that such changes have yet to express themselves through changes in the incidence or gender distribution of anorexia nervosa. Rather than fashion dictating such individual attitudes, I consider it a symptom of individual and group needs—a mirror of personal need. It is the structure, containing forces, and boundaries in society that today are much looser, overthrown by the student rebellions of twenty-five years ago and the emergence of the contraceptive pill. As institutionalized processes in society—such as courtship and engagement—have waned, the need for internal controls, especially in this post-religious world, is likely to take on a more physical form such as anorexia nervosa provides.

My own model for the pathology of anorexia nervosa focuses on the imbalance between calorie input and expenditure as the mechanism generating the disorder through a reversal of the pubertal process. Energy/heat/sexual impulsivity is selectively removed from the system, and residual activity targets essential ingestion of food in an endeavor to restore growth and full biologically mature function.

This final pathway is also open to the male although, unlike the female, the initial focus of dietary concern will not usually be with the very "fatness" that underlies sexuality. In the past I have claimed that some males who have developed anorexia nervosa have engaged in initial calorie restraint because of an actual obesity with which they were unhappy, while other males have sensed, accurately, that such dietary restraint was the pathway to greater impulse control (for example, of sexuality, aggression, alcohol consumption). Still others were dieting because of a sensitivity about "fatness" but with a search for greater femininity. This latter group were more passive and aware of their potential homosexuality. Anorexia nervosa, as it erupted in all such groups, could be seen as a defense against related conflict-laden concerns. Thus, the emergence of the condition required an additional backdrop—an overwhelming sense of insecurity, separation fears, boundary uncertainty, specific sexual identity fears, and so on.

### Male/Female Comparisons

Because males would seem to be protected from anorexia nervosa and resistant to its development, it might be expected that the male anorectic would show (1) greater genetic loading and (2) greater personal and environmental strain. There might also be different clinical features and a different outcome.

In fact, in our data bank of more than one thousand cases of anorexia nervosa, the males and females are remarkably similar, uncannily so in all clinical respects. Nor are there identifiable demographic differences when the 69 males are compared with the 931 females. The only discernible difference in prognosis is that men who vomit have a better chance of recovery than women.

Only when we come to background features is there some evidence of the presence of greater premorbid risk factors for the male: obesity is more common in the fathers and sibs, and "enmeshment" and "overprotectiveness" are more powerfully present in the background family systems. "Leaving home" and "identity crisis" are more commonly identified precipitants.

### Treatment Method Invoked by the Model of Psychopathology

Treatment needs to address:

The avoidant behavior

The underlying dyslipophobia—a normal-body-weight phobia—driving it

The maturational problem underlying the dyslipophobia

Assessment of the psychopathology in the ways briefly alluded to here aims to secure patients' trust and willingness to surrender control over their low body weight in the first instance. The prospect fills them with a panic that threatens to overwhelm them and must be contained within and by the psychotherapeutic relationship. For them, their entire destiny is governed by feelings about their weight. They need help to discover gradually that they are more than their weight.

These patients' target weight is to be set as the average weight for their height *at the age at which they fell ill.* Since that age, they have been emotionally regressed, certainly no more than about nine years of age, and in many ways almost prenatal/intrauterine. For instance, if they fell ill at age sixteen and are now twenty-six and with a Ph.D., no matter. They need to be helped once again to become sixteen and to grow with dignity from the position at which they fell off the developmental rails. The raison d'être of the Ph.D. may eventually come to be a casualty of the recovery. Because at this stage the anorectics can only think of themselves in terms of body weight, this contract makes immediate sense to them: they may begin to believe that you do understand the problem a little.

In the inpatient setting, such conditional control over weight gain is easier than in the outpatient setting. In both settings, the issue of empowerment requires special attention. However promisingly the patients settle in treatment at the outset, nothing is likely to hold them in sustained treatment if the psychotherapeutic relationship is not effective. The psychotherapeutic task is to engage the family whenever possible, to protect against splitting, and to establish a therapeutic relationship with all and sundry that can last for several years against a conditional background of weight gain and its maintenance by the patient, while enabling the individual optimally to grow emotionally from within the framework of no more than about 50 sessions.

With Andrew—male, early-onset, and compliant—my involvement was brief in the first instance, but his problems in a different form came home to roost with me ten years later. Even today, thirty-five years later, I suspect that his outcome could have been even better if I had been available to him (and his parents) more systematically and in the way I described above.

# ANDREW'S CASE

Andrew's case is presented in four sections. They illustrate his recovery from anorexia nervosa and relative well-being thereafter, although he remained dogged for years by recurrent gender-identity doubt and separation anxieties prompting non-anorectic crises in relation to stressful life events. He has now been "well" for twenty years.

1. Andrew was first assessed and treated in hospital for anorexia nervosa in 1961, at age fourteen. He was followed up patchily until age seventeen. His treatment and that of his family was primarily psychotherapeutic.

2. He next presented with an acute identity crisis of psychotic proportions, having just overdosed, at age twenty-five. He required admission to hospital. Treatment was again psychotherapeutic, and he made a rapid recovery.

3. He next asked for help in a dysphoric state, fearful of his aggression toward his girlfriend. He was age twenty-eight and again required hospital admission. He made another good recovery.

4. He is now forty-seven years old and has willingly presented himself and reviewed his life story with me for the purposes of this chapter.

## 1961 (Age Fourteen)

When I was asked to see Andrew on an emergency basis, I elected to meet first with his parents. They were very fearful about the dangers of his condition. They felt disempowered and were floundering in their attempts to help. Some interesting background readily emerged. Mother emphasized her skills as a cook, her long-standing attachment to nourishing her children, and her belief in the centrality of feeding for a home environment. Stripped of this approach by Andrew's resistance to eating, she had no clue as to how to proceed. She had desperately asked him "whether there was anything wrong" but could not get a response. Father, a Frenchman, was an obese chef.

Such starkly relevant markers of underlying family psychopathology are, of course, not always present. In this household, they were associated with other facets of mother's temperament that were readily revealed: her tension, deep insecurity, sense of powerlessness, social anxiety, overprotective approach to her children, and inability to communicate other feelings; also, with father's overpowering but often noncommunicative presence. The initial picture of him, sketched by them both, was of his joviality. He was proud of his French origins. Doubtless, the parents' common belief in the importance of food in the human condition had brought them together. They claimed their relationship was a contented and sexually active one.

Andrew had been born in 1947, the second of three siblings. Edward, now age twenty-three, exhibited food faddiness during adolescence but no body weight disorder. He had had a fairly turbulent late adolescence but was now settled with a girlfriend. The younger sister, Aurelie, age twelve, was said to have been jealous from an early age of the attention given to the patient by his mother and had been a notably poor eater until the age of five.

Andrew had become increasingly finicky with his food one year previously, with progressive reduction of calorie intake. It readily emerged that, until age ten, he had slept in a small single bed in his parents' bedroom. A phase of food faddiness around the age of four or five had worsened, in the parents' view, when the mother persisted in trying to get him to eat more. He had had nightly nocturnal enuresis since infancy, except for one brief period of three weeks when he had slept with his father, three years previously.

At the age of eight, he had suffered from asthma and, subsequently, severe sinusitis for a year or more, during which period he walked in his sleep. He had failed a scholarship examination at age eleven but was now doing well at school. The parents did not believe he had developed any liaisons with girls or had any sexual experience.

The parents' wholehearted wish to commit Andrew to my care seemed to reflect their anxieties about his acute medical state and their inability to help him themselves. They acknowledged that they felt in some way to blame, and I invited them to reflect on their importance in Andrew's life.

Next, I met with Andrew. He was a wan, emaciated young man, lying in a hospital bed. After some initial introductions, I invited him to share with me the nature and development of his condition. I acknowledged that I had already met with his parents but that that must not preempt our discussions. He reported that twelve months previously he had decided he was getting too plump. He had been called "Fatty" once or twice by a friend (this was later revealed to be a sardonic remark regarding his relative leanness even at that time) and, almost certainly more significantly, "pop-bellied" by his brother. Andrew accepted my suggestion that this term had alerted him to his growing physical similarity with his father. He had indeed called his father "Pop" for some while a few years previously. Photographs of the time, however, revealed a relatively tall, lean lad with just the slightest hint of some "puppy fat" around his abdomen.

At this stage he began to reject his father's recent efforts to "build him up"; particularly, he began to avoid hot foods and puddings. Seven months previously, he had attended a talk at school on the evil nature of masturbation and the attendant risk of self-inflicted damage. This lecture had had a profound effect on him, and for the next three months he strove to end the habit.

Four months ago, he found that the need to masturbate had gone. At the same time, his nocturnal enuresis ceased.

At the outset he had weighed 119 pounds. Now, on admission to hospital for investigation, he weighed 96 pounds, at five feet eight inches tall.

Within this first consultation, Andrew admitted that he felt great panic about putting on weight. He had a persistent fear that he was too fat and, otherwise, was only concerned that he was missing school lessons and homework. Apart from this, rapport was good. He was not depressed. He pleaded that he be allowed to leave, promising that he would now eat. His eating improved following the first consultation, and he gained two pounds. His parents then asked that he be discharged back to their care. A diagnosis of anorexia nervosa was made, and he was allowed home on the condition that he see me weekly, together with his parents, for further psychological exploration and treatment.

My view at that time was that his guilt over masturbation, probably rooted in the frequency with which he practiced it and the fantasies associated with it (which I took to derive from his witnessing his parents' sexual intercourse), had been intensified by the experience of the talk at school on the dangers of masturbation. He described the teacher as "dirty-minded" and basically interested in having intimate one-to-one meetings with distressed boys. Andrew's more frequent masturbation had coincided with his pubertal growth spurt; it led to feelings of loss of control over his sexuality and was perceived as associated with his transitory development of puppy fat, which he identified with his father's girth and constitution. Furthermore, the mounting panic had come to be relieved by dietary calorie restraint, and its intensification had totally resolved the problem for him as his sexual impulse and conflict-laden identification with his father became overridden by his starvation. Only later was I to associate the mechanism with the reversal, more or less, of the pubertal process itself. Having found this refuge, Andrew was prepared to pay the price—of having anorexia nervosa. Although it might have resolved some of his mother's mounting separation anxieties, her own panic, guilt, and disempowerment had also driven her to seek help for him. Father, too, was disempowered and had gone along with this pursuit.

During the next three months, Andrew returned dutifully to the outpatient clinic as required. Once outside the hospital, our relationship became more distant despite my attempts to remain engaged and to examine some of his developmental problems. His parents were clearly desperate now to succeed in getting him to eat, although father ceased to attend the clinic. In fact, Andrew continued to lose weight. He began to complain that he was finding light exercise increasingly exhausting. Reluctantly, he admitted that he was not eating the midday sandwiches his mother gave him and that he was refusing breakfast and eating a meager evening meal under protest. At the end of March, he lost more than three pounds in one week. In April, he suddenly developed a puffy swelling of the face and neck that subsided after a few hours. In mid-April, he weighed eighty-eight pounds with his clothes on. He looked and admitted to feeling very ill and was immediately taken back into hospital.

Andrew now weighed only seventy-nine pounds; a figure that suggested he had hidden weights on his body when weighed in the outpatient clinic. His height was still five feet eight inches. He appeared grossly underweight. His skin was dry, cold, rubbery, and had a marked bluish tinge over his abdomen and extremities. His pulse was fifty-six per minute, blood pressure was 80 / 60 (on his previous admission, his pulse had been fifty-two and blood pressure 120 / 80), and temperature ninety-seven degrees Fahrenheit. He was put to bed, and treatment was instituted immediately.

At that time, here in the United Kingdom, a regimen of small doses of insulin plus chlorpromazine was used as a treatment for anorexia nervosa. I instituted this regimen as a pharmacological background to the continued attempts at psychotherapy. I subsequently discontinued the insulin and continued just the chlorpromazine. A normal diet (2,200 to 2,400 calories per day) was prescribed. Andrew started to eat and gain weight. He seemed to put himself in our hands from the outset, and his parents accepted this.

The psychotherapy undertaken at that time, thirty-four years ago, is subject to the distortions of my memory, restrained only by the brief documentation still available to me. Andrew seemed comfortable in my company. We talked about his reemerging sexuality as his weight increased and about the return of his nocturnal enuresis. He was able to consider the possibility that the foundation of this latter habit had been fueled by a wish to separate his mother and father in the bedroom by getting his mother up to attend to him. He could accept that his habit of masturbation had been triggered at an early age by the "closeness" of his mother and father within their bed. However, he could not amplify on this.

Andrew said frankly that he sometimes had realized that his food intake had been restricted, but he had steadfastly been convinced that his weight was satisfactory. He was able to describe how he at times had wanted food but had not dared touch it. He was now aware, however, that he was underweight, that he was hungry and able to eat.

Weight was restored from 80 to 110 pounds in just over four weeks, a much more rapid weight gain than I would plan for now. Andrew tolerated this gain well, although he panicked and lost 5 pounds soon afterward. Thereafter, he stayed at around 105 pounds for some time, still five feet eight inches tall.

Shortly afterward, I moved to work in another hospital, but within nine months I was able to arrange for Andrew and his parents to come again and see me occasionally. The parents now could say more about their incompatibility, though not much, but I was not too concerned because Andrew seemed to be doing fairly well. For a year or more, he had failed to thrive but had held his weight. At this stage, the parents again pressured him because they felt he was still unwell. I was able by then to institute more frequent consultations for the next year, and I continued to see him until he was age seventeen. Shortly after stepping up the frequency of visits, Andrew began to gain weight again.

Still concerned to avoid fatness, he was now keen to build up his lean body mass. He was not concerned about body weight as such under these circumstances.

For the first time, he could begin to share doubts about his masculinity. His bodybuilding attempts were another endeavor to resolve this questioning through a change in his appearance. His masturbatory fantasies were heterosexual, perhaps determinedly so, and he showed a social interest in girls (but from a distance). He took up playing the drums. He went to college to study art. He grew in height to five feet ten inches, and his weight increased to around 170 pounds. He became spotty and slightly overweight. Nevertheless, he appeared much more robust in his bearing and his attitudes. I was busy, and we said good-bye in 1965.

## 1972 (Age Twenty-Five)

After no contact with Andrew for several years, he was suddenly referred, acutely disturbed. He had been admitted to a medical ward after an overdose with fifty aspirin tablets "as an attempt to test my fate." When first seen, he had been in a state of extreme confusion or perplexity, with depersonalization and somatic ideas of disturbed identity of psychotic proportions. I was contacted because of his previous lengthy treatment with me.

What follows is the hospital note of Dr. Ross Kalucy, the physician on the team who undertook Andrew's inpatient psychotherapy during this admission.

---

### ANDREW B: ADMISSION AND DISCHARGE NOTE

Andrew is the second of two boys, and there is a third child, a girl. Andrew for some reason was always seen as a rather delicate and unhealthy child by his mother, and slept in the same bedroom as his parents until the age of nine or ten. The presumptive reason was that there was no room anywhere else in the house. However, at the age of nine he was moved into his brother's bedroom. It emerges, during the course of his therapy, that the arrangement was of profound importance in that he frequently witnessed sexual intercourse between his mother and father. Moreover, it was the habit of his parents to have a commode in the bedroom, and he witnessed his mother and his father using this during the night. During his phase of regression in our present treatment, fantasies concerning this came into evidence.

By the age of nine, Andrew was bed-wetting nightly and compulsively masturbating. He described his fantasies during masturbation as of two kinds representing two needs. One was a masochistic and self-humiliating kind in which he imagined himself being urinated upon by a woman, probably his mother, and the other a rather sadistic kind in which he imagined himself biting and sucking on a woman's backside, again probably his mother. It emerged at a later date that these fantasies related to the infantile experiences in his parents' bedroom and his confusion between their sexual relationship and their excretory functions. When he masturbated, he did not use his hands but lay flat on the bed as if he were having intercourse, pressing his stomach down into the bed and at times having normal heterosexual fantasies. When he developed anorexia, his masturbation disappeared, and this was satisfying to him.

After hospitalization, aged fourteen, he recovered well, at least in terms of his weight. He was left with the belief that his masturbation was an important contributory factor to his anorexia nervosa.

In other ways his progress has varied, with periods of definite well-being. However, he has never settled to a job or course of action and never had a clear view about his future.

Features of continuing psychopathology have included a preoccupation that he regards as the opposite of anorexia—that is, that his body is too small. He has embarked on a long period of bodybuilding. He has been convinced that his legs are too thin and feminine in nature and used to wear two pairs of trousers to school. At other times, he felt that his skin was too feminine or became obsessed by the fact that he had acne, which, as he saw it, related somehow to social circumstances particularly in relation to girls.

In his midteens, he seemed particularly well. He made friends and was working in a band as a drummer (possibly some sort of masturbatory equivalent). At this time, an event of some importance occurred between his brother and his father. The father had always presented himself as a rough, very aggressive, heavy-drinking, working man who had frequent fights with the mother, many of physical intensity. These usually occurred over meals, and in retrospect, as Andrew got better on this occasion, he found them absolutely absurd, but at the time often thought that his father might kill his mother. On one particular evening during an argument, the older brother, Edward, thought that the father might be going to kill the mother and had picked up an iron and struck father across the head. Father fell to the ground and wept copiously for some hours and thereby shattered the boys' image of their father's masculinity and aggressivity. With respect to this, it is interesting that, as Andrew developed his anorexia, the father became impotent for some while (information from the father) and also began to drink more.

It is difficult to know at what stage and what events finally caused the present decompensation in Andrew. Around the age of twenty or twenty-one, he found himself in a perplexed and uncertain state again about his body, himself, and his future and seemed to not know who he was. He ceased working and spent the next year indoors, primarily with his mother, who would not seek psychiatric help for him. He masturbated compulsively and was enuretic nightly. He was very withdrawn and depressed. It was at this time that symptoms such as a conviction that there was something wrong with his testes and that, in particular, the testicular bag was too low, came into prominence.

He recovered spontaneously from this and went to work as a driver with a young man whom he admired greatly, who seemed to be his ideal of a masculine figure—that is, good with men, happy-go-lucky, well organized, forceful, and ambitious. Masturbatory fantasies remained heterosexual. He had a car crash at Christmas that year and was in hospital for some months for a cartilage operation on his left leg. There he met a nurse to whom he began to write, claiming that he loved her. He said, "I wanted to be in love before I really knew her, it was like an insurance policy." He went out with her and found himself, on a particular night, alone in her flat with her. They went to bed, and he experienced an erection. She then told him, apologetically, that she was a somewhat inhibited person, and before he could achieve penetration he lost his erection. He began to doubt himself and was too frightened to try again. He had the feeling that it may have been very painful for her (recalling that this was how his mother had sometimes seemed to react within the parental bedroom). The following morning he tried again but lost his erection and concluded that he was impotent. He has never attempted sex again. He also thought that perhaps inhibited girls made men lose their erections. When discussing this, he concluded by saying, "I've got no strength any more, I can't go forwards or backwards," a statement which somehow summarized his confusion and uncertainty about his identity and himself.

Over the last few years, he has worked on and off and recently again experienced uncertain and confused thoughts and feelings about his skin and body. His compulsive masturbation and enuresis have continued.

Two months ago, a girl had made obvious sexual advances toward him. He did not know what to do, and when the girl inferred that he might take her home, he found himself blushing deeply and had to leave. Shortly after that, during a conversation at work with another girl, she told him that women had better skin than men. This latter statement, he said, completely stunned and paralyzed him; it was "stupid," but it somehow "took something out of me" and "it was as if I had suddenly come across myself, as if I had met myself and as if I couldn't hide any more." This would seem to have been a heterosexual challenge to which he felt incompetent to respond even though it had been appropriately directed toward him. He continued to work but found it a great struggle to face this girl each week and eventually left for a new job a few days before the present admission.

On the first day of his new job, his parents thought that he was "O.K.," but he now says, "I was petrified all day, it was as if I wasn't there" (severe feelings of detachment and depersonalization). He could not return to work and was panic stricken the next two days. He then had a series of experiences which were of psychotic intensity. First, he looked in the mirror and it seemed as if someone was inside him looking through his own eyes. He felt that it was not himself any more. He could not be certain who the other person was but was scared to look in the mirror any more in case the person came through. He felt as if he was occupied by an alien being. He had the sudden conviction again that his testes were too small and a compulsion to tear them off. He looked down at his hands and felt that they were not his. He was not frightened but felt completely cold-blooded about it. He next revealed his panic and perplexity in his mother and father's presence, and they took him into their bedroom for the next two nights, where his enuresis and masturbation stopped. However, his panic mounted.

At interview on admission, it was almost impossible for him to give a coherent story, although many of his actions suggested a more hysterical and stylized feeling of panic with a strong "as if" quality about them, rather than that he was basically schizophrenic. To us, it appeared that in some way he was trying to demonstrate his confusion and uncertainty but that the feelings were not always there to match the action.

His mother was seen. She was a very tense, strange person who seemed to have a somewhat easy acceptance of Andrew in his decompensated state and a rather vague recollection of him in his well state. This was consistent with the fact that later, whenever Andrew was in fact especially well within his recovery phase, she would telephone me to say how worried she was about him because he looked haggard and listless. She noticed dark rings under his eyes whenever I thought he was doing especially well. At the same time, she was very frightened at the initial interview that he might be mad and said that she also felt there was part of herself recognizing the need to separate more from Andrew. She talked a lot about how strange he was in the bathroom: "He is like a woman, he is in the bathroom for so long, he fiddles with his skin all the time, he is so slow." She described the father as hateful to him. She was also resentful that her husband had become "so different" since Andrew's original hospitalization.

Diagnosis on admission was acute identity crisis in an obsessional personality, with strong somatic preoccupations of delusional intensity. The patient was thought to be functioning in a psychotic fashion but not to be schizophrenic.

During the next few days, Andrew lost all signs of psychotic preoccupation, although he still occasionally worried about the appearance of his eyes and reported continuing fears of looking at himself in the mirror. These disappeared within the next week. For the next month, he was quiet and shy but worked hard at his psychotherapy and enjoyed the opportunity of being isolated from his home since I would not allow him home visits. He found visits from his parents very difficult, his mother in particular seeming to overpower him. She remained a most anxious woman.

Mother wept almost every time she met with Andrew. She talked of her great feeling of blame about him but nonetheless continued to see him as sicker than he now was. She felt very depressed that he was being rather rejecting and distant from her. Father, on the other hand, presented himself in his usual rough and rather aggressive way and had no real understanding of Andrew. He seemed concerned, however, and prepared to wait and to fulfill his role as best he could.

I saw brother Edward, who, it now emerged, had undergone similar periods of depersonalization and identity difficulties and left home at age sixteen after his father's "disintegration." Edward had still not settled into a role in life and was basically living off the land. He had taken up many jobs, including being an artist, and was at the present time involved in constructing pictures from clock parts. He had been married and this had failed, although he had been pleased with his unexpected sexual potency. He shared many of Andrew's difficulties in understanding himself and his family and felt that the only chance he had had for survival was to escape.

The sister was seen, and she appeared rather well. She too had left home at about sixteen years of age and had gone to live and work several hundred miles away. She did not wish to talk about why she had done this or how she lived her life, but it was clear that she was much better organized and much less affected by the pathological circumstances of this family. She was living with a man in Spain in what to appeared to be a not too deviant way and was clearer and more assertive than her brothers.

Andrew was involved in many of the ward activities, especially via his music, in which he had some real skills. He went through a period of wanting to be a composer and to write. He taught many of the other patients to play the guitar and spent a lot of time with the anorectics on the ward, chewing over his past experiences and possibly being helpful to them. It was to me as if he was working through some anorectic experience of his own, although he denied any residual traces of this within himself.

He had one experience of some interest when he was made the leader of a group in which there was another patient who was quite psychotic. Andrew found himself becoming too involved with this man, such that the relationship was somewhat like that with his mother. He found himself dominated by the patient and following instructions from him almost without thinking about them. He again became slightly perplexed. His blushing had disappeared by this time, but he found asserting himself in the ward community meetings difficult.

After a further month he decided that he did not want to talk about the past with me any more but that he now would like to talk with Professor Crisp for a couple of hours about his past experiences with him and also his belief that Professor Crisp attributed his troubles to masturbation. Andrew found this an improbable idea. The assertiveness with which this was carried through was a sign of his emerging wellness. The way in which he was able to talk also did a great deal toward making him feel particularly well. He became insistent on leaving hospital in the near future. He now, in effect, separated himself from me in many ways, rejecting our help and

g out on his own to get a job. He took up a job as leader in an
adventure playground, an interesting combination of maternal and
paternal roles and is doing well. He lives with a group of young men
in an apartment and is developing social heterosexual interests. He
is no longer interested in music or composing and is fully occupied
in his job. He is able to accept encouragement from me that he
should again try to establish a relationship with a suitable girl. We
discussed "suitability" in the context of his previous failures with
women and his experience of his mother!

At the present time his prognosis again looks fairly good. The
time may have come when he can be freed up from his stuck identity crisis by further advice regarding his heterosexual behavior. Final
diagnosis: Acute identity confusion state. There is no evidence now
of anorexia nervosa, and he has lost all of his recent psychotic ideas.

## 1975 (Age Twenty-Seven)

Andrew's next contact with us was nearly three years later. Again,
he was admitted, after an urgent assessment; he had contacted
us out of the blue in great distress, asking for help. For the previous few weeks, he had developed an increasing fear that he was
going mad. During the previous two months, he had experienced
terrifying nightmares. More recently, he had developed aggressive feelings toward his established girlfriend that were alarm-
ing them both.

He reported that, after leaving hospital the last time, he had felt
good. He had returned to work in a children's adventure playground
in a London park. He continued to have problems in asserting himself. By 1973 he had met his present girlfriend, who is training to be
a teacher. They have a satisfactory relationship.

Andrew and his newfound girlfriend initially worked together in the adventure playground but then became disenchanted with it mainly because of mounting conflict with an older boy. At this time they were living together and Jane had become pregnant. With his agreement she secured an abortion because she wanted to go on to teachers' training college. In retrospect he feels that this was an important and disturbing event. He had panicked at learning of the pregnancy but at the same time had felt vindicated in terms of his male identity. Around this time he also began writing poems for children. He found another job as a gardener. Eighteen months previously, his nightmares had started, although they were initially less terrifying. His social anxieties had also escalated, not least, he felt, because he now needed to relate to adults rather than children. He left his job after six months and became withdrawn. He started masturbating again, something that hadn't happened since his relationship with Jane had started. He particularly remembered an outburst of aggression following a party when he had smashed a glass. A year previously, he had started a job as a van driver coincidental with Jane starting her teacher's training. Six months previously, he had become aggressive again whilst drunk, causing tears and distress for Jane. A nightmare at this time had the content that he was both towering and cowering in the corner, telling Jane to leave him alone. He secured a new job but remained introspective and especially fearful of meeting with colleagues. His nightmares of the last two months had largely consisted of him dreaming that he was buried alive, being strangled by a large hand; he would wake up sweating and with his pulse racing. He had a sense that the events of this dream were occurring in the room where he had once slept with his parents. After these nightmares he would return to sleep but in the morning would be riven by panic and also would infect Jane with it. Three days previously, they had been to a cinema and seen a mildly pornographic film, following which he had telephoned his mother to seek reassurance about his anxiety. Since that time he had been unable to sleep and was even more terrified of being with people. He has felt increasingly aggressive toward Jane and feared that he might seriously harm her.

Examination of his mental state revealed no delusions or hallucinations and no evidence of depersonalization. He again settled well and rapidly after coming into hospital. The content of his thoughts centered round his fear of losing control of himself and of going "mad." Residual disturbed affects were related more to anxiety than depression.

Andrew remained in hospital for five weeks, engaging in the routine group psychotherapy and unit community therapy meetings. During the first week it was proposed to him that Jane should not visit. During this time Andrew spoke freely about his feelings that, by living with Jane, he was betraying his mother. The parents avoided visiting him. Once again, within the context of his relationship with us, he made an important decision to stay in hospital and, after the first week, Jane was invited to visit for conjoint therapy. Jane was clearly well aware of the constant emotional tug exerted by Andrew's mother. Now that her daughter had also left home, mother was left in stalemate in her essentially conflict-laden relationship with her husband.

Andrew was able to reiterate his long-standing efforts to separate from his mother and his wish to forge a future with Jane. He and Jane determined to stay together. He began to feel more in charge of himself. His nightmares have not recurred. His mother seems to have dropped out of the picture. He became keen to leave hospital and return to living with Jane. He rejected the offer of further outpatient contact. It was made clear to them both that they could contact our service again should they feel the need.

---

## 1994 (Age Forty-Seven)

Twenty years later, I tracked Andrew down to his new home in south London, where he is living with his wife, Jane, and their two children. He was willing to meet with me and talk about his life and the thoughts he now has about the anorexia nervosa and subsequent illnesses and their origins.

He vividly recalled our first meeting when he was fourteen. "I remember the great sense of relief that there was someone who apparently knew that I needed to express myself and say things I was keeping inside."

"And perhaps meanwhile quelling by means of your anorexia nervosa," I replied.

He agreed. "I felt I could speak freely."

This was a salient and humbling reminder of the importance of listening, of being nonjudgmental, and of the helpfulness, at the outset, of my interpretation of the transference—differentiating the "good" me from the "bad" parents—in establishing effective communication with Andrew. I had been unaware at that point of the fundamental importance of these attitudes, which were the basis of Andrew's liberation to begin to talk and to begin to gain weight by eating.

Andrew went on to say how he also remembered the ward and, in particular, one remark of mine: "I can't imagine you being fat." I now have no idea whether and why I might have said precisely that. I would rarely advise such a comment now! It might imply that I would be unable to tolerate the patient at normal body weight, that I was myself disgusted or panicky about fat. But, in Andrew's memory, it had been a liberating remark that enabled him to feel that he could safely gain some weight in the first instance without losing control of either the weight or the attendant reemerging pubertal impulses.

Reflecting again on his parents, he reported that his father had died seven years previously. Prior to that their relationship had improved somewhat. His father had remained emotionally cut off but less volatile and violent. Edward, now age fifty-three, was well and seemed to be living a fulfilling life in France, together with his wife and three children. Their sister, Aurelie—married, with two children, and living in Germany—has been depressed since experiencing a subarachnoid hemorrhage three years ago, from which she has recovered physically. Andrew believes that this illness activated her sense of self-imposed isolation from the family and that she would now prefer to be living back at "home."

He also vividly sketched in his mother, now living in residential care, as anxious and fearful of the outside world as ever and handicapped as always by specific phobias of crowds and open spaces. He now gets explicitly irritated with her and considers that he manages quite well without her. Her long-standing reiterated comment is "Life is a fraud."

Andrew thought that he had always been the "sensitive one" as a child, especially close to his mother and physically like her. He recalled the panic he felt as his body began to change with puberty and as he realized he was expected to be male and could no longer conceal this (doubtless fueled by his mountingly guilt-laden primitive masturbatory fantasies).

He now admitted for the first time that, after his first discharge from hospital, he had gone through a phase of fairly frequent bingeing and vomiting that had lasted for nearly a year. He recalled the experience of being able to eat and yet not gain weight as "amazingly powerful." During this time he kept his distance from me until I reestablished contact, and we had then met sporadically for the next few years. During this period he began to feel physically and mentally stronger but still with "lots of unfinished business." I had not really helped him with this, other than by general encouragement and support. During this period he had striven to prove his "masculinity" with body-building exercises as previously described but had remained locked into his frequent masturbation and the "same old fantasies" until age twenty-four, when he had first attempted sexual intercourse and failed. He still lived at home, and on returning home on this occasion to find his parents engaged in one of their classic battles, he had made a conscious decision to overdose, not especially caring about surviving but also believing that it might provide the only means of reestablishing contact with us. All he now remembers of his state at that time was his sense of helplessness and panic and, on one occasion during his inpatient stay, the experience of "looking in the mirror and seeing my mother looking at me." This experience was transitory, and he remembers reverting to a state of contentless panic.

He attached great importance to the almost daily expert individual psychotherapy he received at this stage from Ross Kalucy on my team. This he recalled as a "lifesaving experience" that "returned me to normality and put me on the right road."

The next three years clearly constituted the key transitional period for Andrew. He met Jane, who was sexually experienced, and their relationship blossomed after some initial stumbling. His bed-wetting had petered out by 1974 or 1975.

By 1975 he felt "strong enough" to write a long letter to his parents in which he blamed them for his developmental problems and said that he now wished to distance himself from them. He wrote to them, "If you and Dad had got on better (he was still primarily addressing his mother), I would not have suffered in this way." Typically, his father never responded, but his mother wrote back saying that she was very upset, but she did not deny the charge. Subsequently, he "regretted making them suffer" by writing in such a way. He now believes that this event precipitated his 1975 admission under our care. He did not reveal it then, although the transitional psychological state that he was in at the time was well recognized and worked with.

In 1978 Andrew and Jane were married, having by then lived together for four or five years.

I asked Andrew how he felt now about having had anorexia nervosa as a male. He has no great concerns about this. At one stage, he had wondered whether he was homosexual by nature—finding himself admiring the physique of his partner during the time they worked together driving a lorry. In retrospect he believes this to have been related to no more than a natural admiration associated with his own bodybuilding endeavors, and that is also my assessment of the situation.

He is inclined to believe that, without anorexia nervosa, he would now be a more aggressive person. He is well known for being gentle but wishes he could "blow a fuse" now and again. Being aggressive would have been identifying not only with his father but also, he thinks, with his mother. He agreed that sex had been a frightening and guilt-ridden experience for him for many years, seemingly unassociated with any genuine intimacy linked to love and security. He recalled having the urge to challenge his father, whom he saw, fearfully, as very powerful.

He considers that he has been well now for twenty years (see Figure 1.1). He reports eating normally. He feels physically strong, weighs a steady 170 pounds, and is five feet ten inches tall (BMI 23 / 24). He has considerable stamina; he exercises healthily.

Andrew would not like to gain weight, and he uses his trouser belt as a measure enabling him to eat sensibly. He also has no wish to lose weight. He still dislikes the appearance of his legs, which he believes (correctly) look very similar to his mother's. He also gets anxious in large groups, especially if he has a leadership role, but he does not avoid them.

Andrew has continued to work with youths and is now training as a child development officer. This training will equip him to work in a senior role in his neighborhood, planning local play and care groups. As a child, Andrew rarely played. His two children, age fifteen and thirteen, are "great." There is no hint of depression—more a sense of maturity and relative contentment.

Andrew had quite severe anorexia nervosa at age thirteen to fourteen. It would probably have become a life-long affliction, but with immediate treatment, he recovered from the avoidant position fairly rapidly. He was left with major impulse-control problems in the first instance, and thereafter with major maturational problems that precipitated two further psychiatric crises during his twenties before they were sufficiently relieved by further individual psychotherapeutic help. As a result of experiences such as these, we would now routinely expect to engage psychotherapeutically with anorectic patients during a five-year period of increasingly attenuated appointments that aim to sustain a continuing, contained "other"-significant relationship for

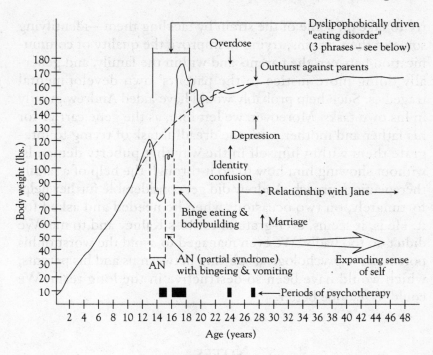

### Figure 1.1
### Andrew's Weight Biograph

An initial episode of a growth-phobic avoidance stance associated with burgeoning puberty was triggered by separation anxiety, an identity crisis, and emerging problems of impulse control. This led on to eating disorder repercussions of a non-anorectic kind over the next several years. Subsequent identity and separation crises did not precipitate further eating problems. They were also addressed psychotherapeutically by the same team, which led to resolution of the main conflicts.
AN = anorexia nervosa

the individual on the necessary time scale for further emotional growth. (Overall, with this model, the average number of psychotherapy sessions spread out through this period is usually about fifty.)

The family conflict in which all of Andrew's difficulties were embedded was never properly addressed within the family itself. These days, I would devote much more time to it systematically within that context. I would expect Andrew's parents' "ups and downs" to be revealed within the first assessment. We could then try to take off some of the strain by tackling them—identifying some of their origins, trying to improve the quality of communication between the parents and within the family, and generally doing more justice to the parents' own developmental tragedies. Such help probably would have aided Andrew greatly in his own tasks. Moreover, we left him, as the gene carrier for his father and mother, with the dreadful task of trying to integrate them within himself in the way that puberty demands, without showing him how to do it through the help of a family therapeutic approach. Andrew did get considerable further help, fortunately, on two occasions when he needed and asked for it. He is, it seems, ever-grateful to Ross Kalucy and to me. We didn't do too badly. We even managed to avoid the worst of his potential for psychological splitting between us and his parents, which would have been so destructive in the long term. We could have done better.

## NOTES

P. 1, *anorectic:* Note on terminology: whereas most clinicians generally use the adjective *anorexic*, some clinicians, like Dr. Crisp, prefer *anorectic* for those individuals who have anorexia nervosa, and reserve *anorexic* for those who have a true loss of appetite.

P. 2, *was duly written up:* Crisp, A. H., & Roberts, F. J. (1962). A case of anorexia nervosa in a male. *Postgraduate Medical Journal, 38,* 350–353.

P. 4, *the maturational problem may never have been articulated:* Crisp, A. H. (1980). *Anorexia nervosa: Let me be.* London: Academic Press, pp. 63–74.

P. 5, *one of the first two cases:* Morton, R. (1694). *Phthisiologia: A treatise of consumptions* (S. Smith & B. Walford, Trans.). London: Princes Arms Press, p. 4.

P. 6, *the need for internal controls:* Crisp, A. H. (1980). *Anorexia nervosa: Let me be.* London: Academic Press.

# 2

# PSYCHODYNAMIC PSYCHOTHERAPY AND ACTION-ORIENTED TECHNIQUE
## *An Integrated Approach*

### Judith Brisman

As an interpersonal psychoanalyst specializing in the treatment of eating disorders, I have been confronted with an ever-present dilemma over the course of the last fourteen years. I want to help my patients understand and appreciate the complexity of human behavior. I also want to appreciate and help them with their urgent wish to assume control over their lives—as quickly as possible. These two goals are often incompatible.

Prior to specializing in the field of eating disorders, I was Director of Group Therapy in the Alcoholism Department at St. Vincent's Hospital in Manhattan. There the counselors—recovering alcoholics themselves—taught me to respect the insidious power of substance abuse and addiction.

"You may think in the sessions you're talking about some important psychological issue," they told me, "but all the patient is thinking about is whether or not he or she is going to make it through the day without drinking. We know. We've been there."

To a newly trained Ph.D., this warning was both humbling and bewildering—and I was to heed it well in my work with the eating-disordered population, substance abusers of a different sort.

After St. Vincent's I went on to develop and direct an outpatient center in Manhattan for the treatment of eating disorders. There I learned to listen even more closely to the concerns of my patients and their families. I deepened my respect for the entrenchment of the eating disorder in these people's lives. I also began to think about my patients' varying capacities to self-soothe and tolerate emotional experience. Many treatment situations seemed to evoke in me the need to intervene with the patient in ways that were directly reparative and structuring, developing with them alternatives to food and dieting as means of self-care.

During this time, I also received training in interpersonal psychoanalysis at the William Alanson White Institute. There I became more aware of the actual interactions that tenaciously evolve between patient and therapist. For example, was my need to intervene directly with some patients derived from a respect for deficits in their developmental makeup, or was it a countertransferential response based on interactional patterns existing between me and the patient?

No matter which way I turned in my work with this population, I could not neglect a respect for any of the philosophies or experiences that were to inform my understanding of the eating-disordered patient. My work with many patients began to involve the use of action-oriented techniques to help structure out-of-control eating rituals. But an ongoing consideration and exploration of what might be transpiring between patient and therapist was to remain integrated into the therapeutic exchange.

Interestingly, I have found that no matter how much I intervene directly in my patients' worlds, no matter how focused I am in helping them structure their eating behaviors, the psychodynamic material is never lost; it is, on the contrary, enhanced. No matter how "real" a figure I am in attending to the eating and food issues, the patient nonetheless experiences me within a narrowed, historically prescribed perspective—and I inevitably conform to the feared or desired visions. The work in treatment entails an ongoing integration and exploration of the constantly evolving interventions and dyadic exchange between patient and therapist.

This chapter presents a means of working with the eating-disordered patient in which psychodynamic and active interventions are integrated into the therapeutic model. The patient is a young woman whom I will call Lisa. Although chronologically a young adult, Lisa's developmental level remained fixed at the stage of adolescence. For example, she actively struggled with issues relating to identity consolidation and separation from her family. Thus, my references to Lisa often consider her as an adolescent despite her actual age. Identifying information has been changed, and many of the complicated details of a three-and-a-half-year intensive treatment are condensed or only superficially presented. Lisa's story, however, accurately reflects the directions and inevitable complications that need to be attended to in work with any eating-disordered patient. The specific treatment with each patient inevitably varies. The concerns one must keep in mind remain unchanged.

## INTRODUCTION TO THE PATIENT

I liked Lisa the minute I met her. A twenty-two-year-old rapid-fire talker with a quick wit, she got down to business immediately. She supplied me with an organized array of information about herself, apologizing for a lack of hearty historical facts but instead offering a description of relevant emotional experiences and a detailed account of the evolution of her eating disorder. The hardest part of my work during this initial interview was to keep my pen rolling fast enough to keep pace with the material coming my way. She was curious, bright, and perceptive about her shortcomings; she kept me alert and engaged, often with a twinkle of her eye or an unspoken invitation to laugh with her.

I smiled to myself, thinking how hard she was working to make me feel comfortable and how effective she was in doing her job! I listened to her history, wondering where Lisa had learned so well to meet the needs of others.

## What Was Not Remembered

Lisa did not actually remember many of the facts of her child-hood and adolescence. Ultimately, a narrative of her life had to be constructed piecemeal in treatment. Lisa tended to record her history, not by events, but either with emotions ("That was a good time"; "High school was hard") or with markers related to food and weight ("Junior year was great because I was skinny"). Thus, the first meeting was as much a statement of the sort of information that was *not* remembered as it was a description of actual events.

Lisa could only reconstruct her early years from stories she had heard and from hypotheses that we would begin to gener-ate as early as that first session. Throughout my work with Lisa, I wondered whether the lack of memory might be due to trauma, overt or subtle, that was never specifically revealed in treatment. Alternatively, however, I considered that Lisa's hysterical style of retaining and relating information was a learned means of interpersonal relating, engendered to facilitate connection and security. From the little information available, it was apparent that Lisa's experience of herself was suffused with that of her mother. It would have been hard for Lisa to retain idiosyncratic memories about her own experiences; she was too involved in living someone else's life.

## What Was Remembered

Born in 1968 to middle-class, caring parents, Lisa was a long-anticipated second child. Her brother had been born seven years previously, and despite many years of trying, Lisa's mother had not been able to successfully conceive until her pregnancy with Lisa. Lisa's mother, who had maintained her role of caretaker of the family, delighted in the second opportunity at parenthood.

Lisa's mother plunged eagerly into the role of participatory parent. She anticipated Lisa's needs and made herself available to attend to them. She helped Lisa with any task at hand and made sure to contribute ideas as to how any experience could be more successfully attempted. She made up projects for the two of them to do and kept Lisa at her side—always. Lisa's father worked hard at a burgeoning business venture. He was steady and reliable, but basically not all that present. And the truth was that no one seemed to miss him. Mother and daughter's time together was always so busy and so much fun.

Despite the obvious complications that would later result from this well-intentioned parenting, what Lisa did remember of her early years, she remembered fondly. She loved her mother and enjoyed the unending time and devotion. She tended to stay at home, rather than engage in playdates or overnights. Mom always had something for them to do together. These years were experienced as more satisfying than not for Lisa—likely because they were times that she and her mother could "merge" with regard to emotions, activities, and time together.

As a child, Lisa was of normal weight and had no apparent eating problems. Once faced with pending developmental changes of adolescence and the inevitable separations from home and from familial values, however, Lisa's difficulties began to emerge. She started to gain weight in high school, and by the end of her sophomore year she was about ten pounds heavier than she would have liked. She describes eating "a ton of junk food all the time"; the subsequent weight gain was inevitable. A humiliating comment from a boy in her class ("Getting a little chunky there, Lisa") was the inspiration for an intense dieting regimen that resulted in weight loss throughout the next year. By the end of junior year, Lisa had lost thirty pounds. At five feet six inches, she now weighed 105 and had stopped menstruating for four months. Lisa's parents were understandably alarmed. For the first time, Lisa's mother wasn't sure what to do but did urge Lisa to meet with a therapist. A short stint of psychotherapy allowed Lisa the expression of feelings that had previously gone unrecognized—feelings of being left out with her classmates, the fear that other girls didn't like her, the concern that she would somehow lose her family. This brief intervention allowed Lisa to relinquish the anorexic hold over her psyche. She put on ten pounds over the summer, regained her period, left treatment, and dug in to make her senior year "different."

Two months into the fall semester, however, despite maintaining a weight of 115 pounds, Lisa experienced a renewed panic regarding her body. This time, instead of voicing her concerns, she turned to bingeing and vomiting to quell rising tensions. "I didn't have the willpower to be anorexic again," Lisa lamented, as she, like many other young women, switched symptomatology in a desperate attempt to exert control over her life. She kept her daily bouts of overeating and purging hidden from family members and friends. Lisa's focus on food took primary importance over social events and classwork.

Lisa never gave up on herself entirely. She maintained B grades in school, and her performance was unremarkable enough to avoid calling attention to her mounting problems. Boyfriends entered the scene in as chaotic a manner as the food—many intense initial contacts followed by disappointing losses. Despite several attempts by boyfriends to pursue physical contact, Lisa remained a virgin. She found the whole "sex thing" disgusting.

Lisa applied to college and, in the spring of senior year, was accepted into a local university. She lived in a dorm and interchanged bulimia, interactions with young men, and interactions with college therapists almost at random—beginning each interaction to "make things better"; ending each interaction in disappointment. During her sophomore year she lost her virginity to a boyfriend who would remain in and out of her life for the next several years. She had, during her college years, sexual relations with two other boyfriends as well. But sex remained, at best, unsatisfying—usually something she was "supposed to do." She had no idea what it was like to be orgasmic.

Relationships with girlfriends were, for the most part, short-lived. Although she sustained two friendships past college years, Lisa often thought other girls didn't like her. "Mom," however, was always close at hand. Lisa's "best friend," her mother, could be reached any time of day or night. These calls, as one might expect, were frequent—perhaps two or three times a day if either was having a rough time.

Lisa graduated with a general degree in liberal arts. She ended college life unsure about a career direction. Her heart had "been broken" several times, and she was wary of entering a new social scene outside the bounds of a college environment. She maintained her weight at 120 to 130 pounds but continued to struggle on and off with bouts of bingeing and vomiting that felt out of control, isolating, and hopeless.

One month after graduation from college, in an impulsive but inspired attempt at autonomy, Lisa left her home and college town and moved to New York City with her college roommate. The two found an apartment to share, and Lisa obtained a job as an assistant in an advertising company. The job was low paying, but Lisa's father would be paying for her share of the apartment, as well as many other expenses, until she got her feet on the ground financially.

Lisa embraced the move to New York with her familiar optimism and hope. She stocked the refrigerator in the new apartment with salads and vegetables, vowing to eat healthfully, relinquish the bulimia, and "this time, change for good." Her vow was kept for three weeks.

In a bout of despair, at 2:00 in the morning after an evening of eating and vomiting nonstop, Lisa called her mother and revealed that she had never been cured of her teenage eating problems, that she had been bulimic for years. By midmorning the next day, Lisa's mother had come up with the names of three specialists in Manhattan, including my own. Lisa called me that afternoon. I was able to see her the following day, and our three-and-a-half-year treatment began.

### Engaging the Patient

Although much information is needed and many complex decisions must be made in a short amount of time, Lisa made my work during the initial interview quite easy.

My primary goal in any initial session is to make contact with the patient, to allow her the experience of being understood. This is usually hard enough. In addition decisions need to be made about treatment recommendations, including the use of medication, medical intervention, nutritional assessment, group work, and the inclusion of the family in the treatment process. After many years of practice, I'm now usually able to make many of these determinations within a first meeting, although I keep open the possibility that I will need to meet with the patient more than once for assessment. Whether the patient is seeing me for an evaluative consultation or for longer-term treatment, my message to her is that this is a joint collaboration in which her input is as important as mine. With Lisa, there was no need for reminding.

I start the consultation with some version of the question "Why did you decide to seek treatment now?" This question opens the door for a description of current concerns, usually involving the eating disorder specifically.

Lisa gave me detailed information about the progression and current state of her symptomatology. Although the anorexic condition in high school had been fairly mild, the bulimic symptoms were entrenched and psychically debilitating.

At the time of the initial interview, Lisa would eat minimally until evening—usually coffee for breakfast, a small salad for lunch, and a piece of fruit before dinner. Once home from work, however, she would allow herself free rein to eat anything she could imagine. Sometimes two deliveries would arrive at her door at the same time—perhaps pizza and Chinese food. Or she would go out to the local deli and buy a combination of cake, cookies, crackers, peanut butter, and always, ultimately, ice cream—"To help it all come up." Lisa never planned these binges. In fact, she engaged in a daily struggle not to overdo it at night and made sure not to keep any food in the apartment; her roommate worked late hours at a nightclub and was never home, so Lisa basically was the controlling force regarding the status of food in the house. But if she was really honest with herself, Lisa found that she looked forward to these evenings of abandon. She avoided making plans, with the ulterior motive to come home and eat. She would rarely be in the apartment for more than twenty minutes before she relinquished her plan to "eat little tonight."

To purge herself of the food Lisa vomited, and by the time she called her mother for help, she was throwing up three or four times a night, eating in between. Patients need to be asked about other means of purging as well, such as laxative abuse, diuretics, fasting, exercise, and enemas. Although vomiting is the most common means of ridding oneself of food, patients can be quite inventive. One woman I met sat in a sauna twice a day, her entire body wrapped in cellophane to accelerate the loss of water from her body; after only twenty minutes, she was guaranteed the immediate satisfaction of seeing the scale go down a pound or two.

Pay special attention to the use of drugs as a means of curtailing appetite. Cocaine and amphetamines in particular are often used by women to avoid the urge to overeat. Lisa had no history of drug or alcohol use, save for an occasional drink or two.

A detailed assessment of the development of symptoms will inevitably lead to other historical data. Further, I am interested not only in the content of what is said but also in how this information is related to me. Here I am opening the door to an analytic engagement with the patient that can begin as early as the first session.

In Lisa's case, I shared my experience of the session with her toward the end of the consultation. I told her that I appreciated the work she put into our meeting and found her very helpful. I commented that initial meetings weren't always smooth and enjoyable for me and that while I delighted in the fluidity of the session, I wondered whether she always made it so easy for everyone. And I wondered what the meeting had been like for her.

In speaking to the patient in this manner, I am doing a number of things at once. Primarily, I am trying to reach the patient with the tools I am most familiar with—those of analytic understanding. I am offering the (as yet unspoken) possibility that there is more to the picture than food. And I am waiting to see what the patient does with the introduction of my thoughts and language. I both learn more about the patient's dynamics and begin to assess the patient's capacity to make use of an analytically oriented approach to treatment.

Lisa felt very understood by my comments. She knew exactly what I meant and even offered examples that contributed to my understanding her means of relating in this manner. She was excited by my "not just buying her stuff," as she put it, and said she often felt as though her experience was completely lost.

Nonetheless, I found myself wondering if Lisa's response was not, in fact, an example of the very issue I had just brought up. I felt so competent and effective at that moment that I wondered if once again I wasn't being taken care of. I would often have this type of interaction with Lisa throughout the treatment, and would come away delighted and, at the same time, doubtful about what was really going on.

### Attending to the Symptom

Lisa was frantic about her lack of control with food. To overlook this aspect of Lisa's experience, to focus just on the "underlying issues" would replicate a history familiar to many of these patients. That is, I would be covertly insisting that I knew more about the patient's experience than she did and would be imposing my language, that of analytic inquiry, onto our interaction. Eating-disordered patients have a facile ability to switch from their own language to another's as a way of complying with what they perceive is needed or expected of them. A therapist's unspoken belief that talk of food and weight avoids discussion of more pertinent issues will be quickly intuited by the patient and will be experienced as a demand to "act differently"—which the patient will do. Here the patient's experience will be relinquished for that of the "caretaking" other, and the patient will be locked in an interplay in which her needs are lost in deference to the needs of others—as they had been repeatedly with parental figures.

Thus, the treatment of the eating-disordered patient entails a complicated exchange involving the language of the patient—discussion about and direct intervention with the symptom—and the language of the therapist: an analytic exploration of feelings and behavior. The crux of treatment is the actual interchange of two people's differing experiences and languages, their hopes and expectations, their mutual disappointments and retreats from each other. Exploration of how two people can interact without merely submitting to or retreating from the other's experience is the goal of this sort of therapeutic work.

## Choosing the Right Treatment

In Lisa's case, I recommended individual treatment on a twice-weekly basis.

In addition to individual psychotherapy, I often recommend group treatment for the eating-disordered patient. Because eating disorders are isolating and involve distorted images of body and self, involvement with others who share these concerns can be an invaluable means of support and feedback. Group also provides a place to explore one's effect on others—and vice versa.

During the second meeting with Lisa, I broached the idea of group therapy as a means of additional support. I suggested a long-standing, interactive, nurturing psychotherapy group run by one of the therapists on staff at my center. Lisa immediately agreed to join, but as we discussed what group therapy meant to her, Lisa's fears quickly surfaced. She was afraid the young women in the group would dislike and reject her, as had girls in the past. Even though this was the very type of concern she would need to address in group, it became clear that Lisa was only considering group because she thought I wanted her to. She preferred not to take on too much at a time when she felt so vulnerable.

We agreed, therefore, that Lisa should, for the time being, put the issue of group on hold. One focus of the work in individual therapy would be to help her more firmly establish what she needed from group and what her goals might be, instead of entering yet one more situation that would potentially end in disappointment. As it turned out, Lisa never did enter group. For many patients, however, this type of initial discussion sets the stage for more effective use of group when they are ready to include it as part of an overall treatment plan.

Lisa and I also considered but agreed to wait with other treatment options—in particular, nutritional counseling, psychopharmacological intervention, and family therapy. These adjunctive therapies should be considered for any eating-disordered patient.

In most cases, nutritional counseling is most effective when the patient has some understanding of the psychological function behind the problematic eating behaviors. Otherwise, the patient looks to a food plan as "the answer," assuming that if she just follows the plan, she will stop bingeing, purging, or starving. The plan fails as soon as psychic distress again disrupts healthy eating. When the patient better understands the role of food in coping with or avoiding stress and has developed means of self-care or self-soothing other than eating or starving, then she can effectively use nutritional counseling to make considered decisions about food choices.

I also like to include the family in treatment after the patient and I have a better understanding of what the family's introduction into the sessions means to the patient, to the family, and to me. With adolescents and young adults, who are living at home or whose family is actively in the picture (paying bills, for example), treatment should at some point involve family sessions. Parents need to be educated regarding the goals and expectations of treatment, specifically how they can best help their child in the therapeutic work of change.

The question is when and how to introduce the family into therapy. With Lisa, because issues of autonomy and separation were so important, I wanted to establish the privacy and security of Lisa's work with me before including her parents. We decided that I would want to meet her family when she and I could better define how they might be of help to her and what issues of entanglement or discord we could specifically address in the sessions.

Physiological issues need attention. All eating-disordered patients should have a medical evaluation by a physician. In some cases—for example, with a deteriorating anorexic or a bulimic who is withdrawing from abuse of laxatives—ongoing work with a physician may be required as part of the treatment plan. The internist can help determine the extent of medical involvement. Another important issue: has the patient had a recent gynecological examination? This question may open the door to future work in the therapy regarding bodily concerns and sexual apprehensions.

Current research indicates that for some patients psychopharmacological treatment—in particular, antidepressant medication—can be effective in ameliorating behaviors such as bingeing or purging. It is important to assess the patient's capacity to make use of a "talk therapy," however, before introducing the idea of medication. This assessment is particularly important with teenagers and older adolescents, whose tentative sense of self can be highly influenced by seeing themselves as "a psych case," as one of my patients put it when we considered her use of Prozac. Referral for consultation with a psychiatrist at the onset of treatment will depend on the severity of the eating disorder and other symptoms, such as anxiety or depression.

Because of Lisa's age and her previous ability to change her experience and behaviors through the use of psychotherapy, it made sense to defer the question of medication until she settled into individual treatment. As it turned out, however, after months of sessions Lisa didn't settle into much of anything. Ultimately, not only would medication be needed, but the family would be called in without the anticipated planning. Despite my thoughtful considerations, the treatment, as Lisa would prove time and again, was not in my hands alone.

## THE INITIAL PHASE OF TREATMENT

Like most other eating-disordered patients, Lisa entered treatment with a specific goal: she wanted to be rid of the eating patterns that left her feeling helpless and out of control.

Any patient who presents with bulimic, anorexic, or binge-eating symptomatology provokes immediate philosophical and clinical dilemmas for the therapist. The patient urgently wants to stop the bingeing or purging—or, in the case of many anorexics, the family wants the patient to stop the starving. The patient (or the family) is looking for directives and to stop the disruptive eating rituals. Discussion about food and weight may be the only language the patient has to communicate that something hurts, something is wrong. She often knows no other way to talk about herself in treatment.

Yet, if the patient is to enter into a treatment that focuses primarily on the symptom, she continues to be trapped in a narrowing world in which who she is remains focused on food, weight, and her body. These patients know how to *do*, not how to *be*. If you teach them to be "good girls and clean up their act," they learn to do it—at the cost of really knowing who they are or what they need. If the real needs and issues behind the eating disorder are not attended to, other symptomatology is bound to develop or, as was the case for Lisa, the disordered eating is temporarily relinquished, only to be resumed again in times of stress or psychic confusion. The therapist needs to hear the frantic concerns of the patient and family and to help the patient immediately and directly address the eating behaviors. In addition the patient needs encouragement to consider that there is more to the problem than meets the eye.

The work of the therapy with the eating-disordered patient thus becomes a mixture of direct intervention with the symptom (speaking the patient's language) while at the same time exploring what that very intervention means to the patient and what purpose the symptom plays in the patient's intrapsychic and interpersonal world (speaking the therapist's language). Eating-disordered patients tend to disavow the effect of interpersonal interactions on themselves and others. Any treatment that does not emphasize what happens between the patient and the therapist seriously neglects an important aspect of the patient's difficulties in living and sets the stage for resumption of disordered eating patterns in the face of future interpersonal stresses or bewilderments.

Treatment begins with listening to the patient's means of introducing herself—that is, in most cases, talk about food and weight. The therapist asks for a detailed description and history of the eating disorder: when the problem began, weight fluctuations over time, what is eaten, what is not eaten, means of purging, and so forth.

Over the course of the initial sessions, the therapist will want to take a careful look at the moments when the patient actually overeats, purges, or obsesses about food. The therapist can encourage the patient to use a journal, not only to record what she eats, but more important, to explore eating and purging behaviors. In particular, patients are asked to note situations, people, and emotions that trigger problems with food and eating. What was the patient thinking or feeling, for example, right before she took that extra bite of food? Can she note what she said to herself when she made the decision to vomit that night?

She made a *decision* to overeat; it was not out of her control. Can she catch and note what she said to herself that allowed her to eat more then she wanted?

During the early sessions the patient thinks and writes often in her journal about "alternative behaviors" she would be willing to engage in before turning to food: self-soothing behaviors, such as resting, taking a bath, letting herself cry; reflecting on her needs other than hunger and putting these needs into words. Alternative behaviors also include questioning where other people are at that moment. Can she call on anyone for support or help? If not, why? Finally, another "alternative" can be the use of food itself, but in a more controlled manner. Can the patient allow herself one piece of cake (for example) to satisfy a craving, and then write in her journal instead of bingeing? Each of these "alternatives" can open the door to a discussion of a wide range of psychological issues—for example, mistrust of others, envy, or abandonment issues. The art of this early work is the interweaving of the interventions regarding food with a broad examination of who the patient really is.

### The Use of Contracts

One means of bridging these different agendas is the use of contracts. A *contract* is an agreement made between the patient and the therapist to structure or abate disordered eating patterns. The patient makes a verbal agreement with the therapist to take one step in delaying or stopping the problematic eating behavior. She agrees to use alternatives, such as those considered above, instead of immediately eating or purging. For example, she may plan that, prior to the next session, she will not binge for one night. Instead, she will write in her journal about what she is feeling, call a friend, or plan a "healthy dinner" instead of an evening of uncontrolled eating. An important part of the agreement is for the patient to take sharp note of how this contract feels to her— and, perhaps, to write her thoughts and feelings in her journal, to be shared in session if she feels ready to do so.

The contract directly addresses the issues that worry the patient, explores and challenges the patient's eating habits, and helps her develop healthier coping skills and self-soothing capacities. "Contracting" also opens the door to an exploration of the patient's relationships. The contract becomes a vehicle for exploring the patient's relation not just to food but also to people—in this case, to the therapist, with whom she has made a negotiated agreement.

I want to know: What does the patient actually do with the contract? Does she keep the agreement? Does she avoid thinking about the contract once she leaves the session? Perhaps the patient keeps the contract in an attempt to be a "good patient" and secure a connection with the therapist in the only way she knows how—through compliance and submission. If she breaks the contract, perhaps she is letting the therapist know that she feels controlled or misunderstood. The patient's world broadens from an addictive relationship with food to an interpersonal exchange, an examination of the mutual effects of patient and therapist on each other.

## The Negotiation of Language

Prior to treatment, Lisa had been bingeing and vomiting daily. She couldn't remember what it was like to have an evening without food in the picture. So, she eagerly embraced the notions of a journal, alternative behaviors, and contracts as tools to help her change. We continued to focus on her daily eating rituals but quickly came up against the inevitable roadblocks.

Lisa liked the idea of paying close attention to what she was thinking or feeling before she actually binged in the evenings. But putting this idea into action, actually knowing what she was experiencing and writing about it, was much harder for her than either of us had anticipated. Lisa didn't seem to have the words for her experiences. About the best she could do by way of description was to say that she felt as if she were "jumping out of her skin." Finding effective alternatives to bingeing was equally difficult. Lisa did not know how to soothe herself. She hated baths, and if she read or watched TV, she still wanted to eat. She refused to call anyone at these times; she couldn't imagine anyone would help, and she wasn't about to set herself up for rejection. On the suggestion of a friend, she tried to meditate but found she couldn't push out of her head all her thoughts of wanting to binge. And if she wasn't thinking about food, she noticed that, even in this private time, she continually brought a stream of people into her head. Merely coming up with alternative behaviors or a contract was proving to be difficult.

This beginning work with Lisa was as critically important for its "failures" as it was for its "successes." These early difficulties opened the doors to an exploration of how Lisa operated in the world and to a consideration of why she was so entrenched in the eating disorder.

We were able to observe that Lisa would not let herself be alone. If she tried—for example, when she refrained from bingeing or began to meditate—she started to feel "too sad." We discussed how "things from the outside—people, food, therapists—were constantly called in to "make the feelings go away." I also began to wonder aloud why Lisa might be so sad in the first place. Unanswered at the time, this question hovered ever-present to color our future explorations and inform us later of the function of the chronic eating and purging.

Not only was the content of these early sessions important, an interesting process was initiated as well. Lisa was frustrated with my "language." Although the sessions were informative and looked as though they would get us somewhere, when Lisa was home alone, she couldn't articulate what she was feeling and continued to binge. She thought that a better "alternative" to the eating might be for her to draw pictures of her experiences instead of to write words. The need for Lisa to insert *her* language into our dyadic exchange (even though it wasn't a verbal language at the time) did not pass me by.

Lisa's pictures took the form of a crying or huddled child. For weeks, the child remained speechless. Lisa didn't know what the child was saying, and I did not want to insert my experience of the pictures in place of Lisa's as yet unformed words. Lisa was annoyed and frustrated that she was the only one who could give the child words. When *I* wasn't actively taking over, defining her experience, she felt I wasn't involved at all.

Despite Lisa's frustration with me, she was able to involve herself fully in her drawing and, for the first time, was effective in having a binge-free evening, substituting the drawing and a healthy meal for the hours of gorging on cake and cookies. One evening without bingeing and vomiting soon became several. What Lisa thought helped were the facts that she could actually get lost in the activity of drawing and also that there was no "right way" to draw. Since the drawing was her idea, she could not fail to live up to my expectations. She did contract for the amount of nights per week she would go without bingeing. In fact, she usually would decide not to binge for two nights and then succeed at three; or she would opt for three nights binge-free and manage four or five.

After several weeks, the paper-doll child developed some words. "I'm all alone," it said. "Everyone thinks they can see me, but I'm hidden away. I'm a dark and private secret. I'm crying most of the time."

Although Lisa knew "this is me," she couldn't understand why she would have such feelings. "My parents love me so much. They are the only ones who will always be there for me. I'm never alone."

We allowed this "kid" (it was genderless) to keep talking. As I told Lisa, it was hard enough work to know what it was saying, let alone why. Perhaps the why would come later.

During these first six months, Lisa made use, in fits and starts, of the contracts and the insights of treatment. She was still frustrated with me for not helping her more, not knowing why she was thinking the things that came to mind, but beginning to make overt and significant changes with the food. In particular, Lisa now had a burgeoning understanding of how she used food—as well as people, boyfriends, and so on—to intrude on her experience and take away less definable discomforts. Through the drawing, she began to give words to these discomforts—sadness, loneliness, despair at being overlooked. Slowly, the evening bulimic rituals diminished in intensity and frequency.

By the end of six months, Lisa could spend a week to ten days at a time without bingeing or vomiting. She maintained a fairly rigid schedule of eating: coffee and a bowl of cereal in the morning, half a muffin for lunch, two apples in the afternoon, and then a "regular" dinner (chicken, fish, vegetables, no bread or dessert) in the evening. But her weight remained stable, and she felt proud of her accomplishments. For the time being, the structured eating regimen gave her a margin of safety against her fear of losing control.

As the symptom diminished, however, and as Lisa's feelings of neglect and despair surfaced, the intensity of the sessions crescendoed. She became increasingly angry, upset, and depressed. Tearfully, angrily, she told me: "So what that I'm not bingeing so much. I hate my life, and I can't cope at work." Voice raised, she repeatedly demanded: "Nothing is working. Tell me what to do!"

## THE SECOND PHASE OF TREATMENT

Now six months into treatment, Lisa dug in her heels. She felt overwhelmed at work and wanted time off. Again and again I heard, "You don't understand how bad it is for me. . . . You're not helping me cope. I'm doing all the work." My attempts at exploring transferential/countertransferential material, the possible repetition of familial experiences, got us nowhere. Using the only language with which she thought she might be heard, as I saw it, Lisa turned back to bulimia with a vengeance. Now she was eating at work, vomiting in the ladies' room, bingeing on the subway home, eating and throwing up two or three times more in the evening, sneaking behind her roommate's back.

I had not expected this vehement outcry and inwardly was somewhat thrown off guard. There was a mounting hysteria to Lisa's behavior, and to be honest I wasn't quite sure how seriously to take her. Part of me wanted to tell her to "cut it out," that I was not going to take over her life, no matter how hard she cried to pull me in. Another part of me was very concerned, wondering what I had missed and what steps to take next. I considered medication but did not want to give Lisa the message that I couldn't take her upset and rage and that I wanted to shut her up.

Lisa didn't give me much time to think. Her bulimia intensified in two to three weeks, outwardly provoked by specific work pressures and departmental deadlines. We urgently discussed ways Lisa could better cope on the job. We questioned what she was trying to tell me about being overlooked and not understood. I shared with her my dilemma regarding medication.

In the midst of this therapeutic work, Lisa quit her job and actively provoked the involvement of her parents. Now they would have to pay all of Lisa's expenses. I received a message from the mother, another call from the father. Now was the time for a family meeting.

### The Family Sessions

Whenever a relative or spouse is introduced into the sessions, complicated issues of trust and confidentiality must be addressed. The individual patient must have absolute assurance that the therapist will not reveal any material from the individual sessions even if the family overtly or subtly questions what has been discussed: for example, "Lisa told you about the effect that move had on her, didn't she?" The family must be told outright that confidentiality is essential if the individual treatment is to proceed effectively. Exceptions to this rule arise, of course, particularly with adolescents and young adults, when destructive behaviors that require parental intervention and limit setting are present. In all cases, the patient and the therapist need to consider what information will be discussed with the family and how this material will be broached.

Families do *not* necessarily need to be informed about bingeing, purging, or starving. This information need only be revealed, ideally by the patient herself, if specific interventions must be discussed with the family—for example, medication or hospitalization—or if the family dismisses the troubles of their daughter.

In treating teenagers or young adults, the therapist must always be alert, on the one hand, to the dilemma posed by the need for appropriate parental involvement and respect, on the other hand, the equally important need to keep therapy a haven for secrets and the exploration of troubling concerns, safe from parental interference.

When family sessions are added, the therapist must listen for the unspoken expectations of both the individual patient and the family. Although everyone involved may agree to the same goals, each individual may bring in other hopes or fears. It is important, then, to make explicit these unacknowledged or unexpressed feelings during the therapy sessions. For example, while the therapist assumes that the sessions are initiated to facilitate or support change, the family may have something different in mind. Lisa's parents certainly wanted to know what to do to help Lisa. Equally important, however, they wanted to meet me and find out why one more treatment was, as they understandably saw it, failing.

Lisa and I agreed on several issues that needed to be addressed with her parents. She wanted to talk about how her mother and father could be more supportive both emotionally and financially as she weathered the current crisis. Lisa also was sick of their constant worry about her eating disorder and wanted them off her back. I told her that my own goal was to try to understand her difficulties better by meeting her parents, getting more information about her family history, and assessing the family's ways of interacting with one another. I also wanted to discuss the general direction of my individual work with Lisa in order to reassure her parents that the treatment was not without focus—even during this chaotic time. As well, I wanted to bring up the issue of medication. Finally, quietly, I also hoped that I could appeal to Lisa's father, who was understandably frustrated, not to withdraw financial support.

Lisa and I met with her parents for six sessions. We did not call Lisa's brother in to the meetings because he lived away from home and was not actively involved in the immediate crisis, and also because Lisa was embarrassed to be in the role of patient in front of him. We left his attendance an open issue to be considered in the future should we feel Lisa could benefit from his input.

Lisa's parents, though annoyed that yet another treatment was looking so bleak, were not bent on pulling Lisa from the sessions. Perhaps they were out of options as to what else to do. In any case, when we met, the sessions assumed the following focus.

First, I outlined how I saw the current situation: Lisa and I had been working on her taking hold of her eating behaviors and her life in general. She had made significant headway and then had become scared. It was unclear whether leaving her job was a good idea or not, but Lisa had done it in such a frightened, impulsive manner that, at the moment, no one was trusting her judgment. Lisa had also let us know, through the out-of-control eating, that she was not feeling capable of making these steps on her own. We (the parents and I) would work together to find ways to support Lisa without taking over completely. Lisa would try to help us understand her decision to leave her job. I emphatically warned that if we were all not careful, we would end up suffocating Lisa with our help. We must not give her the message that she was incapable of running her own life.

Specifically, we discussed restricting the increasingly frequent calls between mother and daughter. We worked with the father to set reasonable financial bounds, which were both supportive and limiting. We explored ways in which the parents could help Lisa take responsibility for her own eating, instead of trying to stop the bulimia themselves by checking in and setting rewards.

We talked with Lisa about what she could do when she was most upset besides eat or call her parents. We explored the parents' reluctance to let Lisa go, Lisa's seductive pleas for help, and ways we all could support Lisa in taking responsibility for herself.

We reviewed the family history emphasizing the father's absence and the mother-daughter symbiotic closeness. The parents rejected the suggestion of ongoing family or couples counseling with another therapist, and understandably, these few sessions did not resolve the complicated family dynamics. They did permit, however, an articulated, structured idea about the family that served as an anchor for everyone to hold on to in the months to come. The sessions opened a dialogue among Lisa, her mother, and father; gave them all directions to consider and pursue; and initiated the process of change that would be evolving over (at least) the next several years. In particular, this brief work set the stage for the father's greater involvement with both his wife and his daughter and an encouragement for all to let Lisa grow up.

The family sessions would later end with specific goals for everyone and with the open invitation for any of the four of us to call another meeting if issues arose that needed discussion. In the months following these initial meetings, Lisa or one of her parents would occasionally bring up with one another the possibility of having another session, but no one took it further. Because Lisa's individual treatment picked up in complexity and development, I did not feel the necessity to bring in the family again. As time passed, I also began to trust that Lisa would handle issues with her parents without my direct involvement.

### Introduction of Medication

Meanwhile, the eating disorder remained out of control, and Lisa reported crying angrily each day because no one was taking her seriously. Still unemployed, she was feeling desperate. At this juncture, it seemed irresponsible not to consider medication.

In both individual and family sessions, I initiated discussions about medication, explaining the indications for its use, answering questions, and giving Lisa and her parents written information so that they would have a better idea of what to expect—and what not to expect. Given the urgency of Lisa's distress, everyone seemed relieved at the possibility of something, anything, that could help the situation.

I referred Lisa to a colleague, a psychiatrist who specializes in the treatment of eating disorders who had worked with me on a number of other cases. After the initial consultation, Lisa was prescribed fluoxetine (Prozac), which she started at five milligrams every other day. She met with the psychiatrist every two weeks for a total of four sessions and then once monthly for the next several months. Lisa felt immediate relief from the medication; she even wondered whether this might not be a placebo effect, in which she was instilling the medication with the power to take care of her in the way she had always hoped someone, something, would. In fact, the rapid positive effects did not last long, and during the next several months the dose was raised to sixty milligrams daily, within the usual therapeutic range for the treatment of bulimia. The result was a significant improvement in Lisa's depression and a noticeable decrease in her urge to binge (even though sometimes she wanted to eat "just because she wanted to"). Lisa was to remain on sixty milligrams of Prozac daily for approximately one year.

As I usually work when sharing a case with another professional, the psychiatrist and I talked once after the evaluation with the patient's permission. We discussed medication and treatment planning. We then agreed that it would not be necessary to talk again unless either of us—or Lisa—had a question about the treatment, for example, a concern that the collaboration between the two professionals was somehow being "split" by the patient.

In general, the goal was to respect the patient's ability to conduct herself responsibly with each of her treating doctors and not to patronize her with ongoing discussions without her being present. This way of proceeding is particularly important for the adolescent who, assuming that parental figures are still in charge, may be inclined to relinquish responsibility for her own care. In Lisa's case, the ongoing relationship with the psychiatrist, who was seen as the dispenser of concrete help, proceeded without incident.

## Intensification of Treatment

The introduction of medication, the limits set on parental involvement, and the hold on employment gave Lisa the sense that she was being taken seriously, which may have been as important as the actual interventions themselves in helping Lisa feel that she was being attended to and, then, calm down. The eating disorder abated once more. Days passed with no bulimic episodes. The crying stopped, and Lisa spent more time reflecting on what she wanted to do next with her life and career.

As the family, her job, and food moved out of the picture, Lisa's relationship with me heightened in importance and, soon, in intensity. What was happening at this point? Was the change in focus merely a learned agreement to speak the analyst's "language"? This was impossible to answer outright. The work at this phase is to listen as closely as possible to the patient-therapist interaction and to continue to posit the question, What is going on here?

Lisa did not relinquish her language of food and weight completely. In fact, she needed to keep the contracts as a part of our work, but defined them more broadly and planned them over longer time periods. For example, instead of paying attention to each night's behavior, Lisa wanted to contract that she would "only be 'bulimic' one time weekly" or that at least three times during a week she would write in her journal or draw when she was home in the evening. At this point, the contract served as a "transitional object" of sorts, a concrete way for Lisa to hold on to the work of our sessions, a reminder to listen to and soothe herself. Once, teasingly, she even referred to her journal as her "blanket" that she carried through the apartment to remind her to quiet down and listen to "what the baby wants." And, as with a blanket, Lisa enjoyed pushing and pulling at the contract to make it fit her needs. "Well, I know I was supposed to write in the journal or draw, but instead, I spoke to my friend and figured out what I needed that way. I can do that with the contract, right? I mean, I still used it to stop bingeing."

But now Lisa was also interested in other aspects of her experience. She was curious about her dreams, which played out themes of engulfment and imprisonment. She noticed that she worried about becoming too dependent on me. She wondered aloud what I expected from her and if she was my favorite patient. She was delighted about feeling more in control of her emotions and of the eating disorder and vehemently attributed the changes to the medication.

I probed, as I could, the depths of these issues. What was her fear of becoming too dependent? What did that mean? Why was it threatening? I thought to myself that, in fact, at that moment in time, she might well be my "favorite" patient. "Why," I wondered? Because she was so involved in the therapeutic process, because we had weathered the crisis, because her parents now were very pleased with me, because I *was* doing great work?

We explored the historical antecedents of Lisa's fear of dependency: her submersion of her sense of self in that of her mother and the resultant suffocation of her own experience. We saw the development of her eating disorders as an attempt to assert a sense of control over her life. We continued to consider how Lisa might be subverting herself in our interchange, what a "connection" to me meant to her, and how I might well threaten her.

And then Lisa came to a session and told me she was planning to take a six-month "leave of absence" from treatment. She had decided that the best thing she could do to foster a sense of self was to travel to California, where she had a friend; the two of them could explore the West Coast and Alaska, something she had always wanted to do. She had thought a lot about it and knew it would be a real growth-enhancing experience.

She had always wanted to do this? Where did *this* come from? I hit the roof. It's not often that I allow myself the freedom to feel spontaneously angry at a patient. Usually, I'm wondering why I am *not* angrier at a particular interaction in a session. Not here. "What are you thinking?" I demanded. "And who is going to pay for this? What about the three-month agreement you made with your father? And why now?"

Although I tried to contain my tone of voice, Lisa burst out crying. And then, to her credit, fought back. "You don't trust me at all. I told you I've thought this out. I thought our work was about my thinking for myself. Now you're telling me what to do, and you haven't even heard what my plans are." We went back and forth until the time was up. It was a true testament to Lisa's inner strength and commitment to the therapeutic work that she showed up at all for the next session.

With some days' time to think, we both returned to the therapy with our individual goals: I wanted to understand what had happened between us; Lisa wanted to show me how wrong I had been. In fact, our dialogue did ultimately affect and circumvent Lisa's decision to leave town. In particular, we looked at how Lisa presented herself in a way that evoked my lack of trust and provoked me to intervene in an angry, authoritative manner. We also considered the abruptness of Lisa's need to leave and the threatening aspects of the treatment.

In retrospect, I realized I also had contributed. We had become enmeshed in a "dangerous" entanglement in which my sense of well-being (in my exchange with her) had become related to Lisa's "achievements." Now I confirmed that the change in focus of the treatment, from food to more psychological issues, was a capitulation for Lisa. Lisa's newfound analytic curiosity was experienced, at least in part, as a submission, urgently provoking the need to "get out." No wonder the "child" she drew had felt so shut out, so alone.

Lisa and I explored the mutual, unspoken negotiations and agreements that we had made with each other. Was she to be my "favored child" in exchange for her compliance and aggrandizement of me? Had we, in fact, "contracted" for a relational exchange, in addition to the overt behavioral contracts, that kept everything on an even keel but narrowed the possibilities of who we were? Was the sadness she portrayed in her early drawings a result, in part, of the subtle dismissal of self, enacted in her earlier relationships and now in the therapy?

We set out to undo the tangled web of our engagement by understanding what had happened and why. The use of the behavioral contract was only the first step in our beginning to explore and appreciate the range of interpersonal agreements that Lisa and I had unwittingly made with each other. Now that Lisa's relationship with me, not the food, was the primary focus and now that the therapeutic arena had begun to encompass previously unacknowledged facets of our relationship, the stage was set for the unfolding of other previously foreclosed aspects of Lisa's identity.

During the next three months, Lisa explored employment opportunities. She ultimately landed an entry-level job in the arts, which over the next two years would blossom into a successful, well-paid career. In sessions, she continued to make use loosely of the contractual work with the eating behaviors; within several months Lisa relinquished the vomiting completely.

## The Middle Phase of Treatment

During the second year of our work together, Lisa and I no longer needed to spend much time addressing the eating disorder directly. Lisa, for the most part, refrained from vomiting. Under stress every month or two, she asked for the structure of specific contracts to "get her through." At this point she embraced writing in her journal more than drawing and used her writings actively in the sessions. Only twice during the year did Lisa resort to bulimic behavior. Her other eating changed as well. On her own, Lisa twice saw a nutritionist, who supplied her with new ideas for food choices. She moved from rigid, controlled eating to experimenting with her forbidden foods, which she successfully kept down—and enjoyed! She had now quite overtly shifted her interest from food to people. Her job flourished, and she began to date again.

We continued to explore the complicated dynamics of her inner and interpersonal worlds. Power, or control, is a common theme that emerges in the treatment of eating-disordered patients. They are awakening from a world marked by fitful fluctuations of control and lack of control—played out daily around food. Within their family environments, control and submission are often the interpersonal means of exchange. Such issues predictably arise in the treatment arena as well.

Lisa and I thus engaged in an ongoing exploration of power, dependency, and "hunger" with regard to food, men, and our relationship. Submission did allow for connection to and care from another person. However, the submission belied a coercive and tenacious pursuit of control. By positioning herself as the "favored child," by meeting others' needs even at the cost of her own, Lisa manipulated a tenuous but persistent hold over others—until, as with many of the men she dated, they imperceptively registered panic and fled.

Lisa also felt, as do many women in this population, like a cheat and a fraud. She dreamed, for example, that she had aced an exam but had stolen the answers from someone else. She noticed her desire to sneak food, rather than to eat outright. She recognized in dreams and associations her medication as the "crib notes" on an exam. Without this cheating, she would never do well.

Lisa was haunted by the experience of feeling "bad" and guilty, but she was not quite sure what she had done wrong. These feelings seemed to result from the belief that she had "stolen" affections, not earned them outright. If she didn't control what everyone thought of her with her constant laborious work at pleasing, she feared others would not stay involved with her. As long as she controlled her own actions, she could control others' experience of her, but she was left with only manipulated affectations, not true caring. A saddened child, lonely and despairing, entered the treatment room in full force. I spent several sessions listening wordlessly to Lisa's mournful sobs.

## THE FINAL YEAR OF TREATMENT

The treatment was now an unpredictable roller coaster of experiential exchange. Lisa progressively took even more risks with me. During some sessions, she was silent. She didn't want to tell me things. She grew annoyed if I yawned. She told me I looked at the clock too often. She peppered the sessions with angry attacks at the rigidity of my style, my lack of flexibility, my insensitivity to my patients.

"If I were the therapist, I would give the patient extra time if she were saying something important at the end of a session—unlike you." "If I were the therapist, I wouldn't charge if someone ran out of money—unlike you." Lisa sporadically canceled a few sessions; she was, for the first time, late.

During this period of "dare," as Lisa allowed herself to express her own ideas with conviction, I, in turn, began to feel quite controlled by her. I didn't dare look at the clock. I stifled yawns. I wondered about my fee policies and worried whether I wasn't a bit harsh.

We explored in these interchanges issues relating to control. The exchange of submission and authoritative demands between us recapitulated Lisa's relationships both with her parents and with the men she dated. This time, however, Lisa was more overt in expressing aspects of herself that had previously been too frightening to unleash or acknowledge. She was as annoying as any teenager could be.

Despite the difficult moments, Lisa was able to hold on to the work of the treatment and to an image of me that was more complicated than her original idealized notions. "I know I still like you, but I can still think you're very rigid, right?" As I didn't like her demandingness but could still like *her*: "I mean, I can't believe you're that dumb that if you didn't like this one thing about me you would stop liking *me*—right?"

During this period, Lisa stopped taking the Prozac "at least for a while—to see how I do alone." Despite her concern in letting it go, nothing much seemed to change.

## Termination Begins

Although we did not initially label it as such, the third year of treatment marked the beginning of the termination process with Lisa. By this point, the eating disorder had abated and was not the means through which Lisa was choosing to experience herself or her relationships. Her language had grown richer and more complicated; a kaleidoscopic fluctuation of emotions and interchanges took the place of a predominantly body-focused sense of self.

Many shifts occurred in Lisa's day-to-day life. Lisa had worked hard during the last two years to define herself as separate from her family. She spent many nights laboring over the decision whether to call her parents and get their advice or support on various matters. Sometimes she called, even as late as 3:00 or 4:00 A.M., in a fit of turmoil that had escalated as she debated not calling. For the most part, however, Lisa held out and developed an increasing sense of personal confidence and self-worth. My overt approval was very important at these times. I would give it freely even though I knew that, in later sessions, we would need to explore, discuss, renegotiate, and disengage from the growing dependency (perhaps mutual?) in our relationship. By the third year of treatment, Lisa was seeing her parents only at holidays or specially arranged visits and speaking to them no more than once weekly. The pain of not calling had passed, and she now enjoyed a growing sense of liberation in determining how she wanted her relationship with her family to be.

Lisa also had accomplished a task inherent in the work with eating-disordered women—with adolescents, in particular. Not only did Lisa take significant steps in separating from her family, she also disengaged from values of the societal "family"—especially those values that insist on skinny bodies for women and dissociation from the self. Lisa, more than many other women her age, now allowed herself full range when it came to eating. At five feet six inches tall and 130 pounds, she thought she could probably lose about ten pounds to look "ideal," but "it was just not worth it." She loved eating these days, did not deny herself much of anything by way of food, and no longer felt compelled to binge. During adolescence Lisa had overidentified with the culture's idea of what a woman should be at the expense of an evolving sense of self that would allow her own complicated and idiosyncratic experience.

Some months into the third year of treatment, Lisa began to date a young man steadily. Her previous dating had been short-lived, with continued disappointments reminiscent of college years. Lisa would get involved quickly with the "perfect man," and within weeks or months he would somehow disappear. The therapy had provided a stable base from which to understand and organize these disruptive rejections. This time, Lisa insisted, was different.

Lisa and her new boyfriend spent almost every day together. At least from afar, he seemed as interested as she. Now the therapy began to feel a bit less important to Lisa. In particular, she did not want to analyze her relationship with this new boyfriend. "Why can't I just enjoy it? Why do we have to put everything under a microscope? That's not how people live their lives."

The sessions became more superficial, with Lisa reluctant to discuss the intricacies of her private life—or the very need for a private life. For the first time, she wondered why she had to keep coming to therapy. And that, in fact, became the new subject at hand.

Initially, I questioned whether Lisa might not once again be running from treatment. With the assumed security that her boyfriend offered, perhaps Lisa could now flee without the fear that I would "coerce" her back into the fold. We went back and forth with this issue, but it seemed to get us nowhere. Fearing I might be missing the point, I eventually switched gears and encouraged Lisa to question why she felt she *had* to come. We discussed her concerns of independence, her fear of missing me, her conviction that, without me in the picture, she would surely "mess things up." But as the sessions continued, Lisa grew more intrigued with the possibility of "trying it on her own." Although I thought many issues could still be considered, I was not as convinced as she that she would "blow it" without me. Perhaps with my confidence in her as an anchor, Lisa ultimately set a date for termination, about six months ahead.

During this next half year, Lisa continued to see her boyfriend and to keep that relationship at arm's length from my "intrusive" explorations. Over time, however, it did not seem to me that things were going all that well. From what I could pick up, her boyfriend had begun to distance himself (albeit more hesitantly than the men in her past), and Lisa seemed more troubled than she admitted.

Again we looked at our interaction. Was Lisa feeding me bits of worrisome news that provoked my parental concern? If she wanted me to "stay out," why tell me anything at all? Why did I feel continually compelled to wonder how well she was doing without my "advice"? We considered that this last ongoing exchange might be Lisa's "going away present," one that would give me a continued sense of importance even after her departure. Three and a half years into treatment, with the work not feeling entirely complete, Lisa left treatment on the anticipated date, symptom-free and nervously eager to get on with her life.

## The Aftermath

After termination, Lisa called twice for "just a little help with something." Returned phone calls instead of actual sessions sufficed. Lisa seemed to need continued permission to be on her own, more than the actual short bits of "advice" that were requested. The calls indicated continued success with the eating disorder and a rocky but sustained relationship with her boyfriend.

# WHAT HAPPENED AND WHY

With regard to the eating disorder, Lisa's treatment was an unqualified success. With more far-reaching goals in mind, however, the outcome is less clear.

In particular, I remained concerned about Lisa's characteristic style of relating. I was never quite sure how much of our work was integrated into Lisa's experience of self and how much it merely taught her new ways to change behavior in order to win my favor. I wondered whether, by supporting her termination, I cut short vital struggles and in that way gave Lisa the message that anger and difficulties could only go so far. Was she running from treatment as she had at the start? While she was dating, her relationships were far from stable, rocked by the issues of control and submission enacted in the treatment. What material would have emerged if I had pushed a more prolonged therapy?

In the three years that Lisa and I worked together, one issue in particular was glaringly unresolved—the issue of sex. Lisa had sexual relations with a few men during the time I knew her, but she continued to experience, at best, disinterest and, at worst, disgust with sexual activity and her genitalia. She liked to be held and kissed, and she knew (of course) what to do to please her partner. But being touched sexually left her cold. She basically felt nothing and had never been orgasmic—with a partner or "on her own." She had absolutely no memories of any sexual trauma in her past and didn't remember sex being an issue one way or another in her family. Her mother had conducted, as Lisa put it, "the typical mother discussions" regarding menstruation and sex, and although "a little uptight when it comes to sex," her mother was, Lisa described, "basically a regular mother." Lisa could not elaborate what she actually meant. Her father, she reported, kept out of the way of the "girl stuff."

I tried to engage Lisa in an exploration of her inhibited sexuality in any way I could. But any time I pursued this line of discussion, Lisa would get anxious and say she didn't know what to talk about. Her mind would go blank. Alternately, she would get angry, noting that she had other things on her mind. This was my issue, not hers. No matter what route of questioning or exploration I initiated, nothing happened. No doubt, we were reenacting in the treatment her thwarted sexual experiences with her partners. But even trying to explore *that* idea didn't help. No matter what I did in this arena, Lisa was not going to let me in.

It is possible that Lisa's protective stance in the arena of sexuality (both with her boyfriends and with me) was one last entrenched vestige of her need to set boundaries and not lose herself in the experience of her partner. Or perhaps it was reflective of her adolescent level of development. Most adolescents are loathe to reveal any details about their sexual lives, needing to keep some piece of the developing self private. The quality of Lisa's few references to sex, however, was so heightened and her self-reported sexual experiences so shut down that the privacy was suggestive of distress, not of healthful self-preservation. In evaluating the success of Lisa's treatment, I cannot help but wonder whether I missed critical historical information suggesting sexual trauma or incestuous activity. If I had more vehemently insisted on Lisa's remaining in treatment, would the questions about sexuality or abuse have been answered?

The way I think about this issue with Lisa is informed by newly evolving perspectives in both interpersonal and feminist schools of thought. Here, the focus of analytic thinking has shifted from the more classical pursuit of truth to an exploration of the fluid, ever-changing effect therapist and patient have on each other while they create a narrative together about the patient's past and current life. This change in focus has critical relevance to the work with eating-disordered patients. At first, these patients are often at a loss when it comes to recognizing what transpires interpersonally between themselves and others. They can be, as was the case with Lisa, quite capable of discussing pieces of information about themselves, but they maintain a narrowed vision and experience as to their effect on others and vice versa.

Trying to establish a narrative about the patient's life, trying to understand what actually happened and what didn't, cannot possibly be attempted unless one also explores what the patient is doing with that very pursuit of "truth." Therein lie the concerns I have voiced regarding submission, desire to please, and the like.

It remains unclear whether continued treatment with me at that point would have been of benefit to Lisa or would have been experienced by her as one last replication of submission and dread. Likely, it would have been both. I had made a decision that Lisa needed to be supported in her "moving away from home," that it might be time for her to be on her own. That very decision was likely informed by interactions in the therapy that I am not even aware of. Having taken that route, however, the work that followed involved keeping a watchful eye on the interchanges and events to follow and listening as closely as possible to how Lisa was experiencing all of this. It was yet another aspect of the ongoing negotiated but always ambiguous relationship between therapist and patient.

Treatment of the eating-disordered patient is an ever-evolving interplay between the language of the therapist and that of the patient. My work often begins with steeping myself fully in the patient's psychic and interpersonal life in an effort to shift the focus for the patient from food and weight toward that of an interpersonal exchange. In doing so, the work then entails an ongoing analysis of the dyadic interaction, an exploration of the use of the symptom in this interchange, and an overt attempt to understand and disentangle myself from the narrowed means of exchange that inevitably develops. With Lisa, the therapy moved toward the exploration of issues involving dependency and separation, submission and control, and the ever-negotiated integration of my language with hers.

No two treatments are ever close to the same. Some patients immediately experience contracting as a thwarting pressure—

deterring, not facilitating, therapeutic action. In these cases, I quickly abandon this approach and I listen for subtler means of hearing and speaking my patients' language. Other patients cling desperately to any concrete bit of structure they can get. Here, the work over time may well be to wean the patient from the contracts and a dependent hold on the structuring aspects of treatment.

Despite how it may sound, I do not *constantly* explore the intricacies of my relationship with the patient! Weeks can pass as we discuss the patient's past or current life experiences. Some sessions are spent troubleshooting difficult situations; others focus on movies or sociological events. Often I wonder what the patient is doing with me at that moment. Often I forget to think about it.

The demanding work of therapy with the eating-disordered patient involves the constant interplay between knowing what one is doing, and a certain not knowing, a losing one's self in the language and experience of the patient and in the process of the session. The irony of any analytic work (and this is particularly important with this population) is that as soon as the therapist has a concrete approach in mind, as soon as he or she knows exactly what to do, the therapy inevitably turns out to be on the brink of becoming authoritative and doctrinaire—an issue not to be overlooked with a population of women who have relinquished control to their parents, their spouses, and their culture.

People are complicated. As treatment progresses, the therapy may well provide more questions than answers. It is with the ongoing consideration of those very questions that the patient's and the therapist's lives continue to evolve, continue to be affected and transformed during the course of treatment and over time thereafter.

## NOTES

P. 34, *Lisa's hysterical style:* For a more detailed description of hysterical means of retaining and processing information, see Lionnells, M. (1986). A reexamination of hysterical relatedness. *Contemporary Psychoanalysis, 22,* 570–597.

P. 36, *she turned to bingeing and vomiting:* Research shows that approximately 50 percent of anorexics develop bulimia when they resume eating. About 25 percent of bulimics develop anorexic symptomatology in their attempts to lose weight. Holmgren, S., Humble, K., Norring, C., et al. (1983). The anorectic bulimic conflict. *International Journal of Eating Disorders, 2*(2), 3–14.

P. 41, *Eating-disordered patients have a facile ability:* Brisman, J. (1994). Addictions. In *Handbook of interpersonal psychoanalysis* (pp. 301–316). New York: Analytic Press.

P. 41, *The crux of treatment:* For discussions of the complicated exchange between the eating-disordered patient and the therapist, see Brisman, J. (1994). Learning to listen: Therapeutic encounters and negotiations in the early stage of treatment. *Eating Disorders, 2*(1), 68–73; Bruch, H. (1973). *Eating disorders: Obesity, anorexia, and the person within.* New York: Basic Books.

P. 43, *Parents need to be educated:* Siegel, M., Brisman, J., & Weinshel, M. (1988). *Surviving an eating disorder: Strategies for family and friends.* New York: Harper & Row.

P. 43, *medication—can be effective:* Lewis, O., & Brisman, J. (1992). Medication and bulimia: Binge/purge dynamics and the "helpful" pill. *International Journal of Eating Disorders, 12*(3), 327–331.

P. 44, *If you teach them:* Bruch, H. (1985). Four decades of eating disorders. In D. Garner & P. Garfinkel (Eds.), *Handbook of psychotherapy for anorexia and bulimia* (pp. 7–18). New York: Guilford Press.

P. 44, *other symptomatology:* Zerbe, K. (1993). *The body betrayed: Women, eating disorders, and treatment.* Washington, DC: American Psychiatric Press.

P. 46, *the use of contracts:* Brisman, J., & Siegel, M. (1985). The bulimia workshop: A unique integration of treatment approaches. *International Journal of Group Psychology, 35*(4), 585–601.

P. 56, *What is going on here?:* For an interpersonal perspective to the therapeutic interaction, see Levenson, E. (1972). *The fallacy of understanding.* New York: Basic Books; Levenson, E. (1983). *The ambiguity of change.* New York: Basic Books.

P. 60, *Power, or control:* Boris, H. N. (1988). Torment of the object: A contribution to the study of bulimia. In H. Schwartz (Ed.), *Bulimia: Psychoanalytic treatment and theory* (pp. 89–110). Madison: I.U.P.

P. 62, *Her language had grown richer:* Brisman, J. (1992). Bulimia in the late adolescent: An analytic perspective to a behavioral problem. In J. O'Brien, D. Pilowsky, & O. Lewis (Eds.), *Psychotherapies with children: Adapting the dynamic process* (pp. 171–187). Washington, DC: American Psychiatric Press.

P. 63, *Lisa had overidentified:* Ericson, E. (1968). *Identity, youth, and crisis.* New York: W. W. Norton.

P. 66, *interpersonal and feminist schools of thought:* Levenson, E. (1991). *The purloined self: Interpersonal perspectives in psychoanalysis.* New York: Contemporary Psychoanalysis Books; Mitchell, S. (1993). *Hope and dread in psychoanalysis.* New York: Basic Books; Steiner-Adair, C. (1991). New maps of development, new models of therapy: The psychology of women and the treatment of eating disorders. In C. Johnson (Ed.), *Psychodynamic treatment of anorexia and bulimia* (pp. 225–244). New York: Guilford Press; Stern, D. (1990). Courting surprise. *Contemporary Psychoanalysis, 26*(3), 52–478.

P. 67, *trying to understand what actually happened and what didn't:* Research actually swings sharply from one extreme to another, indicating that anywhere from 4 percent to 65 percent of women with eating disorders report a history of physical or sexual assault. Zerbe, K. (1993). *The body betrayed: Women, eating disorders, and treatment.* Washington, DC: American Psychiatric Press; Bulik, C. M., Sullivan, P. F., & Rorty, M. (1989). Childhood sexual abuse in women with bulimia. *Journal of Clinical Psychiatry, 50,* 460–464; Jacobson, A., & Herald, C. (1990). The relevance of childhood sexual abuse to adult psychiatric inpatient care. *Hospital Community Psychiatry, 41,* 154–158; Palmer, R. L., Oppenheimer, R., Dignon, A., et al. (1990). Childhood sexual experiences with adults reported by women with eating disorders: An extended series. *British Journal of Psychiatry, 156,* 699–703; Shure, J. (1989). Sexual abuse linked to eating disorders. *Renfrew Perspective, 3,* 1–6; Tice, L., Hall, R.C.W., Beresford, T. P., et al. (1989). Sexual abuse in patients with eating disorders. *Psychiatric Medicine, 7,* 257–267.

# 3

# How Long Is
# Long-Term Therapy
# for Anorexia Nervosa?

## Paul Hamburg

For the past ten years I have been privileged to belong to a dedicated multidisciplinary team at the Massachusetts General Hospital that evaluates and treats hundreds of patients with anorexia nervosa and bulimia nervosa. As our collective clinical experience has grown, we have become aware of a remarkable phenomenon: some patients who have suffered from intractable eating disorders for several decades, with a dreadful prognosis at the time we first began to treat them, have achieved breakthroughs toward recovery after many difficult years of treatment.

We have often shared these stories of unexpected change at our weekly clinical meetings to cheer each other during the inevitable moments of despair that characterize long-term therapeutic work with severely ill and treatment-resistant patients. Often, we have urged each other to write about such patients in order to document their courage and persistence in the face of severe illness. Particularly at a time when scarcity of resources and philosophical myopia have institutionalized therapeutic despair, the reality of transformative change after long years of illness and treatment commands serious attention. It is in this spirit that I have chosen to present the story of Ms. Q, a woman who entered treatment demoralized and debilitated by decades of anorexia nervosa and yet went on to make incremental but astonishing changes over the course of long-term psychodynamic psychotherapy.

## THE STORY OF MS. Q

When I met Ms. Q six years ago, she was thirty-four years old. For seventeen years, she had lived in the austere, blank world of anorexia nervosa; her appearance was skeletal, and both her voice and her gestures carried the self-image of a young adolescent girl—dutiful, talented, but with hardly a trace of detectable authenticity or liveliness. Her most recent therapist of four years had been compelled by illness to eliminate difficult patients from his practice, and not surprisingly Ms. Q had been among the first to go. I was alternately daunted by her history of extreme low weight, medical precariousness, intransigence, and chronicity and impressed with the sheer fact of her survival. After hearing her story and feeling the emptiness of her current existence, I wondered what psychotherapy could offer a patient like Ms. Q after so many years of unremitting illness.

Had we encountered each other two decades sooner, at the time her personal development froze, she would have had more to talk about than her current litany of food rituals, exercise classes, and stories from her bell jar life in the condominium her parents had bought, now filled with stuffed animals, porcelain figures, and memorabilia of a life barely lived.

She was once a promising violinist, a star student at a nationally renowned conservatory, the apple of her mother's eye. By age sixteen, she had performed abroad with a symphony orchestra. She could have told me about her daily hours of rigorously enforced practice, about the beatings with a heavy stick that her mother would inflict when her interest or concentration flagged, about the friendships that withered because her mother forbade social contact with unsuitable children. Her stories back then would have been full of longing for a childhood that was abbreviated by parental ambition. She would have spoken of a handful of surreptitious dates, of adolescent desire now buried under the powder-dry ruins of the ensuing decades so fully devoted to self-denial and starvation.

By the time she graduated from high school, Ms. Q was solidly launched on her second, more persistent career as a hunger artist, a career that rapidly truncated the expression of her musical talent and landed her in a psychiatric hospital for the beginning of a tortuous chain of treatments.

### Family History

Ms. Q's parents were immigrants from Asia, survivors of hardship and loss during the Second World War. Her mother rarely spoke of those times, but quite recently, when she saw the film *The Joy Luck Club*, confided to her daughter without further elaboration that her own wartime history paralleled the tragic circumstances depicted in Amy Tan's narrative. Her father was a successful businessman who divided his time between Asia and New York. Both parents were immersed in intricate financial projects involving international investments, the details and outcomes of which were unfathomable to Ms. Q. The family's financial standing had always been a source of doubt and mystery for Ms. Q. Her parents spent lavishly and conspicuously (fur coats and diamond necklaces) and moments later pleaded impoverishment: "Your illness has finally driven us to bankruptcy."

Her only sibling, a younger brother, grew up relatively unscathed by the turbulence of the family, finished college, married, and moved to the Midwest, maintaining only a distant connection to his parents. Ms. Q was her mother's special favorite, and she received an indigestible surfeit of maternal expectation and possessive love. Mother and daughter were entangled in an embrace of power. Much later, Mrs. Q was able to express her remorse at treating her daughter so much like a treasured possession: she acknowledged that her way of loving might well have choked off Ms. Q's growth as a separate individual. During the early years, however, Mrs. Q was completely unreflective regarding the potentially harmful consequences of her stance as a parent and unable to pull back from the daily struggle.

For her part, Ms. Q complied with what was asked of her: she gave up dating, withdrew from schoolmates, practiced long hours each day, prepared for her concerts, and dressed up in pretty clothes for each performance. But one day she refused to eat. Her parents took her to see an internationally renowned expert on eating disorders, and at her recommendation, Ms. Q began to receive outpatient treatment for anorexia nervosa. Early treatment had no apparent effect on the emergence of her symptoms. Despite plummeting weight and escalating preoccupation with her body image and self-starvation, she continued to pursue her academic and musical studies.

Ms. Q attended a small liberal arts college for women, where her education was interrupted several times by medical and psychiatric hospitalizations. When she was healthy enough to attend classes, she did well academically. After receiving her bachelor's degree, she pursued further study in music, moving to the New England city where she has lived ever since. After receiving advanced training in baroque performance, she revolted against her musical shackles. At the time we first met, she had not played a musical note for more than a decade.

For a while she worked intermittently as a proofreader and editor for a publishing company. She remained fully dependent on her family, however, and as her eating disorder became more chronic, she stopped working altogether. For many years she could think of no reason to work again. Her family purchased a condominium where she lived with minimal adult responsibilities, sent her monthly checks to cover personal expenses, and paid all her medical bills.

Ms. Q's next attempt at negotiating with the adult world was to take up the study of ballet. Dance had appeal for two reasons: it made use of her aesthetic sensibility and it provoked her parents' venomous cultural disapproval. She began this pursuit rel-

atively late, compared with the natural history of most successful dancers. At first she was able to master the fundamentals of
classical technique and was considered promising by capable
teachers. She participated in several public performances. But
over time, her dancing career disintegrated much like the musical one that preceded it. Rather than achieve a professional level
of competence and confidence as a dancer, Ms. Q found herself
learning the same routine steps over and over again. She became
a disturbing fixture at a number of local dance classes, moving
slowly from advanced to intermediate to beginner's level, well
known to all her classmates as a familiar skeletal figure punish-
ing herself with hours of vigorous daily practice toward no discernible end. Occasionally, she would be banned from the studio
because her emaciated presence so upset the class.

### A Relentless Disorder

For several years she alternated between periods of severe calorie restriction with a medically dangerous low weight and binge-
purge periods accompanied by temporary weight gain. With rare
exception, her practice was to weigh little more than the bare
minimum set by her treatment team as the threshold for hospitalization. As an inpatient, she would gain weight under duress,
but on discharge she would refuse or would be unable to maintain her weight gain. Over a period of many years, her physicians
reluctantly came to accept that she hovered at the edge of biological catastrophe. They remained prepared to rescue her when
difficult life events prompted her to eat even less than usual.

Ms. Q complied without serious complaint with whatever
treatment her parents and doctors recommended, which is to say
she participated in the ritual of treatment. At no time did she
resist coming to therapy sessions, going to the hospital when that
was recommended, attending a group when referred, chatting
with her nutritionist about dietary change, or being weighed by
her physician. Within this territory of apparent compliance, however, her resistance to change was absolute. She disclosed nothing

of her feelings. She absorbed nothing from the concern or didactic zeal of her treatment team. She came to each new treatment—even each new therapy session—a therapeutic virgin.

When asked about her opinions, feelings, or understanding of subjects close to her personal experience, Ms. Q's standard response was a disingenuous, startled, "I don't know. What do *you* think?"

## Previous Therapies

Over the years, Ms. Q exhausted several experienced therapists. Her caregivers were based at established academic eating-disorder programs—her parents made certain that Ms. Q received competent care. Her internists struggled—successfully—to keep her alive, to maintain her bones and body in the face of unrelenting malnutrition. After the period in her twenties when she required frequent hospitalization for emergency weight management, Ms. Q settled into stable precariousness. Behavior therapists focused on her food rituals and distorted body image; she complied with their prescribed thought exercises and left each meeting with a new plan of action—only to return the following week unable to execute even the smallest increment of change. "I tried, but for some strange reason, it was too hard."

Psychodynamic therapists explored the intricacies of her unconscious, her family dynamics, and her musical career. She spoke about her life from a great emotional distance, parodying interpretations and connections, while she internalized nothing. Ms. Q was as impervious to the nourishment of human relationship, connection, and understanding as she was to food. If her physicians and therapists had hopes of witnessing demonstrable change in Ms. Q's nutritional, medical, or psychological state during these many dreary years of early treatment, they must have been bitterly disappointed.

Socially, Ms. Q remained completely isolated, without friends or acquaintances. She idealized her dance teachers, both men and women, with whom she often had power relationships quite reminiscent of that with her mother. They would alternately encourage and punish her, investing varying measures of hope and sternness into her development as a dancer. In the end, most of these relationships faltered. A single teacher was an exception to this rule. She treated Ms. Q with persistent kindness and respect, and Ms. Q returned to her repeatedly despite periodic ruptures in their attachment. In relating to her peers, Ms. Q lacked rudimentary social skills. She would plunge rapidly into gladiatorial competition so vigorous and offensive as to alienate them one and all.

After decades in the United States, Mr. and Mrs. Q returned permanently to their Asian home; their enmeshment in their daughter's life scarcely diminished by virtue of a ten-thousand-mile gap between them. Once or twice a year, Mrs. Q would stage a dramatic visit, heralded by dread and nervous anticipation. When her mother arrived, Ms. Q would inevitably be considerably thinner than expected. Mrs. Q would make angry rounds among the treatment team, liberally spreading blame and despair. Sometimes she would threaten to stop paying for her daughter's treatment. At other times she would bring gifts and gratitude. She emanated a heady mixture of concern, guilt, rage, supplication, and cunning. She would intersperse her questions about Ms. Q's care with a wide range of her own somatic concerns, seeking advice, referrals, and emotional support, trying to appropriate whatever might be of value to her daughter.

Mr. and Mrs. Q provided the material support for their daughter, paying most or all of her expenses. Their approach to family finances, however, placed their own personal power at center stage in a confusing theater of appropriation and secrecy. When Mrs. Q purchased the luxurious condominium for her daughter, she retained the deed in her own name. Each called the apartment "mine." From time to time, Mrs. Q would call from across the ocean to berate her daughter about money: "You are bankrupting the family. Your illness will kill us all. We have no more money." A month later Mrs. Q would arrive for a visit, bearing gifts of diamond jewelry and a fur coat: "You are going to be the death of us," she would moan. She would slip extra hundreds of dollars to her daughter: "Don't breathe a word to your father. He would be terribly distraught." The next day, "You must stop your therapy. We simply can't afford this nonsense any longer."

Mrs. Q would describe international finance schemes "worth millions of dollars if we succeed. (They did not.) Tell Dr. H that I want to create a foundation for his research in eating disorders." Between these financial gyrations, Mrs. Q would complain to her daughter about the ailments of her own body, both imagined and real. Whenever Ms. Q tried to speak to her mother concerning her budding wishes for financial independence, her mother would say, "You mustn't worry yourself about money, my dear." Then Mrs. Q would threaten to disinherit her, and for a few weeks Ms. Q would scramble to prepare herself for imminent austerity. Then mother would recant with, "I just want you to have this extra money, but you should realize that it is taken from your grandmother's funeral account." At no time could Ms. Q or I obtain even the most approximate picture of her parents' actual financial standing or the extent of her expectable inheritance, if any.

This was where my work with Ms. Q began, in a confusing sea of medical precariousness and angry family dependency. She was a woman whose emotional development had arrested early in adolescence. Her social functioning was dramatically impaired in both human relationships and work. She was living a barebones existence, nutritionally and spiritually. Her days were filled with dreary rituals: cutting small morsels of food into even smaller pieces, pounding her body with exercise and dance classes, waking up hungry and going to bed hungry. She claimed she wanted nothing. From this intransigent prison of petrified desire, we had to seek a way out together.

## Theoretical Perspectives

My eating-disordered patients have taught me the need for flexibility in psychotherapeutic practice. I have learned from them that no single theoretical framework is sufficient to encompass all the complexities of their symptoms or their lives. They have helped me draw on a variety of conceptual sources in formulating and modulating their treatment.

One essential source is self psychology. Its painstaking attention to the therapeutic relationship as a curative factor provides the fulcrum for all other interventions; by listening with empathy, the therapist locates possibilities for effective action. Self psychology views anorexia nervosa as a disorder of relationship and the therapeutic relationship as the engine of recovery. In the early development of the anorexic patient, the basic functions of a healthy self—sustenance, nurturing, soothing, and containment—have withered in the face of a bleak and encroaching parental environment. The therapeutic relationship becomes the human matrix around which the damaged self can grow strong.

Self psychology articulates an empathic field that is essential for therapy to take place. Two supplementary approaches—cognitive-behavioral therapy and a more interpretative version of psychoanalysis—may provide guidance for direct intervention when destructive behaviors and distorted thinking threaten the survival of the patient. In these critical situations, understanding and being-with are simply insufficient. There is a requirement for effective therapeutic action. Such interventions are not inherently inconsistent with a self-psychological perspective, which would find in them the therapist's provision of missing psychological functions for the patient's marginal self. When confronting the distorted perceptions, behaviors, and thoughts so characteristic of anorexia nervosa, the therapist needs some theoretical backup to justify moments that are bound to feel unempathic and tense. Traditional psychoanalytic and cognitive-behavioral theory remind the empathic clinician that there must also be room for interruption, interpretation, and the expression of difference in order for treatment to be effective.

There is a fine line in therapy between appropriate activity and the deleterious enactment of a power struggle. Keeping on the right side of this line is a matter of forbearance; the therapist needs to time confrontational interventions carefully and limit them to situations where life and health are truly in jeopardy. In practice, treating patients with severe eating disorders requires a judicious mixture of empathy, interpretation, support, and behavioral intervention.

## GETTING ACQUAINTED: THE EARLY PHASE OF TREATMENT

In the beginning Ms. Q's individual therapy was a repetitive enactment of an impasse, valuable mainly as my period of education in the parameters of her idiosyncratic, narrowly encoded world. What I experienced many times over was the absence of sufficient room in that world for another human being. Ms. Q scarcely grieved the loss of her former therapist, with whom she had worked closely for five years. It was as if we were simply obeying stage instructions: he left the scene, and I arrived. Whatever difference there might be between us was hardly worth noting.

Ms. Q also spent four years in a therapy group for patients with eating disorders. Although she often leaned on the other members of the group for support—as when her mother was planning a transcontinental visit—and claimed her full share of group air time, at the very end of the group's life Ms. Q could not remember the name of a single other group member. When other members spoke with great emotion about difficult aspects of their own recovery, she would listen only long enough to detect an opportunity to say, stretching credibility, "I have exactly the same situation in my life," and leap into a purely personal digression. At other times she would appear to fall asleep.

The autistic quality of her private existence was an enormous impediment to both individual and group therapy. In her universe people existed only as powerful beings. Sometimes she idealized these beings. Most often she ignored them, unless they posed a sufficient threat; in that case she fought against them with great fury. As her therapist, I was destined at times to occupy each of these positions.

These difficulties of relationship were matched by the paucity of effective language available to Ms. Q. My early education regarding her world made me as aware of the emptiness of her speech as the minimalism of her day-to-day life and the abject degree of her aloneness. She used language to fill a void in the therapy room, rarely to evoke, to connect, or to express the truth. Quite the contrary, for Ms. Q, language appeared to have only a very quirky relationship to ordinary reality. Empty speech could fill time and mislead. Therapy sessions were typically devoted to microscopic narratives concerning meals not eaten, exercise classes attended and missed, malls walked through, and grocery stores browsed in without purchase. As Ms. Q walked through the door to begin such a session, she might turn to me and say, "Well, you just aren't going to believe all that has happened since we last met."

## Language and Power

To Ms. Q's mind, language generally represented an assertion of power by one person over another. For instance, if a physician were to explain that extreme malnutrition might threaten the basic physiological processes that sustain life, Ms. Q would read this statement as a semantic ruse designed to control her life. Asked if she believed that her physician was speaking the truth, she would become puzzled, as if the concept of an objective truth separate and distinct from the speaker's will to power simply made no sense to her.

One day, after I had begun to appreciate the depth of her skepticism regarding the existence of nonpersonalized truths, I asked her whether the scale that weighed her at the internist's office could only report her actual weight or instead could underestimate or overestimate it at will. As I suspected, she was convinced that the scale could invoke a number according to some moral or juridical principle unknown to her but unrelated to any underlying physical reality. In her view the scale was no different from a powerful person whose pronouncements might affect her life.

For Ms. Q, language, truth, and fact were captive to interpersonal struggles that took on implications of good and evil, life and death. The collapse of language critically abbreviated the therapeutic space between us. It placed her in a curious position, at once subject to the world's endless whims while also occupying a dizzying position of personal power. She dared to claim that, unlike other humans, she needed neither biological nor psychological nurture.

Ms. Q's particularly perplexing form of lying brought chaos directly into the treatment. In her battle to keep starving herself, Ms. Q manufactured elaborate lies regarding the food she ate, the frequency of her visits to the nutritionist, and her weight. While considerable craft and energy appeared to go into these inventions, I slowly learned that Ms. Q fundamentally lacked the capacity to understand what made her false claims different from the truth.

I came to appreciate the difficulty of treating Ms. Q in a therapeutic mode whose linchpins were relationship and language, two realms that had lost their usefulness to her because of the retreat, deprivation, denial, and introversion that marked the course of her illness. Trust, warmth, a sense of connection, and empathy were all qualities that barely existed in her experiential lexicon. And the ordinary exchange of words that we attempted to pursue in the course of psychotherapy had very little credibility for Ms. Q. It was difficult to imagine how, merely through the effect of our discourse, these essential aspects of a healthy self could ever emerge from the therapeutic work.

### Countertransference Issues

These first years of our work together served to make me aware of the extraordinary predicament of Ms. Q's life. By bumping into barriers at every turn, I learned about the extreme constraint she lived with year after year. During this time I kept lowering my expectations, cutting my suggestions into tiny morsels just as she divided her meager daily rations. And even these microchanges most often proved impossible.

During this frustrating period a number of countertransference difficulties emerged—intense feelings aroused in the therapist by the patient's particular mode of relationship. These feelings periodically threatened my ability to maintain a basic attitude of care, hopefulness, and attention. Provoked by Ms. Q's absolute resistance to change as she invited me yet again to make helpful suggestions, I felt tempted to enact her dreaded image of a controlling, powerful person. It was difficult to respond empathically to her intransigence, her superficial compliance, or her emotional disconnectedness. I was racked with boredom as hour after hour of therapy was filled with the vacuum of her empty narrative. I found myself drawn toward despair; in a world where a year of treatment is considered heroically long, how could I justify the expenditure of her parents' financial resources and my limited time and energy pursing the nineteenth or twentieth year of treating Ms. Q's unrelenting illness?

To keep such sentiments from sabotaging the treatment, it was enormously helpful to have the support of a treatment team, including—besides myself—a group therapist, a nutritionist, and an internist. Treating such patients alone is next to impossible. It was also helpful to review her case periodically with colleagues who were able to detect beginnings of incremental change well before they passed the threshold of my own awareness.

My day-to-day efforts during these early years of treatment closely paralleled Winnicott's Zen-like aphorism regarding his work: "In doing psychoanalysis I aim at: Keeping alive, Keeping well, Keeping awake." Staying alive included retaining a vestige of hope despite the desolation of Ms. Q's discourse. Detecting signs of life in her—and even in me—during our sessions was often difficult. I realized that she barely knew anyone was there with her; she had absolutely no sense or curiosity about who I might be in particular, what I might feel, or what made me tick. When I spoke, it was most often to indicate that I was alive and to give some hint as to who I was and reassurance that I was still listening to her story. At these times I interrupted her aloneness.

Periodically my interventions were challenges that upset the litany of truisms, quotations, and thoughtless phrases that peppered her narratives. At these moments I briefly interrupted her total-itarian mind-set. More often I wondered if my comments were ever heard, except to take their own place amid Ms. Q's reserve of ritualized quotations that she would call on to fill silences in other conversations, perhaps in her group or when meeting with her nutritionist: "My *doctor* always says that . . ."

## BUILDING BRIDGES:
## A MIDDLE PHASE OF TREATMENT

After two years of difficult groundwork together, Ms. Q and I slowly shifted gears into a more dynamic phase of the treatment. The clearest index of change was her budding interest in achiev-ing financial independence from her parents.

During the previous two years, Ms. Q had made several unsuccessful forays into the workplace, motivated by a desire to comply with what she interpreted as my wish for her to be a pro-ductive citizen. In each instance the minimal social and cogni-tive demands of the job, even though it was beneath her education and native intelligence, proved to be insurmountable. At a prominent consulting firm where she had talked her way into an entry-level administrative position, Ms. Q found a way to delegate every task assigned to her. For a few months her total lack of productivity was overlooked, but once her supervisors realized that she was unlikely to improve her substandard per-formance, they terminated her employment.

At the perfume counter of an urban department store, Ms. Q's responsibilities were limited to basic sales and inventory, but she was unable to master these simple tasks. Worse yet, she engaged in a mortal struggle to discredit her colleagues on the sales floor. Several fellow workers resigned or asked for transfers. Finally, she lost the job. Undoubtedly, her cognitive impairment (sec-ondary to chronic malnutrition) kept her from learning the new skills required to keep any job. But an equally devastating obstacle to employment was her seeming oblivion to the social norms of any situation that involved other people. Her confusion regarding social cues was aggravated by unbridled displays of aggressive competitiveness whose alienating impact remained largely outside her range of awareness.

With each job failure, she became more discouraged. She also became intrigued, however, by the concept of a paycheck and the power it might come to represent. This was the single piece of new motivation to emerge in the first two years of our work together, so it naturally became the focal point of our discussions. If potential financial independence was of such compelling interest, then what might she be willing to sacrifice to achieve it? If she could not learn new skills at her current nutritional plateau, could we begin to discuss an increase in her food intake and weight with the specific goal of improving her cognitive function?

As it happened, a particularly turbulent maternal visit, accompanied by dire threats of financial ruin and sudden severing of the umbilical support lines, occurred in the midst of these discussions. At this juncture, Ms. Q stated in no uncertain terms that she hated to have her psychotherapy held hostage by her mother's power struggles.

"I want to pay for my own therapy," she insisted. I realized, even through the filter of my skepticism, that we were on new ground.

### Hints of Change

Shortly after her mother's departure, Ms. Q enrolled in a vocational rehabilitation program designed for more disturbed patients, most of them with schizophrenia or severe affective illness and chronic thought disorder. The goal was to improve her social skills and to develop better coping strategies for the specific demands of the workplace. Ms. Q took to this program like a fish to water. Knowing that in many respects she was healthier than her fellow students, she was able to relax her usual level of competitive anxiety and thereby expose more of her vulnerability and need. The program included active support for interviewing and postplacement meetings to help alleviate problems that develop early in the course of employment.

Ms. Q's first job after graduation from the rehabilitation program was as a security guard in a major museum. She found the atmosphere gratifying, tinged as it was with high fashion and culture; this veneer enabled her to ignore the lowly status of her actual work. Although her job consisted basically of arriving on time, being there, and leaving at the end of the day, she found it quite demanding. Each encounter with a fellow guard, each negotiation of a coffee break, each limit she had to set with a visitor represented a small victory or a crisis. Every therapy session began with, "I have so much to tell you," followed by a microscopic analysis of museum life. Experiencing the real world with its inconsistencies, layoffs, fiscal cutbacks, unionization, special favors, and interpersonal dramas was a difficult change for someone accustomed to the life of a self-starving hermit.

While at the museum, Ms. Q attempted some social connections as well. She selected several fellow guards as potential friends, only to later discover (with my help) that one new acquaintance was psychotic and another was strangely inconsistent—even potentially dangerous. Her choices were marginal people, most of them decades older than Ms. Q. Usually, she broke off these connections when they became strained or demanding.

One real friend, however, did emerge from the group—a retired telephone operator in her sixties, never married, lonely, her life almost as ritual-bound and disconnected as Ms. Q's. It was quite touching to witness their discovering each other, accepting strangeness, and finding ways to connect against all the odds. They began to spend holidays together and met for coffee twice a week, continuing to be friends long after Ms. Q had moved on from the museum. For Ms. Q, this was the first experience of an adult relationship that included genuine empathy. At times she would become frightened that her friend, Mildred, "doesn't have a life." She worried that in twenty years she would share her friend's fate. At other times Ms. Q marveled at Mildred's consistent quiet interest in Ms. Q's life, sympathy for her troubles, and pleasure at her successes. In turn, when Mildred was ill in the hospital, Ms. Q worried about her. These simple aspects of human relationship were, for her, remarkable novelties.

Regular work, paychecks, and positive feedback from her employer bolstered Ms. Q's independence project. After several museum jobs, she began to notice that it was boring to work in a job that did not involve any skilled activity on her part. She wondered whether she could do better for herself. At her own initiative, she began to explore how to acquire more marketable skills. From several possibilities, she chose a venerable secretarial school and secured a bank loan to finance her education.

Without telling her parents, Ms. Q entered school. She proved to be an excellent student, albeit a whirlwind relentlessly vying for the top grade in every class. She mastered typing and stenography, and after considerable hesitation, began to use a computer for word processing and other business tasks. Over time, she developed a special fondness for computers, mastering desktop publishing, basic graphic design, and slide presentations. On graduation from secretarial school, she was offered an excellent entry-level job despite the major economic recession peaking at the time in New England.

This first job following secretarial school marked a significant turning point in Ms. Q's psychosocial development. For the first time she was earning enough money to pay her own way in the world. Her new job came with a progressive health insurance plan that partially covered the cost of her therapy. She personally assumed responsibility for the bills not covered by insurance. She renegotiated her financial arrangement with her parents, markedly reducing their subsidy for housing and subsistence. Not surprisingly, her mother reacted with a mixture of relief, pride, and alarm. She recognized that independence meant psychological health but fretted about her loss of maternal power. For Ms. Q, her new financial independence represented a significant departure from her mother's control—as well as from her own internal constraints.

## Use of Metaphors

Ms. Q's achievements in work and relationships were attained during a period of more intensive and less barricaded work in psychotherapy, heralded by a change in the discursive pattern of our sessions. Until this time our meetings had been dominated by Ms. Q's wordy, concrete, and passionless enumerations regarding her restricted everyday life, punctuated from time to time by my own attempted interventions, which she politely tolerated without allowing them to affect her in any pertinent way. It was hard to characterize these meetings as a form of dialogue. I had often wondered how I might help soften this quality of alienation between us.

I found myself groping for new words. Besides staying attuned to her meandering, austere narratives, I tried to construct experiments in language to offer her models of a more complex, less see-sawing articulation of her own experience. Without much planning or design, my search led to a chain of interlocking, extended metaphors about "prison," "bridge," and "home." In retrospect, I see that these metaphors became the spontaneous groundwork of interpretation, the threshold of symbolic language in the treatment. Over time these figures of speech helped us approach a consensual order in our discourse. These metaphors emerged as signifiers from the images of Ms. Q's anorexic world, but over time they helped transcend its boundaries and enacted in language the possibility of a journey beyond that world.

Metaphor, with its complex symbolic structure, expands on the imaginary dualities of the anorexic's inner world, where all truth is subjected to the yoke of personal power. The architecture of metaphor offers a signifying structure while retaining play; Winnicott located metaphor in the transitional space between the private world of mother and baby and the alienation of adult existence. Consequently, metaphor can be a powerful, evocative language that contains space for the imagination and the hope of expressing a personal truth. Through its figures, the arbitrary, merciless voice of the scale and the silent signifier of the starved body can be balanced by a more complex articulation of experience allowing for ambiguity and playfulness. Metaphor offered Ms. Q an alternative to the outright rejection of language represented by her starving and her lies.

"Prison" described the narrowness of Ms. Q's mode of dwelling, while also reflecting the safety of restriction. We would speak of her apartment as a prison when she would feel trapped there and realize that no other person had passed through its doors for months and months. Her body would feel like a bony prison where her self was trapped and unable to find expression or fulfillment. At times, therapy would also feel like a prison where she felt captive to her parents' desire to see her cured. The difficulty of change could be imagined as the despair of a prisoner who has become so acclimatized to the restricted world of confinement that the outside seems hopelessly foreign and complex—better to rail at the jailers than to contemplate freedom.

"Bridge" referred to the truth of two sides, to their division, and to the journey from one side to the other. Therapy at its more hopeful moments was conceptualized as a way across the divide between her anorexic world and an unseen other bank. She could speak about the precariousness of crossing and her fear of being engulfed by the waters below. Would this transitional structure hold, as construct or as metaphor? Would the language of therapy be stronger than lies and manipulation? Our complex negotiations concerning food plans and diets were part of a bridge between a starved body and the future, sometimes dreaded as portending grotesque obesity, at other times embodying her wish to be "normal."

"Home" captured the possibility of building, within her body as well as her surroundings, a dwelling place that breathed life.

We spent hours speaking together about the subtly changing climate of her apartment, the meaning of new objects permitted entry there: the new violin, the now beloved personal computer. At times even a friend was allowed to visit. The kitchen stove, never used before, now saw an occasional meal cooked on it. Her closets full of never-worn clothes and makeup became accessible to daily use. Her redecoration schemes drifted beyond the hollow themes of an imagined Walt Disney childhood toward images that reflected her love of dance and music. Both her house and her body began to feel at times like places where life could be contained and where a certain excitement might even be felt.

## CROSSING THE BRIDGE: A LATER PHASE OF THERAPY

Progress regarding weight and nutrition did not always parallel progress regarding work and relationships. One particularly worrisome crisis regarding medical safety occurred, in fact, during a period of considerable movement, when I detected early glimmers of her reanimation: new, warmer friendships, a willingness to maintain a full-time job, a wish to support herself and pay for her therapy, and a newly articulated yearning for freedom. The austerity of her interior world had softened a little, nudging me toward optimism.

My optimism should have been interrupted by visions of an even gaunter face, an even more angular chin, only partially obscured by her careful application of makeup. But lulled into complacency by the seeming success of our work together, I was shocked to discover that Ms. Q had been lying to me for several months, had avoided meetings with her nutritionist, and had lost weight beyond her agreed-on baseline for medical safety.

Under threat of hospitalization, which would have been an undesirable interruption in her increasingly valued work and social activities, Ms. Q was able to eat enough to gain several pounds. One incentive that helped assuage her customary terror regarding any increase in weight was her recent acknowledgment that her capacity to learn actually did vary according to her level of malnutrition. She wanted badly to succeed, and she tentatively accepted the need to eat more because it promoted a goal that now mattered to her.

Without the force of desire, such a shift of paradigm in her anorexic worldview was inconceivable. In our conversations her priorities see-sawed. For Ms. Q, eating more required tangible prior proof of increased life potential. Unfortunately, better nutrition was often a prerequisite for new opportunity in work and relationships. And increased occupational and social involvement brought complexity and stress to her life, along with opportunities for eventual gratification. The most difficult work in Ms. Q's therapy was to expand this choked circle of existential restriction. Ms. Q demanded guarantees; I had none to give.

Besides remaining empathic to her extreme reluctance to forsake practices that had enabled her to survive for so long, albeit in such precarious fashion, I also had to do battle with her stubbornness. For weeks on end she would dispassionately repeat familiar formulas: "You don't know that it's hard for me to eat." "I do try." "I can't change without support." "I'm doing everything I can."

## The Recognition of Time

When I pushed harder, Ms. Q's anger would bring her to life in the room, and we could meet in a struggle. Unlike earlier confrontations about food and weight, these sessions, however intense they became, were always punctuated by Ms. Q's spontaneous avowal that despite all evidence to the contrary, she remained personally committed to change. Her experience of time had altered. She no longer retreated into the timelessness so characteristic of the anorexic's world.

The anorexic denies the reality of her own body. By refusing to submit to its requirements for care and nurture, she paradoxically denies her mortal nature even while she risks death. Denying the body makes it possible to deny the passage of time and ultimately the reality of death. Without a body, time is suspended in an ageless frame. Sitting with Ms. Q year by year, I regularly had to remind myself that she was a grown woman; her manner, appearance, and vocal inflection so seductively lured me to imagine her as a young, naive girl.

Ms. Q's first moments of recognition of the passage of time overwhelmed her with a sense of enormous loss. So many decades had passed without change. Would there still be time enough to live? At first she retreated from such insight in anxious haste. Sometimes she would walk in the shopping mall near her condominium and watch couples pass by with their children. She would fill with envy. On the surface, she envied people in affectionate relationships, adults able to bond and have children—Ms. Q wanted a child of her own. As we spoke further, what emerged was a more primitive longing to be such a well-loved child herself. What she wanted most of all and could never have was a chance to begin her life all over again.

## THE RELATIONSHIP

These themes of desiring, missing, having, and losing permeated our work together. As Ms. Q became self-sufficient for the first time with some limited success in the working world, she began to wish for a love relationship. After many disappointments trying to date men less capable of attachment than she, she befriended a forty-five-year-old music teacher, Mr. R. He had never fully separated from his parents and still lived next door to the small suburban house where he had grown up. His mother cooked meals that she left for him every day. Mr. R was well respected as a devoted elementary piano teacher for his dozens of young pupils who came to his house for their lessons on weekday afternoons and often on Saturdays and Sundays as well. He was a hoarder whose living space consisted of passage-ways between piles of accumulated stuff. Mr. R was embarrassed about his way of life and only permitted Ms. Q to visit his home once during the entire course of their year-long relationship. Even then, he made her promise she would confine her visit to the living room/music studio.

Mr. R and Ms. Q met through a dating service where he had placed an advertisement. Besides their shyness and social awkwardness, they also shared an interest in music and a fondness for childish play. They gave each other little stuffed animals and trinkets on every imaginable occasion. Sometimes they went out together to a movie or a concert. Mostly they spent a few hours every weekend sitting together in Ms. Q's apartment. He would play music for her, and they would talk about their future. Sometimes they held hands. Physical closeness was equally frightening for both of them, so it was a year into their relationship before the question of spending a night together first arose.

They both led highly ritualized lives, with every waking moment planned to exasperation. Joining forces for a night proved quite a task. He would have to cancel Sunday morning lessons, something he was quite reluctant to do. She would have to miss a ballet class. Her bedtime was enshrouded by an array of infinitesimal food rituals, his by equally time-consuming and private preparations for sleep. Months went by without resolving these logistical obstacles. Meanwhile they continued to speak about a future together and dreamed of living in the same space and joining forces in life.

During the course of this relationship, Ms. Q was often quite motivated in her therapy, seeking to overcome her many internal barriers to intimacy. At other times she would complain bitterly about Mr. R. He was hopelessly attached to his mother. He was changing his habits but only so slowly. Conversely, she would panic whenever it seemed that their relationship might actually become more intimate. Both sides of her ambivalence aroused anxiety. But she maintained her weight and even spoke about gaining a few pounds in the hopes of becoming more attractive and desirable to him.

### Defying Her Mother

In the midst of the ephemeral growth of this new relationship, Mrs. Q scheduled a visit. This time she was arriving to visit a thirty-nine-year-old daughter who had finally become financially independent, was medically stable, and was seriously dating a man for the first time since high school. Ms. Q awaited her mother's arrival with a mixture of excitement and dread. Within a day of her arrival in the United States, Mrs. Q threw down her gauntlet.

She issued an ultimatum to Ms. Q: either Mr. R had to go, or she would expunge her daughter from her heart. Her surreptitious investigation had turned up a flaw in Mr. R that she refused to overlook. Several years earlier, he had had resected a skin growth that proved to be a malignant melanoma. Mrs. Q would not allow her daughter to be involved with a man who might be under a death sentence: "I do not want my daughter to have the pain of burying a husband."

She demanded that Ms. Q summarily tell Mr. R that their relationship was over. After momentarily considering a capitulation to her mother's demand, Ms. Q summoned all her fortitude and stood firm. She sent her mother off to New York to stay with other relatives. Mrs. Q could only return if she apologized for her behavior and if she accepted her daughter's relationship with Mr. R.

Not one to change course regardless of the consequences, Mrs. Q stuck to her position. For an entire year mother and daughter exchanged no words. Their perverse bond had ruptured. Somewhat to my surprise, Ms. Q withstood this loss almost without a ripple of regret. She sustained her rage against her mother for months, railing at her for her lack of generosity, her choking possessiveness, and her failure to appreciate the remarkable changes taking place in her daughter.

### Capacity for Empathy

Several months after Mrs. Q's rageful departure for Asia, her daughter came to a therapy session looking perplexed. Mr. R had been irritable and fatigued; he seemed preoccupied and looked pale. At first, he would not discuss his worries with her, but then revealed that he had found several suspicious new spots on his skin and was awaiting word from his dermatologist. She presented this information to me as if she had read an article about a distant city in the daily newspaper. What could it mean?

Within a few weeks it was all too clear. Mr. R's melanoma had returned in multiple sites, including distant metastases. He faced a very uncertain prognosis despite intensive chemotherapy, immunotherapy, and radiation treatments. Most likely, he would die within a year. Ms. Q gave some initial thought to the possibility of leaving her friend immediately. After all, it would be easier to leave than to be left. She was furious already that he was rarely able to visit her, that he became increasingly introspective and less interested in the details of her daily life. He was even more inseparable from his parents. "If he can't meet any of my needs, why should I stay with him?"

His illness became a severe test of Ms. Q's newly found capacity for empathy. She decided to stay with her friend no matter what happened to him but from day to day had enormous difficulty knowing how to be. Her spontaneous response to every new setback was to be furious. It was hard for her to distinguish between her anger at fate and her anger at Mr. R. Despite our discussions in therapy, he sometimes bore the brunt of her discontent. At other times she was able to muster up a measure of sympathy and treated him with relative kindness. When he was discouraged, she gave him pep talks and persuaded him to take walks, continue teaching, and sustain hope. When she was a harsh taskmaster, our work together resembled a crash course in compassion. It was difficult for Ms. Q to practice commiseration with her ailing friend when she had such minimal experience of being kind to herself.

Despite optimal medical care, Mr. R lost ground rapidly. After only a brief initial remission, his cancer spread inexorably. I became an interpreter for Ms. Q of the steady flow of complex medical information. Six months after he had first noticed the new spots on his skin, he was bedridden, confused, slept most of the time, and barely recognized her. One night, he suffered a brain hemorrhage and was rushed to the hospital. At my urging and despite her considerable fear of trains, taxis, and unfamiliar places, Ms. Q made her way to his bedside seventy-five miles distant in a neighboring state. His stupor seemed to lighten for a moment as she spoke to him and held his hand, and he tried unsuccessfully to say something to her. The next day Mr. R died.

Ms. Q was stunned by her loss. She could not believe the finality of Mr. R's death. Like a child not quite cognizant of death's irreversibility, she kept expecting a reprieve. During Mr. R's illness, I had tried periodically to provide measured doses of medical realism to offset her own tendency to absorb and magnify every grain of optimism she would encounter in Mr. R, his doctors, or his parents. Often she could repeat information she had learned, but she clearly could not follow its ominous implications. The powerlessness of Mr. R's doctors was unfathomable to her.

As perplexing as she had found the demands of empathy during his illness, Ms. Q now found her own grief even more bewildering. Her strong sentiments were unfamiliar, and she knew neither how to interpret them nor what to do about their ferocity. Unable to imagine recovering from this loss, she was alternately engulfed by despair and fury. As intensively as we worked together to bring some perspective to her flood of feeling, Ms. Q resorted to the one measure she knew was effective to organize a world breaking apart in chaos. She starved herself.

Soon she had returned to the familiar precipice of severe malnutrition, becoming increasingly obsessive as she deteriorated, approaching once again the edge of medical catastrophe. Her work suffered. At a relatively new job, she lost herself in computer projects only peripherally useful to her employer but more entertaining to her than the required routines of the job. In the solitude of her malnutrition and obsessive rituals, she lost her newly acquired capacity to respond to social cues in the workplace. Soon her probation period came to an end, and without any warning she lost her job.

At age forty, after twenty-three years of treatment for anorexia nervosa, Ms. Q's world was again in shambles. She was as emaciated as she had ever been, despondent, angry, and stuck. The life she had struggled to build seemed damaged beyond repair. What argument could possibly persuade her to pick up the pieces and resume her struggle? Had the glimpse of a world beyond her anorexic prison been so traumatic that she would choose to return to her confinement forever? As much as I actively promoted the view that her relapse was an understandable reaction to a grievous loss, I could not help wondering if this untimely stroke of fate might prove irremediable.

## Crisis and Recovery

As the months passed following Mr. R's death, Ms. Q slowly began to recover her equilibrium. At first she avoided all triggers to remembering her friend. She did not listen to music, go to places they had been together, or engage in reminiscence. I tried to explain the process of grieving to her.

Slowly, she allowed herself to remember and to cry. As she felt more, she loosened her grip on the past. Her extreme idealization of Mr. R faded; she even conceded that had he survived, their life together might have been compromised by his attachment to his mother and his ritualized existence. Perhaps she would eventually have left him, had he not left her in this way. With respect to work, Ms. Q decided that she wanted a job where her growing computer skills were valued. She did not want to be a mere assistant to someone else. She liked desktop publishing and design. Why not get paid for what she actually liked to do? With respect to her solitude, she decided to answer several personal advertisements from eligible men and placed her own ad in a local magazine.

But as her grief subsided and as her determination to survive returned, Ms. Q remained stuck with respect to eating. Despite acknowledging the need to eat more, she had worked her way into such a corner with restrictive dieting that she simply could not change direction. Over the weeks I thought she looked more wan and gaunt, although she claimed that her weight had not decreased further. Perhaps she had not lost more weight, and it was only my patience thinning out.

I decided to intervene more forcefully and offered her a choice between inpatient hospitalization for the purpose of weight stabilization and participation in a new six-week evening hospital program. To my relief, Ms. Q readily agreed to this latter plan. She stated that she now felt determined to change her eating behavior and resume her interrupted attempts to build a life but that she needed more support with the nutritional piece of this plan. She fully expected to return to a medically safe weight.

"I have lost too many years already. I can't waste any more time. Even as I was crying all through Christmastime about losing Mr. R, I suddenly realized for the very first time ever that even if it is this painful, something is definitely better than nothing."

Ms. Q's story remains unfinished, her future uncertain. Our work in therapy is far from over. What is clear is how different a person she is now than she was six years ago. From the extreme impoverishment of her anorexic world—dependent, alone, brittle, and harsh—a more complex person has emerged. She is now capable of wanting something in the world and of struggling to attain it. She is willing to overcome adversity and to face loss. To sit with her now is to be in the company of another person. To use her phrase, she is no longer her mother's china doll. While these changes have been painfully slow in coming and almost imperceptible to me as they occurred, I am astonished today to realize in retrospect the overall distance we have traveled together.

In an era dominated by the economics of managed care and short-term, symptom-focused treatments, Ms. Q's story should challenge our assumptions about psychotherapy for anorexia nervosa. When should the therapist despair? When do we stop investing optimism and energy into a patient's treatment? If Ms. Q had not been fortunate enough, amid her many misfortunes, to have the financial support of a family with means, she would not have had prolonged and intensive psychotherapy for over two decades. By most conventional standards, her particular form of anorexia nervosa would have been classified as chronic and incurable. Her care would have been restricted to minimal support and emergency medical intervention, and her mere survival would have been judged a clinical success. I am not sure that I thought otherwise at the time I first heard her story. I recall no expectation that she would be able to change so profoundly, that she would grow from a near robot into a complex, animate, and affectively real human being.

From my labors as Ms. Q's therapist, I have learned something of inestimable value. In this current climate of therapeutic nihilism, we must remember that change is possible even when it least seems so. We cannot afford to discard individual lives because the road is so difficult and long. This work requires forbearance, extensive outside support, some inventiveness, and theoretical flexibility. Especially during such politically troubled times, we would do well to ponder what Ms. Q can teach us about the value of psychotherapy, of persistence, and of refusing to give up.

# 4

# COGNITIVE-BEHAVIORAL THERAPY FOR BULIMIA NERVOSA

## Bruce Arnow

This chapter focuses on cognitive-behavioral therapy (CBT) for the treatment of bulimia nervosa. By looking at a single case, I hope to offer more detail than is usually available in research papers or general manuals about how to apply certain key clinical strategies that characterize this approach.

Discussions about clinical procedures are not meaningful, however, without clarity about the therapeutic goals. Different psychotherapies do not simply make use of different procedures to achieve the same outcomes; rather, different therapies often strive for different ends. Thus, discussion of any specific approach to psychotherapy must begin by spelling out what therapist and patient are attempting to accomplish. Before discussing a case example of CBT for bulimia, I would like to comment briefly on the goals of this form of psychotherapy.

## GOALS OF COGNITIVE-BEHAVIORAL TREATMENT

As a Ph.D. student in the early 1980s, I began to learn about and observe how behaviorally oriented exposure therapy was conducted with agoraphobic patients. In many such cases, the procedure involved having the therapist accompany groups of phobic patients out of the office and into the community to facilitate and encourage exposure to previously avoided situations. Patients were often taken to a local shopping mall, where they practiced going into stores, waiting on line, going up to the second and later the third floor of a department store, discussing possible purchases with store clerks, and so on. The strategy was to reduce fear and avoidance through repeated exposures to incrementally increasing fear-evoking situations. The therapist functioned much like a coach, giving encouragement, discussing strategy for coping with panic, and dealing with fear and resistance through persuasion.

At the same time, a close friend who was a student in a Ph.D. program at another institution had begun to take courses at an analytic institute. When I described to him the treatment I observed, he was incredulous. The therapeutic process was so different from the one in which he had begun to immerse himself that he had a difficult time making sense of it. It didn't, he said, even seem like psychotherapy. My references to the growing number of controlled studies testifying to the efficacy of such treatment left him unimpressed. Puzzled by his lack of interest in the outcome literature, I asked how he thought the interpretive therapy in which he was becoming involved would compare against the treatment I was describing in helping agoraphobics "get to the grocery store." His reply was, "I'm not really that interested in whether or not they get to the grocery store."

I would not hold my friend to his comment now. Nor would I draw sweeping conclusions about the goals and objectives of a particular form of therapy from the conversation of two fairly green Ph.D. students. Psychoanalytic practitioners are not indifferent to the resolution of presenting symptoms. I do think, however, that our discussion underscored important differences in the scope and emphases of different approaches to psychotherapy. The goals pursued by different therapies fall on a continuum, with the most circumscribed approaches to treatment on one end and the more diffuse on the other.

The goals of the analytically oriented therapies are on the diffuse side of the spectrum, with psychoanalysis defining its end-point. There is variability in the language used by different analytic theorists of different schools to describe treatment goals, but few would disagree that such treatment focuses on increased understanding of the individual's internal life—uncovering unconscious motives and elucidating the roles of intrapsychic conflict and early experience in shaping the individual's life patterns and self-concept. Treatment is defined as an exploration whose goal is to uncover the meaning of behavior. It is hoped that the process will result in the reduction or elimination of specific symptoms, if such symptoms were instrumental in bringing the patient into treatment, but that is not necessarily the primary goal.

Cognitive-behavioral therapy, on the other hand, occupies the circumscribed end of the continuum. It is symptom focused. The emphasis is on modification of more molecular processes involved in maintaining problematic behavior, rather than on the global characteristics of patients. This is not to say that there is no interest in internal life. In fact, CBT focuses on those beliefs, values, and cognitive processes believed to maintain symptomatic behavior. But that is a means to another end, rather than an end itself. The goal of treatment is to modify specific target behaviors and/or attitudes by changing the thoughts, beliefs, feelings, and patterns of action that maintain them.

There are a few recent and notable exceptions. For instance, Marsha Linehan's dialectical behavior therapy for the treatment of patients with borderline personality disorder incorporates a wider view of the scope and outcome of treatment than many of the cognitive-behavioral therapies for Axis I disorders. But even here, the therapeutic goals—such as reducing parasuicidal behaviors, reducing "therapy interfering" behaviors, and increasing skills for coping with emotional dysregulation—are markedly more specific than one would find in discussions of therapeutic goals among analytically oriented practitioners working with the same population.

The application of specific procedures designed to effect specific and measurable outcomes is the hallmark of CBT. To return to the discussion between my friend and me, he argued that placing the emphasis of treatment for agoraphobia on mobility, rather than on the inner world of the patient, focused therapeutic effort on a peripheral aspect of the problem. From the vantage of cognitive-behavioral treatment, getting to the grocery store is much closer to the heart of the matter. If the patient is agoraphobic, the goals of treatment involve managing panic and reducing avoidance, rather than coming to understand and cope differently with dependency needs. If the chief complaint is bulimia, the treatment aims are to facilitate reduction or elimination of binge eating and purging, rather than, for example, working through issues of separation and individuation.

## A Rationale for CBT for Bulimia Nervosa

The rationale for cognitive-behavioral treatment for bulimia nervosa is based on two related issues. One is the individual's attitudes toward weight and shape. The second is restrained eating.

We live in a time in which women, particularly young women, are under extreme pressure to be slender. Thinness is revered not only because it has come to be synonymous with beauty but also because it has come to denote competence and self-control. Our culture's emphasis on a slender body has been documented in some interesting ways. For instance, in one study with a sample of high school students, 80 percent of the senior women wanted to lose weight, and 30 percent were actively on a diet. By contrast, among the men, 20 percent wanted to lose weight, and only 6 percent were actively dieting. Another indication of the pressure on women to be thin can be seen in the leading magazines catering to females; observe the amount of space devoted to dieting tips. One study completed a frequency count of such articles in three leading women's magazines and found none in magazines of the 1920s; 0.1 per issue in the 1930s and 1940s; approximately 0.5 in the 1950s, 1960s, and 1970s; and 1.25 per issue in the early 1980s.

Another group of investigators examined the published measurements of centerfolds in *Playboy* magazine and found that, between 1959 and 1979, the bust measurements and hip measurements became smaller, whereas waist measurements became larger, pointing to a feminine ideal that was becoming more androgynous. During the same period of time, the percentage of average weight for age and height also decreased significantly. Of further interest, as the feminine ideal became thinner and more angular, the weight of the average American female between ages seventeen and twenty-four increased by five to six pounds. These conditions have set the stage for fear of fatness in some women and the overvaluing of weight and shape.

Few women are unaffected by such pressures. Some are more vulnerable than others. Think for a moment of self-esteem as a pie composed of many different-sized slices representing the different attributes that together constitute self-regard. We might imagine the pie to be composed of such characteristics as strength of character, responsibility, intelligence, kindness, honesty, career accomplishment, the capacity to be a good friend, attractiveness, and other virtues that would combine idiosyncratically, in different combinations for each individual. For some, athleticism, musical ability, or leadership might be critical. For others, important components of self-esteem might include being a loving parent or providing some form of community service.

What we find among bulimics is that weight and shape inordinately influence self-esteem. Attractiveness, defined in terms of one's weight and shape, is by far the largest slice—in many cases completely crowding out other virtues.

It is the overvaluing of weight and shape that is thought to lead to restrained eating; restrained eating, in turn, begets binge eating. Self-induced purging is then an attempt to compensate for the excess calories. The desire to maintain a weight below one's set point initiates a cycle beginning with extreme attempts to diet. Bulimics characteristically develop a variety of rigid "food rules" concerning amounts of food that may be consumed or types of food that should not be consumed under any circumstances. Thus, it is not unusual to see bulimics who are trying to consume only five hundred to eight hundred calories daily or who have self-imposed strictures forbidding the consumption of any sweets or carbohydrate-rich foods such as breads. Such efforts to restrain intake lead to a state of physiological deprivation. Once the individual is sufficiently deprived, the motivation to continue dieting may be disrupted by a variety of cognitive or affective factors often referred to as *disinhibitors.*

An example of a *cognitive disinhibitor* is the following thought after eating one donut that is on a tray at work: "I've blown it, the day is lost, I might as well just continue to eat and start all over again tomorrow." *Affective disinhibitors* include negative mood states, such as anger, depression, and anxiety, that may overwhelm the dieter and decrease the motivation to continue adhering to a difficult regimen. The consumption of alcohol or the use of street drugs may also interfere with self-control and lead to binge eating.

So, the rationale for CBT is as follows. Social pressures to be thin combine with certain individual factors such as low self-esteem to lead a percentage of women (and a much smaller percentage of men) to markedly restrict their caloric intake and choice of foods. In their attempts to maintain their weight at a level below their body's natural set point, these individuals establish a set of unrealistic and rigid guidelines regarding food consumption. Extreme efforts to restrain eating inevitably lead to episodes of binge eating.

The same concern with weight and shape that led to restrained eating leads to vomiting or laxative abuse to "undo" the effects of the binge. Moreover, binge eating tends to result in the individual redoubling her efforts to diet. Once vomiting or laxative abuse is incorporated into the person's behavioral repertoire, her ability to control intake becomes further eroded. These behaviors remove the normal constraints against binge eating because they appear to protect against the consequences of overeating. As binge eating becomes more frequent, the person comes to rely more and more on vomiting or laxative abuse to control weight.

It is beyond the scope of this chapter to review the enormous number of studies investigating the relationship between restrained eating and bingeing. However, I will briefly describe one experimental paradigm, variations of which have been carried out in a number of these investigations.

The basic experiment involves bringing a sample of subjects—defined as restrained eaters (chronic dieters) or unrestrained eaters (nondieters) on the basis of their response to a questionnaire—into the laboratory. They are told that they are participating in an ice-cream taste test. Prior to the "taste test," half of the subjects receive a milk shake "preload" (consisting of one or two milk shakes), while the other half do not. The restraint hypothesis predicts that the unrestrained and restrained eaters will demonstrate different consumption patterns in this situation. The unrestrained eaters who consume the preload are expected to eat less ice cream than those who do not consume a preload, presumably because they are full. In contrast, restraint theory predicts that restrained eaters will demonstrate the opposite pattern; those restrained eaters who consume a preload are expected to eat more than those who do not consume a preload presumably because ingesting the milk shake disrupts their efforts to diet and unleashes a counterregulatory eating episode.

In fact, in many studies, this is exactly what happens. In one study carried out by Herman and Mack, restrained eaters who consumed a milk shake preload subsequently consumed an average of 163 grams of ice cream, whereas those who did not consume a preload averaged only 97 grams. Unrestrained eaters demonstrated the opposite pattern: those who had a preload consumed 119 grams of ice cream, whereas those who did not consumed an average of 205 grams. Such data suggest that restrained eaters attempt to regulate their weight through cognitive means—that is, through various rules and guidelines—whereas unrestrained eaters are guided more by physiological sensations of hunger and satiety.

# THE STORY OF JANE

At the time of the initial consultation, the patient, whom I will refer to as Jane, was a thirty-five-year-old Caucasian homemaker, married for fifteen years, with three children. She had formerly been a participant in a study at our clinic investigating the efficacy of Prozac for bulimia and was referred by the psychiatrist who had been monitoring her medication for that study. She had been taking sixty milligrams of Prozac daily. The study did not involve psychotherapy.

Jane reported that the medication appeared to be helpful initially, and that for a time her binge eating and purging were reduced, but that after a while the medicine had "stopped working," and after the study was over she had elected to withdraw from it. When I first began seeing her, she estimated the frequency of self-induced vomiting at one to three times daily. This was confirmed in her self-monitoring records, which I will discuss shortly. She reported being obsessed with how many calories she was ingesting and with worries about gaining more weight. She did not use laxatives. She frequently skipped meals. She did not exercise.

Jane reported having been concerned about her weight for as long as she could remember, though she had never been overweight. Bulimic episodes began when she was about nineteen years old. She was unable to link the onset of the disorder with any particular stress or relationship problem, but once in treatment she was able to relate that her eating style had become more restrained as she went through her adolescence. Sometimes she purged following a binge; at other times she purged after a normal meal or after a snack that she considered too large. Five feet seven inches tall, her weight was 138 pounds at the time that I began seeing her.

Jane's family history was unusual and, in several respects, traumatic. She was the elder of two children. The most striking event in her early history was her mother's death when Jane was three years old. At that time her father placed Jane and her sister in a convent boarding school. She remembered her experience in the boarding school as secure and denied any history of physical, sexual, or emotional abuse. Among her most vivid and poignant memories was one of trying to be the best little girl in the boarding school—praying fervently, doing extra chores, and in all ways trying to please the nuns who were caring for her.

Jane's father remarried when Jane was eight years old, and the family was reunited. She became very close to her stepmother. For the first few years, all members of the family appeared to be doing well. Jane had always excelled academically, winning numerous awards and, in general, seeing to it that she was a straight A student. She was very pleased with her relationship with her stepmother and never exhibited any behavioral difficulties. Her younger sister, however, soon began to experience significant problems, including shoplifting, defiance, and poor academic performance. Later, as an adolescent, the sister became involved with alcohol and drugs. These problems persisted throughout adulthood, compromising the sister's ability to relate to the family and outsiders and to maintain steady employment.

Throughout her life, Jane reported feeling an intense sense of obligation to both her father and her stepmother, but most intensely toward the latter. She felt that her stepmother had given up the opportunity to have children of her own in order to marry her father and care for his children. From Jane's standpoint, her stepmother received few rewards from efforts to parent her younger sister; Jane was determined that, unlike her sister, she would repay her stepmother for her sacrifice. Apart from her kindness and generosity, having a life that appeared perfect was part of that repayment; so was a perfect appearance.

Although I probed for evidence that her stepmother expressed concern about her or her sister's weight or that she promoted Jane's general sense of obligation either implicitly or explicitly, I was unable to find any. On the contrary, Jane's descriptions of her stepmother suggested a very accepting person.

Bulimics are notorious for the high expectations they place on themselves, and Jane was obviously no exception. Having a perfect body was only one of the many demands for perfection that she placed on herself. She noted that her house was in perfect order most of the time. If it fell short of her standard at the end of the day, she would have difficulty sleeping and would go downstairs and straighten up, fluff pillows, and in general, she related wryly, make sure that "each morning they woke up to a house that could be photographed for *House Beautiful*." She spent considerable time working on their garden. I did not get the impression that she gardened because she found it relaxing or rewarding; rather, it seemed to be part of her effort to make herself acceptable and to present herself to the world as perfect.

Every twelve to eighteen months, Jane would repaint the inside of the house from "top to bottom." She spent each evening helping her children with their homework—not just checking it when the children were done, but doing it along with them. In addition, she spent an enormous amount of time engaged in volunteer activities. She had no time to relax. She felt guilty whenever she sat down and took time for herself. When she did, she often would binge and purge.

Jane described her marriage as happy and stable. From her description she and her husband seemed compatible in most areas and appeared to have a marriage relatively free of conflict. She was deeply ashamed about her symptoms of bulimia and had only told her husband about the problem eighteen months prior to her first consultation with me. She reported that he had been supportive and concerned and had encouraged her to seek treatment.

Despite the apparent harmony in the relationship, Jane described certain features of their interaction that appeared to contribute to some of her difficulties. For instance, Jane's husband had made it quite plain that he preferred her to be thin. From her description he didn't express his preferences in a demanding or entitled way—it was more that he might tease her if he noticed she gained weight—but nevertheless, he made clear his investment in her weight and shape.

In addition, her husband, who was professionally successful and extremely hardworking himself, seemed to see nothing wrong with Jane's unceasing labors. She reported that before he left for work he frequently left lists of chores he thought needed to be completed and would ask about them when he came home. I asked once whether her husband thought it odd that she painted the house so frequently or whether he had ever suggested they hire painters to do the job. She replied, no, that he seemed to like the idea of her doing such work herself.

### General Impressions

It is ironic that among certain bulimic patients, particularly those without notable Axis II pathology, the very features in their character that make them highly susceptible to social pressures to be thin also make them appealing patients. Jane's adaptation to losing her mother and to being separated from her father at so early an age was to ensure that she was always acceptable to the important people in her life; she did this by being exquisitely attuned to their expectations and by trying earnestly to meet them. She worked hard in her therapy, and she seemed quite appreciative of the help she was receiving. She arrived on time for her appointments and always was careful to give adequate notice when she needed to miss a session. She appeared to be quite engaged in the process. She was easy to collaborate with.

A number of authors have noted that bulimic patients often present a "false self" adaptation. One has the impression that, in their intense desire to please and make themselves acceptable, they lack an inner core or their identity is submerged beneath a veneer of superficial compliance. Although I have treated many such patients, Jane was not among them. Despite her history and general adaptive strategy, she had a clarity of values and of priorities that caused me to feel that I was in the presence of a person of considerable strength.

Alongside her capitulation to social pressure to be thin and her desire to present to the world a picture of perfection was a person with a clear sense of purpose regarding her family life, a well-defined sense of right and wrong, and clear and realistic ideas of what she expected from the people with whom she interacted. She had a way of avoiding conflict, and she often did go along with requests that may not have suited her, but she did not do so without an awareness of the dissonance involved.

## Beginning Treatment

Jane made clear that her reason for seeking treatment was to resolve the symptoms of bulimia. She had already tried medication, and that had proven ineffective—at least as administered in the study in which she participated. So, I began treatment by having her keep a complete record of her food intake and purging behavior. I asked her to make an entry each time she ate, recording the date, time, setting, degree of hunger, type and amount of food consumed, degree of fullness, whether or not she purged, and sensations after purging (see Figure 4.1 for a sample of Jane's self-monitoring records early in treatment).

Helping the patient normalize her eating pattern is a key component of the first stage of treatment. Self-monitoring focuses both therapist and patient on the current eating regimen, including the meal pattern, the frequency and timing of bingeing and purging episodes, and the "food rules" that are important in maintaining the pattern. Moreover, the act of self-monitoring keeps the patient focused, between sessions, on the problem and provides the information necessary to devise therapeutic tasks aimed at ameliorating the difficulty.

I find that, in the first session, I cannot do much more than take a history and obtain a detailed account of the current problem, begin to get a sense of the patient, and introduce the idea of self-monitoring. Because bulimia is a secretive and frequently shame-inducing behavioral pattern, I am careful to ask whether the patient anticipates any difficulty in completing the self-monitoring records. Jane indicated it made sense to her that I would need to have a clear picture of the behavior and that she did not anticipate any difficulty.

Nevertheless, I thought it was important to anticipate any reluctance she might have about sharing with me her eating and purging patterns by saying that I have worked with a great many people with this problem and that I have seen patients whose binges were as high as 15,000 calories and who purged as often as twenty to twenty-five times daily. I don't know for sure whether telling patients about some of the outer extremes of behavior I've seen is helpful in putting them at ease; it seems to me that it has been.

When I look at a patient's food record for the first time, I pay closest attention to the pattern of meals, particularly whether meals are skipped, the amount of food that is consumed during both binge- and non-binge-eating episodes, what types of food the patient is eating and not eating, and the types of episodes associated with purging (for example, regular meals or binges). There are often problems in most or all of the above areas.

If there is evidence of skipped meals, that is the issue we address first. Jane's food records indicated that she was in the habit of eating at least a small breakfast each day but that she did not consistently consume lunch and dinner. Frequently, she would consume one but not the other. I asked which of those two meals she might be most comfortable beginning to add. Adding a meal was defined not only as ingesting the food but also as abstaining from purging for a period of at least two hours following the meal. Jane felt most comfortable working on adding dinner consistently.

One issue I keep in mind in the earliest phase of treatment is that success must be defined in moderate and reasonable terms. Perfectionism and "black and white" thinking are well-documented patterns among bulimia nervosa patients. I have had the

| Day/Time | Location | With Whom | Degree of Hunger Before Eating (0-10) | If Binge Mark (✓) | Food: Types and Quantity | Activity While Eating | Degree of Fullness After Eating (0-10) | Vomiting (V) Laxatives (L) | Sensation/ Feelings After Vomiting | Comments |
|---|---|---|---|---|---|---|---|---|---|---|
| 2:25 a.m. | Home | alone | 10 | ✓ | chips, cereal & milk, chocolate cake | Reading | 10+ | ✓ | Guilty ++ | |
| 6:30 | Home | husband | 8 | | cereal & non-fat milk | Talking | 8 | | | but not so fat |
| 10:00 a.m. | Home | daughter | 8 | | coffee & milk | Talking | 8 | | | |
| 12:30 | Menlo Park | daughter | 8 | | 1/2 club sandwich & fries, 1/2 ice cream, diet coke | Talking | 10 | ✓ | Guilty | but not so fat |
| 3:00 | Home | alone | 10 | ✓ | chips, cheese, cookies, milk | — | 10+ | ✓ | Guilty | but not so fat |
| 4:15 | Home | kids | 8 | ✓ | coffee, cookies | — | 10+ | ✓ | Guilty | Why did I do this? |
| 7:00 | Home | family | 8 | | chicken & salad, 1/2 baked potato, french bread, small scoop non-fat ice cream | Talking | 8 | | | Wish I hadn't eaten bread, ice cream |
| 11:50 | Home | alone | 10+ | ✓ | french bread without butter, cookies | — | 10+ | ✓ | | Wish I hadn't bought bread |

| Day/Time | Location | With Whom | Degree of Hunger Before Eating (0-10) | If Binge Mark (✓) | Food: Types and Quantity | Activity While Eating | Degree of Fullness After Eating (0-10) | Vomiting (V) Laxatives (L) | Sensation/Feelings After Vomiting | Comments |
|---|---|---|---|---|---|---|---|---|---|---|
| 10:00 a.m. | Home | husband | 8 | | corn flakes & banana, 1/2 bagel without butter | Talking | 9 | | | |
| 2:00 p.m. | Home | husband | 8 | | tea & 2 cookies | – | 8 | | | |
| 7:00 p.m. | Concert | family | 9 | | turkey sandwich, few chips, ice cream | Talking | 8 | | | Wish I hadn't eaten ice cream |

**Figure 4.1
Daily Food Record**

experience of suggesting that a patient add a specific meal and not purge for a period of two hours afterward and then listening to the patient the next week report that she has complied perfectly but still feels like "a failure" because she purged at other times during the week and hasn't "solved the problem yet." Therefore, when Jane indicated a willingness to add dinner to her regimen, I made a point of telling her to focus only on that, not to attempt further changes, and to count herself as having made progress if she was able to keep that one meal down each night regardless of what else took place during the day.

Providing a compelling rationale for the directives is extremely important. I prefer to do this in the second or third session, with self-monitoring forms in hand so that I can use the patient's unique pattern in presenting the rationale. Figure 4.2 displays a diagram that I frequently draw for patients as an aid in providing a rationale for treatment.

In Jane's case, I used the diagram to make the points that she frequently skipped meals, that her pattern of extreme dieting initiated a set of conditions under which feeling depressed or thinking she had violated a food rule would often precipitate a binge episode, and that her anxiety about weight gain caused her to purge. I noted that her response to such episodes was to redouble her efforts to more fully restrain her intake, which reinitiated the cycle. This explanation made sense to her, but she indicated considerable anxiety about the fact that although I was suggesting that restrained eating was a key issue, she was already heavier than she was comfortable with.

To support the notion that eating less was not the answer to her difficulty, I told her that while purging gives the illusion of "getting rid of" unwanted calories, in fact it is impossible to purge all of the calories; some are inevitably retained. Moreover, because her binges tended to be on high-fat foods, she was probably taking in, through the pattern of restrained eating punctuated by binges, far more calories on a week-by-week basis than she realized. I also noted that, while every individual is different and no guarantees could be made, in my experience in provid-

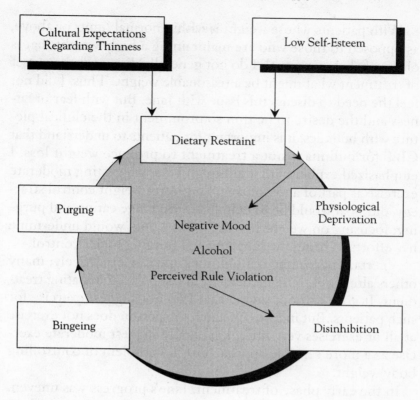

**Figure 4.2**
**Restraint, Disinhibition, and Bulimia**

ing this kind of treatment, patients did not typically gain weight. She seemed somewhat doubtful about this proposition.

At this point, I thought it would be helpful to take a step to reduce her anxiety about weight gain. Because she did not exercise, I suggested that she initiate a moderate program. I told Jane that, as concerned as she was about her weight, she was attempting to control it by diet alone and that this was unlikely to be successful. She seemed to welcome the suggestion and indicated that although she felt she had little time for exercise, she would give it a try.

With patients whose weight is within normal limits or above, as opposed to those who are maintaining a body weight that is obviously below normal, I do not generally discuss at the outset of treatment what might be a reasonable weight. Thus, I did not feel the need to discuss this issue with Jane. But with fear of fatness and the desire to be thin so prominent in the clinical picture with bulimics, it is important for patients to understand that CBT for bulimia is not a treatment to produce weight loss. I emphasized explicitly that although I was suggesting moderate exercise as part of a reasonable, long-term weight control strategy, our goal would be to help Jane stop binge eating and purging; focusing on weight loss as a goal, I said, would undermine her efforts to bring the bingeing and purging under control.

A certain percentage of bulimics exercise excessively; many others already exercise moderately at the point of initiating treatment. It goes without saying that I do not suggest exercise for such patients. But in cases in which the person does not exercise at all or exercises very little, I generally suggest moderate exercise as a more sensible approach to the problem of controlling body weight.

In the early phase of treatment, Jane's progress was uneven. She faithfully kept up with self-monitoring and worked on adding dinner to her daily intake regimen. Within three weeks, she was eating dinner each night and not purging for two hours afterward. I then suggested she add lunch. Within two or three weeks, she was eating lunch consistently. Nevertheless, seven weeks into treatment, although the total number of purge episodes had decreased and she was eating three meals daily, she was still purging—sometimes following a snack, sometimes following a binge—about ten times per week.

One of the more difficult issues with Jane, as it is with many bulimics I've seen in treatment, involved her beliefs about the nature of the problem itself. Jane conceptualized her problem as one of self-control and willpower. She wondered why she suffered such intense food preoccupations and why she had so much trouble controlling her urge to eat when being thin was so important to her. Persuading her that she needed not to work on increasing her willpower, but rather to eat more healthy food at regular intervals was difficult.

At this point we needed to address the amount of food she was eating. When I examined her food record seven weeks into treatment, it was clear that while she was reliably consuming three meals daily, almost everything she ate that was not purged was half a portion: half a sandwich, half an apple, half a chicken breast, half a baked potato, half a glass of wine, and so on. I began trying to persuade her to eat full portions.

Again, this prospect was very frightening to someone who was already feeling that her weight had crept up beyond a tolerable point. I made the point that her constant food preoccupation was probably related to insufficient caloric intake. She was skeptical, noting that because she had gained weight even in the past year, it was inconceivable that she was taking in too few calories. I again pointed out that she was absorbing a certain number of calories from her binges before purging. In addition, I noted that she had been sedentary, whereas now she was exercising. Once again, taking a stepwise approach, I asked her to begin eating whole portions, meal by meal. As she was already eating a full bowl of cereal with some fruit for breakfast, she began working with dinner and later concentrated on eating full portions at lunch.

During this time I asked her to rate her level of food preoccupation on a zero to ten scale, with zero indicating no preoccupation and ten indicating extreme preoccupation. After two weeks of doing this, she realized that the intensity of her food preoccupation and her urge to binge did indeed decline as she began eating full portions.

## Overcoming Binge-Purge Triggers and Symptom-Maintaining Attitudes and Beliefs

Thus far, the discussion had centered on the work of helping Jane abandon an eating regimen that makes binge eating and purging more likely and of adopting in its place a pattern of food intake that would facilitate her recovery. But in addition to emphasizing her meal pattern, we also worked on identifying those cognitive patterns associated with bingeing and purging.

I pay attention to two levels of cognitive process with bulimics. One level involves "triggers," those thoughts that have some immediate association with binge eating or purging. These include, for example, thoughts about the consequences of eating certain foods ("I'll get fat from having eaten this") or thoughts about appearance ("I look so fat today"). The second level involves more enduring attitudes and beliefs about the importance of weight and shape. I often address the immediate antecedent thoughts during the early stage of treatment. I don't usually take up the patient's more enduring attitudes toward weight and shape until later in treatment, once eating has been normalized.

At about session five, I asked Jane to keep track of those thoughts that were immediately associated with binge eating or purging. She used the back of the food self-monitoring forms to do this. When approaching this material, I find it important to keep in mind the difference between cognitive distortions associated with purging following normal eating and purging following a high-calorie binge. When the patient's purging takes place following a high-calorie binge, I tend to focus more on the cognitive process that led to the bingeing. But when purging takes place following normal eating, I focus more on those cognitions associated with purging.

In Jane's case, as in many others, purging took place after both modest- and high-calorie eating episodes. After a snack or normal meal, one set of thoughts that frequently led to purging had the theme of "I ate too much, this is too many calories, I'll surely get fat if I keep this down." Often, the amount of food was quite modest (for example, a sandwich and a piece of fruit for lunch), and I would ask what made her think she would gain weight by eating what amounted to a modestly normal lunch.

We found, in the course of our discussion, that Jane had unrealistic ideas about how and why she might gain weight. I explained that, in general, at her weight, 1,500 calories daily would be a conservative estimate of the amount she should be able to take in and remain stable in weight. With exercise, she should be able to take in somewhat more. A lunch of 400 to 500 calories was within those guidelines. Jane's attitude was skeptical but open.

One suggestion I made that seemed to make a difference was to think of eating more food "as an experiment." This suggestion seemed to acknowledge her anxiety at the same time that it encouraged her to try a different strategy. The question in Jane's mind, of course, was not whether eating more regularly would help control binge eating. Of that, she had little doubt. Whether eating regular, normal-sized portions would help her keep from gaining additional weight was the "experiment."

In addition to concerns about the number of calories she might be taking in during any one eating episode, like many bulimics Jane experienced anxiety following eating that stemmed from a hypothesized association between the physiological sensation of fullness and weight gain. Feeling slightly hungry, or with "an empty stomach," was comforting. In contrast, she viewed feeling full as promoting weight gain. Thus, she sometimes purged after normal or moderate eating if she "felt too full."

I reminded her that fullness after a meal was normal and had no real bearing on whether or not she had overeaten. I noted that you can drink two cans of diet soda with a total of fewer than five calories and feel very full. I asked her to continue to monitor her thoughts and to remind herself of our discussion whenever she found herself with the impulse to purge after eating a modest amount. As treatment progressed, she became more and more able to do so.

Readers who are familiar with the clinical literature on cognitive therapy may note that I did not use any formal thought records or self-monitoring forms to facilitate changes in cognitions. Although I did ask Jane at different points to *identify* and write down problematic thoughts so that we might understand their contribution to her difficulties and discuss them, I have never been comfortable using dysfunctional-thought records as a way to facilitate cognitive *change*. Such records involve having the patient record a "dysfunctional" thought followed by a more rational counterthought, often along with a quantitative estimation of the individual's belief in the latter or a rating of the accompanying emotional state, depending on the problem being addressed.

In my own work, I have never found repetition—the repeated substitution of one thought for another—to be an effective intervention in bringing about a change in perspective. It has often seemed to me that because patients don't yet believe the more "rational" thought that they are recording, the exercise can come to be experienced as artificial and alienate them. I'm sure that, in the hands of another therapist, the use of such records can be quite helpful in facilitating cognitive change, but like all therapists, I have found the success of a particular intervention has much to do with the "operator," and in this case my own doubts or discomfort with the procedure has limited its effectiveness.

I therefore rely almost exclusively on in-session discussions of symptom-maintaining cognitive patterns to bring about change, often asking, as the literature on cognitive therapy suggests, that patients examine the evidence for particular propositions or asking that we consider together alternative interpretations of events. In addition, when treating bulimics, although keeping records of eating and purging behavior is most essential, I have found that there is a limit to how much self-monitoring patients can do—and how many forms patients can fill out faithfully and productively.

To facilitate the identification of symptom-maintaining cognitions, one strategy I employed was to have Jane delay bingeing for a period of half an hour when she experienced the urge and, during the delay, write down her thoughts. We instituted this procedure about ten weeks into treatment, when her eating pattern had become considerably more regular. One issue we discovered through this exercise was the connection between self-criticism and binge-purge episodes. At times Jane would find herself with a free hour on her hands. She then had the desire to relax and read a book but would criticize herself for this impulse. The thought she reported was "how lazy and worthless I am." Frequently, she then would not read or relax but, instead, would binge-eat and purge. At other times, the same thought would occur to her when she looked at her garden and found it not up to her standards or when something about the house needed attention and she didn't have the energy or desire at that moment to do anything about it. Jane's underlying attitude was that, to establish her worthiness, she must always be engaged in productive activity.

I pointed out that the message in her recorded thoughts was that she owed the world—her father and stepmother, her husband—a huge debt of gratitude for caring for her and that she must justify the caring through unremitting service and a commitment to perfection. This explanation resonated for Jane. We discussed her early history, her sense of loss and abandonment, and her strategy of perfectionism and commitment to meeting the needs of others as a way of ensuring the viability of her adult relationships. She was able to realize that, in most of the important relationships in her life, she felt a significant sense of indebtedness. For instance, she viewed her stepmother as someone who had given up the opportunity to have children of her own to raise Jane and her sister. Because her sister's life had turned out tragically and because she had, in effect, failed to "repay" their stepmother's kindness and sacrifice, Jane felt an added burden to lead a life that appeared in all ways perfect and successful.

She was able to see that she viewed her relationship with her husband in a similar way: if she did not continuously justify his caring, it would be withdrawn. One way she ensured that he would not abandon her was by her unremitting productivity. In the course of these discussions, she came to see that she was ignoring the mutuality in her relationships and viewing them as more fragile than, in fact, they were.

## Body Image and Self-Esteem

I generally do not take up the relationship between self-esteem and weight and shape until the patient's eating pattern has progressed to a point where three adequate meals per day plus one or two snacks are being consumed—that is, to a point where the person's eating pattern itself no longer appears to be a major contributor to episodes of disinhibition. In Jane's case, it was not until session fifteen that we began this discussion.

It is always of interest to me how much of the patient's sensitivity to weight and shape is related to specific feedback from significant others. In many families of the eating-disordered patients I've seen, there appeared to have been an inordinate emphasis on physical appearance. And certainly, I've seen many married women with eating disorders who indicated that their husbands were very invested in their thinness.

In Jane's case, when I asked about her husband's attitude toward her weight and shape, she reported that he had made clear his preference for thinness and that he had "teased" her about her weight gain. I asked what it was like for her to be on the receiving end of his "teasing"; she indicated that although she found it unpleasant, she couldn't be angry because she herself thought she had gotten too heavy. Nevertheless, she realized that her own sensitivity to weight and shape was in the way of her struggle to conquer the eating disorder, and without any prompting from me, she had a discussion with her husband in which she told him that his comments were not helpful and secured his cooperation in stopping them. I found myself surprised at her determination and frankly was equally surprised at her husband's readiness to cooperate.

Even more important, however, were Jane's own attitudes toward her body. She had maintained a weight of 115 to 118 pounds as a late adolescent/young adult, and she seemed to use that weight as a benchmark against which she constantly compared herself and to which she fervently wanted to return. We had several discussions in which I gently attempted to point out how unrealistic this attitude was. We discussed this from a number of angles, including how one's metabolic rate slows as one gets older and how she had given birth to three children. I also asked her about friends and acquaintances with whom she had maintained contact over the past fifteen or so years: whether any people she knew had exactly the same shape they did when she first met them. She conceded that all of those she had known over that period had at least thickened; some had grown heavy.

I also asked whether she judged the worth of these people by their shape (I try to be careful not to ask this question of patients I believe will answer in the affirmative—those who are younger and more competitive with other women). She indicated that she did not, and we began to discuss the pragmatics. What were the consequences of equating her worth with her weight and shape? Did she think, given our earlier discussion about the slowing of the metabolic rate and of a tendency in all of us to gain weight as we age, that she would ever feel good about herself as long as she held her self-worth hostage to an ideal she was unlikely to meet?

I find these discussions about the relationship of weight and shape to self-esteem somewhat difficult. Much about cognitive-behavioral therapy for bulimia involves outright persuasion. I try to persuade patients that trying to control weight through extreme restraint is futile or that vomiting reduces the ability to control food intake or that laxative abuse simply has no effect on calorie absorption. I attempt to persuade patients that self-control is not the problem and that extreme restraint leads only to increased food preoccupation. I point out that constantly weighing oneself yields misinformation and contributes to hypervigilance, thereby impeding recovery. Even when the patient is skeptical, I am rarely uncomfortable promoting these ideas, perhaps because they do not challenge our agreed-upon aims of symptom management.

But discussing the relationship of weight and shape to self-esteem is a different matter. It involves a challenge to the patient's values. Therefore, I approach this issue somewhat differently.

I discussed with Jane, as I have with many other patients, that our culture makes unreasonable demands of women, demands that it does not make of men. There is powerful evidence not only in media images but also in the individual's daily life that thinness is revered and conventional beauty is rewarded. As Ruth Striegel-Moore has pointed out, female identity is bound up with the ability to establish gratifying relationships, and the ability to establish such relationships is influenced significantly by physical attractiveness and thinness. I shared with Jane the study that noted the frequency of articles on diets in women's magazines and the study that contrasted the rates of dieting in young women and young men. I tried to encourage in her a more critical attitude toward these cultural pressures. She was receptive, perhaps particularly because she had a preadolescent daughter. In my tone I acknowledged the pressure, acknowledged the demands to be thin, and encouraged Jane to question her attempt to adhere so strictly to the cultural demands and to consider the consequences.

One cannot really break the link between body image and self-esteem. Our culture is too hard on the overweight. But in the course of our discussions, Jane could see that using as a standard the weight that she had maintained as an eighteen-year-old was unrealistic and destructive to her. As she became more accepting of her current weight, and she understood the futility of trying to control her weight through extreme self-denial, her panic associated with eating subsided.

We met for twenty-four sessions over a period of nine months. At the beginning of treatment, we attempted to meet once weekly, but on occasions, because of scheduling conflicts on either my part or Jane's, we were unable to do so. Later on, as her symptoms abated, we met approximately once every two weeks. Progress was somewhat slow over the first ten visits of treatment, but there was a steady reduction in bingeing and purging after that (see Figure 4.3 for samples of Jane's self-monitoring records during the last month of treatment). During the last two months there were no episodes of binge eating and purging; having met the treatment goals, Jane elected to stop treatment.

### Outcome Analysis

The foregoing case illustrates the application of CBT with a patient whose chief complaint was bulimia nervosa. In order to facilitate reduction in her symptoms, I focused on two major areas. First, I attended to her eating habits. I helped her establish a three-meal-per-day pattern that also included snacks. Most of Jane's symptom-maintaining "food rules" pertained to amounts of food, rather than to types of foods, and I took specific care to intervene in ways that encouraged her to eat an adequate amount of food at each setting. This was done in a gradual, stepwise fashion, concentrating on one meal at a time. The second area involved intervention to alter her attitudes toward weight and shape—specifically to reduce the salience of weight and shape as a determinant of her self-esteem and to reduce her sensitivity and alarm to changes in her body that, for the most part, were a function of aging.

Despite the severity and duration of the symptoms, and despite the traumas in her childhood, Jane presented with a great many strengths. We easily established a sound working alliance. She was a very appealing person who was both very bright and competent.

Another factor that probably contributed to her good treatment response was that although Jane presented with characteristic weight and shape concerns for this population and longed to be twenty pounds lighter, she was not actually defending a weight that was too low for her. Although therapy did not bring about weight loss, she did not gain weight either. In general, I have had fewer good outcomes with those patients who begin treatment at a weight that is below normal and for whom the treatment involves accepting a higher body weight.

At age thirty-five, older than many bulimics presenting for treatment, Jane may have been more "ready" to undertake the steps necessary to give up her symptoms. In addition, her pattern of eating and purging seemed to be directed only toward weight control. In that sense, her presentation closely fit the model of bulimia that underlies CBT and so created a good fit between patient and treatment. Patients whose bulimic symptoms appear to be serving other functions, such as mood regulation, or (as is sometimes the case with younger patients) who appear to be engaged in an ongoing, open struggle for autonomy with parents or others respond less well. Although I did not

| Day/Time | Location | With Whom | Degree of Hunger Before Eating (0-10) | If Binge Mark (✓) | Food: Types and Quantity | Activity While Eating | Degree of Fullness After Eating (0-10) | Vomiting (V) Laxatives (L) | Sensation/Feelings After Vomiting | Comments |
|---|---|---|---|---|---|---|---|---|---|---|
| 6:15 a.m. | Home | husband | 7 | | corn flakes & skim milk | Talking | | | | |
| 12:30 | Home | alone | 9 | | bacon & lettace sandwich, baklava, milk | T.V. | | | | |
| 3:30 | Out | alone | 8 | | diet coke, 2 cookies | Driving | | | | |
| 6:30 | Home | alone | 8 | | 5 small crackers & low-fat cheese spread | T.V. | | | | |
| 7:15 | Home | family | 9 | | lasagne, green salad, baby corn salad, skim milk, 1 scoop low-fat ice cream | Talking | | | | |
| 10:00 p.m. | Home | family | 7 | | cup of coffee | T.V. | | | | |

| Day/ Time | Location | With Whom | Degree of Hunger Before Eating (0-10) | If Binge Mark (✓) | Food: Types and Quantity | Activity While Eating | Degree of Fullness After Eating (0-10) | Vomiting (V) Laxatives (L) | Sensation/ Feelings After Vomiting | Comments |
|---|---|---|---|---|---|---|---|---|---|---|
| 10:00 a.m. | Home | alone | 8 | | corn flakes & skim milk, 1 slice toast, coffee | T.V. News | 7 | | | |
| 12:40 p.m. | Out | daughter | 8+ | | B.L.T., coffee | Talking | 8 | | | |
| 4:00 p.m. | Out | daughter | 7 | | coffee & bran muffin | Talking | 8 | | | |
| 7:00 p.m. | Home | kids | 8/9 | | B.B.Q. chicken, salad, slice apricot pie, skim milk | Talking | 9 | | | |
| 9:30 p.m. | Home | husband | 7 | | cup coffee | Talking | 7 | | | |

Figure 4.3
Food Records Later in Treatment

meet her husband or directly observe them together, the apparent strength of her marriage and her husband's flexibility were also helpful. Most of all, she was very motivated to be free of her bulimic symptoms—sufficiently motivated to experiment with changes that aroused considerable anxiety.

When evaluating the progress of bulimic patients, in addition to tracking changes in the frequency of bingeing and purging episodes, I look for evidence that changes have occurred in both the areas of eating habits and concerns about weight and shape. Jane made substantial changes in both. Changing her eating habits was difficult and aroused considerable anxiety, but she was able to make the effort and, before too long, experience positive results. Whereas her self-monitoring records at the outset of treatment revealed a pattern of skipped meals and an effort to restrict caloric intake below a reasonable level, by the end of treatment she was eating three adequate meals daily and at least one or two snacks. Her choice of food was varied and did not exclude any of the major food groups. Letting go of long-cherished notions regarding weight and shape was also not easy, but she was open enough and sufficiently flexible to consider alternative ways of thinking in that area as well. By the end of treatment, Jane arrived at a more realistic view of her weight and shape and gave up her quest—sadly, perhaps—to return to her late-adolescent/young-adult weight level.

Although we did not specifically address issues apart from Jane's presenting symptoms, I believe there were, in fact, additional gains. She mentioned that she found it very helpful to "take inventory" of herself. She expressed particular appreciation for the insight she gained into how her early experiences shaped her general interpersonal orientation, specifically her sense of obligation and indebtedness and her strategy of using her exquisite sensitivity to meet the needs of others automatically without considering enough her own preferences, needs, and resources.

She became more assertive in her marriage not only by asking her husband to stop making comments that amplified her weight and shape concerns but also by making him aware of her desire to reduce her compulsiveness about the maintenance of the house. At one point during treatment, she and her husband initiated a project of remodeling their kitchen, and rather than do the painting herself, at Jane's insistence they hired painters.

Additional evidence of her increased ability to set limits and to engage with others in ways more consistent with her resources emerged in certain interactional patterns with her children. As treatment progressed, Jane began to realize that doing her children's homework with them not only exhausted her but also possibly got in the way of their developing autonomy. She transformed her role from that of a collaborator to a resource. Rather than do homework with them, she made herself available to check it over when they were finished and to answer any questions when a problem arose that they were unable to solve themselves. This was not an issue that we ever explicitly discussed; as part of "taking inventory" she realized that, with the children, as with other relationships, she was putting forth effort that exceeded what was appropriate both for herself and for them.

So, in Jane's case, symptom-focused CBT for bulimia resulted not only in resolving the presenting complaint but also brought about other positive changes.

## COMBINING CBT FOR BULIMIA WITH OTHER FORMS OF PSYCHOTHERAPY

It is my hope that the foregoing case discussion illustrates some of the "nuts and bolts" of applying cognitive-behavioral therapy for bulimia nervosa. For didactic reasons I intentionally chose a case in which the patient's goals were limited to resolution of the bulimic symptoms and in which treatment was applied in relatively pure form without having to consider Axis II or other Axis I conditions. Of course, each individual is different, and one cannot carry out treatment in exactly the same way with all patients. In many instances bulimic patients present other issues that may necessitate integrating other forms of therapy with these interventions.

Although it is beyond the scope of this chapter to discuss fully the contingencies that dictate major changes or additions to CBT with bulimic patients, I would like to comment briefly on indications for combining such treatment with other forms of psychotherapy and on some of the issues that arise in doing so.

Perhaps the first question to address is whether integrating CBT for bulimia with other models of psychotherapy should even be considered; agreement about this is far from universal. In a recently published manual on CBT for binge eating and bulimia nervosa, the authors are cautious on this point, noting that "changes [in the protocol] may not result in improved outcome." They note the advantage of focus that comes with time-limited treatment and point to data gathered in clinical trials indicating continued improvement in patients for several months following CBT for bulimia.

This is an instance where the aims of the academic researcher and the clinician diverge. Controlled psychotherapy outcome studies are usually designed to address one focal problem; a group of subjects are selected who meet the criteria for a specific diagnostic category, and all those in the active condition receive the same treatment. But in the clinical setting, patients may present a variety of problems requiring the therapist's attention. It is more the exception than the rule in clinical practice to treat someone who is functioning well in all areas with the exception of one isolated difficulty. In some cases, successful symptom-focused treatment of bulimia nervosa may lead to beneficial changes in other domains of the person's life. For Jane CBT resulted in significant changes in her interpersonal functioning without our directly addressing this area. But in other cases, comorbid problems are more serious and additional treatment may be necessary.

Bulimic patients may arrive for treatment with a variety of problems, but it is among those with enduring interpersonal problems sufficiently severe to qualify for an Axis II diagnosis that I often find I must take a broader approach to treatment. I routinely refer patients with active substance abuse problems for drug and alcohol treatment before attempting to treat them for bulimia. Circumscribed problems, such as specific anxiety disorders, can usually be treated in a cognitive-behavioral format; the therapist must simply decide with the patient which problem to target first. Marital problems can often be treated concomitantly by another therapist. Depression in the bulimic patient often resolves or improves significantly as a result of CBT aimed at resolving the bulimic symptoms. But significant interpersonal problems by definition affect multiple domains of the individual's life, not the least of which is the ability to engage in and profit from a symptom-focused approach to treatment. In one study examining the effects of pharmacotherapy, CBT, and their combination for bulimia completed at Stanford, subjects with coexisting "cluster B" personality disorders (borderline, narcissistic, histrionic) fared significantly worse in all three treatment conditions.

## Factors in Treatment Selection

A brief case example will help illustrate the kinds of patients for whom CBT for bulimia should be combined with other treatment. I was recently asked to consult on a case involving a thirty-five-year-old woman who requested help with bulimia. She noted over the phone that she felt "desperate" for help and "out of control." When she contacted our clinic, she initially refused to give her name to the receptionist, saying she wouldn't do so unless offered an appointment for the next day. When the time was offered, she gave her name, but then called back thirty minutes later and asked to be seen that day. When informed that this was impossible but that she could be seen in the emergency room, she declined and said she would come tomorrow.

The patient arrived at the agreed-on time the next day. Her manner was guarded. Her answers were terse, and the therapist found it difficult to obtain enough information about her eating habits and other matters to have a clear picture of what was going on. Finally, the therapist indicated that she would have a very difficult time helping the patient without more cooperation. The patient seemed taken aback, but then said, "Well, I suppose I ought to begin by telling you my real name." She had begun therapy by giving a false name.

During the next meeting, the therapist began taking a history and learned that the patient's father had had an explosive temper, had beaten the mother, and at the very least had verbally abused the children—but in particular, the patient. He had called her vile names and had often told her he wished she were dead. The mother had been ineffectual, distant, and seemed not only unable to, but actually disinterested in, protecting the patient. The patient, who had been married and divorced twice, had once been close to an older sister but had had a falling out with her some years before when she found that this sister had slept with her first husband.

This was a patient whose history of abuse and betrayal obviously had had enormous consequences for her interpersonal and intrapsychic life; from the very first contact, her hostility and suspiciousness about the motives of others compromised her ability to enter into a collaborative relationship with the therapist. Not surprisingly, at the outset of treatment, she refused to complete the self-monitoring forms and complained that the therapist wasn't "really interested" in her. My recommendation was that because the patient's capacity to form a collaborative therapeutic alliance was so impaired that she was unwilling to comply with basic procedures in CBT, she be referred to a psychodynamic therapist at the outset to explore the issues that had impaired her basic trust and ability to collaborate. Later, if progress was made, another attempt at CBT could be initiated.

What often happens in such complicated cases is that the full breadth of the patient's problems is not addressed. If the therapist attempts to attend only to the bulimic symptoms—which is what this patient requested—he or she may not give enough attention to the long-standing interpersonal problems that affect the patient's life in myriad ways. Further, in cases such as this, the impediments to creating a working therapeutic alliance have to be at least partially resolved for symptom-focused treatment to begin. If the therapist elects to focus solely on the interpersonal issues, on the other hand, the patient may experience the therapist as unwilling to respect her chief concerns, complicating the efforts to create an alliance. In both cases, the patient is short-changed and the therapy may founder.

### Integrating Behavioral and Psychodynamic Treatment

In the past fifteen years, interest in integrating different models of psychotherapy has increased dramatically. Much of the literature in this area has been devoted to attempts to integrate behavioral and interpersonally oriented dynamic models of treatment, probably because these models have complementary strengths and weaknesses. The strength of behavioral models is in the treatment of specific symptoms; their weakness is the relative inattention to recurring patterns of interpersonal interaction that are often a source of significant difficulty to psychiatric patients of all kinds. Analytically informed models are the mirror image. Their strength is their ability to address complex interpersonal problems; their weakness is their frequent ineffectiveness at addressing the treatment of specific Axis I disorders.

Many of the suggestions I have found most helpful in integrating cognitive-behavioral with interpersonally oriented dynamic therapy have come from the writings of Paul Wachtel. His ideas on cyclical psychodynamics emphasize the ways the individual's past experiences and internal conflicts are enacted and confirmed in present interactions with others. He has argued against the notion of therapist neutrality, proposing that the concept of transference be expanded to accommodate examination of the patient's responses to the therapist's active intervention, including behaviorally oriented procedures and instigations.

Despite these helpful concepts, I have found integrating CBT with dynamic psychotherapy for those bulimic patients with comorbid Axis II diagnoses to be extremely challenging. One reason is that patients experience these problems differently; the level of awareness regarding the presence of these difficulties and their consequences can vary significantly. CBT for bulimia focuses on a problem that the patient must at least ostensibly acknowledge and want to resolve. Although it is true that the patient and the therapist may, at the outset, conceptualize the *solution* differently (for example, the patient believes more "self-control" is necessary, whereas the therapist conceptualizes the problem in terms of ending the binge-starve cycle), there is little disagreement about the nature of the problem itself. In contrast, the patient with serious interpersonal problems often fails to see them clearly. For instance, the patient with a narcissistic personality disorder may come to treatment enraged over having been rejected by a partner but doesn't see that her sense of entitlement, lack of empathy, or harsh criticism of the other has contributed to the difficulty. The patient who requests treatment specifically for bulimia yet who has obvious serious interpersonal problems as well may not be readily able to address the latter difficulties, which then may interfere with the symptom-focused treatment that is requested.

Most important, CBT's therapeutic process as developed for the treatment of bulimia is vastly different from the process of even the most interpersonally oriented dynamic therapies. Its process is prescriptive. The model explaining the development and maintenance of the disorder, as well as the steps necessary for resolution, are precisely formulated. The goals of treatment (abstinence from binge eating and purging and more realistic views regarding weight and shape) and the means for achieving those goals (for example, breaking the binge-starve cycle, eating forbidden foods in moderate quantities, changing one's thinking to achieve a more "rational" view regarding weight and shape) are quite specific. Much of the therapist's effort is geared toward educating the patient about the model and persuading the patient to take the prescribed steps.

This stance creates a particular kind of relationship; one in which the therapist is adviser, mentor, and coach—with a clear point of view and an investment in helping the patient make specific changes. Much of the writing on psychotherapy integration has focused on the behavior of the therapist and, in particular, on the ways the therapist can accommodate his or her conceptual scheme to permit a wider range of intervention choices. As instructive as this literature has been, it has not sufficiently acknowledged the ways the patient's experience of the therapy also complicates efforts to deliver a truly integrative treatment.

The prescriptive process in CBT for bulimia shapes both the patient's in-session behavior and her perception about how therapy operates to produce change. It is impossible to spend a great deal of time in treatment coaching a patient on what and how much to eat without inducing in the patient an attitude that change occurs through understanding the steps laid out by the therapist and complying with these as best as possible.

The interactional pattern that develops between patient and therapist in CBT for bulimia is profoundly influenced by the early interventions. A rhythm is created in which the patient seems to wait for the therapist's direction. I don't mean to imply that the patient is rendered passive; on the contrary, it is made clear that her behavior between sessions will determine the outcome. But the in-session process is antithetical to facilitating the kind of interaction in which the therapist and patient together engage in reflection about the patient's internal life or about what the patient's reaction to the therapist—even an active, directive therapist—reveals about her motives or interpersonal patterns. To put it differently, the patient-therapist dance that is characteristic of dynamic therapy is vastly different from that of therapist and patient in CBT. And it is impossible to perform two different dances at the same time.

My own efforts to work with bulimic patients who also present with serious Axis II conditions have involved, therefore, combining and sequencing cognitive-behavioral treatment with dynamic therapy, rather than attempting to integrate these treatments seamlessly. Broadly speaking, for those patients whose presenting complaint is specifically bulimia and who express the desire to be treated for that problem, I generally find it most helpful to attempt to provide CBT and, if possible, to wait to address the longer-term interpersonal difficulties. As Barr Taylor and I wrote in an earlier work on the treatment of patients with anxiety disorders, focusing on the patient's chief complaint—even though other problems are not being fully acknowledged—is often necessary to create a workable therapeutic alliance. In some cases, the patient leaves treatment without ever addressing the other difficulties; in other cases, direct help with a specific symptom enhances the patient's trust in the therapist and in the potential of psychotherapy to provide benefit, and thus facilitates the investigation of enduring interpersonal problems. I have not found the transition from cognitive-behavioral to dynamic therapy to be particularly difficult.

For some bulimic patients, it is not possible to wait to address the interpersonal problems. Among this group are those who are aware of chronic interpersonal problems and want treatment for both problems simultaneously and those whose personality difficulties impede the patient's ability to constructively engage in CBT for bulimia. Some of these latter patients are simply too hostile or disorganized and distressed to focus on the tasks of CBT. For others, after discussing with the patient that the two areas require different approaches, I have often split the session into two parts: in the first part using cognitive-behavioral techniques to address the bulimia, and in the second part using a more dynamic format.

This protocol is not unlike what dynamically oriented psychiatrists do when they prescribe medication in the context of dynamic treatment. Some time is typically spent in the beginning of the session discussing dosages, instructions, and side effects, after which the format of the session changes. I have sometimes found that the patient and I can go over the tasks involved in cognitive-behavioral treatment in fifteen to twenty minutes before shifting gears to a more dynamic format. While the bulimic symptoms do not abate as quickly in this format— one cannot reduce the time spent on CBT by half without loss— it is possible to provide good treatment in this way, and many patients do make slow but steady progress.

I concur with others who, after reviewing controlled studies of treatment outcome for bulimia nervosa, regard cognitive-behavioral therapy as the "first-line approach" with this population. Considering that CBT is a short-term treatment, outcomes are quite good, and studies show that gains are maintained at one-year follow-ups. Although patients with serious personality disorders are less likely to respond, I do not attempt to prejudge before initiating CBT whether or not they will be able to profit from it. One advantage of this form of treatment is that the patient's ability to become engaged in therapy can be clearly assessed at the outset through the willingness to comply with initial directives, such as the self-monitoring and the efforts to begin normalizing the eating pattern. As treatment is highly focused on presenting symptoms, if the patient is going to respond, this too is evident early on in treatment; so, if necessary, the treatment approach can be altered before the patient has made a large commitment in time and money. While not everyone responds to CBT, I believe it is the best place to begin with patients who present with bulimia nervosa.

# NOTES

P. 101, *In many such cases:* For a discussion of exposure therapy, see Taylor, C. B., & Arnow, B. (1988). *The nature and treatment of anxiety disorders.* New York: Free Press. See also Barlow, D. H., & Cerny, J. A. (1988). *Psychological treatment of panic.* New York: Guilford Press.

P. 102, *The goals of the analytically oriented therapies:* For a discussion of the issue, see Wachtel, P. L. (1987). *Action and insight* (Chap. 12). New York: Guilford Press. See also Gill, M. M. (1984). Psychoanalytic, psychodynamic, cognitive behavior, and behavior therapies compared. In H. Arkowitz & S.

B. Messer (Eds.), *Psychoanalytic therapy and behavior therapy: Is integration possible?* (pp. 179–187). New York: Plenum Press.

P. 103, *The emphasis is on modification of more molecular processes:* Goldfried, M. R., & Castonguay, L. G. (1993). Behavior therapy: Redefining strengths and limitations. *Behavior Therapy, 24,* 505–526.

P. 103, *Marsha Linehan's dialectical behavior therapy:* Linehan, M. M. (1993). *Cognitive-behavioral treatment of borderline personality disorder.* New York: Guilford Press.

P. 104, *in one study with a sample of high school students:* Dwyer, J. T., Feldman, J. J., Seltzer, C. C., & Mayer, J. (1969). Body image in adolescents: Attitudes toward weight and perception of appearance. *American Journal of Clinical Nutrition, 20,* 1045–1056.

P. 104, *One study completed a frequency count:* Agras, W. S., & Kirkley, B. G. (1986). Bulimia: Theories of etiology. In K. D. Brownell & J. P. Foreyt (Eds.), *Handbook of eating disorders* (pp. 367–378). New York: Basic Books.

P. 105, *Another group of investigators:* Garner, D. M., Garfinkel, P. E., Schwartz, D., & Thompson, M. (1980). Cultural expectations of thinness in women. *Psychological Reports, 47,* 483–491.

P. 107, *It is beyond the scope of this chapter:* For an excellent review of such studies, see Ruderman, A. J. (1986). Dietary restraint: A theoretical and empirical review. *Psychological Review, 99,* 247–262.

P. 107, *In one study carried out by Herman and Mack:* Herman, C. P., & Mack, D. (1975). Restrained and unrestrained eating. *Journal of Personality, 43,* 647–660.

P. 111, *bulimic patients often present a "false self":* For instance, see Johnson, C. (1985). Initial consultation for patients with bulimia and anorexia nervosa. In D. M. Garner & P. E. Garfinkel (Eds.), *Handbook of psychotherapy for anorexia nervosa and bulimia* (pp. 19–51). New York: Guilford Press.

P. 113, *Perfectionism and "black and white" thinking are well-documented patterns:* See Butterfield, P. S., & Leclair, S. (1988). Cognitive characteristics of bulimic and drug-abusing women. *Addictive Behaviors, 13,* 131–138; Heatherton, T. F., & Baumeister, R. F. (1991). Binge eating as escape from self-awareness. *Psychological Bulletin, 110,* 86–108; Katzman, M. A., & Wolchik, S. A. (1984). Bulimia and binge eating in college women: A comparison of eating patterns and personality characteristics. *Journal of Consulting and Clinical Psychology, 52,* 423–428; Lingswiler, V. M., Crowther, J. H., & Stephens, M.A.P. (1989). Affective and cognitive antecedents to eating episodes in bulimia and binge eating. *International Journal of Eating Disorders, 8,* 533–539; Mizes, J. S. (1988). Personality characteristics of bulimic and non-eating disordered female controls: A cognitive behavioral perspective. *International Journal of Eating Dis-*

*orders,* 7, 541–550; Ruderman, A. J. (1986). Bulimia and irrational beliefs. *Behavior Research and Therapy,* 24, 193–197.

P. 116, *Figure 4.2 displays a diagram:* For an alternative diagram, see Fairburn, C. G., Marcus, M. D., & Wilson, G. T. (1993). Cognitive-behavioral therapy for binge eating and bulimia nervosa: A comprehensive treatment manual. In C. G. Fairburn & G. T. Wilson (Eds.), *Binge eating: Nature, assessment, and treatment* (pp. 361–404). New York: Guilford Press.

P. 125, *As Ruth Striegel-Moore has pointed out:* See Striegel-Moore, R. H. (1993). Etiology of binge eating: A developmental perspective. In C. G. Fairburn & G. T. Wilson (Eds.), *Binge eating: Nature, assessment, and treatment* (pp. 144–172). New York: Guilford Press; Striegel-Moore, R. H., Silberstein, L. R., & Rodin, J. (1986). Toward an understanding of risk factors for bulimia. *American Psychologist,* 41, 246–263.

P. 132, *In a recently published manual on CBT:* Fairburn, C. G., Marcus, M. D., & Wilson, G. T. (1993). Cognitive-behavioral therapy for binge eating and bulimia nervosa: A comprehensive treatment manual. In C. G. Fairburn & G. T. Wilson (Eds.), *Binge eating: Nature, assessment, and treatment* (pp. 361–404). New York: Guilford Press.

P. 132, *the aims of the academic researcher and the clinician diverge:* For an excellent discussion of this issue, see Persons, J. B. (1991). Psychotherapy outcome studies do not accurately represent current models of psychotherapy: A proposed remedy. *American Psychologist,* 46, 99–106.

P. 133, *the effects of pharmacotherapy, CBT, and their combination for bulimia:* Rossiter, E. M., Agras, W. S., Telch, C. F., & Schneider, J. A. (1993). Cluster B personality disorder characteristics predict outcome in the treatment of bulimia nervosa. *International Journal of Eating Disorders,* 13, 349–357.

P. 135, *Many of the suggestions I have found most helpful:* See Wachtel, P. L. (1977). *Psychoanalysis and behavior therapy: Toward an integration.* New York: Basic Books; Wachtel, P. L. (1987). *Action and insight.* New York: Guilford Press; Wachtel, P. L., & McKinney, M. K. (1992). Cyclical psychodynamics and integrative psychodynamic therapy. In J. Norcross & M. Goldfried (Eds.), *Handbook of Psychotherapy Integration* (pp. 335–370). New York: HarperCollins.

P. 138, *As Barr Taylor and I wrote:* See Taylor, C. B., & Arnow, B. (1988). *The nature and treatment of anxiety disorders* (Chap. 4). New York: Free Press.

P. 139, *I concur with others:* Fairburn, C. G., Marcus, M. D., & Wilson, G. T. (1993). Cognitive-behavioral therapy for binge eating and bulimia nervosa: A comprehensive treatment manual. In C. G. Fairburn & G. T. Wilson (Eds.), *Binge eating: Nature, assessment, and treatment* (pp. 361–404). New York: Guilford Press.

# TREATMENT OF BINGE-EATING DISORDER IN GROUP COGNITIVE-BEHAVIORAL THERAPY

**Carol B. Peterson and James E. Mitchell**

Binge-eating disorder (BED) is characterized by recurrent overeating episodes in which the individual consumes an objectively large amount of food and feels a loss of control over his or her eating behavior. Unlike individuals with bulimia nervosa, clients with BED do not engage in compensatory behaviors like self-induced vomiting, laxative and diuretic abuse, protracted fasting, or excessive exercise to counteract the effects of the binge-eating episodes. Binge-eating disorder is listed as an example of Eating Disorder Not Otherwise Specified (ED NOS) in the appendix of the most recent *Diagnostic and Statistical Manual of Mental Disorders (DSM-IV)*. To meet criteria for the diagnosis, individuals must engage in binge eating an average of two days per week for at least a six-month duration and report marked distress about their symptoms.

According to epidemiological studies, the rate of BED in the general population is 2 percent and is more common in women than men. Perhaps because of their tendency to ingest large amounts of food without compensatory behaviors, individuals with BED tend to be overweight. Among overweight individuals seeking weight loss, rates of BED are approximately 20 to 30 percent. There also is evidence that the prevalence of binge eating increases with degree of overweight. Descriptive studies have revealed that BED is associated with elevated rates of major depression, substance abuse and dependence, and personality disorders, compared with rates in samples of obese individuals without BED.

Treatment approaches for binge-eating disorder have evolved from interventions for related disorders, including other eating disorders (especially bulimia nervosa), depression, and anxiety disorders. Preliminary studies indicate that certain medications, including antidepressants, are helpful in reducing the frequency of binge-eating episodes, though not necessarily eliminating them. More promising treatments include various types of psychotherapy, including cognitive-behavioral and interpersonal psychotherapy. Specifically, three studies have found that group cognitive-behavioral therapy (group CBT) reduces and, in many cases, eliminates binge eating—although relapse rates are high. Another type of therapy, interpersonal psychotherapy (IPT), also has been found effective in group format in reducing binge-eating symptoms in one study.

At the University of Minnesota our own group CBT treatment for BED evolved from a manual-based treatment for bulimia nervosa used for several studies we conducted in our research facility during the past decade. The manual and treatment protocol have been modified to treat individuals with BED, most of whom are significantly overweight. We have used this manual-based treatment with clients in our outpatient and research clinic for the past five years.

Our decision to use group CBT rather than individual sessions in treating BED was based on three primary considerations:

1. The published research on CBT for BED has usually involved group modalities.
2. Group psychotherapy is more cost-effective than individual therapy, a consideration of importance in the current economic

climate with a focus on managed care and diminishing resources. This issue is especially important because of BED's classification as an Eating Disorder Not Otherwise Specified (ED NOS) in the *DSM-IV,* which leads to further problems in receiving reimbursement from some third-party payers.

3. Group psychotherapy provides a number of benefits not available in individual psychotherapy, including the instillation of hope and the development of socializing techniques.

Our group treatment program is conducted on an outpatient basis. Our current protocol consists of fourteen sessions over an eight-week period. Sessions are held twice a week for the first six weeks, then are tapered to once each week for the final two weeks. Because the treatment is usually conducted as part of a research project, all individuals enrolled in the program participate in an extensive screening and assessment phase prior to treatment. We also ask participants to complete a number of self-report questionnaires throughout the course of their participation. All treatment offered as part of research protocols is free of charge to participants.

To recruit group members, we usually place advertisements in local newspapers, offering free treatment for individuals with binge-eating problems. We also receive referrals from the outpatient Eating Disorder Clinic affiliated with our hospital. In addition, we disperse information about our groups to local eating-disorder therapists, clinics, and health maintenance organizations. Treatment providers in these settings are especially willing to refer individuals to our facility when their own clinics do not offer treatment for binge-eating problems.

When potential group members call us, we give them a brief introduction about the type of treatment we provide. We also screen them for inclusion into the study by asking information about current binge-eating patterns, drug and alcohol use, and whether they are receiving any other type of psychiatric or medical treatment. Individuals who do not meet criteria for our research studies or who are inappropriate for group therapy are referred to alternative treatment resources. When the treatment is offered as part of a research project, we send subjects who meet criteria a copy of the consent form, which has more detailed information about the study. We then invite them to attend an orientation session, during which they meet the group therapist and other members of the research staff.

We find this type of preliminary orientation session especially important in a research setting, which patients often fear will look and feel like a laboratory. They are usually (although not always) relieved to see that our offices and staff are welcoming. Interestingly, individuals who express trepidation during the initial phone call about participating in group therapy (for example, "I'd really prefer individual therapy because I just don't feel comfortable talking in groups") are reassured and put at ease during the orientation "preview." Conversely, the orientation also helps identify individuals who really would prefer alternative types of treatment prior to the beginning of therapy.

# THE STORY OF ELLEN

Ellen responded to a Sunday newspaper advertisement offering free treatment to women with BED as part of a research protocol. A thirty-six-year-old Caucasian female, she presented for treatment with a twenty-year history of binge-eating episodes. At the time of the evaluation, her weight was 180 pounds with a height of five feet two inches, yielding a body mass index (BMI, an individual's weight in kilograms divided by the height in meters squared) of thirty-three. Because healthy BMIs typically range from twenty to twenty-five, Ellen's BMI of thirty-three would be classified in the range of significantly overweight.

Ellen and Bob, her husband of ten years, own a home in a nearby metropolitan suburb. They have two children: Jennifer, age five, and Christopher, age two. Ellen transitioned from working full-time to part-time in her job as a marketing representative when Jennifer was born. Bob, also thirty-six, is a bank executive.

## History of Eating and Weight Problems

Like many individuals with BED, Ellen reports being mildly overweight as a child and describes having "used food for comfort." According to Ellen, both of her parents were obese. Ellen remembers her mother's preoccupation with being overweight and her unsuccessful attempts at weight loss. Fearing that she, too, would develop a serious weight problem, Ellen began to diet at age twelve in an attempt to lose weight. After approximately one year of inconsistent dieting, Ellen remembers having strong urges to overeat and "losing control" when consuming food.

Our data on the development of BED indicate that approximately half of all individuals with BED engage in dietary restriction prior to the onset of binge-eating episodes. The other half report the onset of binge eating prior to dieting. This pattern contrasts with what is typically seen in the development of bulimia nervosa, in which individuals usually engage in excessive dieting prior to the onset of the bulimic symptoms.

Although Ellen's overeating episodes started out with relatively modest portions (for example, extra cookies after dinner), the size and frequency escalated over time. She reports that, by age thirteen, she was consuming a half-gallon of ice cream at one sitting after school at least three days a week. Ellen was upset by her behavior and attempted repeatedly and unsuccessfully to stop:

> I would start out each day determined to stay on my diet. I would eat a grapefruit for breakfast and a salad or yogurt for lunch. Then, I would get home from school and I'd be so hungry that I'd end up overeating. It was awful. I swore every night that the next day would be different, that I would "be good." Then, I would lose control and just give up for the rest of the day, promising myself that it would never happen again.

According to Ellen, she continued to gain weight through her high school years and into her early twenties. Although she heard about people who "got rid of food" through vomiting, laxative abuse, or self-starvation, Ellen was concerned about the long-term health risks of such behaviors.

Throughout her development, Ellen made repeated attempts to lose weight. At one time during late adolescence, her pediatrician prescribed diet pills; however, these made Ellen "jumpy," and she subsequently discontinued their use. Since adulthood, she has enrolled in a number of structured dieting programs. She is usually successful in losing weight down to 160 pounds but quickly regains the weight afterward. She reports that she is able to cut back on her food intake while dieting but that she "rewards" herself with food after successfully losing weight ("I deserve to eat what I want after being hungry for so long") and begins to overeat soon after.

At the time of the evaluation, Ellen was binge eating approximately two or three times per week. Most of these episodes occurred in the late afternoon or evening and consisted of a box of cookies or a half-gallon of ice cream. Ellen reported feeling a loss of control during these episodes, stating that she was unable to stop herself from eating once she started. She also described eating more rapidly than usual, eating even when she was not physically hungry, and overeating to the point of discomfort. She reported feeling extremely distressed about these episodes and "disgusted" with herself afterward. Ellen told the staff that she was "desperate" to change her behavior: "I'll do anything—really I will. This out-of-control eating has just got to stop."

A semistructured clinical interview conducted during the assessment session revealed that, in addition to binge eating, Ellen had a lengthy history of problems with depression. By *DSM-IV* criteria, she had experienced at least three episodes of major depression since her early twenties. The most recent episode occurred two years ago, after the birth of her second child. Although she no longer reported concomitant physical symptoms, such as sleep and energy disturbance, at the time of the evaluation she indicated that her mood was often "low."

Ellen also tended to be highly self-critical and at times experienced feelings of worthlessness. Although the content of these thoughts often focused on her concerns about weight, shape, and eating, she also reported ruminating about whether she was "good enough" as a wife and mother.

> Sometimes I just wonder if I do a good enough job. I feel like I try so hard to make Bob and the kids happy, but it just seems like I can never do enough for them. I also worry about whether they think I'm slacking off at work, since I've been only working part-time since the kids were born. Sometimes, I'm okay with everything, but other times, it just seems like I don't do anything well enough.

### Past Treatment

Ellen had sought treatment on a few occasions in the past. After she graduated from college at age twenty-two, she met with a counselor from her church "for support." In describing that time in her life, Ellen reports that she felt "alone and lost" for six months while she was looking for a job. She had difficulty sleeping and concentrating. She also had more problems with her eating. She reports that her church counselor was quite helpful and that her symptoms remitted completely after she started working.

Ellen's depression remained in remission for seven years. Following the birth of her first child, however, she became quite depressed and met with a psychologist for seven months for insight-oriented psychotherapy. Ellen reports that this treatment was quite helpful in alleviating her symptoms of depression. In the course of this treatment, she also developed the understanding that the onset of her binge-eating behaviors was related to her family context during adolescence, at which time eating became a form of self-nurturance. Although insight-oriented therapy improved her depression and helped her understand the origins of her overeating, her binge-eating episodes persisted.

Recently, Ellen had sought treatment for her eating problems but was told by her insurance company that they would not provide coverage for treatment of "overeating"; she was concerned about the expense of paying for treatment out-of-pocket. She responded to our advertisement because it offered treatment free of charge.

### Social History

Ellen was born and raised in the metropolitan suburbs. Her mother, a housewife, has struggled with obesity and depression throughout her adulthood. Her father, who worked as a salesman for a large corporation, was an alcohol abuser until successful treatment following a heart attack ten years ago. He also has a weight problem.

Both of Ellen's parents are still living, although their health is poor. She visits them weekly but speaks with them by phone more frequently. Ellen also has an older brother living out of state but does not communicate with him on a regular basis because they "don't have much in common."

Ellen met her husband, Bob, at a church outing when she was twenty-four. They became engaged a year later and were married at age twenty-six. She describes the first few years of their marriage as "blissful" but notes that they have not spent much time with one another since the children were born. Ellen describes Bob as "supportive, but he does not really understand this eating thing."

Ellen has a few close friends but tends to spend the majority of her time outside work with her children. She likes to knit, listen to music, and go to the movies in what she describes as her "limited" free time.

### Medical Evaluation

Ellen denied all physical symptoms and medical problems except for mild arthritis and occasional tension headaches. Otherwise, her medical history was unremarkable. Blood pressure and cholesterol levels were normal. Serum electrolytes, obtained to help confirm that she was not engaging in self-induced vomiting, were within normal limits. She denied a personal or family history of diabetes.

Compared with many patients we evaluate with BED, Ellen was in relatively good physical health. In part because of their obesity, many individuals with BED present for treatment with hypertension, cardiovascular disease, Type II diabetes, or severe arthritis. We emphasize to patients the importance of continued monitoring by their own physicians because medical issues are not a primary focus of our treatment program.

Some patients report feeling ashamed to visit their physician because of fear of being criticized for failing to lose weight. At times we obtain a release of information in order to communicate by phone or letter with the patient's physician. We find it helpful to emphasize the importance of gradual weight loss for individuals with BED to minimize the risk of relapse.

### Initial Treatment Sessions

After contacting our center, Ellen attended our orientation program, which provided information on the structure and type of treatment, as well as on the typical expectations of group participants. At this time she met the group psychotherapist, the assessment coordinator, and the team physician. She then attended the pretreatment evaluation meeting where she gave us the details of her eating disorder and history.

At the first group session, Ellen met the other six members, all of whom were women with BED. After group members introduced themselves to one another, we (the group leaders) provided information about the format of the group and the content of group sessions. Members were provided with a copy of the schedule (see Table 5.1).

We then described the rationale for CBT as treatment for binge eating and the goals of the program, emphasizing that CBT is a type of therapy that focuses on *changing thoughts and behavior patterns that contribute to the binge-eating episodes*, as well

## Table 5.1
## Group Therapy Schedule

| | | |
|---|---|---|
| Wednesday | Session 1: | Introduction |
| Monday | Session 2: | Cues and Consequences |
| Wednesday | Session 3: | Normalizing Eating |
| Monday | Session 4: | Thoughts, Feelings, and Behaviors |
| Wednesday | Session 5: | Restructuring Your Thoughts |
| Monday | Session 6: | Cues and Chains |
| Wednesday | Session 7: | Self-Control and Mood Enhancement |
| Monday | Session 8: | Body Image |
| Wednesday | Session 9: | Self-Esteem |
| Monday | Session 10: | Stress Management and Problem Solving |
| Wednesday | Session 11: | Assertiveness |
| Monday | Session 12: | Weight Loss Issues |
| Wednesday | No Meeting | |
| Monday | Session 13: | Relapse Prevention, Part I |
| Wednesday | No Meeting | |
| Monday | Session 14: | Final Session: Relapse Prevention, Part II |

as developing alternative coping strategies. We noted that this type of treatment is time-limited, active, and focused on management of symptoms. Regular attendance and completion of homework assignments are essential for the treatment to be effective. We also emphasized that much of the therapeutic work in CBT takes place outside the clinic, between treatment sessions.

We believe it is important to inform members in the first session that although weight-loss issues would be addressed in the later sessions, the primary goal of the program is to alter binge-eating patterns. This therapeutic rationale stands in stark contrast to most of the weight loss groups in which individuals with

BED have participated in the past, and members often have mixed reactions:

> *Ellen:* How much weight will we lose in this program?
>
> *Therapist:* I'm glad you raised that issue Ellen, and I'm sure other people are wondering about it as well. [Others nod in agreement] Basically, our goal in this program is to help you manage your binge-eating behavior—specifically, to reduce and hopefully eliminate your binge-eating episodes.
>
> *Laura:* But won't we lose weight then?
>
> *Therapist:* Maybe. Many people do, but it's important to know that people don't necessarily lose weight in the short term when they stop binge eating. We do recognize that many of you come to treatment here with the primary goal of weight loss. For how many of you is that true? [Four hands raise, including Ellen's]
>
> *Therapist:* Well, from what we know, it's not easy to lose weight—if that is your goal—when you're still binge eating. For this reason, we suggest you try to approach weight loss in phases. First, focus on managing the binge eating. Then, we will discuss some weight-loss strategies later on in treatment.

Another group member stated that, from her own experience, she doubted "anyone could lose weight if they're stuffing their face with food all the time." The other members agreed—although, like Ellen, they appeared disappointed that the group leaders were unwilling to promise them weight loss. As the discussion, continued, however, Ellen agreed that, apart from her weight, the lack of control she experienced during her binge-eating episodes was extremely distressing to her and warranted the focus of her attention.

Next, we reviewed the materials presented in the first portion of the manual and encouraged group members to follow along in their own manuals. The initial session focused on psychoed-ucational information detailing what is known about BED: the rates of the disorder in the population and among individuals seeking weight loss, how it is more common in women than men, and typical associated symptoms.

The session then turned to a discussion of consequences of binge eating. The group members volunteered a number of problems associated with binge eating, including depression, anxiety, irritability, self-loathing, obesity, and physical discom-fort. Ellen raised the issue of social consequences, especially feel-ings of isolation and shame when she engaged in binge eating during her husband's absence. She also expressed concern that she might serve as a poor role model for her young children. The group members agreed with Ellen's points and described their own experiences of secretive eating and social isolation.

At the end of the first session, we distributed self-monitoring forms (see Figure 5.1) and provided instructions: we asked mem-bers to write down what and when they ate, the context, associ-ated thoughts and feelings, and whether or not they thought it was a binge. Members were informed that they should complete the forms as soon as possible after eating.

We also described different types of binge-eating episodes and asked members to note on their self-monitoring sheets which type they had experienced. *Objective* binge-eating episodes (OBs) are characterized by two features:

1. The consumption of a clearly *large amount of food* in a discrete period of time
2. A feeling of *loss of control* during the binge-eating episode

The members had a number of questions about these defini-tions, especially what was meant by "loss of control." One group member said, "I should be able to control it, but I don't." We explained that feeling "loss of control" is characterized by the sense that one could not prevent the eating from occurring or stop once it has started.

| Time | Food and Liquid Consumed | Place | OB or SB | Context | Thoughts | Feelings |
|------|--------------------------|-------|----------|---------|----------|----------|
|      |                          |       |          |         |          |          |
|      |                          |       |          |         |          |          |
|      |                          |       |          |         |          |          |
|      |                          |       |          |         |          |          |
|      |                          |       |          |         |          |          |
|      |                          |       |          |         |          |          |
|      |                          |       |          |         |          |          |
|      |                          |       |          |         |          |          |

**Figure 5.1**
**Self-Monitoring Form**

OB = objective binge; SB = subjective binge

The group members also had questions about what we meant by a large amount of food. Ellen said that putting mayonnaise on a sandwich felt like a binge to her because she tried to avoid eating high-fat foods. We used this example as an illustration of a *subjective* binge-eating episode (SB), which is characterized by a feeling of loss of control but not necessarily consumption of a large amount of food. When asked, the group members agreed that even if they might have felt as Ellen did at times, a sandwich with mayonnaise was *not* clearly a large amount of food. Ellen affirmed that it probably did constitute a subjective binge-eating episode because she felt out of control of her eating when she added mayonnaise or dressing to food.

At the end of the session, we emphasized the importance of making a commitment to change and of making treatment the top priority. We also reviewed possible consequences that members could expect as they stopped binge eating. First, because binge eating often serves as a coping strategy to manage uncomfortable feelings, members might feel increasing levels of anxiety, sadness, irritability, and emotional discomfort. We also predicted that members might feel ambivalent about treatment at times, especially when discouraged. We suggested that even on nights when they had the urge to skip a session, they should still attend and try to discuss their feelings in the context of the group. Finally, we suggested that members start identifying sources of social support that could help them through the difficult recovery process.

The group members, including Ellen, walked out to the parking lot together after the conclusion of the session. They appeared to interact well with one another, laughing and smiling as they departed.

### Behavioral Cues

At the beginning of the second session, we asked group members to share their self-monitoring sheets and to review how their week had progressed since the previous session. A number of members, including Ellen, observed that self-monitoring alone had reduced the frequency and size of binge-eating episodes.

"When I knew I'd have to write it down and read about it later, I was a lot less likely to put it in my mouth," Ellen remarked.

Treatment outcome research indicates that self-monitoring alone can lead to a reduction in symptoms in bulimia nervosa. In our opinion, self-monitoring is one of the most crucial elements of CBT, and its importance should be emphasized in early sessions.

We asked group members if they had noted any patterns to their symptoms. A number of members observed that their binge-eating episodes occurred when they were at home watching television. Most members reported that binge eating usually occurred in the late afternoon or evening, especially after they had experienced anxiety, sadness, or anger during the day. One of Ellen's self-monitoring sheets is shown in Figure 5.2.

Review of self-monitoring led to the topic of the evening: behavioral models of binge-eating behavior or "cues and consequences" of symptoms. We explained that behaviors are "cued" by what happens before them. Behaviors (and the associated thoughts and feelings) are then followed by "consequences" (see Figure 5.3).

We asked members to identify specific cues and consequences associated with their binge-eating episodes. Although members were silent at first, Josephine finally responded, "Oh, you mean like what I was saying about how I usually binge eat while watching television?" We agreed that her example was an excellent one and could be classified as a "situational" cue. Members then began to list other situational triggers, including viewing food advertisements, walking by a bakery, and cooking dinner. Ellen reported that driving by the donut store on the way home from work was often a cue for her episodes.

When asked for examples of social or interpersonal cues, Ellen mentioned fighting with her husband. Many of the women agreed that interpersonal conflict was a common trigger, as were social isolation and loneliness. Psychological triggers were common, including boredom, upsetting memories, mental images of obesity, and distressing feelings. We also asked if anyone had observed that dieting served as a cue. Many members reported that hunger in general and dieting in particular triggered binge-eating episodes.

We then explained the behavioral principle of reinforcement: repeated pairing of a cue with a behavior may result in the cue "triggering" the behavior. To prevent binge-eating behavior, cues

| Time | Food and Liquid Consumed | Place | OB or SB | Context | Thoughts | Feelings |
|------|--------------------------|-------|----------|---------|----------|----------|
| 7:45 am | 1/2 grapefruit<br>coffee<br>1/2 piece dry toast | kitchen table | | breakfast | "This is okay – my eating is in control" | calm, relaxed |
| 10:00 a.m. | 1 orange | desk at work | | snack | "I'm hungry - this is good for me" | tense about work |
| 12:00 p.m. | low-fat yogurt<br>10 crackers<br>5 pretzels | lunch room | | eating lunch with friends at work | "I'm trying to be good"<br>"I shouldn't eat the pretzels" | happy to be with friends, anxious about eating the pretzels |
| 3:00 p.m. | Oreos (25-30) | kitchen | OB | hungry after work | "I blew it with the pretzels, so I might as well eat a cookie"<br>"I had too many - I might as well binge" | anxious, fat, disgusted |
| 6:00 p.m. | diet frozen dinner | dinner table | | dinner with family | "I'll diet tomorrow" | still upset about cookies, distracted |

## Figure 5.2
## Ellen's Self-Monitoring Form

OB = objective binge; SB = subjective binge

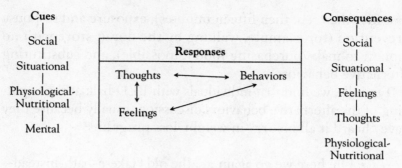

**Figure 5.3**
**Cues, Responses, and Consequences**

need to be identified and altered. Strategies for rearranging cues include the following:

- *Avoiding* stimuli (for example, do not watch television or walk by the bakery if these trigger binge eating)
- *Restricting the stimulus field* (for example, restrict eating meals only to the table so that other settings—the car, the kitchen, the movie theater—are no longer "cues" for binge eating)
- *Strengthening cues for desired behavior* (for example, if binge eating does not occur when eating with a friend, plan to eat meals with friends)

Ellen suggested that because driving by the donut shop often triggered a binge, she would attempt to take an alternate route home from work. She also decided to schedule more meals with friends because dinners often evolved into binge-eating episodes when she was eating alone.

In addition to rearranging cues, *changing responses to cues* can also reduce binge eating. We emphasized that behavioral theory indicates the importance of "breaking" the relationship between the cue and the binge-eating behavior. Strategies for altering responses to cues include building in a pause (for example, wait for progressively longer periods of time after a cue before eating—

first five, then ten, then fifteen minutes), exposure and response prevention (for example, walking by the donut store with no money, to make purchasing food impossible), and substituting alternative behaviors.

Typically, we find that individuals with BED balk at the beginning of the alternative behaviors discussion, usually because they have "heard it all before" in weight-loss programs:

> *Lisa:* Oh, here we go again . . . the old "take-a-bath-instead-of-eating" routine. As if that works.
>
> *Therapist:* What do you mean, Lisa?
>
> *Lisa:* Everyone always tells you to do something else instead of eating—take a bath, go for a walk, stuff like that. But it doesn't work. All you do is think about food while you're taking a bath. [Other group members laugh]
>
> *Therapist:* Yes, it is simplistic to think that alternative behaviors will necessarily work as a substitute for something as powerful as binge eating, especially at first. But we suggest that what's really important is to break the relationship between the cue—watching TV, fighting with your husband, whatever—and the binge-eating response. Even if it's only a brief delay, it's an important step in breaking that association. So in our opinion, lying in the bathtub not binge eating after being exposed to a cue, even if you're thinking about food, is an important step in breaking that binge-eating response.

We asked group members to spend considerable time developing lists of alternative behaviors as potential substitutes for binge eating. Ellen and other members were skeptical, so we asked them to generate ideas that could distract them from binge eating even momentarily.

Ellen had difficulty with this task at first but was eventually successful in identifying a number of alternatives to binge eating. Her list included the following:

1. Reading a story to her children
2. Calling her best friend
3. Going for a walk
4. Listening to her favorite music
5. Playing with the dog
6. Organizing her desk
7. Working on a knitting project
8. Playing golf

Although a number of members included going to the movies, Ellen crossed this activity off her list because the smell of popcorn was usually a cue for her to binge eat.

### Consequences of Behaviors

After members reviewed cues of their symptoms, we discussed positive and negative consequences of binge-eating episodes. Some of the members appeared surprised when we mentioned positive consequences; they insisted that binge eating caused them nothing but misery. We emphasized that one of the primary reasons binge eating is so difficult to interrupt is its reinforcing properties. We asked members to identify positive and negative social, situational, psychological, and nutritional consequences of binge eating.

> *Ellen:* Positive consequences? If it was positive, why would we be in treatment?
>
> *Therapist:* Well, think about it, Ellen. Does binge eating help you out in any way?
>
> *Ellen:* Well, when I'm stressed out, nothing makes me feel better like binge eating. I guess that's positive, in some strange way.
>
> *Josephine:* And you can count on food always being there—I wish the same could be said for my husband. [Group members laugh]

The members agreed that binge eating provides relief from emotional discomfort on a short-term basis, although guilt and shame are also present. Binge eating also provides an effective means of procrastinating and of avoiding interpersonal conflict and rejection.

The group members had an easier time identifying negative consequences of binge eating, including social isolation, poor concentration, mood lability, self-loathing, and obesity. We explained that binge eating is often perpetuated because the short-term consequences tend to be rewarding, whereas the negative consequences are often delayed. (Consider that hangovers do not usually prevent people from drinking again.)

We explained the principles of contingency management. To alter consequences, desirable behaviors (for example, eating dinner without binge eating, driving by the donut shop without purchasing any) should be rewarded. We asked members to identify "material rewards" (for example, gifts they could purchase for themselves) and "mental rewards" (for example, stating: "You did a great job . . . congratulations!") they could use in changing their eating behaviors. Ellen stated that she had tried this technique before but had had difficulty because she "felt stupid." We discussed the fact that many women with BED struggle with self-esteem problems and are deficient in self-nurturing skills, which makes self-reward a difficult task. We emphasized, however, the importance of positive consequences and rewards, both for reducing binge eating and for establishing healthier self-esteem.

### Setting Goals

Finally, we discussed techniques for goal setting. We asked members to identify long- and short-term goals for themselves. We emphasized that goals need to be realistic and to be broken down into small steps. Ellen stated that her goal was "stopping binge eating once and for all." We suggested she break this goal down into steps—stopping binge eating for a certain number of hours,

then days, then weeks—rather than expect an immediate [
manent change. She agreed that the modified goals felt m
manageable and less overwhelming.

Members then designed specific long- and short-term goals
and designated specific rewards they would give themselves for
each goal attained. Ellen's short-term goal was to get through
Saturday afternoon without binge eating, after which she would
reward herself with a professional manicure. Her long-term goal
was to stop binge eating for thirty days in a row, following which
she would buy a new set of golf clubs. We also encouraged Ellen
to use mental rewards and self-talk to reward herself for smaller
steps along the way.

### Normalizing Eating Patterns

The third session was a continuation of the second, with the
focus on cues and consequences related to nutritional and physiological factors associated with binge eating. We reviewed the
results of the Keys study reported in 1950, in which healthy males
were placed on a low-calorie diet and monitored over time. The
men exhibited signs of semistarvation, including concentration
impairment, mood disturbance, and food preoccupation. When
allowed access to unlimited food, the subjects engaged in binge-
eating episodes and temporarily regained weight above their original level. Over time, however, their eating behaviors and body
weight eventually normalized.

These results suggest that binge-eating behavior may be an
"adaptive" response to food deprivation that evolved as a protection for our species during periodic famines. Although food is
abundant in our society, severe dieting may "trick" the body into
adapting for a famine and thus may ultimately result in binge eating. We also reviewed the results of studies about restrained eating, in which individuals who engage in rigid dieting are more
likely to overeat when they consume a "forbidden" food.

We suggested to the group that the research on the physiological and psychological nature of binge eating indicates the

importance of eating regular meals and snacks and of including a variety of foods in moderation. We also suggested that normalized eating may promote a healthier metabolism. We provided nutritional information about serving sizes and recommended amounts for each food group, including a statement that fats and sugar can be consumed in moderation.

The group had strong reactions to our suggestions. A number of members, including Ellen, insisted that the regular consumption of meals and snacks would definitely promote weight gain and that incorporating a variety of food was "unhealthy":

*Lisa:* Are you serious about this? No wonder we won't lose weight in this program.

*Ellen:* If I ate three meals a day and two snacks, I would gain at least five pounds.

*Therapist:* We know it's scary for some of you, but consuming regular meals and snacks will probably reduce the urge to overeat substantially. The majority of people in our programs do not gain weight, and it's an important step in normalizing eating patterns.

*Ellen:* I still don't know if I could do it.

*Therapist:* Well, you might want to set smaller goals, maybe eating three regular meals at first, then adding the snacks.

*Josephine:* What I can't believe is that you're telling us to eat foods that are high in fat: I've got my family, my doctor, and every commercial on TV telling me to avoid fat completely—for my health, but especially to lose weight.

*Therapist:* I'm sure it is confusing to hear contradicting messages. And we're certainly not encouraging you to eat a high-fat diet. However, it's important and healthy to include some fat in your diet. And we do know it's risky if you have binge-eating problems to avoid it completely, because you may be more likely to overeat when you are exposed to foods you don't let yourself eat.

Ellen seemed to be relieved by this clarification but continued to express concern that eating regular meals and snacks would prevent weight loss. We agreed but reiterated the importance of gaining control over eating behavior before attempting to lose weight.

We asked Ellen about her typical eating habits. She said that she would wake up every day intending to "be good" by staying on her diet of one thousand calories. She would usually skip breakfast ("I don't need those calories") or have half a grapefruit and dry toast. At lunch, she would usually eat a salad with no dressing, or yogurt and fruit. By the afternoon she was usually quite hungry and would set out to eat one cracker for a snack. Her hunger level, however, would be so extreme that she usually would quickly eat a number of crackers. Feeling guilty, she would end up eating the entire box because she "had blown it anyway." Sometimes, she would "get back on track" by eating dinner with the family; at other times, a second binge would occur after dinner, typically consisting of ice cream or cookies.

We noted that hunger was a very clear cue for Ellen to overeat. We suggested that eating breakfast, a snack, and a more substantial lunch would reduce the likelihood of extreme hunger and subsequent binge eating following her afternoon snack. We encouraged her to continue eating dinner on a regular basis. Ellen agreed that she consumed so many calories during her binge-eating episodes anyway that "anything that might get rid of them, even if it means eating more during the day, is probably worth a try."

Ellen balked at incorporating fat and sugar—foods she typically forbid herself from eating outside binge-eating episodes—into her diet, however, because she thought these types of foods were too likely to serve as cues for overeating. We agreed that many people with BED need to avoid certain high-risk foods at first in order to stop binge eating. She agreed to set, as a long-term goal, permission to eat these forbidden foods.

> *Ellen:* I just can't imagine eating ice cream right now,
> though, even if I did give myself "permission" to eat it.
> It's too strong a cue.
>
> *Therapist:* Yes. And oftentimes foods may be too high-risk to
> incorporate early in treatment. What about a smaller
> step? Butter on your toast?
>
> *Ellen:* Yeah, maybe I could try that.

## Identifying Cognitions

Phase two (fourth and fifth sessions) of our group treatment focuses on cognitive restructuring techniques and integrating these strategies with behavioral interventions. On entering this phase of treatment, Ellen noted her improvement since the beginning of treatment: her binge-eating episodes had decreased in size and frequency, and her self-esteem had improved as a result of "feeling more in control." She was frustrated by the fact that she had not lost any weight, but seemed more willing to postpone this goal temporarily.

Ellen noted that although she had been successful at rearranging behavioral cues of binge eating and was beginning to eat more normally, certain "triggers" persisted. Stressful days at work and disagreements with her husband inevitably resulted in overeating episodes. She emphasized that these interpersonal "cues" were unavoidable, although she had attempted to incorporate delay techniques when she felt the urge to binge.

We used Ellen's examples when introducing the principles of cognitive therapy to the group. Specifically, we discussed how responses consist of thoughts, feelings, and behaviors, all of which influence one another. We asked the group members to consider binge eating as an example of a behavioral response and to identify feelings associated with this behavior. Examples included relaxation, tension reduction, sadness, loneliness, anxiety, anger, and shame. The members pointed out that some of these feelings preceded and others followed the binge-eating behavior. We then used Ellen's interpersonal cues as examples and asked the members to identify thoughts following the cue associated with the binge-eating behavior.

Ellen identified the following: "He'll never understand—I might as well binge"; "Cookies will make me feel better"; "The people at work think I'm incompetent."

Other members agreed with her suggestions and added, "It's because I'm fat"; "My kids never listen to me"; "I'll only have one piece, then I'll stop"; "My boss criticized me—I might as well quit."

We used these examples to help the members understand how thoughts influence feelings and behaviors. Although Ellen seemed to grasp the concept of "thoughts" quickly, many members were confused. In further detail, we described automatic thoughts as "internal dialogue or monologue" and used the example of cartoon characters who think, rather than speak, their thoughts. One of the group members volunteered, "Right now, I'm thinking about whether I remembered to lock the door of my car and what I'm going to make for dinner when I get home." These examples helped clarify what we meant by thoughts. In general, we find that "here and now" examples in the session help illustrate cognitions vividly.

We explained to the group that although thoughts, feelings, and behaviors all influence one another, it is more difficult to alter feelings and behaviors. Focusing on changing thoughts can be effective in changing accompanying feelings and behaviors. In particular, examining and changing thoughts associated with binge eating can reduce binge eating. Although some of the group found this explanation simplistic, Ellen agreed that her thoughts clearly influenced her symptoms:

> I can just feel it. . . . When I get home from work, I've had a stressful day, and I'm thinking, "No one at work appreciates me. I'll never be successful there." And then my kids start crying, and I feel like a bad mother too. And then I think, "Well, everything is terrible, so I might as well eat because it's the only thing that will make me feel better." And then I start out

with a plan to eat only one cookie. But one cookie is never enough, and I end up eating three or four. Then I think, "Okay, I've blown it now—I might as well eat the whole box." And the binge goes from there.

Ellen and the group members agreed that these are exactly the types of thoughts that lead to binge eating.

We then explained different types of dysfunctional "thinking errors" that can lead to mood and behavioral disturbances. These include

- *Overgeneralizations,* in which a rule is extracted from one instance (for example, "I'll never be able to control my eating")

- *Catastrophizing,* in which situations are viewed in an extreme, pessimistic perspective without basis in fact (for example, "I'm a failure")

- *Black-or-white, all-or-none, or dichotomous thinking,* in which situations are viewed as an either/or dichotomy (for example, "Because I had one extra cookie, I might as well eat the whole box")

- *Minimizing,* in which weaknesses are exaggerated and strengths are minimized (for example, "I might have done that well, but anyone could have done it")

- *Self-fulfilling prophecy,* in which a belief is acted on to ensure its occurrence (for example, "I won't be able to control my eating at that dinner party")

- *Mind-reading,* in which the individual falsely assumes to know what others are thinking or feeling (for example, "That woman looked at me—she must be thinking I'm fat")

Ellen laughed when we described these examples and pointed out that her descriptions of her own thoughts prior to the onset of a binge-eating episode included many of these types of patterns. She stated that she tends to be especially prone to dichotomous thinking and catastrophizing. The other members cited a number of their own examples of these types of dysfunctional thoughts. We instructed group members to monitor their thoughts, feelings, and behaviors and to note any thinking errors they tended to make as part of their homework assignment.

### Cognitive Restructuring

After focusing on identifying cognitions, we reviewed specific cognitive restructuring techniques. Specifically, thoughts can be evaluated by either *testing* them out or *questioning* them to determine their accuracy. We started with the testing strategy and emphasized to the group that this technique involved becoming a "scientist."

In monitoring her thoughts, one of the members, Roberta, found that she often thought, "My friends would like me better if I lost weight." The group members strongly disagreed with this statement and emphasized that *their* feelings for her would be unaffected by weight loss. We wanted to validate Roberta's concern, however, and suggested she test it out prior to the next session. Roberta agreed to ask her best friend whether her feelings would change if she lost weight.

Then Ellen asked Roberta whether her feelings for her best friend would be influenced by her friend's body weight. Roberta appeared surprised and replied, "Of course not. She's my dearest friend—I don't care what she weighs." The group asked, if that was the case, why should Roberta's weight matter?

We find that one of the greatest assets of conducting CBT in a group is the use of decentering techniques with members to highlight cognitive errors in self perception:

> *Roberta:* It's funny—I guess you're right about the fact that my feelings for my best friend would not be influenced by her weight. I guess I have a different set of rules for myself than for others.
>
> *Ellen:* Yes, when you were talking about how your friends would like you more if you lost weight, I was thinking,

"Of course not, Roberta's wonderful the way she is. I don't care what she weighs." But then I realized that I have the same belief for myself: I assume that people will like me more if I were thinner. It's easy for me to see that Roberta's not thinking accurately, but it's harder to do for myself.

*Therapist:* Seeing how that process works for Roberta might give you some objectivity in examining your own thoughts.

We then discussed methods for challenging thoughts in more detail. We provided three steps for questioning one's thoughts:

1. What is the evidence in favor of and against my thought?
2. What are the implications of my thought?
3. What are the alternative explanations for my thought?

We also suggested starting out by determining whether the thought was an example of a dysfunctional thinking error, like an overgeneralization.

Ellen then presented an example from the night before. She had not experienced a binge, but rather felt that she had eaten too much at dinner when she was not particularly hungry. Prior to dinner she had been bathing her children and trying to get them to bed. Her oldest child was uncooperative and refusing to brush her teeth. The youngest was also crying. Ellen looked to her husband for help, but he rolled his eyes at her and continued to read the paper. Frustrated with her oldest child, she finally gave her a time-out. The child began to cry but came back after her time-out, brushed her teeth, and went to bed.

When Ellen sat down to dinner, she found herself thinking, "I'm a bad mother; I can't even control my children's behavior." She felt sad, discouraged, anxious, and frustrated. Her husband watched television during dinner and seemed uninterested in Ellen's parenting concerns. Ellen took an extra helping of chicken, although she stopped herself from eating anything else.

Ellen first challenged her cognition, "I'm a bad mother," by realizing that it was probably an overgeneralization. When we asked her to consider the evidence in support and against this thought, she agreed that, in general, she is a very effective parent and loves her children very much. The other group members insisted that, in their opinion, she had handled a difficult situation very successfully. Ellen agreed that an alternative explanation for the event was that although her children usually cooperate, bedtime difficulties are quite common and are no reflection of her parenting abilities. In reevaluating the event, Ellen stated that she felt calmer and less discouraged about it. She agreed that if she were in the situation again, she would be less likely to overeat. Roberta pointed out that Ellen's husband did not sound particularly helpful. Ellen shrugged and said, "He had a busy day at work; I only work part-time, after all."

For the following sessions we continued to focus on cognitive restructuring. The group worked well together in challenging and testing their thoughts. The members were able to evaluate their thoughts on their own by the sixth session. Ellen commented that it was "a little like doing surgery on your mind: you look at your thoughts, figure out what needs to be fixed or taken out, and perform the operation."

### Cues and Chains

At session six, we also introduced the concept of cues and chains: cues, responses (including thoughts, feelings, behaviors), and consequences are often linked together in successive fashion. We find that this technique is helpful in integrating cognitive and behavioral strategies in managing binge eating.

Using Ellen's example from the week before, we asked her to work backward from the time at dinner when she ate the extra piece of chicken (as illustrated in Figure 5.4). The behavior at the end of the chain was overeating; the thoughts preceding involved her inadequacy as a mother and feelings of depression and discouragement; the cue had been struggling to get the children to bed; prior to that she had been very hungry and had felt impatient about eating dinner. In constructing the chain, Ellen worked her way backward to lunch and realized that she had only eaten an orange at the office because she was "too busy." She had not eaten a snack. The group exclaimed that it was no surprise that she was hungry for dinner, given how little she had eaten at lunch. Ellen admitted that skimping at lunch probably initiated the chain of events. We reemphasized "breaking" the behavioral chain as early as possible. Eating lunch to prevent extreme hunger, for example, is usually much easier than resisting a second helping at dinner.

### Later Sessions

Sessions seven through eleven focused on issues less directly related to binge-eating symptoms but still very important. By the beginning of this phase, most of the members, including Ellen, reported few objective binge-eating episodes. One member, Laura, was having considerable difficulty but was pleased with the fact that her binge-eating episodes had decreased in size. The group supported one another warmly. They walked to the parking lot together and often talked for an additional fifteen minutes after the sessions ended.

### Impulsivity, Self-Control, and Mood Enhancement

Session seven focused on impulsivity, self-control, and mood enhancement. Because many individuals with BED have a history of impulsivity problems, we asked the group in what ways they have had problems with self-control other than eating. Although members were shy at first, a number of them admitted to past problems with alcohol, shoplifting, and gambling. We explained general strategies for self-control, including response delay, alternative behaviors, and self-talk and visualization.

We also encouraged members to identify situations in which they were more likely to engage in impulsive eating and other

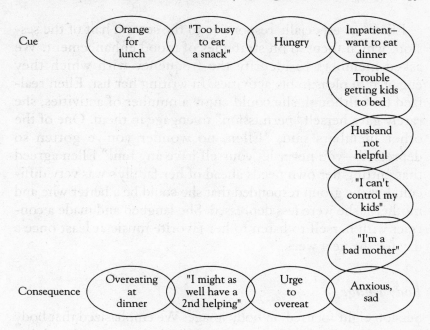

**Figure 5.4**
**Cues and Chains**

such behaviors in order to avoid these situations or plan for them ahead of time. In response, three of the members exclaimed, "Whenever there is alcohol." Ellen did not find alcohol a problem but did report having more difficulty with social situations in which others are behaving impulsively. We also discussed using deep breathing and relaxation techniques, especially in high-risk situations.

Finally, we suggested beginning to experiment with exposure-response prevention: exposing oneself to a high-risk situation without engaging in the behavior. Ellen remarked that she was attending a large office party on Friday that would give her the opportunity to "try it out." The group members suggested ways of maximizing success, including eating ahead of time, deep breathing, and enlisting a friend's help while at the event.

Ellen was especially responsive to the second half of the session, which focused on strategies of mood enhancement. We asked members to identify the frequency with which they engaged in pleasurable activities. In writing her list, Ellen realized that although she could enjoy a number of activities, she rarely gave herself "permission" to engage in them. One of the other members said, "Ellen, no wonder you've gotten so depressed—you never let yourself have any fun!" Ellen agreed that putting her own needs ahead of her family's was very difficult, but the group responded that she could be a better wife and mother if she were less depressed. She laughed and made a contract with herself to listen to her favorite music at least once a day for the next week.

### Body Image

Session eight focused on body image. We emphasized that body perception is a "multidimensional" phenomenon involving vision, touch, thoughts, and feelings that is determined by a number of individual, familial, and societal factors. The group discussed sociocultural variables at length, especially the pressure in our society to be young and thin and the stigma against people who are overweight.

Many of the members agreed that they felt being overweight was their "fault" and had difficulty accepting that genetics might have contributed to it. Roberta commented, "The prejudice that our society tolerates against fat people would never be tolerated toward other religions or races. Everyone thinks it's our own fault." The other members agreed, although some hesitated in accepting the idea that body weight is genetically determined—in part because "then you can't control it."

We believe it is important to challenge the widespread myth that anyone can be the size and shape they want with "adequate" diet and exercise. We therefore emphasize the importance of genetic factors in contributing to weight and body size. This idea is often met with frustration and resistance on the part of group members, although it is an important step in promoting self-acceptance. Perhaps one of the most difficult aspects of the body-image group sessions is focusing on self-acceptance while allowing for the possibility of moderate weight loss.

We then suggested techniques for using CBT to improve body image. The group looked at us skeptically at first, until Ellen reminded Roberta how she thought her friend would like her more if she lost weight. Roberta reported that she had asked her best friend, who said that her feelings for Roberta were totally separate from weight. Roberta admitted that her friend said she was beautiful "as is." We agreed that Roberta's experience was an excellent example of using CBT to challenge one's thoughts and beliefs about body size and shape.

We encouraged the members to explore their own thoughts and feelings about their weight and shape, especially the degree to which they allow their weight and shape to determine their self-evaluation. We also suggested working toward acceptance by recognizing and emphasizing some positive aspects of appearance.

The group members provided one another with feedback about physical attributes. The group agreed, for example, that Ellen had beautiful hands, eyes, and teeth. We also suggested exploring fantasies of how one's life would be different with weight loss and the degree to which these fantasies are realistic. The group members laughed and agreed that they often view losing weight as "an answer to every problem in the world."

*Ellen:* I think about losing weight, and it seems to be the answer to everything: I'd be a better mother, better wife, better employee. I also think that I'd never be depressed again and that everything would be easier.

*Therapist:* Do you think those expectations are realistic?

*Ellen:* Probably not, but I've been thinking that way for years.

### *Self-Esteem, Stress Management, and Assertiveness*

We used cognitive restructuring extensively in the following three sessions (sessions nine through eleven) on self-esteem, stress management, and assertiveness. The self-esteem session focused on rewriting self-statements about oneself by using more accurate language. For example, Ellen described herself as "a people pleaser." We asked her to elaborate by using nonpejorative and specific language. Her revised statements were more accurate:

> I tend to be very intuitive with and sensitive to people. Sometimes, especially when I'm overwhelmed by problems at home and work, I put other people's needs ahead of my own. However, I am working on taking better care of myself—like listening to music every day!—and can still be sensitive to other people.

The stress management and assertiveness sessions revealed the extent to which Ellen was unhappy with aspects of her marriage. She realized that attempting to please her husband all the time was increasing her stress and causing an emotional burden. Ellen reported doing all of the housework and child care because she "only worked part-time and Bob works full-time." She found herself resenting doing all of the chores by herself, however, including "picking up after his mess." Ellen also realized that she hardly spent any time alone with her husband and rarely held "meaningful conversations" with him. Ellen emphasized that she loved her husband very much but felt frustrated by their communication style and division of household duties.

The group was very helpful to Ellen. The members shared a number of their own experiences and suggestions. During stress management, Ellen realized that she could not do all of the chores alone. The group also emphasized that she should seek emotional closeness from sources other than her family members—for instance, joining a play group to get support from other mothers. Another member suggested hiring a cleaning service.

Ellen agreed that her goals at home and work were often unrealistic. She used cognitive restructuring techniques to modify her goals and to generate alternative coping strategies.

The discussion of Ellen's marital situation continued during the assertiveness session. The group encouraged Ellen to discuss her concerns and frustration with her husband. Ellen stated that she had attempted to talk with him in the past but usually ended up losing her temper. We reviewed the differences in assertive, aggressive, and passive communication styles. Ellen agreed that she had never been assertive with Bob in a constructive fashion. She was concerned, however, that she had so many complaints that she might overwhelm him.

One group member suggested that Ellen make a list of her priorities. She decided that her main request was that he stop leaving his clothes and sporting equipment all over the house. She practiced her assertive communication by using a role-playing situation in group and set a goal (and a manicure reward) of talking to Bob over the weekend. At the following session, she was very pleased: Bob had agreed to make more of an effort around the house and was even willing to consider paying for a cleaning service. The group gave Ellen a round of applause.

### Relapse Prevention

By the beginning of the relapse-prevention phase, all of the members except one (Laura) were free from binge eating. Ellen was especially pleased because she also had lost four pounds.

Session twelve reintroduced the topic of weight loss. Continuing the themes from the body image sessions, we emphasized the importance of self-acceptance and of not "putting your life on hold" prior to weight loss. We asked members to write a list of activities they were postponing until weight loss and then to make plans for doing them now. Ellen realized that she used to love sailing but had not done it for years because of her self-consciousness and a feeling that she did not "deserve" to go sailing until she was thin.

Everyone in the group agreed that clothes shopping was a dreaded activity. After discussing it, the group decided that purchasing clothing that was attractive and flattering was a worthwhile activity. Although some members feared "it's a waste of money if I'm going to lose weight," the other members emphasized that clothing can always be altered and that the benefits to self-esteem might be tremendous.

We agreed that gradual weight loss could be a healthful goal and suggested achieving it through increasing exercise and reducing (but not eliminating) fat intake. We also provided in-depth written material addressing this topic. Some of the group members groaned that they had "heard this all before." We agreed that this approach was not a novel one, but a necessary lifestyle change for gradual weight loss. The group members then discussed strategies for incorporating exercise into their daily activities, including gradual goals, systematic rewards, exercise "buddies," comfortable clothing, and finding "fun" activities. Ellen realized that golfing without the cart involved considerable walking and would be a painless way of increasing her aerobic exercise.

The final two sessions (thirteen and fourteen), which were conducted once a week rather than twice a week, focused on relapse prevention strategies. We encouraged group members to continue reintroducing high-risk foods and situations into their daily activities. Ellen admitted that although she was more willing to consume fats, she was still frightened of sugar. The group members constructed lists of the high-risk foods and situations they still avoided, starting with the easiest first. We instructed members to move up the hierarchy gradually, moving ahead only when they had "mastered" the first step. Ellen agreed to try two cookies after dinner and to plan to go for a walk afterward to reduce the likelihood of binge eating.

We explained the difference between a "slip" or "lapse" versus a "relapse." A slip or lapse is characterized by an episode of binge eating or partial return of symptoms; a relapse involves a full reemergence of symptoms. We find it important to explain the difference and to prepare clients for the likelihood of lapses (or at least urges to binge eat) in the future. A lapse can escalate into a relapse if an individual views his or her slip dichotomously (for example, "I've blown it; I might as well binge the whole weekend").

We asked the group members to write out plans for what they would do if they had a lapse or a relapse. We suggested including meal planning, calling friends, and rereading the manual. Ellen wrote a step-by-step plan for both lapse and relapse situations that included self-monitoring, alternative behaviors, talking with her minister, writing down her thoughts, and setting up a reward system.

At the final session, we asked members to review the progress they had made in treatment. The group members were highly complimentary of one another, including the member who was still binge eating and another member who had experienced a slip the night before. The group members commented on how successfully and quickly Ellen had stopped binge eating. They also remarked how much happier and more confident she seemed. One noted that she seemed to be wearing more brightly colored clothing. Ellen agreed that she was pleased with her treatment and that although she was disappointed about losing less than ten pounds, she had decided to start wearing her favorite color of clothing anyway.

The group members said good-bye to one another and exchanged phone numbers in order to keep in contact. We also said good-bye to the group but scheduled individual "exit" interviews for each of the members to discuss their follow-up plans in greater detail.

## EVALUATION OF TREATMENT OUTCOME

We have presented Ellen as an example of successful treatment of BED in group CBT. From our perspective, she responded well to the therapy and eliminated her binge-eating symptoms.

Her mood and self-esteem also improved. She was also able to seek social support more effectively.

Ellen was an ideal candidate for this type of psychotherapy for a number of reasons. Perhaps most important, she was extremely motivated and determined to stop binge eating. Motivation is essential for CBT because this type of therapy requires a substantial out-of-session time commitment in the form of self-monitoring and homework assignments. In addition, Ellen was intelligent and high functioning. Once in therapy she became a hardworking group member. She was willing to disclose information about herself and to rely on the group for help in coping with difficult situations. She was helpful to other group members and provided emotional support and suggestions on a number of occasions.

In this type of therapy, individuals with prominent Axis II personality disorders, especially Cluster B types (borderline, narcissistic, antisocial, histrionic), often have difficulty engaging in treatment and interacting appropriately with other group members. Individuals with marked personality disturbances can more effectively receive CBT for BED in individual therapy, where Axis II symptoms can be addressed simultaneously.

Active substance abuse or dependence also necessitates alternative treatment. There is considerable debate about whether substance-related treatment should precede interventions for eating disorder symptoms or whether the comorbid problems should be addressed concurrently. Regardless of the ideal approach, a CBT group devoted exclusively to BED would be inappropriate for anyone with active substance abuse or dependence.

Another consideration in Ellen's case was her co-existing depression. Although the relationship between mood disorders and binge-eating symptoms is well documented, the nature of the causal relationship is unclear. Because Ellen's diagnosis was major depression in partial remission, we decided to enroll her in the group therapy program with hopes that her depression would improve as her binge-eating behavior subsided. Had she reported a significant number of clinically significant depressive symptoms at the onset of treatment, we would have considered the possibility of adjunct psychopharmacotherapy (assuming she was participating in a research protocol that allowed concurrent medication). Specifically, we would have suggested a selective serotonin reuptake inhibitor like Prozac (fluoxetine), Zoloft (sertraline), or Paxil (paroxetine). In contrast to treatment of uncomplicated unipolar depression, however, we would have prescribed higher doses of these medications for Ellen (for example, sixty milligrams of fluoxetine) because these higher doses have been found to suppress binge-eating behavior.

Ellen's symptoms of depression improved considerably with treatment. At the time of her evaluation, her score on the Beck Depression Inventory was twenty-two. At the conclusion of the group, her score had decreased to thirteen. Although this score is still clinically significant, we decided against suggesting an antidepressant medication. Instead, we referred her to an individual therapist in our clinic who specializes in interpersonal psychotherapy and couples counseling.

In Ellen's opinion (and we agreed), her residual depressive symptoms were related to the psychosocial difficulties stemming from her marriage. She believed that if she were happier in her marriage, she would feel more optimistic and less discouraged about her future. Ellen stated that CBT had helped her realize that she "deserved to be happy in a relationship" and that her husband was not always supportive to her in ways she needed. She approached him about the possibility of couples counseling, and he agreed to attend some sessions with her.

Although we consider Ellen a treatment success, she, herself, was quite disappointed that she had not lost more weight. She agreed that she was "on the right track" but asked for additional ways in which to facilitate weight loss. We referred Ellen to a nutritionist, affiliated with the university, who has experience working with individuals with BED. We suggested that Ellen continue limiting her fat intake, increasing her exercise, and eating regular meals. She agreed but expressed sadness and frustration that "there isn't a quicker way." Of note, she had modified her ideal weight to 150 pounds, which she believed was a healthier ideal than her previous goal of 120 pounds. We also asked Ellen to return to our clinic for follow-up evaluations one month, six months, and one year after the end of treatment. The purpose of these visits are twofold: (1) they allow us to collect data for our research projects and (2) they give us the opportunity to monitor for relapse, a crucial consideration with patients with BED, given the high rate of relapse.

Ellen was a representative case in a number of ways. Her gender, age, BMI, family history, symptom course, and comorbid psychopathology were all consistent with our clinical experience, as well as with empirical studies documenting descriptive features of BED. Like many of our clients, she was employed and was married with children. She also resembled many clients in her primary goal of weight loss.

Perhaps one difference between Ellen and other individuals with BED was her absolute resolve to give up her symptoms. Many individuals who present to our clinic are somewhat ambivalent about "giving up" their symptoms. Although Ellen relied on binge eating for self-soothing and comfort, she quickly found alternative strategies and used cognitive restructuring techniques effectively. She was also extremely motivated and worked diligently on therapeutic materials outside sessions. Many individuals have more difficulty with this type of treatment because of ambivalence and/or inconsistent motivation, although we have treated a number of clients who, like Ellen, respond to CBT rapidly and successfully.

Although our understanding of binge-eating disorder is still in its infancy, clinical and empirical findings indicate that CBT is an effective treatment for a number of people. In a climate of diminishing resources for health care, CBT has the additional advantage of efficiency because it is time-limited and symptom-focused. Group CBT for BED is also more cost-effective than individual therapy—and, from our experience, CBT has a number of benefits when implemented in group modality. As researchers and clinicians, our next task involves determining which clients with BED will benefit from group CBT and developing alternative modalities and treatment strategies for clients who do not or cannot respond to this type of intervention.

# NOTES

P. 143, *(BED) is characterized by:* American Psychiatric Association. (1994). *Diagnostic and statistical manual of mental disorders* (4th ed.). Washington, DC: Author, p. 729.

P. 143, *the rate of BED in the general population:* Spitzer, R. L., Devlin, M., Walsh, B. T., Hasin, D., Wing, R., Marcus, M., Stunkard, A., Wadden, T., Yanovski, S., Agras, S., Mitchell, J., & Nonas, C. (1992). Binge eating disorder: A multi-site field trial of the diagnostic criteria. *International Journal of Eating Disorders, 11,* 191–203.

P. 143, *Among overweight individuals seeking weight loss:* de Zwaan, M., & Mitchell, J. E. (1992). Binge eating in the obese. *Annals of Medicine, 24,* 304–308.

P. 144, *Descriptive studies have revealed:* de Zwaan, M., & Mitchell, J. E. (1992). Binge eating in the obese. *Annals of Medicine, 24,* 304–308; Telch, C. F., & Agras, W. S. (1994). Obesity, binge eating, and psychopathology: Are they related? *International Journal of Eating Disorders, 15,* 53–61.

P. 144, *certain medications, including antidepressants:* Mitchell, J. E., & de Zwaan, M. (1993). Pharmacological treatments of binge eating. In C. G. Fairburn & G. T. Wilson (Eds.), *Binge eating: Nature, assessment, and treatment* (pp. 250–269). New York: Guilford Press.

P. 144, *group cognitive-behavioral therapy (group CBT) reduces:* Smith, D. W., Marcus, M. D., & Kaye, W. (1992). Cognitive-behavioral treatment of obese binge eaters. *International Journal of Eating Disorders, 12,* 257–262; Telch, C. F., Agras, W. S., Rossiter, E. M., Wilfley, D., & Kenardy, J. (1990). Group cognitive-behavioral treatment for the nonpurging bulimic: An initial evaluation. *Journal of Consulting and Clinical Psychology, 58,* 629–635; Wilfley, D. E., Agras, W. S., Telch, C. F., Rossiter, E. M., Schnieder, J. A., Cole, A. G., Sifford, L., & Raeburn, S. D. (1993). Group cognitive-behavioral therapy and group interpersonal psychotherapy for the nonpurging bulimic individual: A controlled comparison. *Journal of Consulting and Clinical Psychology, 61,* 296–305.

P. 144, *(IPT), also has been found effective:* Wilfley, D. E., Agras, W. S., Telch, C. F., Rossiter, E. M., Schnieder, J. A., Cole, A. G., Sifford, L., & Raeburn, S. D. (1993). Group cognitive-behavioral therapy and group interpersonal psychotherapy for the nonpurging bulimic individual: A controlled comparison. *Journal of Consulting and Clinical Psychology, 61,* 296–305.

P. 144, *several studies we conducted in our research facility:* Mitchell, J. E., Pyle, R. L., Eckert, E. D., Hatsukami, D., Pomeroy, C., & Zimmerman, R. (1990). A comparison study of antidepressants and structured intensive group psychotherapy in the treatment of bulimia nervosa. *Archives of General Psychiatry, 47,* 149–157; Mitchell, J. E., Pyle, R. L., Pomeroy, C., Zollman, M., Crosby, R., Seim, H., Eckert, E., & Zimmerman, R. (1993). Cognitive-behavioral group psychotherapy of bulimia nervosa: Importance of logistical variables. *International Journal of Eating Disorders, 14,* 277–287.

P. 145, *Group psychotherapy provides a number of benefits:* Yalom, I. D. (1985). *The theory and practice of group psychotherapy* (3rd ed.). New York: Basic Books, pp. 3–18.

P. 147, *Our data on the development of BED:* Abbott, D. W., de Zwaan, M., Mussell, M. P., Raymond, N. C., Seim, H. C., Crow, S. S., Crosby, R. D., & Mitchell, J. E. (1994, April). *A comparison of binge eaters who begin to binge before and after dieting.* Data presented at the Sixth International Conference on Eating Disorders, New York, NY; Mussell, M. P., Mitchell, J. E., Weller, C. L., Raymond, N. C., Crow, S. S., & Crosby, R. D. (1995). Onset of binge eating, dieting, obesity, and mood disorders among subjects seeking treatment for binge eating disorder. *International Journal of Eating Disorders, 17,* 395–402.

P. 147, *typically see in the development of bulimia nervosa:* Pyle, R. L., Mitchell, J. E., & Eckert, E. (1981). Bulimia: A report of 34 cases. *Journal of Clinical Psychiatry, 42,* 60–64.

P. 148, *A semistructured clinical interview:* First, M. B., Spitzer, R. L., Gibbon, M., & Williams, J.B.W. (1994). *Structured clinical interview for Axis I DSM-IV disorders: Patient edition* (SCID-I/P Version 2.0). New York: Biometrics Research Department, New York State Psychiatric Institute.

P. 154, *self-monitoring forms:* Adapted from Fairburn, C. G., Marcus, M. D., & Wilson, G. T. (1993). Cognitive-behavioral therapy for binge eating and bulimia nervosa: A comprehensive treatment manual. In C. G. Fairburn & G. T. Wilson (Eds.), *Binge eating: Nature, assessment, and treatment* (pp. 361–404). New York: Guilford Press.

P. 156, *self-monitoring alone can lead to a reduction in symptoms:* Agras, W. S., Schneider, J. A., Arnow, B., Raeburn, S. D., & Telch, C. F. (1989). Cognitive-behavioral and response-prevention treatments for bulimia nervosa. *Journal of Consulting and Clinical Psychology, 57,* 215–221.

P.163, *Keys study:* Keys, A., Brozek, J., Henschel, A. J., Mickelsen, O., & Taylor, H. L. (1950). *The biology of human starvation.* Minneapolis: University of Minnesota Press.

P. 163, *studies about restrained eating:* Polivy, J., & Herman, C. P. (1985). Dieting and bingeing: A causal analysis. *American Psychologist, 40,* 193–201.

P. 169, *specific cognitive restructuring techniques:* Beck, A. T., Rush, A. J., Shaw, B. F., & Emery, G. (1979). *Cognitive therapy of depression.* New York: Guilford Press.

P. 170, *dysfunctional thinking error:* Garner, D. M., & Bemis, K. M. (1985). Cognitive therapy for anorexia nervosa. In D. M. Garner & P. E. Garfinkel (Eds.), *Handbook of psychotherapy for anorexia nervosa and bulimia* (pp. 107–146). New York: Guilford Press.

P. 172, *a history of impulsivity problems:* Yanovski, S. Z., Nelson, J. E., Dubbert, B. K., & Spitzer, R. L. (1993). Association of binge eating disorder and psychiatric comorbidity in obese subjects. *American Journal of Psychiatry, 150,* 1472–1479.

P. 174, *body image:* Cash, T., & Pruzinsky, T. (1990). *Body images: Development, deviance, and change.* New York: Guilford Press.

P. 175, *possibility of moderate weight loss:* Brownell, K. D., & Rodin, J. (1994). The dieting maelstrom: Is it possible and advisable to lose weight? *American Psychologist, 49,* 781–791.

P. 176, *self-esteem:* McKay, M., & Fanning, P. (1987). *Self-esteem.* Oakland, CA: New Harbinger.

P. 178, *in-depth written material addressing this topic:* Are you eating right? (1992, October). *Consumer Reports,* pp. 644–655.

P. 178, *"lapse" versus a "relapse":* Marlatt, G. A., & Gordon, J. R. (1985). *Relapse prevention: Maintenance strategies in the treatment of addictive behaviors.* New York: Guilford Press.

P. 180, *Cluster B types:* American Psychiatric Association. (1994). *Diagnostic and statistical manual of mental disorders* (4th ed.). Washington, DC: Author, p. 645.

P. 180, *Axis II symptoms can be addressed:* Beck, A. T., & Freeman, A. (1990). *Cognitive therapy of personality disorders.* New York: Guilford Press.

P. 180, *substance-related treatment:* Mitchell, J. E., Pyle, R. L., Specker, S., & Hanson, K. (1992). Eating disorders and chemical dependency. In J. Yager, H. E. Gwirtsman, & C. K. Edelstein (Eds.), *Special problems in managing eating disorders* (pp. 1–14). Washington, DC: American Psychiatric Press.

P. 180, *the relationship between mood disorders and binge-eating symptoms:* Swift, W. J., Andrews, D., & Barkalage, N. E. (1986). The relationship between affective disorders and eating disorders: A review of the literature. *American Journal of Psychiatry, 143,* 290–299.

P. 181, *higher doses of these medications:* Mitchell, J. E., & de Zwaan, M. (1993). Pharmacological treatments of binge eating. In C. G. Fairburn & G. T. Wilson (Eds.), *Binge eating: Nature, assessment, and treatment* (pp. 250–269). New York: Guilford Press.

P. 181, *Beck Depression Inventory:* Beck, A. T., Ward, C. H., Mendelson, M., Mock, J., & Erbaugh, J. (1961). An inventory for measuring depression. *Archives of General Psychiatry, 4,* 561–571.

P. 182, *high rate of relapse:* Wilfley, D. E., Agras, W. S., Telch, C. F., Rossiter, E. M., Schnieder, J. A., Cole, A. G., Sifford, L., & Raeburn, S. D. (1993). Group cognitive-behavioral therapy and group interpersonal psychotherapy for the nonpurging bulimic individual: A controlled comparison. *Journal of Consulting and Clinical Psychology, 61,* 296–305.

P. 182, *empirical studies documenting descriptive features of BED:* Brody, M. L., Walsh, B. T., & Devlin, M. (1994). Binge eating disorder: Reliability and validity of a new diagnostic category. *Journal of Consulting and Clinical Psychology, 62,* 381–386; de Zwaan, M., & Mitchell, J. E. (1992). Binge eating in the obese. *Annals of Medicine, 24,* 304–308; Spitzer, R. L., Devlin, M., Walsh, B. T., Hasin, D., Wing, R., Marcus, M., Stunkard, A., Wadden, T., Yanovski, S., Agras, S., Mitchell, J., & Nonas, C. (1992). Binge eating disorder: A multi-site field trial of the diagnostic criteria. *International Journal of Eating Disorders, 11,* 191–203.

CHAPTER

# 6

# STRUCTURAL FAMILY THERAPY

## H. Charles Fishman

*Go to the heart of danger—there you'll find safety.*
LARRY HARTZELL, MARTIAL ARTIST

My first contact with Joy was on a late Friday afternoon in the spring of 1991. She was requesting refills of her psychiatric medications. She had just been discharged from a partial hospitalization program, where she had been treated following her second inpatient psychiatric hospitalization that year. Each hospitalization had been precipitated by a serious suicide attempt.

Joy dated her psychiatric difficulties from age fifteen, when her bulimia began. It waxed and waned in severity for the next twenty years. During that time, she was addicted to heroin for a year, supporting her habit through prostitution.

Despite difficulties, she married in her twenties, obtained a college degree, and had a son. Throughout this time, her bulimia continued. Her psychiatric difficulties were exacerbated when she and her husband embarked on a course of infertility treatments. She became increasingly depressed, resumed her old habits of cutting herself and head banging, and then became actively suicidal.

That afternoon, Joy presented as an attractive, thin but not emaciated, thirty-two-year-old resident of Philadelphia who was visibly upset. Speaking with blunted affect, she described her present mental state. She felt good about her hospitalization and her stay at the partial hospitalization program, which she saw as something of a breakthrough. Now she understood the cause of her difficulties over these many years: she had a borderline personality disorder. She understood that she would never be "normal" and would probably be on medications for the rest of her life.

When I attempted to explore her relationships, she resisted. She was concerned only about her disorder. But then she said in passing that if her marriage did not change in two weeks, she was going to kill herself. After considerable urging, she agreed to bring her husband to the next session.

The facility where I was working at the time was a small outpatient clinic that worked heavily with severely troubled patients referred by case management companies. Joy was referred to me by one of these large companies, specifically because late on a Friday afternoon, she had run out of medications. I was the founder and executive director of the Institute for the Family. The goal of our organization was to provide high-level family systems psychotherapy to cases that ordinarily would have been hospitalized.

## THE INTENSIVE STRUCTURAL THERAPY PROGRAM

The orientation of the eating disorders program at the Institute for the Family derives from general systems theory. The initial psychotherapeutic conceptualization was based on a research project at the Philadelphia Child Guidance Clinic. The study focused on a group of anorectic and hyperlabile diabetic adolescents. It was discovered that the youngsters' symptoms went out of control only at home. At these times, their requisite insulin would rise from a maintenance level of twenty units per day to as much as five hundred. First, the children were given individual therapy; then, the parents were given marital therapy—to no avail. Only when the entire family was included were the symptoms controlled.

Because the diabetes went out of control only when the children were home with their families, the researchers sought to identify specific interactional patterns in these families. They found conflict avoidance, triangulation, diffusion of conflict by a third, rigidity, and enmeshment. They coined a term to describe these families: "psychosomatic families."

The original study was done with younger adolescents who were anorectic. At the Institute for the Family, we found that this model, with certain modifications, may be applied effectively with older anorectics and with bulimics and compulsive overeaters.

One of the major changes in the model has been to involve not only the patient's family but also the patient's larger context. Older eating-disordered patients tend to have been symptomatic longer and usually have more complex social systems than their adolescent counterparts. There are, as well, more people in the patient's context who are influential and must be included in the treatment. We can achieve a greater therapeutic intensity through working with this larger system.

Today's family is not only more complex, it is also more stressed by a number of factors, especially the economy, a declining standard of living, limited job opportunities, and the greater frequency of divorce. In many families, both parents work two jobs. Divorce exacerbates emotional and economic stress through lack of parental cohesion and the financial hardships of two households. Work with larger systems is essential to increase support for these burdened families.

In addition, we choose to deal with key personality characteristics of the patient to increase the therapeutic intensity. One factor that, in our experience, is central to eating disorders is conflict avoidance. This is an individual parameter that is seen isomorphically (in similar shape) across contexts. Clearly, on some level, the patient's contemporary context may be maintaining this pattern. But nevertheless, this individual characteristic provides a good handle for the treatment. Empirically, I have found a continuum: to the extent that there is conflict avoidance, the symptomatology is manifested; to the extent that conflict is addressed, the symptomatology is controlled.

The model, which I call *intensive structural therapy* (IST), is based on four theoretical tenets.

1. *The problem is being maintained by the patient's contemporary social context:* all individuals and institutions that affect the patient's system. The model utilizes extended family, friends, co-workers, colleagues, and other therapists in the therapy.

   In addition, at times, part of the contextual problem is the *absence* of essential resources. In such cases, the therapist must create a new context. The term we use is the *recontextualization of the family*, that is, the introduction of a new context into the patient's system to help ameliorate the problem. Our eating disorders program uses the incorporation of other contexts— women's groups, vocational counselors, financial counselors, and even martial arts classes, as we will see in the case to be described. These contexts augment the therapeutic intensity of the family therapy.

2. *Every system contains a homeostatic maintainer (HM).* Ascertaining the HM is a powerful way to assess a system. The identity of the HM can best be determined by perturbing the system: the person who activates at that point to bring the system back to the status quo is the HM. When direct observation is not possible, the experienced clinician can get a good idea of the HM through inquiry.

   The HM concept is used to plan treatment and intervene decisively. As therapy proceeds, if the focus on the identified HM does not yield change, the therapist should search for other forces in the system that are maintaining homeostasis.

3. *Certain isomorphic (structurally equal) patterns pervade the context.* For example, the same pattern may be seen between the patient and the nuclear family, between the patient and co-workers or supervisors, and between the patient and friends. Therapy is directed toward transforming these isomorphic patterns.

Used together, the concepts of the HM and isomorphism help the clinician recognize what is maintaining the problem. Furthermore, applying the idea of isomorphic patterns avoids the theoretically untenable position of identifying a single person as maintaining the homeostasis yet does not deny the observation of systemic contributions of varied levels of influence. Some members of the system may exert more influence than others. Of course, the influence may rotate—for example, at one time it may be the husband who is more the obstacle to change, at another time it is the wife—but at any given point one person may be identified as being most powerful in maintaining the homeostasis. Indeed, it is therapeutically useless to identify *every* member of the system as maintaining the homeostasis. The idea that everyone maintains the system is true only globally, as when one looks at a system from Mount Olympus.

4. *Therapeutic crisis induction can be invaluable in transforming systems.* In work with psychosomatic families, which are characterized by rigidity and extreme conflict avoidance, the therapeutic emergence of crisis is often the essential step in transforming the systems.

The eating disorders program at the Institute for the Family is based on several fundamental postulates. First is a belief in the perfectibility of people. Second is a belief that the self is multifaceted, so if a person's context is transformed, different and more functional facets of personality can emerge. The therapist can therefore confidently expect profound change in people. Third is a belief that etiology and maintenance are separate processes. The etiology of an eating disorder, on the one hand, is not available to observation; it is lost in history (and perhaps biology) and can only be speculated on. The maintenance of the disorder, on the other hand, can be readily understood. We can see the interactional patterns between members of the system that reinforce the problematic behavior maintaining the symptoms. For example, when working with young anorectics, the therapist can readily see how the division between the parents maintains the anorectic behavior. Often, as the parental discord increases, the child becomes more symptomatic; conversely, as the two adults begin to come together and actively work together, their child's symptoms diminish.

## ASSESSMENT

Because the problem is seen as existing in the organization of the contemporary context, the essential first task is to evaluate the patient's context. What are the relevant contemporary social forces, and how do they maintain the problem?

Joy's family system consisted of her husband and eight-year-old son. After assessing the system, I did not see her extended family as significant in the maintenance of her problem. (This is contrary to customary family therapy thinking, which assumes that the patient's extended family must be involved in the treatment for significant change to occur.) In this case, the family was alive although relatively distant. The usual intrusiveness that one finds in these systems was absent. The family did not create stress in Joy's life, either through their presence or absence. Furthermore, they lived sufficiently far away that I didn't see them as social supports who could help Joy and her family in their day-to-day lives.

Another influential context was that of the psychiatric practitioners. The "borderline" diagnosis created a sense of hopelessness in Joy and her family. The label hampered changes in the system. Because this "reality" organized the couple to avoid conflict, the husband could not challenge Joy to mobilize her life. Moreover, when Joy was feeling appropriate indignation with her husband, she did not have the credibility to challenge him or anyone else in her life. She was easily dismissed by others (and by herself) as mentally ill. Thus, the dysfunctional system did not change. Furthermore, Joy has said that thinking of herself as borderline sapped her self-confidence to socialize, to be with other people. This depletion only increased her isolation and exacerbated her symptoms.

For the last two years, Joy and her husband had been treated for infertility. They desperately wanted to have a second child. Unfortunately, the process of infertility treatment—the roller coaster of elation and disappointment and, even more significant, the effect of the drugs, which replicate pregnancy and at times menopause—had the effect of augmenting her emotionality, making her more susceptible to depression.

From the onset of therapy, it was apparent that Joy's marriage was a great source of stress for her. It was also clear that, in the family's organization, the husband and son had a close relationship that excluded Joy. Her major involvement was with the unpleasant tasks, such as telling her son when to go bed.

Joy did volunteer work at a local church. The female minister was one of her best friends. With her other good friend, who baby-sat for her son, she had a conflictual relationship (discussed later in this chapter).

As I noted earlier, in IST the clinician searches for the HM and the isomorphic interactional patterns in which the forces of homeostatic maintenance are embedded. In this approach we look at all the contexts. We assume the problem is maintained by the contemporary system. Two essentially influential systems in an adult's life are work and friends. In Joy's situation, these contexts were much more important than her extended family. In this system, I saw the HM as being both the husband and the psychiatric community. The psychiatric diagnostic system does not address context—the patient's interpersonal problems. The *DSM-IV* describes only the clinical symptoms that Joy exhibited when she was under stress. In our model, it was essential to address the interactional patterns and social forces that were causing the stress.

In fact, Joy was actively triangulated by this discordance between models. Indeed, one tension in the therapy was that, for the first few months of our work, Joy attended a group at the partial hospitalization program where she had been treated. The group's conceptualization of her as a disordered personality was diametrically opposite to mine. This tension, though not responsible for her difficulties when therapy began, served to make our work more difficult. I noticed at one point that crisis calls from Joy came only on Fridays; this was the day after she had been to her group. This clash of models was increasing her stress and thus her symptoms.

The isomorphic patterns were conflict avoidance and isolation. To the extent that she did not address the stressful relationships in her life, she was more symptomatic, and the system did not change. Within these psychosomatic systems, any conflict is considered undesirable. Of course, such a rule goes against nature, where only conflict and imperfection usher in changes that lead to evolution. In these systems, conflict must emerge for systems to change.

# TREATMENT

The model of therapy derives from that described in *Family Therapy Techniques*. The specific technique I use to address conflict avoidance is *enactment*: the family members introduce dysfunctional interactional patterns in the therapy room, and the therapist works with them to change these patterns. A strong emphasis is placed on changing the patterns right in the session.

Another technique I frequently use is *unbalancing*. The therapist sides with one member of the system, increasing the intensity of the session by empowering one member to confront the other. At the same time, a change in perception occurs: by siding with one person, the therapist often forces the other party to see that person with increased respect.

## The First Session

With her husband—a heavy-set, balding man with a soft voice—sitting to her left, Joy began the session in a manner that seemed comfortable to her: almost dreamily, she catalogued her psychiatric difficulties. She seemed oddly at ease at this task, or at least well trained in it. My goal was to get her to abjure this passive, hopeless, and self-destructive view of herself. She must become a catalyst for change within her system. She could not do it if she believed that she had an indelible flaw that predestined her for self-destruction.

> *Therapist:* Tell me more. When you say you did all these unpredictable things in your life, I don't know how you'd describe them.
>
> *Joy:* Like what?
>
> *Therapist:* I don't know, you say. Your whole life, there were various things you did that were very upsetting.
>
> *Joy:* I tried to kill myself twice, or suicide attempts—I'm beginning to understand the difference—once I think when I was thirteen, and once again I think when I was fourteen. I was a prostitute for a while when I lived in Chicago. I'm bulimic. I've been bulimic since I was seventeen.
>
> *Therapist:* Are you still bulimic?
>
> *Joy:* Yeah.
>
> *Therapist:* When were you a prostitute? What was that all about?
>
> *Joy:* Make money. Fast.
>
> *Therapist:* Were you using drugs as well?
>
> *Joy:* Yeah.
>
> *Therapist:* What kind of drugs?
>
> *Joy:* Cocaine. Not regularly. Just when I do a job, they always have it. I was raped two times, both of which I think were my fault.
>
> *Therapist:* How's that?
>
> *Joy:* I led them on.
>
> *Therapist:* Where were your parents during all of this?
>
> *Joy:* Home.
>
> *Therapist:* I know, but why weren't they in your life?
>
> *Joy:* 'Cause you don't tell your parents this stuff. 'Cause then they won't let you go out of the house.

Perhaps Joy is rationalizing here to avoid the conflict that would have arisen had she told her parents of her rape. On the other hand, her parents might not have been capable of dealing with this sort of news, and she may not have been avoiding conflict, but rather saving everyone from profound upset beyond what they could handle.

There is also a pattern of isolation. A tell-tale sign is that her parents were not perceived as a protective force in her life. She doesn't even understand my question, "Where were your parents?" by which I meant, why weren't they looking after you? She simply says, "Home," showing that she is unable to see the parents as able to offer her protection or even to help her reactively.

*Therapist:* How old were you during all of this?

*Joy:* I was raped when I was thirteen. I'd never had sex before. The next time I think I was sixteen or seventeen. But this is not the kind of thing you tell your parents. I had an abortion when I was seventeen. And I did tell my mother because I was too young; she had to sign for them to do it. And I was all scared, too. And she said she was so happy that I told her because she said most kids wouldn't tell their parents.

I mean, I know that part of my cutting myself and hurting myself and smashing my head into the wall is to get away. I just have this incredible desire to get away from reality, from what I'm feeling. So, that's why me more than anyone else in the world. I have this incredible need to get away from the pain. Me particularly, I guess. And that's why I ended up in the hospital. . . . You know, that's how I wound up on medication, and that has something to do with, I'm sure, my relationship with my husband, Michael, and I'm not sure exactly what at this moment. But part of feeling alone when I'm with him . . . you know.

*Joy:* (Later in the session) I have something wrong with me. I don't function normally, and for us to sit here and pretend that I do, and just talk about me and Michael and our relationship—I mean, that's fine, and I can even see that this is valuable in dealing with someone who's a borderline personality, because one of the things they recommend is that you do family work. I'm afraid that you're not going to pay enough attention to that, or something . . .

*Therapist:* I think you might be afraid that I'm not going to treat you like a patient. Everybody treats you like a patient; I want to treat you like a woman who doesn't have a full life, who doesn't have all these things wrong with her. I want to deal with the positive parts of yourself.

My goal in the therapy was to transform Joy's context, both internal—how stress led her to be bulimic—and external—how she handled relationships and how she isolated herself. The bulimia was the result of dysfunction in these domains. But by transforming the external, the internal was ameliorated.

*Therapist:* You've been focusing on the negative parts, and I'm not sure that's all that you need. Look at this room. It's a hall of mirrors. You can go back and forth in the mirrors forever. One mirror reflects the other, back and forth. If you believe firmly in your heart that you are flawed as a person, you will do everything you can to prove that hypothesis because nobody wants to be wrong. If you believe, instead, that you have tremendous potential and there's lots that you've done in your life that's positive, that has nothing to do with "borderline," that's one of the things that should be worked on. (Slightly later) The idea is not to focus on your problems, it's to make it so that you are confident of yourself.

*Joy:* I'm just so confused.

*Therapist:* I understand. I feel for you, and the psychiatric field is unbelievably confusing. It's a mess.

*Joy:* (Crying) I mean, I want to believe what you're saying. . . . And maybe what we do here will make a difference finally, but nothing else has. My whole life, nothing else has.

I saw this as a special moment of linkage between the self of the therapist and the self of the patient. She came driven by the inertia of being called borderline and of the horrendous life events that she had faced: suicide attempts, bulimia, drugs, prostitution. I was commiserating and empathic, both for the pain—for the years that she suffered these symptoms—and also for her confusion, created by my introducing an alternative therapeutic reality.

But here we also see the struggle between two models. I sensed her fear that I would not treat her like a patient. For a long time, her identity had been based on the opinion of others that she was flawed. She actually seemed to be afraid that I was *not* going to pay enough attention to that. I was struck by her utter despair and a certain pushiness as she tried to obtain validation that she was, indeed, handicapped. I countered with another definition of self; I would not treat her in the way she was trying to compel me to. I could say, "I think you are borderline, but there's help for borderlines." Instead, I chose to abandon that label, which I think she used destructively, part of seeing herself as "unable." Acceptance of the label would have missed the opportunity to wean her from her pernicious sense of self.

This struggle was made more difficult, and yet all the more essential, because of her isolation. Her influential context consisted of her mental health providers and her conflicted family. In this rarified world, scant input confirmed her as a whole person, a nonpatient. Even her best friend was closely involved in her psychiatric struggle; she cared for Joy's child while Joy visited her multiple doctors and groups.

I attempted to provide a context that was as powerful as her present one. In this redefinition of the context, I sensed that this may have been the first time she could not manipulate people by declaring herself incapable or sick.

The initial task of the therapy was to win the battle of the models, to get Joy to see herself as capable and able to address the dysfunctional relationships in her life. If she saw herself as ill, she could not fight; she remained locked in the position of the patient. If she saw herself as a competent person, she could empower herself to transform the contexts that were rendering her symptomatic. The implicit precursor to this change was that Joy be willing to accept that her context was relevant in the maintenance of her difficulties and that it must be addressed and changed.

It is important to note that I was empathic when I said, "The field is unbelievably confusing. It's a mess." I was attempting to let her know that she had connected with me at the affective level. Without connecting with her pain, I would have been too rational and thus ineffectual. Her experience with many of the significant people in her life had been one of disconfirmation: she was declared either mentally ill (the psychiatric establishment), too emotional (her husband and the alliance of her husband and son, who saw her as emotionally out of control), or weak (her own self-doubts, demons fed by her isolation).

This was a turning point in therapy. It was the first of a number of therapeutically induced crises in the course of the therapy. I saw this crisis as addressing her inner directives that organized her self, the most profound inner talk—the way she addressed herself. I was trying to retrieve the positive opinion of self. But cognitive changes are not enough. They would reframe the problems but would not have sufficient intensity to transform the system. Joy's problem was not simply how she saw herself, but rather how her social system supported this reality. Her systems had to change to support her changed concept of self. Armed with this changed definition of self, Joy could be supported (and challenged) to revise the dysfunctional relationships by changing her patterns of conflict avoidance and self-isolation.

## Work with the Family Context

The work with the family is the cornerstone of IST. In most situations, it is the people closest to us who are responsible for our psychological well-being.

The second session included both Joy's husband, Michael, and her seven-year-old son, Billy. It was clear to me that the therapy would have to address her identity as mother and the triangular relationship with her husband and her son. I had to support Joy in challenging patterns that had been oppressive to her, to continue the process, to both depathologize her from a weak, voiceless mental patient and to empower her to transform the relationships in her life.

> *Therapist:* (To Joy) Are you the only person in the house who helps with homework?
>
> *Joy:* Yeah. Michael doesn't know it exists.
>
> *Therapist:* I guess Michael has no formal education, is that right? (I know he has been a teacher; Michael laughs)
>
> *Joy:* Yes. He doesn't take any responsibility, really. Some things can't change. (To son) Why don't you go out and play with some toys? Daddy and I want to talk to the doctor for a minute.
>
> *Billy:* I'm not going out there by myself. I'm scared.
>
> *Joy:* Just out into the lobby.
>
> *Billy:* (Energetically burrowing into his father's lap) I'm scared.

The lobby is only a few doors down. Of course, the boy's resistance may come from a sense that he cannot leave his parents alone, that they need him to diffuse their conflict. Is this the boy's role at home? Is he caught in a triangulation, impeding his parents' resolution of their conflicts—and his own development?

Joy tries to take the boy out. He whimpers, and she lets him go back to his chair.

> *Therapist:* (To Joy) You were saying that you always do
>     too much.
> *Billy:* (Burying his face in his father, who is totally passive)
>     Help me.
> *Michael:* What can I do?

The boy's enmeshed connection with his father is clear. He asks his father for help, and the father responds by commiserating with the child, not by supporting his wife. Even his helplessness suggests a hopelessness against an irrational force. I see this as a further insult to Joy, an implication that she is not a reasonable being.

> *Billy:* (Looking beseechingly at his father) You can do nothing?
> *Michael:* Then wait for us out there.
> *Billy:* I don't want to. Daddy, I'm scared. Help me.

Joy gets up, obviously burdened, and dutifully leaves the room with the boy. She returns, and almost comically, the boy follows her back into the room. His reappearance further demonstrates his disrespect for his mother and her powerlessness.

I see the family problem emerge in the room. Not only are father and son inappropriately close, but this coalition also somehow leaves Joy to do most of the unpleasant tasks of parenting. In addition, perhaps most disempowering for Joy, is the pernicious disrespect for her.

Behavior patterns like this are creating the stress that leads to the emergence of Joy's eating disorder symptoms. These dynamics diminish Joy's self-esteem and predispose her to isolate herself further—and to accept the unacceptable conditions of her life.

> *Therapist:* (To Joy) This is a pattern you need to change?
>     (Joy nods) I think you need to get Michael to take Billy

out of the room. He needs to support you in this. You should not be doing all of the unpleasant tasks of parenting.

*Michael:* (Takes Billy out and returns) One of the things that concerns me is how scared he is. At the house, he won't go into the next room because he's afraid to leave us.

*Therapist:* As your marriage gets happier, he'll be more willing. (Husband nods) He's concerned about you guys.

I am addressing the complementarity of the family: to the extent that his parents are so embattled, he must be close to them. Should they become less embattled, he will have less concern and will be able to distance from them. I emphasize the point that their son will be more normal if their marriage improves in order to increase the father's initiative with his wife. Because the father is so involved with his son, seeing the connection may make him more supportive of my therapeutic efforts.

*Therapist:* So what about Michael helping out? You were a teacher, weren't you?

*Michael:* Uh-huh.

*Therapist:* And your background is in history, isn't it?

*Joy:* I was a teacher too, a history teacher and a math teacher.

*Therapist:* Well, if you don't use your mouth and your voice to get something to change . . .

*Joy:* I guess I feel there's not that many things I do with Billy. Homework is one thing I do with him, and I'm screwing it up, obviously. He doesn't think I'm doing it right. His homework is bad because I'm doing it with him, and . . . I just don't know what to do with that.

*Therapist:* Well, can't you and Michael do different subjects?

*Joy:* He's only in first grade. He comes home with spelling homework, and he comes home with math homework.

*Therapist:* When you say that Michael's just not that involved with raising the youngster . . .

*Joy:* Well, I think he's very involved in playing with Billy. I'm
    always the heavy.
*Therapist:* So really, what we're talking about is sharing that
    burden, not the difference between arithmetic and
    spelling and stuff like that.
*Joy:* (To husband) Do you know what that means? Do you
    understand what he's saying?
*Michael:* Oh, absolutely.

Joy's question implies that she thinks her husband is stupid.
My reading on this is that she had, until now, given up trying to
get Michael to hear her entreaties.

*Joy:* I do, too.
*Therapist:* This is an extended honeymoon he has with this
    young man.
*Michael:* But we have a big disagreement about what's
    required. And how to do it. That's the problem. Joy
    draws lines in the sand and says don't go across this line
    or else. And I don't agree with that line, you know.
*Therapist:* You think it's too rigid. Or arbitrary.
*Michael:* It's always arbitrary. She'll make a stand on a point
    that I don't agree we should make a stand on.
*Therapist:* (To Joy) So why don't you defend yourself?
*Joy:* I don't know, it's not worth it. I . . . I . . . I don't know
    how to do this. I feel like I draw lines when they're nec-
    essary, and I try not to, because I don't believe in that
    either. I think there should be as much playtime in this
    life as possible and that we shouldn't be drawing lines
    and that organization is only to allow for more playtime.
*Michael:* (Laughing) That's simply not true. You and Billy
    have power struggles. You want him to do it *now* because
    you said so, and you want me to get involved, and I'm
    not interested. If it's something like we agree on a
    bedtime and it's eight-thirty and that's the time, I have
    no trouble enforcing that. But it's when all of a sudden

you've decided this is the way it's going to be, I don't
back you on that. I don't, and that's probably not a good
thing. I don't know how to deal with it. But I'll be happy
to help with homework, as far as that goes.

*Joy:* Good. The first thing you could do is to know that he
has homework and to look for it, to know that a child
needs to have homework done, to be bathed, to be fed,
all those things that come with having a child. All those
awful things that come require time schedules.

Joy competently gets her husband to cooperate to a much
greater extent with the domestic chores. At the same time, her
husband challenges Joy to be more responsible. In the past, it
was difficult for him to do so; her diagnosis functioned as a kind
of medically sanctioned shield that encouraged conflict avoidance; it kept the system stuck and the marital relationship unau-
thentic. The spouses could not confront each other and deal
honestly with differences. Buying into Joy's pathology, her husband could not encourage her to act and live more normally, and
she lived in a kind of isolation. He often would not try to stop
her from making choices that he knew were reinforcing negative attributes.

During the six-month treatment, there were weekly sessions
with the family. As Joy changed, the therapy dealt not only with
the problems with which they had presented but also with the
emerging problems of a changing system. For example, Joy's
place in the family changed—from the sick, disqualified family
member to a competent person who was to be respected. The
son was confused by these changes, as were the adults, at times.

## The Introduction of Martial Arts

In IST we work with the patient's contemporary context both by
restructuring present relationships and by recontextualization,
adding contexts to help transform the patient's self. Introducing
a new context facilitates the therapy by bringing forth different,
more functional facets of the self.

In Joy's case, I used martial arts as the new context. Joy kept avoiding issues by calling herself too weak to address them, and she often referred to her lack of power. I believed it essential to provide a context that would counter this organizing core, for her sense of weakness was reinforcing her pattern of conflict avoidance. To the extent that she felt weak, she would avoid conflict, and this conflict avoidance led to indignation, bulimia, and depression. I had challenged her idea that she was "only a borderline" and thus frail and damaged. I told her we would work to counter this feeling that she was weak. What better way to deal with weakness than try to turn the weakness into strength?

In a sense, bringing in a martial artist is almost like bringing in a re-hab specialist as a tangential therapist. The main orchestra continues to be normal family therapy; I was not simply referring her—it would be absurd to pin the whole therapy on martial arts or Tai Chi therapy—but was seeking to maximize the leverage of family therapy. By introducing a specific context, that of strength building, I was attempting to give her a corrective relationship so that she would have the confidence to address and resolve her other relationships.

After the third session, I brought in the martial arts instructor: a burly man in his early thirties wearing a military camouflage suit entered the therapy room and began by describing his model of martial arts.

> *Instructor:* You don't have to do anything but stand there. It's patented. Six million Chinese aren't wrong. I need your upper body built up, from your chest to your arms. I'm going to move everything upward and change your attitude about things.
>
> *Joy:* Push-ups and stuff?
>
> *Instructor:* Oh, yes.
>
> *Joy:* (Laughing) I can do two, so . . .
>
> *Instructor:* Hey, no problem.
>
> *Therapist:* Would it be possible for you to begin the first lesson here in the room?

Following one of the basic tenets of *structural family therapy*, I was introducing a different therapeutic experience into the therapy room. The instructor nodded. The chairs were pulled aside, and Joy and her family lined up, facing the instructor. As Joy, her husband, and their son began the exercises, the teacher gently challenged the three, especially Joy, to push themselves beyond their stopping point.

After this session, Joy had a course of lessons at the instructor's studio. She had to stop after she had a strained back, but to this day, three years later, she describes the martial arts as pivotal in enabling her to challenge her husband and to have the confidence to deal with her other troublesome relationships.

### Psychotropic Medications and the Medical Context

I was beginning the process of decreasing the medication. Joy had been complaining of memory difficulties and hair loss. When she had been off antidepressants for about a week, her eyes looked brighter and she reported that her memory had improved.

> *Therapist:* So, how are you doing otherwise?
>
> *Joy:* Better than I expected. I'm a little confused about my women's group, what my purpose is there. I was doing great til I got there, and I just don't understand. . . . I have to reestablish what I'm doing there and try to figure out if it's something that's working for me.
>
> *Therapist:* What did you talk about in women's group?
>
> *Joy:* I talked about the karate and stuff, about fear . . .
>
> *Therapist:* Were they supportive of the karate?
>
> *Joy:* Yes, they were, actually, very. I talked about going off the medication, and the nurse was concerned and said she thought it was a bad idea. I just stood up for myself and said, "I know what I'm doing." And I'll know if it's not going right. I said, "Listen, my hair's falling out, I feel terrible, I don't remember anything."

This triangulation of patients between mental health professionals is endemic in our field. I might have asked Joy to choose one program or another, but I did not believe I had the credibility to ask her to make the choice. Ideally, one should work with other professionals to provide congruent treatment. In this case, however, the differences were irreconcilable.

## The Work Context

Structural therapy is sometimes accused of being unrelated to the deepest inner directives that are accessible under hypnosis and perhaps in individual therapy. Joy's therapy makes clear that we *are* addressing her subjective experience. Deeply embedded fears yield when the therapist organizes other contexts that validate the new thinking about the self.

One of Joy's major fears concerned her ability to function outside the home. Her recent work experience had mostly been volunteer. In IST the clinician considers the nature of the workplace and tries to determine whether it will undermine or foster the development of a new self-esteem. Would Joy's volunteer work at a church give her increased self-confidence so that she could more forcefully advocate for herself? I thought not. It seemed to promote isolation, and it provided little intensive skill growth. I wanted to see her in a setting where she would enhance her social relationships and develop new skills.

During a session in the second month of treatment, we were discussing the couple's financial situation.

> *Therapist:* What's a relevant issue?
> *Joy:* Save money.
> *Therapist:* Let's not talk about saving money, because saving money is passive.
> *Joy:* I know what I need. I need to get a job.
> *Therapist:* I think you need a place where you can go every day, not necessarily the whole day. (To husband) Do you encourage Joy to get a job?

> *Michael:* Oh, absolutely. . . . But I don't confront her, I
>    haven't for years.
> *Therapist:* To the extent that you don't confront her . . .
> *Joy:* (To Michael) I wish you would.
> *Therapist:* (To Michael) Don't back down. (To Joy) I think
>    getting a job would be a wonderful thing because it
>    would socialize you. You'd be normal.

They discussed options. Joy was incredulous when I suggested that she have a job by the next week. I did this to create a crisis, to force the issue so that new patterns could emerge. I was also anticipating passivity and stalling, which I countered by requesting immediate change. They negotiated and said, "Well, in a week and a half."

I also wanted to see how the husband would react because he had fallen in with the idea that his wife was a chronic borderline, a cripple, who could not be pushed. I encouraged the husband to both support and challenge his wife. To the extent that he challenged her to get out and do more, he implicitly confirmed her and gave her a vote of confidence.

In this session, I was seeking a vision of the rewards that could come from being in a competent working position. There was a specific directive to visualize herself in a situation of competence and to anticipate the thrill of not just being passive, but on the ball. Like reading biographies, these glimpses give people a sense that they can have alternative scenarios for their lives. I was impressed by her readiness: she would nod and indeed would seem to see herself as competent. She then would discuss pertinent associations to work—and how much she enjoyed it.

This process I call "accessing" the competent self. With each context introduced, I was searching for her competent self. Let me emphasize, however, that visualization is a small and even trivial part of the accessing process. The competent self is attained through changing the contexts of a person's life. Beyond that, the self is transformed when Joy herself is empowered to affect these contexts—for example, when she got her husband to share in the housework or when she prevailed on her boss to pay her a salary. The goal is that these contexts change to confirm her as a person.

Joy was weaned of medication. In response to the therapist's urging, she and her husband decided to start a business venture together. He played the piano and she sang. They went to nursing homes and performed for the patients.

The therapy continued for five months—two or three times a month. At one point, Joy told me that she and her husband had decided to adopt a baby and asked if I thought she could handle it. I said, "Definitely." I thought she and her husband could handle the inevitable stress, and I said I would be glad to support their application. Joy called me the next day, saying she had decided to quit her other group because when she asked for a letter of support for the adoption agency, they refused. They said she could not possibly handle the stress. At that moment, she decided they were too negative and were holding her back.

The therapy also included a session with her best friend, who took care of Billy when Joy went to her various treatments. The session dealt with the artificiality of their relationship. Each woman had resentments toward the other that they had never confronted. It was difficult for Joy to address her friend with these issues because she was beholden to her for caring for her son. Nonetheless, she was able to confront her friend (and vice versa) so that they could have a more honest and less stressful relationship. We also dealt with her boss at the church, who was a good friend and with whom she had a similarly complex relationship. As a result, she succeeded in raising her status from that of a volunteer to a paid employee.

## THE AFTERMATH OF TREATMENT

When therapy was terminated, Joy and her family were stable. They were content with one another. Joy was working at the church in a more responsible position. Their son was doing well.

And although her husband was unhappy with his boss, he was becoming increasingly essential to the organization.

Once symptoms have been ameliorated, the question remains, Will the changes be maintained? I gave the family my usual refrain: I work like a family doctor in the sense that after I help people through a difficulty, I try to be available should they need additional therapy. Although things were stable at the time, one cannot control fortune, and I would not presume to suggest that a course of therapy immunizes families from further difficulties.

Joy and her husband adopted two children from Lithuania, a brother and a sister aged six and three. The children spoke no English, and their new parents spoke little Russian. Joy and Michael expected problems, and although the children did not seem quite right, they thought things would work out in time. After three months, however, they learned that both children had fetal alcohol syndrome. Both were severely disabled and had been sexually abused. And the couple was coping with this enormous problem while their son, Billy, was entering adolescence.

For the three years since the children arrived, Joy and Michael have struggled with these extremely hyperactive youngsters. Although the older is controlled with Ritalin to some extent, they nonetheless suffer severe stress. At one point the pressure was exacerbated by Joy's contracting a severe case of Lyme disease. A few months afterward, her husband left his position at a large corporation and became a consultant. He traveled extensively for his job, which required him to be away from home three nights a week. His absence increased the stress on Joy; she had responsibility for three children—two hyperactive and seriously handicapped and one a twelve-year-old boy.

I have seen the family sporadically over these three years. Joy and her husband have coped with the stresses courageously. Their marriage has been taxed to the limit at times, but they have stayed together, and Joy's bulimia and suicidality have never returned. Clearly, the changes were profound for Joy to have remained asymptomatic for these immensely stressful years.

Why was the therapy successful thus far? One cannot say that the change was due simply to the fact that she no longer was being treated for infertility. These changes were both internal and external. To this day, Joy credits a conscious decision to confront her husband and her context, rather than become sick again. Her distress has been transformed: she sees the difficulties as stemming from her context, not as the result of a flaw in her mental architecture. But we clinicians are always reserved in our self-congratulations. At this point, we are only three years post-treatment.

Although this is an anecdotal case, this model is applicable generically to eating-disordered patients: anorectics, bulimics, and compulsive overeaters. A follow-up evaluation of the eating disorders program found that, for the first twelve patients, ten of them had amelioration of symptoms and significant systemic change. The patients who did not do as well were an older compulsive eater and one patient who had no family system available. The compulsive overeaters are, in my experience, more difficult to treat because it is harder to create a crisis.

I told Joy at one point that I was writing an article on the therapy and asked her if she would be willing to give her perspective on the treatment. She enthusiastically agreed.

## JOY'S LETTER

I had been given many diagnoses and opinions from many well-meaning specialists in the mental health field. They included Manic Depressive with rapid mood swings, Severe Anxiety Disorder, Borderline Personality Disorder, Depression, Bulimia, and Anorexia. I was on seven different medications, all prescribed in an effort to enable someone as sick as me to live a somewhat normal life. I was very dependent on my "medicine." I would not consider missing a timed dosage of any one of them for fear that I (or one of my many disorders) would break through. On a particularly frustrating day I would use my diagnosis as a consolation: "It's O.K.," I'd say, "I'm too sick to expect much of myself anyway."

I was hospitalized a number of times and spent a year in a day program that was designed to help "mentally ill" people cope with their daily lives and learn to become independent. It was a wonderful program that included things like goal setting, time management, support groups, and daily meetings with professionals in the mental health field. All I had to do to receive the maximum benefit from this program was to accept that I had a mental illness, that I would always have a mental illness, and that I would need to be on medication for the rest of my life. Daily, I would tell doctors in one way or another that I was not willing to accept that as fact, and that I was interested in getting well and moving on with my life. Daily, they would tell me that I not only needed to accept my "mental illness" status, but that they could not help me until I did. Eventually, I stopped talking with them about it, but secretly hoped I could prove them wrong someday. . . . It became a private vendetta, one which I eventually found difficult to maintain. Well-meaning people would tell me or insinuate that this sort of denial thinking was, in fact, part of the "illness" itself.

I did eventually graduate from this program, considered "stable" on my seven different medications. (I was, however, still bulimic, had frequent anxiety attacks, and resorted to self-destructive behaviors when things got too stressful.) My release was conditional; I needed to find a psychiatrist who would monitor my medication. I met with this doctor once a month, and he refilled my prescriptions. We spoke very little.

I needed more. I wanted to work on my life, my relationships, figure out why I was *so* angry all the time. I had one or two sessions with 5 different doctors, all of which I walked out of very disappointed and/or angry. I didn't know what I was looking for but I did know that none of these were it. My sixth try led me to the Institute for the Family, run by Dr. Fishman.

I was still terrified of my medication lapsing, so our first inter-action was on the phone; me pleading with him to refill my many prescriptions. I made an appointment for a few days later.

The minute I met him, I knew something was very different. He didn't want to hear long stories of my mental health history. As a matter of fact, he didn't want to talk about my past very much at all, except to find out briefly what brought me here. He basically wanted to know how I was doing right now. Where did I want to go, and what were my plans for getting there? A part of me reacted violently to this "taking responsibility for my life" approach. "How dare he!" I thought. "Doesn't he know I'm 'sick,' way too sick to be expected to participate in this line of reasoning?" I was very angry. I almost left, but I didn't. You see, there was another (very medicated) part of me that was yearning for this sort of recognition, this kind of opportunity, this chance to use my own inner strength to make something of my life. Here was someone who believed in me, who validated my strengths. My therapy became about what I *could do* well, and looking for ways to do more of it. No longer was I focused on the limitations of my "illness." As a matter of fact, it seemed to be a sort of unspoken rule in this place to leave "limitations" and "illness" outside the door before you came in.

In this process, I came to believe in myself again and I began to flourish. Soon I was able to stop my medications, one by one. I was required to bring the people I was in close relationship with into my sessions, one at a time. This was a very important part of my treatment. We didn't talk "about" my life, we worked within it. One of the things I discovered is that I tend to isolate myself, especially when things get tough. We had worked on this in my previous day program a bit, but we called for support only within our groups in the program. Dr. Fishman essentially was asking me not only to do this in my daily life, but to bring my friends and family right into his office, so I could get my support network set up right here and now. There were times when this was the last thing in the world I wanted to do. (I would have much preferred to talk about how hard it was.) But as difficult as it was, I felt like "I" was really doing my life; I was at the helm.

I discovered in this process why I was so angry all the time. I felt alone (I isolated myself), I felt powerless (I hung around with amateur "shrinks" and let them define me). "I" was disappearing. In our sessions, I let people in my life know, one by one, that I wanted their support in where "I" was going. I established that I was strong and capable *and* that I could be even more so with their support. I learned to ask for this support in effective ways.

I would say that the most impactful insight for me has been the realization that I am, in fact, *not* "mentally ill," I am very, very sensitive. I've had difficulty setting boundaries, and I tend to take on too much, which I try to do alone. Once we broke it down into these basic components, it was much more manageable. I've been able to make powerful changes. I actually keep a note which I read when things get hard and I need to remember. It begins with "I am *not* mentally ill—I am a very sensitive person." I look to see what I need to do to take better care of myself. Mostly it begins with calling a friend; telling the truth about something uncomfortable, or telling someone how much they mean to me. Above all it means remembering that I am a super-woman to do what I do in my life, and that I need to let up on myself.

Another incredible outcome: my bulimia began to disappear. I felt like I just didn't have a craving to overeat anymore. We never worked directly on my eating disorder; as a matter of fact, we rarely mentioned it. Instead we worked on making effective changes in how I do my life. I began to see that my eating was *directly* related to who is in charge in my life. If I let others tell me how it is, if I can't tell someone the truth when I need to, or if I'm withholding love in any way, it directly affects my eating. The more I worked on these areas, the more my eating became normal. My bulimia is basically not "my" bulimia anymore. I've learned to see my now very occasional bouts with it as a signal—a signal that something is out and that it's time to take a look at what I can do to take care of myself better.

# NOTES

P. 188, *research project at the Philadelphia Child Guidance Clinic:* Minuchin, S., Rosman, B., & Baker, L. (1978). *Psychosomatic families: Anorexia nervosa in context.* Cambridge, MA: Harvard University Press.

P. 189, *"psychosomatic families":* A later discussion is found in Coyne, J. C., & Anderson, B. J. (1988). The "psychosomatic family" reconsidered: Diabetes in context. *Journal of Marital and Family Therapy, 14*(2), 113–123; and Rosman, B., & Baker, L. (1988). The "psychosomatic family" reconsidered: Diabetes in context—A reply. *Journal of Marital and Family Therapy, 14*(2), 125–132.

P. 190, *The model, which I call* intensive structural therapy *(IST):* Fishman, H. C. (1993). *Intensive structural therapy: Treating families in their social context.* New York: Basic Books.

P. 194, *The model of therapy derives from that described in* Family Therapy Techniques: Minuchin, S., & Fishman, H. C. (1981). *Family therapy techniques.* Cambridge, MA: Harvard University Press.

# COMBINING INDIVIDUAL AND FAMILY THERAPY IN ADOLESCENT ANOREXIA NERVOSA
## *A Family Systems Approach*

### Ivan Eisler

*Sitting looking around this sparsely decorated hospital
waiting room, I begin to ask myself how I ever ended up in this
situation. Yet more importantly, when is it all going to end? It
is impossible to pinpoint when it all began. One could adopt
Freudian concepts of it being conceived in my early childhood,
or alternatively it could be attributed to that fateful
decision to diet before going to Greece.
Whenever it began, it feels like it will never end. So much
to deal with, so much to change and accept. As I begin to dissect
my innermost being, I ask the daunting question, "Who am I?"
Yet who are any of us? Am I merely taking normal self-awareness
to extremes, or am I paying the price for an inability to cope?
Despite endless encounters in hospital units, confrontations and
arguments over food, am I any nearer answering the question?*

This is how Sara (not her real name) starts her written account of
her journey through anorexia nervosa and her experience of therapy. This chapter is my account of this journey, or at least the part
in which I accompanied her and her family in the struggle to

make sense of this bewildering illness. The story is unfinished—partly because, at the time of writing, the therapy is only just reaching its final stages and has not completely ended, but more important, because therapy itself can never be more than an interlude in a person's or a family's life and the outcome will therefore always remain, in some ways, uncertain.

Although I will, from time to time, return to Sara's narrative to balance the picture, this is primarily my perspective of the therapy. Describing in detail the course of therapy is inevitably subjective. It is quite different from writing a formal academic paper about a piece of research, reviewing an area of literature, or even writing about psychotherapy in general. In such cases one aims to be as objective as possible focusing on general conceptual ideas or offering interpretations or generalizations of specific research findings. It is a process of looking in from the "outside"—indeed, sometimes from a distance—at what therapy is about.

When one works as a therapist, the position is very different because one is part of the therapy process itself. Using my conceptual understanding of therapy, consulting with colleagues, or simply reflecting on what happened during the therapy session may allow me, partly, to step outside the process and gain an outsider or "meta" perspective; however, this view will always have its limitations. Writing this chapter, I have tried to retain this inside view of the therapy process of which I was part.

As a therapist, I must have a sense of direction that guides me in what I do, but at the same time I know that therapy with any particular individual or family has unique features and unfolds in unpredictable ways. In writing this account of the course of a therapy, I tried to highlight not just the way it may illustrate the general model of a family systems approach in the treatment of anorexia nervosa but also the much more personal and idiosyncratic experience of being a participant-observer in the process of therapy.

Since the early 1980s, I have worked as a member of a clinical/research team at the Institute of Psychiatry and Maudsley

Hospital in London that has been investigating psychotherapies for eating disorders. Our research work has been an integral part of the specialist Eating Disorder Services at the Maudsley Hospital, which includes an inpatient Eating Disorders Unit and separate outpatient services for adults and adolescents. The general ideas that I present in this chapter are strongly influenced by my collaboration with many colleagues, who are too numerous to acknowledge individually. There are two colleagues, however—Chris Dare and Liz Dodge—whose contribution to the specific work described here I would like to acknowledge. They were always available throughout the course of the therapy when I needed an "outside" perspective to help me think through what I was doing. In addition, when I was seeing the whole family, Liz would usually sit behind the one-way screen, sometimes joining me in the room to add her voice. Her comments on the several drafts of this chapter were therefore particularly valuable.

This is also the appropriate place to thank Sara's family and, above all, Sara herself. It is difficult to convey in a few words what one has gained as a therapist from one's clients. I hope the chapter, itself, will convey this. I want to thank the family for agreeing to let me write this chapter about them and for their useful comments on the draft. I was particularly pleased that Sara agreed to let me quote from her own written account of her experience of anorexia. Her writing (which includes essays, poems, letters, and the extended account of her "story," from which I am quoting) has been an important resource for Sara, which she has used to help herself.

## WHY FAMILY THERAPY?

In accounts of the etiology of anorexia nervosa, the patient's family relationships have generally been given a prominent place. As clinicians we often have a strong sense that there is something very specific about the families we see: we may observe particular patterns of interaction that seem to emerge again and again with different families, giving us a sense of familiarity; this awareness may lead to the idea that addressing the family issues might be a way of dealing with the eating problem itself.

A number of accounts in the family therapy literature of the "typical" anorexic (or "psychosomatic" family) have been influential in the development of family-focused treatments. The evidence for a specific family constellation in anorexia nervosa, however, is unconvincing. The accumulation of research findings suggests that the differences between families of individuals suffering from an eating disorder and control families are generally quite small, particularly when community samples are considered. The families we see in specialist eating disorder clinics may have some distinct features, but these are most probably a consequence of selection factors or of the protracted nature of the illness in these cases and are just as likely to be a consequence of the illness as a predetermining factor.

But if the models of eating disorders that view the family as a major etiological factor are wrong, what rationale is there for believing that family therapy can be a useful treatment approach? A simple, though not entirely satisfactory, answer is to point to the increasingly persuasive evidence for the efficacy of family therapy. Our own controlled treatment studies have shown that, particularly for adolescent anorexia nervosa, family therapy is highly effective and that successful outcome is mostly maintained in the long term. To explain such findings does not require that we view the family as the origin or source of the problem. There is little doubt that regardless of how the problem arose in the first place, the eating disorder symptoms become intertwined with family relationships, dominating family life in a way that makes the whole family feel paralyzed, stuck, and unable to find a way out of their predicament. We involve families in treatment partly because we recognize that the distress is experienced by the whole family, but more important, because we see the family as holding the keys to the solution. We view family therapy as a treatment *with* families, rather than *of* families. In other words, we aim to help families find ways of solving their problem, and we do not assume that this requires correcting "family pathology."

When an eating disorder develops, certain features of family life (for example, disagreements between parents, adolescent concerns about growing up and leaving home), which may be part of the normal life cycle stage that the family has reached, suddenly begin to loom large. Any distressing event, such as a bereavement, a serious illness, or impending family breakup, takes on a new significance in the context of the life-threatening eating disorder. Feelings of anxiety, helplessness, and guilt and blame begin to dominate. A sense that it may be safer to do nothing than to risk doing something that may make things even worse becomes all-pervasive. The family feels unable to deal with the crisis, and in their attempts to maintain a grip on the situation, aspects of their family functioning become overemphasized or skewed. The clinician is easily misled into seeing family pathology, rather than, in the first instance, evidence of the family being stuck.

As the family moves through the developmental stages of its life cycle, it has to find ways—while meeting the needs of all members—to maintain stability, as well as to negotiate change in response to a variety of internal and external pressures. Sometimes the adjustments are relatively minor; at other times—as is the case when children are moving from adolescence to adulthood—the changes required may be considerable. These transition points in the family life cycle are points of vulnerability, points when unresolved individual or family issues or the impact of significant life events may combine and lead to the development of symptoms of one kind or another in one of the family members.

The issues that are central to the particular stage of family development begin to be difficult to separate from the family's thinking about the problem itself. Thus, if an eating disorder emerges in the context of a family moving toward a postparenting phase of family life, issues of closeness and distance, individuation and separation, take on a central significance in relation to the eating disorder. The parents will feel pulled in opposite directions—on the one hand, desperately wanting to help their daughter by taking charge and, on the other hand, fearing that if they are too intrusive, they will make things worse. Although both parents will be struggling with this dilemma, often one of them will become the voice of greater involvement, while the other will highlight the importance of not being too intrusive. Their internal dilemma of how to relate to their child thus becomes externalized as a more or less open split between the parents.

In trying to resolve their difficulties, the family may get entangled in patterns of interaction around the eating disorder and thus tighten a web in the very act of trying to break out of it. The symptom is only one of the many strands in the weave, but without it the web loses its hold. The aim of family therapy is to help the family pull out this particular strand that seems to bind everything else together.

## THE STAGES OF FAMILY THERAPY

I will briefly describe the model of treatment that has been developed in the context of our investigation of family treatments for eating disorders. The model presented here is of an outpatient treatment of anorexia nervosa in an adolescent. There are, of course, important differences in our style of work with families of adult patients, bulimic patients, or in cases in which the family is engaged in treatment as part of an admission to an inpatient unit.

In our therapy we may see families in conjoint meetings, see the parents separately with parallel sessions with the adolescent, have joint sibling sessions, and in some cases also include an extended period of individual therapy. Although theoretical labels are always to some extent misleading, the conceptual framework that informs our treatment approach is perhaps best described as a family systems orientation. The following quote from Elsa Jones provides a succinct summary:

When an individual complains of personal distress or when others, family or professionals, regard that individual as distressed, the usual Western psychological response has been to deal with that person alone. However, once the meaning, maintenance and resolution of individuals' feelings or actions are seen as being connected to their ongoing relationships with others, it begins to make sense to involve those others in the therapeutic process. This has implications not only for how many people will be invited to meet together for the purpose of therapy; once the therapist thinks of behavior and its meaning as being influenced by interaction and context, it becomes necessary to evolve theories which take account of phenomena other than those within the internal personal or biological world of the individual.

## Addressing the Symptom

The starting point for the treatment is the engagement of the family in the context of a crisis, where there are often serious concerns about the youngster's life. Our customary practice is to invite the whole family to an initial session, so that we can help them start thinking how best to use all their resources as a family to help their daughter or son. In inviting the whole family to attend, we are aware that we may reinforce the family's sense that they are seen as the source of the problem.

This perception can become the first stumbling block for the therapy. If the family feels blamed, they will sometimes agree that they are at fault but as a consequence end up feeling even more helpless than they did before. Alternatively, and this is more common, the sense of being blamed by the therapist will cause the family to get locked into battles with the clinical team, at times around seemingly trivial issues; or they will discontinue treatment and perhaps look for help elsewhere.

Although we recognize that the issues that have brought the family in to treatment are complex, when the referred patient is a child or adolescent, we begin our treatment in a very single-minded way. Our first step is to help the parents take charge of their daughter's eating. We do this for several reasons. Given the life-threatening nature of the illness and the critical point at which the family approaches us for help, the family will readily accept, in most cases, that unless and until the immediate crisis is dealt with, nothing else can be done. It is apparent that this approach is likely to succeed only if the therapist can convey his or her belief that parents do have the resources to take on such a task despite their sense of helplessness and failure and their protestations that they have already tried everything possible without any success. As I will describe later, the degree to which the parents "succeed" at this stage is variable. The crucial step is achieved when it is clear that parents believe they have an ally in the therapist in their fight to combat the anorexia. The patient will often at first feel betrayed and abandoned and protest that now no one is on her side, but paradoxically she may at the same time be secretly relieved that she no longer has to struggle on her own with her anorexia.

The main impact of this first step is clear: if the parents are able to take effective control of the eating, the most immediate crisis is averted, and they begin to rediscover their faith that they can be competent parents. Indirectly, this realization becomes the first step of disentangling the eating disorder from some of the individual and family issues with which it has become interwoven.

To succeed, at least some of the patterns that the family has become locked into have to change. By sanctioning the parents to do the one thing that the youngster, as well as the parents, fear most, the symptom loses some of its grip on the family. The parents are most likely to succeed in taking control if they become deaf to their daughter's pleas not to take away her last bit of autonomy. In fact, paradoxically, they increase the distance between themselves and their child, rather than engulf her completely, as they had feared.

Their concern that they may be too controlling and intrusive can be partly allayed by discussing the caring and lifesaving aspect of what they are doing. To help the parents maintain an implacable attitude toward their daughter's self-starvation, however, the therapist may also need to focus some of the discussion on the future, drawing a distinction between what the parents are having to do now and the situation in the near future when their daughter will seek to establish age-appropriate areas of independence.

When the duration of the illness has been short, taking this first step is sometimes all that is needed for the family to move on without the need for any further sustained help. A follow-up of a small group of young anorexics who had received family therapy in a general practice setting showed that often no more than two or three family sessions were needed to achieve a good outcome. In the setting of a tertiary referral eating-disorder clinic, however, the therapy more often continues through several further phases.

## Maintaining the Momentum of Change

Once the immediate crisis of the initial referral has been overcome, there is a tendency to want to move on very quickly and start dealing with other issues. The family at this stage will often start bringing to the therapist's attention some of the matters that hitherto have been pushed to one side by the eating problem. These matters may have to do with school attendance, relationships between siblings, the parents' marriage, and so forth. Although the therapist will acknowledge that these are important issues that the family may need to discuss, he or she will be careful not to let them become a distraction from the continuing need to deal with the eating disorder symptoms. In particular, if marital disagreements between the parents are raised, the therapist will emphasize the distinction between marital and parental disagreements and ask the couple to consider whether focusing on marital issues at this stage would help or hinder them in their parental task.

With the strong focus on the parents during the first stage of treatment, it is important for the therapist not to lose sight of the children in the family. The anorexic youngster at this stage may be relatively inaccessible and show her anger and bewilderment by refusing to engage with the therapist. More commonly, she may respond positively, if somewhat guardedly, to the therapist's informed questioning about her preoccupation with food and weight, about her sense of being out of control, and about her fears of letting others take control. Siblings also need to know that the therapist is aware of their sense of bewilderment and anxiety and that their perspective on what is happening is also of importance in helping the therapist understand things.

### Moving on to Individual and Family Issues

Once the eating disorder symptoms no longer dominate the family's thinking and the links between the symptoms and the patterns of individual and family functioning are weakened, the therapy can move to more general areas. The eating-disorder problem at this stage may be completely in the background, and instead, the issues of specific concern to each particular family are brought for discussion.

Therapy seldom follows a simple upward curve, and it is not unusual for the symptoms to force themselves onto center stage again at some point during treatment. This resurgence will commonly occur at points when questions of terminating treatment arise. When such *crises* occur, they are often useful reminders either that still-unresolved issues may need to be addressed or that the therapy is already moving into areas that seem too difficult or too painful to discuss. The knowledge that the family has previously found the resources to tackle the eating problem can act as a reassuring and stabilizing factor for both the therapist and the family.

## THE STORY OF A FAMILY'S JOURNEY

The following is an account of a two-year-long therapy with Sara and her family. During the first stage of treatment, I saw the family together and then moved on to seeing the parental couple and Sara separately. After approximately three months, my meetings with the parents became less frequent, but I continued to see Sara on her own—first fortnightly and then on a regular, weekly basis. I had occasional meetings with the whole family and also saw Sara with her brother, Robert. Now that the therapy is coming to an end, I have started seeing the whole family, including Robert, together again on a more regular basis and am also continuing to see Sara individually.

Sara came to the outpatient eating disorder clinic with her parents when she was seventeen years old. By the time of referral to us, Sara had had two admissions to hospital: the first an extended stay on an adolescent unit, the second a brief admission to a local adult psychiatric clinic. From the referral information, we knew that the first admission had been quite difficult and extended over a number of months. During that time Sara developed a close, confiding relationship with one of the doctors, and when the doctor left the unit for another job, Sara felt terribly let down and abandoned. She took an overdose and for a time afterward remained very reluctant to let anyone close to her. Eventually, she started making good use of her relationship with her key nurse. During Sara's stay in hospital, there had been regular meetings with the whole family, which continued for some time after her discharge. Sara made good progress while in hospital and continued doing well for a time after discharge, seeing her key nurse on an outpatient basis.

It had been thought that Sara might benefit from individual psychotherapy, and attempts were made to find an appropriate resource for this. Because of her age, which placed Sara between the service provisions for children and services for adults (a difficulty made worse by the reorganization of the Health Service that was going on at the time in the UK), finding suitable psychotherapy for her proved difficult. Sara's mother made numerous attempts to find help but was frustrated at every turn. The family became exasperated and increasingly skeptical that anyone was willing to provide help. They felt angry and let down, and when Sara's condition gradually deteriorated to the point where a further admission to hospital became necessary, they blamed the lack of professional support.

Sara's admission to the local psychiatric unit (her second admission to hospital) was short-lived. Sara found the experience so distressing that she convinced her parents she was willing to do anything to help herself if they took her home. By the time the family came to see us at the Maudsley Hospital, Sara had managed to slow down her weight loss through regular support from the family doctor, who saw Sara on a weekly basis, and by intense involvement from Sara's mother. She devoted all of her spare time to her daughter, sitting with her at every meal, persuading and cajoling her to eat, talking her through her anxieties, and patiently absorbing Sara's outbursts when things got to be too much.

The referral information about the rest of the family was not too detailed, but there was an indication that although Sara's father was much less involved with her, he, too, had a clear commitment to her and wanted to help. We learned that there also was a brother, who was no longer living at home but continued to have regular contact with the family.

### Initial Treatment

My first few meetings with the family (not including, at that point, Sara's brother, Robert) amplified the referral information. Sara was a rather sullen, painfully thin, but nevertheless attractive young woman. She sat next to her mother, Jane, and most of the time seemed content to let Jane speak on her behalf. When asked a direct question, Sara spoke in a quiet voice, generally agreeing with her mother's descriptions. Jane would often check things out with her daughter. Their closeness enabled Jane to express Sara's anxieties for her, with Sara frequently nodding in agreement.

I was very conscious that her parents were being careful—in different ways—not to do or say anything that might upset Sara. Jane was very protective of Sara and made clear her resolve not to put her daughter through any unnecessary ordeals. At the same time, however, she also clearly knew how seriously ill Sara was and was determined to ensure she received the kind of help that was needed. Jane and Sara agreed that the most important thing was for Sara to get individual therapy so that she could get something for herself. While Jane was careful in how she talked about Sara's predicament, she could also be quite blunt and would be quick to correct Sara if she felt that Sara's answers to my questions might be misleading. If Sara protested, however, Jane would in most cases quickly back down.

Sara's father, James, tended to remain outside the conversation, although he closely followed what was being said. From time to time, he would join in, adding to and amplifying what Jane had to say. On the few occasions when he expressed a different point of view, he was careful to do so in a nonconfrontational way. He never contradicted Sara unless she directly challenged something he had said. James's wariness "not to put his foot in it" seemed to be directed not just at Sara but also at Jane—and, in some ways, even at me. When James spoke, Jane and Sara would often exchange glances and sometimes join in open disagreement with his perceptions. At which point, after brief protestation, he would usually give in. To illustrate:

Jane had just explained how Sara had been expecting things to be more difficult during the Christmas period (this was an early January session). With James being at home more and Robert also visiting, there would be a lot of disruption, compared with when it was just Sara and Jane on their own most of the time.

> *Mother:* In fact, after the initial bit of that, when she felt the place was crowded and noisy, she seemed to cope quite well. She got used to it. In fact (turning to Father), it was probably worse for you and Robert. Where Sara and I have established a routine, if you like, and I know exactly what's going on and what's not going on. I think it was much harder for you, wasn't it? . . .

*Father:* I think for Robert as well . . .

*Mother:* Yeah, and Robert.

*Father:* . . . because Robert and I do not have a routine.

*Sara:* (In an irritated voice) Everybody has a routine, it's just not as obvious as ours is.

*Mother:* (Laughs uneasily)

*Father:* (With a somewhat indulgent smile) . . . not a hard and fast routine, Sara.

*Sara:* (Her annoyance becoming more obvious) Everybody has a routine in what they do.

*Mother:* (In a very matter-of-fact voice) So that was hard and there were various tensions about, weren't there.

*Therapist:* (To Sara) Sounds like you feel you're being criticized when people talk about you having a routine.

*Sara:* Yeah, everybody has a routine. (To Father) *You* get up in the morning, *you* have a bath, *you* go to work, *you* always take the same thing for lunch, *you* always come home the same time, give or take five or ten minutes. So what's different in that from what I do? O.K., our routine is a bit more rigid and the rest of it, but everybody has a routine. I had a routine of going to school and getting up. *That's* a routine, isn't it?

*Father:* Yes, I certainly have a routine of what time I get up every day in the morning, because I am tied to the time I have to get in to work . . .

*Sara:* Yeah, so my routine is . . .

*Father:* . . . because I am tied to the time that I need. (Starts explaining as if Sara were a little child) And that is because if I don't, I don't get paid, and if I don't get paid, we don't have any money coming in. That's a different *type* of routine.

*Sara:* Yes, but it still is a routine.

*Father:* It's not a routine imposed by me.

*Mother:* (Who has been watching the interchange carefully, joins in explaining to Father) She is just saying that it is still a routine.

(After a pause turns to Sara) I think what Dad means is, that it does not affect . . . , that if things don't happen exactly according to the routine, it doesn't affect things . . .

*Sara:* Yeah, I know, I am just saying that everybody has a routine.

*Mother:* Yes, that's true.

*Therapist:* (To Mother) It seems like you have to be the advocate for both sides.

*Mother:* (Smiles and nods)

*Father:* (Grins) Isn't that what mothers are for—and wives?

*Mother:* I just stand in between them, because otherwise (turning to Father) there would just be an explosion.

*Sara:* (Quietly) No, there wouldn't.

*Mother:* No? Alright, O.K.
(Sounding for the first time somewhat exasperated) I often have to explain to Dad, though, why you are behaving in a certain way, *don't I?*

*Sara:* He can't understand if you've explained *ten billions* of times.

These observations of the family fitted well with the information we had from the referrals, and it would be easy to see them as confirming a picture of the stereotypical "psychosomatic" family: (1) an "overinvolved" mother and a "peripheral" father, (2) a cross-generational alliance between mother and daughter that excludes father, and (3) a pattern of interaction in which mechanisms of conflict avoidance are prominent. One could also see how much seemed to revolve around the anorexic symptoms. But although this description is accurate at one level, it is also misleading, as I will try to demonstrate later.

Another aspect of the first session was important because it set the focus for a significant part of the early work of the therapy. When I told Sara I would like to weigh her, she refused adamantly and got visibly upset. Jane seemed torn between trying to comfort Sara and trying to explain to me why I should back off. Jane explained that Sara was weighed by their family doctor at the same time every Monday morning and that, in her view, it was better not to challenge this routine because it would simply upset Sara and make it more difficult for her.

I agreed that, having been told Sara's weight, it certainly would not make sense to spend the whole of the first session having a fight about this. But I also pointed out that weighing Sara here was an important part of the treatment. I turned to Sara and explained that it was not just a matter of having accurate information about her progress; it was precisely because she found the whole issue of being weighed so difficult that it was all the more important I should be able to see firsthand what it was like for her. At that point, Jane joined with me and agreed.

On two more occasions during the first session, it appeared that another confrontation might develop—the first over whether Sara would agree to have blood tests done, which again were already being done regularly by the family doctor; the second over the date of our next session—but in both cases the parents jointly asserted their authority over Sara.

During the next few sessions, we returned several times to the topic of Sara being weighed by us. Jane explained that, in the weeks preceding their appointment with us, she had managed to get Sara to agree (as part of the conditions of Sara not having to go back into hospital) to a minimum level of food intake that would at least maintain her weight, which would be monitored by their family doctor. She talked about her concern that to challenge Sara too strongly would jeopardize the precarious balance they had achieved.

## Understanding the Family Dynamic

Several aspects of this early exchange were important and paradigmatic. Jane was unsure that I would be able to understand Sara and tried to protect her daughter from my ill-conceived attempts to challenge the obsessionally rigid patterns of behavior around food and weight. She anxiously anticipated that Sara might react to any such challenge in a way that would undermine the progress she felt she had helped Sara achieve so far. Jane's great closeness to Sara and her at times fierce protectiveness stopped her from pushing Sara too hard and meant that she also tended to become Sara's shield when others tried to challenge her.

It is worth reflecting that it is precisely this kind of pattern that, as professionals, we tend to label as *over*protectiveness. I suspect this is, at least in part, because we feel hampered and constrained in our clinical role, particularly when the parent's protective behavior seems to come between the child and our attempts at therapeutic interventions. If one focused only on the ways in which Jane protected Sara from being challenged, it would be easy to miss that it was also Jane's closeness to Sara that had allowed her to find a way of helping her. It was precisely because she was close to Sara that Jane was able to draw a line, beyond which she would not let Sara go. She was making sure that Sara was eating regularly and was trying to get her to change her eating habits. Jane was also aware that, in trying to take things very slowly, the danger was that they might fail to recognize when things were, in fact, at a standstill or even moving backward.

Metaphors are often a useful way of bringing together the therapist's and family's understanding of what is happening. The following metaphor evolved out of my conversation with the family and seemed to characterize the situation in this early part of the treatment: it was as if the family was in a small boat that had been sinking fast until they found a way of plugging the hole. Now, they were no longer sinking, or were only sinking slowly, but the boat was up to the brim with water and anything could send it under. They knew they had to start bailing out the water and start rowing toward shore, but they felt paralyzed, afraid to move, lest they capsize the boat.

The psychological dynamics of Sara's rigid routines around weight and food were quite clear to the family: they recognized that although these routines lowered Sara's anxiety, they also reinforced the symptoms and protected her from having to face troubling relationship issues. They agreed that, in the long term, Sara would only recover when it became possible to challenge these routines.

There is little doubt that the relationship between Jane and Sara had become closely intertwined with Sara's anorexia. Anorexia had brought them closer together; it was at the heart of Jane's intense preoccupation with Sara and was the main reason that she tried to anticipate Sara's feelings, needs, and fears. If one were to consider this relationship, divorced from the anorexia, as simply a relationship between a mother and a daughter approaching adulthood, it would indeed appear unusual. In a relationship between a mother who is desperately trying to save her child's life and a daughter who is starving herself to death, afraid of life and not sure who else she can trust, the closeness becomes understandable.

Both Jane and Sara were clearly conscious of the contradiction in their relationship. Both of them have at times said that while they found their relationship a major source of comfort and strength, they were also sometimes troubled that it was too close and overpowering. Sara's way of managing this closeness was to fall back on her rigid, obsessional anorexic behavior, a tactic that increased her distance from her mother. This anorexic behavior would then heighten Jane's anxiety and make Jane all the more determined not to fail Sara; the existing pattern would be reinforced.

Sara repeatedly stressed how important the relationship was to her and how difficult it was even to contemplate that some aspects of their relationship might have to change:

> I guess, looking back now, maybe we did become consumed by each other. But who wouldn't, faced with a similar situation where she was the only one who seemed to really understand and know what I was going through? Equally, I was the only one who knew what she had to contend with as Dad's behavior reached crisis point. She was able to share her pain and misery as much as I could mine, so in a sense we became each

other's key to survival. I begin to realize now that all along I have focused on my relationship with Dad as the problem. I'm not saying Mum and I have a problem in our relationship, but that I can see now the influence she has had. Mum was perfect, so to question our relationship felt like a huge act of betrayal. The things that I can identify as issues in my relationship with Mum are far harder to deal with, as I still tend to deny they exist. It feels like I would hurt Mum so much after all she has done for me. Yet in any mother-daughter relationship, the mother's influence usually has a profound effect. Why should ours be different?

The unique sense of acceptance I received from my mother and the love we still share is the most precious thing in my life. In her book *My Mother, My Self*, Nancy Friday suggests that the intensity between mother and daughter will be passed on down the generations as daughters seek to share the same closeness they experienced with their own daughters. Just as they felt unable to express their own individuality, so too do their daughters, and thus the pattern continues.

I never felt that my Mum prevented me from being myself. Indeed, whilst we do think alike, she seldom inflicts her opinions on me, and like everyone we do have our rows. Does our intimacy stem from her own childhood when her mother died when she was young? Did the more distant relationship she shared with her father's second wife ensure she would never let me feel the loneliness she had suffered? Or am I grasping at straws? For it seems obvious that any family faced with the disruption of anorexia would find highlighted both the positives and negatives of their existence.

James's more peripheral role in the family can also be seen as part of the overall pattern. The anorexia kept him at arm's length from Sara. Sara complained bitterly that her father did not understand her and that he was not there when she needed him most. In these interchanges Jane generally became the mediator. She would usually support Sara against James but in doing so would adopt a more moderate tone; at times she would also try to put his point of view across to Sara.

James's position in the family can also be viewed as a distance regulator of Jane's relationship with Sara. In moving closer to James, Jane would distance herself, at least briefly, from Sara; this distance relieved Sara, to some extent, of her feeling of guilt from pushing out her father but also made her isolated; Jane then had to move back toward her. It was always clear that James's position was not an expression of disinterest or unwillingness to help, but rather of his being disqualified (or that he disqualified himself) from helping actively.

Here again is Sara's account:

> Is it because he is such a horrible person? He is, in fact, capable of many roles: the victim, the scapegoat, the loser, the alcoholic, and even, now, the redeemed. But what I will always remember my Dad for most is in his role as the absent father. Should I be grateful that he didn't beat me or abuse me? At least I would have known that he felt something for me, even if it was only hate and anger. When I was younger, I wasn't really conscious of him at all. He was just there. Sure, he would drive us anywhere and served to provide the stereotypical father/mother family life.
>
> We never talked much. It was as if he was just there to make up the numbers, a sleeping partner, yet it didn't bother me then. We weren't exactly close as a family, and I gained that from outsiders. I didn't even realize the huge problem he had with drink. What I did realize, though, was that, after being trapped by anorexia, it did bother me. He increasingly irritated me to the point where I couldn't even stay in the same room as him.

And later Sara adds:

> I'm not going to convey all the complexities surrounding my relationship with Dad, as much of it I am still trying to deal with myself. What I do realize is that as I became increasingly

more disillusioned with the male relationships I was having, I craved a far less complicated type of affection which only a father could give. As I began to long for this more and more, it perpetuated the gulf between me and Dad, and I felt I had to punish him further.

## Challenging the Symptoms

From the start I thought that the very aspect of Sara's family relationships most closely interconnected with her anorexia was also the resource that needed to be mobilized to help break the power of the symptom. This predicament posed a dilemma for me that paralleled the parents' own dilemma.

I felt that if I was to engage the parents around the task of more forcefully challenging the anorexic symptoms, I had to have their confidence that I would support both them and Sara. I also had to convey my belief that they would succeed. Because of their previous experiences, Jane in particular was convinced that only someone who could gain Sara's trust would be able to help. At the same time, I knew that Sara was continuing to lose weight, albeit quite slowly.

The dilemma was that only someone whom Sara could trust would be able to challenge her. Yet, any attempt at challenging her seemed to demonstrate that one did not understand her and could not be trusted. This interactional dynamic was played out within the family, in my relationship with Sara and her family, and also in the relationship between the different professionals involved in supporting Sara. The problem in addressing this dynamic was that it was difficult to talk about it without appearing to blame someone. Sara felt accused of being manipulative. Jane thought she was being labeled as overprotective. And James sensed that he was seen as detached and uncaring.

The third session provided a brief exception to the usual pattern. I had seen Sara on her own and had then proceeded to see the parents while Sara was in the waiting room. After approximately thirty minutes, when we were talking about the increasing probability of admission to hospital and the parents had united in expressing their anger and feeling of being let down by previous attempts at treatment, Sara suddenly burst into the room, screaming at the top of her voice that she wanted to leave right now. At first I was only partly aware of what had provoked this outburst, but it became clear from the ensuing interchange:

> *Sara:* (Shouting at Jane) You have been here for nearly an hour. You don't know what its like for me sitting out there.
>
> *Father:* I will drive as fast as I can when we leave.
>
> *Sara:* No you won't. And I am going to be the one who will have to face having my tea late. You don't know what it's like.
>
> *Mother:* Sara, you are making things worse. Go and wait in the waiting room.
>
> *Sara:* No.
>
> *Therapist:* Sara, I haven't finished my discussion with your parents yet, and it is important that we finish what we have been talking about.

At this point, to my surprise, James got up and tried to calm Sara down. Jane looked absolutely dejected and drained. When Sara continued to protest, though not quite as loudly, Jane got up and took over from James, who sat down. After some further protestations from Sara, Jane insisted firmly that Sara allow us to finish.

I was surprised that James had been the first one to take action. He persisted (and might have succeeded) until Jane joined in. At that point, he vacated the scene, and the more customary pattern reasserted itself.

The issue of Sara's weight was a central theme for the first few sessions—partly because of the way it was bringing forth the main issues around which the family was locked, but also because there was a very real threat to Sara's life. Her weight was down to 63 percent of average body weight (matched for age and height). She was at her lowest weight since her illness started, and we knew that unless the weight loss was reversed, admission to hospital was unavoidable. Our previous clinical experience, as well as the results of our controlled treatment studies, however, had taught us that if the family could be helped to challenge the symptom, there would be a solid foundation on which to build further therapeutic endeavors.

Our usual approach is to try to get the parents to take on the responsibility of tackling the symptom. Where one parent is more involved and the other apparently more detached, the different position that each parent has can be used to advantage. As long as the parents see that they are involved in a joint task—and do not feel blamed by exploration of their differences—they will often find creative ways of mobilizing their own strengths.

Although Jane and James went some way along this path, two factors were making it difficult to achieve this aim. Both were linked to the progress that Sara had already made since her last admission. First was, paradoxically, the success that Jane had already achieved in getting Sara to make small but crucial changes to her eating pattern. James felt that the most useful thing he could do was not to interfere—not because he did not want to help, but because when he tried, it usually had the effect of upsetting Sara, and he feared he would undermine the progress Sara had made with Jane's help.

Jane herself, although saying she would like more support from James, was reluctant to let anyone do anything that might upset the delicate balance that had been achieved. The paradox was that unless the status quo was challenged, what the family was trying to stave off—admission to hospital—was, in fact, rapidly becoming the only alternative.

The second factor making it difficult to move ahead was Sara's relationship with her family doctor. The family doctor was very committed to Sara, and she trusted him. He had played a crucial role in helping stabilize the situation but now had also become part of the status quo. The impasse within the family seemed to be mirrored by the impasse between the professional systems. I felt that I was in a similar position as James: he could not do anything that might undermine what Jane had achieved. Similarly,

I did not want to do anything that might undermine the family doctor's role. I had expected that talking about the extreme seriousness of Sara's illness would help me join with the parents and start the process of challenging the anorexic symptoms. In doing this I also seemed to be challenging the family doctor's importance. When I discussed the situation with him, it was clear that he was aware of this situation. He agreed that it was important for our clinical team to take on the full responsibility for Sara's treatment and that he would make this clear to Sara and her family.

At the next meeting with the family, I was joined by our team's medical colleague who had examined Sara. He used his full medical authority to highlight the very real risks that Sara was facing and made it very clear that if he were to take medical responsibility for outpatient treatment, he would have to be in a position to directly monitor Sara's weight, blood levels, and so forth. Unless Sara agreed, he would recommend immediate admission to hospital, if necessary, as compulsory treatment under the Mental Health Act.

I discovered later that Sara would have agreed fairly readily to admission to hospital. She had become quite frightened that she might die and also thought that if she went in to hospital, she would relieve her mother of some of the burden she was carrying. Jane, however, was determined to find a solution outside the hospital. She joined with us in insisting that Sara be weighed there and then. Sara became very tearful and asked to have some time on her own with Jane. After they returned, Jane said that Sara had agreed to be weighed but did not want to know what her weight was. I agreed that, at least for the time being, I alone would be the "keeper of her weight," although I emphasized that at some point I would have to talk with Sara about her fears and preoccupations with weight; therefore she would not always be able to keep her eyes closed while standing on the scale.

This was one of several important turning points in the therapy. From that point Sara continued to gain weight at a very slow but steady rate. Although at several points much later in the treatment her weight temporarily dropped, it was never to a dangerously low level. The observable shift was at one level quite small. The main change was in my position in relationship to Sara and to her family. Now we clearly had a joint agenda, for I had accepted the family's own way of bringing about change.

There was, however, also a downside. As Sara was moving out of the danger zone in weight, both Jane's central role in helping Sara and James's role as "outsider" were reaffirmed. Looking back, I am not sure whether there was scope for change in other directions at that point. With another family I might have persisted longer in trying to explore how both parents might actively contribute to helping their daughter. A number of factors persuaded me not to challenge the family's preferred solution at this point: Sara's antagonism to her father and James's response, which suggested that he felt he had no right to expect anything else; the relationship between Jane and James; and also my own sense that, if I was to retain any therapeutic maneuverability, the most important thing was to address the immediate crisis. Thus, once it was clear that Sara was regularly gaining weight, I agreed with the family that the direction in which they were moving and the making of gradual changes were probably the right things for them. I emphasized once more, however, the risk of slow, gradual change being sometimes difficult to distinguish from standing still or moving backward.

### Couple Issues or Parental Issues?

Clinicians sometimes assume that if they see evidence of a poor marital relationship, the child's problem is a consequence of getting caught up in a marital dispute. They then conclude that where the symptomatic child is clearly seen to act as a mediator between the parents, effective treatment will need to include some work on the marital relationship. At a theoretical level, two kinds of arguments seem to support such a view.

First is the somewhat simplistic idea that, in the development of an eating disorder, a poor marital relationship is a major underlying causal factor that, if left unaddressed, is going to undermine any attempt at treatment. What reinforces such a view is the experience that a youngster may make significant improvements while away from home (for example, in hospital), only to relapse after returning to the family.

This argument ignores the fact that the influences between parents and child are not unidirectional and that while the parents' relationship is, of course, likely to affect the child, the impact on the marital relationship of an ongoing life-threatening illness in the family's midst is likely to be equally significant. There is also little empirical evidence that marital disharmony is any more common in eating disorder groups than in comparison groups.

The second argument is more subtle and makes no assumptions about the etiological role of the marital relationship in the development of the eating disorder: the parents' relationship and the symptomatic behavior of the child mutually influence each other, and the eating disorder symptoms may then indeed play a central role in mediating the marital relationship. There is little doubt that, at least in some cases, this argument is supported by clinical observations.

Nevertheless, it is doubtful that addressing this problem is best achieved by targeting the marital relationship directly. First, as I argued earlier, this strategy can easily be misunderstood as an expression of the clinician's belief that the poor marital relationship is indeed "the cause" of their daughter's problems. This belief simply reinforces feelings of guilt and blame. Second, it is not at all clear that the marital relationship itself must change if there is to be long-term improvement in the child. What is needed is the severing of the link between the symptom and the marital relationship. In our experience, this severance is achieved more effectively by helping the parents address parenting issues, rather than marital issues.

Jane's and James's marital relationship had not been a direct topic of discussion in the early sessions, but a number of indications suggested it was not an entirely easy one. After I started seeing the parents on their own, they raised this issue more directly and asked whether they ought to seek marital counseling. I made it clear that I was not in a position to judge whether marital counseling was appropriate for them or not because that was not the problem they had sought help with initially and, consequently, we had never discussed their marriage. I suggested that, given that they had both made it clear that their wish to help Sara was their number one concern, they had to think through whether dealing with their marriage at this point in time was going to help or hinder them in this task.

The discussion continued over the next two meetings with the parents. Jane and James found it difficult to decide, realizing that although enhancing their marital relationship would make it easier for them to work together as parents, they also felt that, for the time being, they really needed to concentrate their efforts on helping Sara. I continued talking with them about the way they could help each other as parents. Eventually, after considerable discussion by themselves, James and Jane decided that marital counseling would have to wait. They openly acknowledged that they decided against marital therapy partly because they were afraid of what it would lead to. They smiled when I commented that, having taken such a long time over making this decision, they had actually already started doing their own marital therapy.

Plainly, it is not possible to completely separate parental and marital issues in a couple's relationship. But by drawing a distinct boundary between the two, one can more easily start to address some of the feelings of anger and blame, of feeling unsupported or excluded without blaming or undermining the marriage. One also starts drawing a boundary between the marital relationship on the one hand and the daughter and the eating disorder symptoms on the other.

As Jane and James started to think about these two areas as distinct, some important issues started to surface. Jane started talking more openly about how hurt she still felt because of James's history of drinking. For many years, James had denied that alcohol was a problem, and Jane, in trying to protect the children from seeing their father as an alcoholic, covered up for him. She was very surprised when I asked her whether she was aware how she also protected James and whether she saw any similarity to her protectiveness of Sara.

After the first three months of therapy, my meetings with James and Jane became much less frequent and focused mostly on James's relationship with Sara and how Jane tried to act as mediator. Jane now hated this role and had a strong wish for James to find a way of getting through to Sara. She recognized that she generally ended up deflecting their anger or frustration. Jane started making very conscious efforts not to be either Sara's or James's advocate.

It was increasingly clear that James's drinking was a potent factor in the family structure. It explained why he had disqualified himself in the family—especially when he tried to assert his views. Jane and Sara had repeatedly complained that James was always hiding his feelings, and both wanted him to be more honest. When James expressed more clearly how he saw things and what he felt, however, he generally got a very negative response from both of them. On such occasions, after brief protestations, James would pull back.

An important change took place about eighteen months after I first started seeing the family when James started seeing an alcohol counselor. For Jane this was an important acknowledgment on his part that his drinking had been a significant problem. It somehow also seemed to give more space for her to think about herself, and soon afterward she asked to see me on her own. She had said she wanted to discuss her relationship with Sara, to see how she could become less involved with her as she thought she might now be stopping Sara from moving on. In fact Jane used the meeting primarily to talk about herself and about her relationship with James. She was very positive and reflective, but what perhaps struck me most was how much more able she was to think about her own needs. Interestingly, it was at this very time that Sara was also changing most obviously.

## *Turning Points*

Figure 7.1 shows the progress that Sara made in her weight during the course of the therapy and indicates a number of what I call *turning points*, at which I felt that significant changes took place. I cannot be sure whether Sara or her family would accord them the same significance; equally, there are likely to be other points that are of significance to them that I thought less important.

In some ways, using the term *points* is misleading because it implies that change took place from one instance to the next. Clearly this is not the case because a number of things would always be happening simultaneously and mutually influencing each other. The turning point or discontinuity is, therefore, in the "eye of the beholder." I have deliberately omitted describing the beginning and ending of therapy as turning points—even though these may be of great importance—because they are, so to speak, outside my field of vision.

I have already described what I consider to be the first turning point in therapy, which was symbolized by Sara agreeing to be weighed at the hospital. The real shift, then, was in my relationship with the family. This shift was followed by slow but steady progress. During this period Sara at times would talk in a fairly detached way but with some insight about her predicament. At other times she would be quiet and seemingly uncommunicative.

As I was seeing Sara on her own, in parallel with sessions with her parents, one immediate issue was the question of boundaries. At the outset I explained to Sara that what she and I discussed together would be confidential. The only exception to this, and it was an important exception, would be if I thought she was endangering her life. Highlighting the issue of confidentiality, as well as stressing its limits, was important because it emphasized both that I respected Sara as an individual and that I assumed a certain degree of responsibility in our relationship.

Although a number of changes had occurred during the early months, they were very small, incremental changes that became

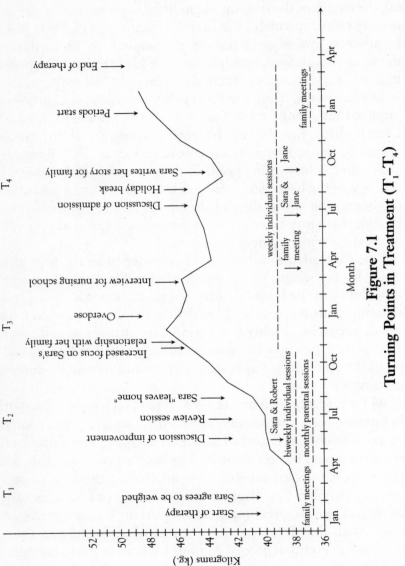

**Figure 7.1**
**Turning Points in Treatment ($T_1$–$T_4$)**

The chart shows Sara's progress in weight and some of the significant events that took place during the course of treatment.

visible only over a period of time. It seemed as if change needed to be imperceptible or attributable to a "chance" event to be tolerable. If in one session Sara talked more about herself than usual, in the following session she would tend to be much less forthcoming.

The second turning point came about approximately six months after the beginning of treatment. Sara's brother, Robert, had not attended the initial family meetings, but it was clear that even though he was living away from home he was an important person in Sara's life. She valued that, according to her, he was one of the few people who did not simply give in to her "anorexic" demands. When I suggested it might be useful if he came to some sessions with her, she readily agreed. Also arranging the time when they could both come proved important because it required that Sara modify one of her rigid routines about meals.

Robert's presence in the session had a noticeable effect on Sara. She was more relaxed and less guarded than usual. It also became easier to talk about some subjects that had been difficult to address in individual sessions. Previously when the question of Sara's progress had come up, for instance, she would quickly assert that nothing had changed and that things were as bad as ever. When Robert asked me whether I thought Sara was better, I hesitated and then explained my dilemma: on the one hand, I clearly knew that Sara had changed in a number of ways and that to ignore that was tantamount to saying she had made no effort so far. On the other hand, talking about her progress was difficult because it made it sound as if everything was O.K. Sara listened to my conversation with Robert, and as my comments were made to Robert rather than to her, she seemed content not to join in. During the next few individual sessions, Sara talked about her feeling that no one was worried about her any longer and acknowledged that this was one reason that she found it hard to continue to put on weight.

Another important factor at the time was the approaching planned review session. A review session is often a useful way of punctuating the therapy, and at the time I had agreed to "take things slowly," I felt that having such a point ahead of us would be important. As the session approached, Sara expressed her concern that if things were going too well, I might stop seeing her. It is perhaps also significant that, during this time, Jane and James were seriously thinking about seeking help with their marriage, a notable change in their relationship.

At the review session Sara described her anorexia as unchanged: she was still terrified of putting on weight, saw herself as fat, and although she was eating more and had put on weight, her eating habits were as rigid as ever. In other areas, however, she acknowledged that she had changed. Her relationship with her mother was changing: she was finding it easier to be away from her even though she thought she still had to cling to her at times. She was also aware of the change in the relationship between her parents but was unwilling to discuss the change and how it might make things different for her.

Following this session, Sara became more forward-looking. Also for the first time she spoke about her wish to feel differently about her father. Sara had been working in her spare time as a care assistant in a nursing home for elderly people; she now decided to spend more time there during her school holidays. She persuaded her parents that she should at least temporarily make use of the staff accommodation there. Although she continued to come home on most days, she in effect started to lead an independent life, which included taking on the responsibility for her eating.

The importance of Robert's role in this shift is seen in what Sara wrote about her relationship with her brother:

> Robert is in ways very much like Dad. His reluctance to say how he really feels and [his tendency] to play the clown if things get tough are all, I guess, his ways of coping. During his final year at university, the last thing he wanted was frantic phone calls about his sister's latest antics. His letter writing was never very long, yet the continual postcards I received

with the odd sentimental comment amid the jokes and humor lifted my spirits. The turbulent relationship we shared at home has matured into a solid friendship now that he is away, and he provides an escape when things get too much. I never felt he really understood what I was going through, it was just all too damn crazy for him. My habits would baffle him, I would yell if he touched any food that was mine. . . . Remember the day you put the butter knife in MY marmite!!!! But at least he tried to understand.

It was in fact during a weekend at his flat that I made one of my biggest breakthroughs. I was forced into having breakfast unsupervised for the first time, as he refused to get up at 8 o'clock on a Sunday morning! For this I will be eternally grateful, as it gave me confidence to escape the stress of living at home and move into the staff living quarters at work.

The third and fourth turning points both involved a crisis that at one level involved a setback but also allowed for more change and eventually led to significant improvement. The third turning point followed a period of some three months during which Sara seemed to be making much faster progress both in terms of her eating problems and in thinking about herself and her relationships with her family. We had agreed earlier that when she was ready, I would be willing to see her once a week (rather than fortnightly) to do more intensive work on these issues. She now decided to take up this offer.

Among other topics we started discussing ending treatment in the future and relating this to her past losses of significant people in her life. Sara found this an extremely difficult topic, which she linked to the fact that she felt she was becoming too dependent on me. In the following sessions she became much more preoccupied with her weight again, started talking about wanting to lose weight or at least remain static, and on several occasions refused to be weighed.

With the approaching Christmas break, Sara's relationship with her family also became an important theme. She had decided to work over the holiday even though part of her longed for a family Christmas. She worried, however, that she had already caused her family enough troubles and did not want to spoil their holiday. She felt isolated and alone in her struggle, and with the anorexia receding, she was losing her sense of identity. She thought that because she was doing so much better in terms of her weight, everyone was losing sight of the fact that she still had numerous difficulties. Her sense of desperation increased, and on New Year's Eve she took quite a serious Paracetamol overdose. Although she later described being of two minds about dying (and did, in fact, let Jane know what she had done), it was clearly more than a mere gesture. It highlighted to everyone how fragile her progress had been and the extent to which she felt isolated.

Sara again became much more dependent on people around her to provide her with support and a "safety net." For a while my role became a much more active one, liaising with the family doctor and other professionals, at times becoming quite directive and insisting that when I felt Sara's behavior was too risky, I would have to make decisions she might not agree with, such as, involving her parents in decisions about her safety. At the same time, however, this period also included some of the most productive therapeutic sessions so far.

Over the following weeks, Sara's weight fluctuated, but each weight gain seemed to be followed by a greater weight loss. The fourth turning point came several months later. Sara was struggling during this time. She had worked hard to get accepted for nursing training—something she desperately wanted to do—and she thought this fervor should have motivated her to get better. At the same time she felt that if she succeeded in obtaining a place in one of the nursing schools, she would end up having to cope entirely on her own—away from home, with no more therapy. It was not only her weight that fluctuated: she again went through several periods of feeling that life was not worth living. She found it hard to see how she was going to move forward and considered the possibility of inpatient treatment.

Sara was at one of her lowest points when a summer holiday break in therapy took place. She lost a considerable amount of weight during this period but afterward was more able to talk about her loneliness, her sense of being stuck, and her wish to move on. She also talked about her despair and anger at being abandoned. Gradually, over the following weeks, a change became apparent in Sara's relationship with me. One week, she would come to a session and talk with complete insight about herself and her family relationships, and she would talk about anorexia as if it were a thing of the past. The following week, she would be angry and critical of me for not letting her know whether I cared about her, would storm out of the room, and a while later would come back and thoughtfully talk about how she felt. As she herself commented, she felt safe to show all her emotions, and if I did not like it, that was just too bad because that was what she really felt.

Many, if not most, of the shifts in Sara's thinking and perceptions happened outside the therapy sessions—often following a particularly turbulent or upsetting session, after which she would go away and think through what had happened. It was during this time that she wrote the long, personal account of her experience of anorexia, of her relationship with her family, and of her experience of therapy and sent a copy of this to each member of her family. It was Sara's way of letting her family—her father, in particular—know the hurt she had felt but also her hope that in time she could move beyond this. This letter was probably the main marker for this fourth crucial turning point.

## Changing Relationships Within the Family

Despite the considerable changes that have taken place, the basic structure of relationships has remained essentially the same. What has changed is that the relationships appear to be more flexible, allowing both closeness and independence to co-exist.

Thus, Jane and Sara continue to be very close, and Jane makes it clear that Sara will continue to be her number one priority as long as Sara needs her. Jane and James are, at times, notably closer, although on occasion it is clear that there are still unresolved issues between them. Probably the greatest change for them is that they are able to really hear each other out. Today Robert is careful to preserve his role as the one who has left home and is therefore "outside" the family, but he continues to have a strong relationship with each other family member. Although he is probably closest to Jane, he has become closer to James than he used to be, and he seems to move easily among all three members.

The one aspect of the family structure that has remained rigidly fixed, at least on the surface, is the relationship between Sara and James. Although both of them would clearly like the situation to change, the distance between them has, if anything, increased. Sara's position both inside and outside the home has become a more direct *distance regulator*, taking anorexia, to a considerable extent, out of the equation.

To understand the changes that took place in the family, it may be useful to look at the changes in my role in relation to the family, and to Sara in particular, over the course of the therapy. The family initially related to me with some caution. They were desperate for help but, given their sense of having been let down previously, were understandably wary.

It took several sessions before I felt that I had really engaged the family. I was able to do this around the parents' anxiety about Sara, but it was crucial to accept the family's pace and preferred direction of change. Although slow, the pace created a sufficiently safe context to allow Jane to go on helping Sara and to allow Jane and James to start thinking about both their own relationship and their relationship with Sara. The background of these changes made obvious the split between Sara and her father, which culminated in a clear shift in the relationship between Jane and James as Sara sought more independence for herself and moved out of the parental home.

After Sara moved to the staff accommodation at work, she hardly ever saw James but maintained her close relationship with

Jane by going home regularly when James was out at work. Anorexia became a much less prominent part of her relationship with her mother as Sara took on the responsibility for her own eating—although Jane continued to follow Sara's progress. With Sara away at least part of the time, Jane and James found more time for themselves and began to rediscover some of the positive aspects of their relationship. Jane continued for some time to act as mediator between Sara and James.

The middle phase of the therapy was marked by a notable change in the relationship between Sara and me. As I described earlier, this change was most obvious following Sara's suicide attempt, but the change had probably started some time before. At times our discussion had a very clear parent-child quality in which, on a few occasions, I was quite directive. At one point I became increasingly concerned about Sara's weight loss, and when she expressed reluctance to be weighed, I insisted that I had to know her weight. She complied reluctantly and was clearly angry that I was treating her like a little child. Afterward, she was able to reflect on the mixture of anger and relief she had felt and also on how difficult it was for her to think about herself as a child, teenager, or adult.

During this period I had little contact with James, apart from one family meeting. Jane, however, remained very much in the picture even after I stopped seeing James and her regularly. She would telephone from time to time and, on several occasions, asked to see me. She also would be very much involved at times of crisis. My perception was that although the relationship between Jane and James was growing closer, James continued, in other ways, to be outside the family. His position was mirrored by Sara, who was living away from home but spending most of her spare time with the family.

The greater flexibility of relationships within the family became most evident during the last phase of the therapy, which was marked by James seeking treatment for his alcohol problems and by Jane being able to think more about her own needs. With the prospect that Sara's anorexia might be a thing of the past, her poor relationship with James became more central. It seemed to the family as if this last piece of the jigsaw puzzle needed to be put into place so they could all move on. It was as if everything had been frozen in time; if James could convince Sara that he regretted having let her down and if she could forgive him, they could restart their lives where they had left off.

There was a very striking difference at this time between what Sara was like when I saw her on her own and how she was when I saw her together with her family. In individual sessions she could be a mature nineteen-year-old as well as a vulnerable little girl. With the prospect of therapy coming to an end, both sides of her became more prominent; we talked a lot about how both were important parts of herself and how they could co-exist. In the family meetings, however, Sara would show only one side of herself. She would sit to one side and talk very little, giving the impression of an angry, truculent child. On occasions she would storm out of the room, shouting that she could not bear it anymore. Later Sara would explain to me that she did not feel safe to be herself in the family meetings because she was not sure I was on her side.

I understood her to mean that she was afraid to show her vulnerability because she was unsure how her family, especially her father, would respond. It was not immediately clear why she should also stop from showing her more mature side. It seemed that the whole family had moved on and that all of them wanted to find a way of putting the pain and the distress behind them. They showed a great deal of awareness of the issues that concerned them and also a willingness to listen to one another. I was sure that Sara knew she would be taken seriously. Perhaps it was precisely this knowledge that was making things so difficult. The greater the possibility that Sara could move on and have an adult relationship with both her parents, the less there was space to show how vulnerable she also still felt at times. In relationship to James, growing up seemed to mean that she might never have the opportunity to experience her father as someone who could look after her and protect her. In one of the final family meetings, James expressed his sense that they were all ready to move on and yet feeling stuck: "It is like being at crossroads with all the lights on green and no one is quite sure who should go first."

In coming to the end of my account, I am aware of all that remains unsaid. This story is only one of a number that could have been written; each member of the family has his or her own story and each is different. Perhaps the one version of the story that has received the least attention is James's account. In many ways his addiction to alcohol bears important similarities to Sara's addiction to starvation. His self-blame and both Sara's and Jane's hurt at being let down have made it difficult to hear his part of the story in full.

I have also only touched on the role of other important people in Sara's life. Over the course of her illness, Sara developed and maintained a number of important relationships with people who had tried to help her; besides relationships with her mother and me, they were with the family doctor, a pastoral counselor, a doctor who had looked after her during her stay in hospital, and a nurse from the same hospital. Sara experienced all these caring relationships as *dependable*, but they also made her feel *dependent*. These important relationships provided crucial support for Sara and her family; at times, there also was a danger in that these relationship would make it difficult for Sara to move on.

I started this account by saying that this is an unfinished story, and I want to end on the same note. The incompleteness is not just in the fact that the therapy still has some sessions ahead or that a number of unresolved issues still remain. I do not know what will happen in the remaining sessions; but more important, I cannot know how things will continue after the therapy has ended. Although it would be nice to finish the story by saying how all the main issues have been resolved and that Sara is now free to move on to the next phase of her life, I would give the wrong impression of what psychotherapy has to offer. Psychotherapy is one chapter in people's lives that may offer them new resources and help them find new choices in life.

Sara is about to embark on a new chapter in her life. She is starting her nursing training, which will entail moving completely away from home. She is excited by this prospect, but she also fears how well she will cope. Anorexia is not yet completely a thing of the past, but it does not rule her life in the way it used to. It has left some unresolved issues for her in how she feels about herself and her family. Jane and James, like all parents whose children are about to launch themselves into the world, share the excitement and the anxieties that Sara has. Like other parents, they are more likely to focus on the risks than Sara herself does. Continued difficulties between Sara and James, in addition, make it uncertain whether Sara can use their home as a secure base to which she can return when she needs to. Robert, whose relationship with Sara has become increasingly strong, is an important counterbalance, sharing with Sara some of the difficulties he had to overcome when he left home to go to university but also just being around to have an uncomplicated good time with Sara. The crucial point is that Sara and her family now have choices of where to go next. Although they may not know what the future holds, it is no longer an uncertainty that stops them from moving on.

## NOTES

P. 220, *A number of accounts in the family therapy literature of the "typical" anorexic (or "psychosomatic" family):* Minuchin, S., Rosman, B., & Baker, L. (1978). *Psychosomatic families: Anorexia nervosa in context.* Cambridge, MA: Harvard University Press; Selvini-Palazzoli, M. (1974). *Self starvation: From the intrapsychic to the transpersonal approach to anorexia nervosa.* London: Chaucer.

P. 220, *The evidence for a specific family constellation in anorexia nervosa:* Eisler, I. (1994). Family models of eating disorders. In G. I. Szmukler, C. Dare, & J. Treasure (Eds.), *Eating disorders: Handbook of theory, treatment, and research* (pp. 155–176). New York: Wiley.

P. 220, *Our own controlled treatment studies have shown:* Dare, C., Eisler, I., Colahan, M., Crowther, C., Senior, R., & Asen, D. (1995). The listening heart and the chi square: Clinical and empirical perceptions in the family therapy of anorexia nervosa. *Journal of Family Therapy, 17*(1), 31–57.

P. 221, *These transition points in the family life cycle are points of vulnerability:* Carter, E., & McGoldrick, M. (1989). *The changing family life cycle: A framework for family therapy.* Needham Heights, MA: Allyn & Bacon.

P. 222, *I will briefly describe the model of treatment:* Dare, C., Eisler, I., Russell, G.F.M., & Szmukler, G. (1990). The clinical and theoretical impact of a controlled trial of family therapy in anorexia nervosa. *Journal of Family and Marital Therapy, 16*(1), 39–57; Eisler, I. (1993). Family therapy for anorexia nervosa. In S. Moorey & M. Hodes (Eds.), *Psychological treatments in human disease and illness* (pp. 209–222). London: Gaskill.

P. 222, *the conceptual framework that informs our treatment approach:* Eisler, I. (1993). Families, family therapy, and psychosomatic illness. In S. Moorey & M. Hodes (Eds.), *Psychological treatments in human disease and illness* (pp. 46–62). London: Gaskill.

P. 222, *quote from Elsa Jones:* Jones, E. (1993). *Family systems therapy.* New York: Wiley, p. 2.

P. 225, *young anorexics who had received family therapy in a general practice setting:* Mayer, R. D. (1994). *Family therapy in the treatment of eating disorders in general practice.* Unpublished master's thesis, University of London.

P. 256, *it is no longer an uncertainty that stops them from moving on:* Mason, B. (1993). Towards positions of safe uncertainty. *Human Systems, 4*(3,4), 189–200.

# TREATMENT OF A PATIENT WITH BULIMIA NERVOSA IN A MULTIGROUP INTENSIVE DAY HOSPITAL PROGRAM

## Allan S. Kaplan and Harold I. Spivak

Despite considerable research over the past decade, the optimum and most efficacious treatment for seriously ill treatment-resistant patients with bulimia nervosa remains not well defined and somewhat contentious. The search for innovative approaches to the management of these intractable patients is ongoing. In 1985, I (Kaplan) with my collaborators, Dr. Paul Garfinkel and Dr. Niva Piran, conceptualized and initiated the Day Hospital Group Therapy Program (DHP) for eating disorders at The Toronto Hospital. We felt it represented an innovative, cost-effective approach to the treatment of such patients. We set up the program to provide integrative, intensive, outpatient care in a day hospital setting through the cumulative effects of group psychotherapy, nutritional rehabilitation, family therapy, and where indicated, pharmacotherapy. In this chapter, we briefly describe this program and review the advantages and disadvantages, as well as the indications and contraindications, of such an approach for the treatment of bulimia nervosa. We then detail the treatment of a patient with bulimia nervosa who successfully completed the program.

# DESCRIPTION OF THE PROGRAM

The DHP operates five days a week, 8 hours a day, treating a maximum of twelve patients at a time for between six and fourteen weeks duration (see Table 8.1). The average length of stay for a patient with bulimia nervosa is ten weeks. The program is staffed by a multidisciplinary team consisting of a full-time psychologist, psychometrist, occupational therapist, nutritionist, social worker, and two nurses, as well as a part-time psychiatrist. The goals of the program are threefold:

1. The normalization of the disturbed eating behavior, with the stated objective clearly being the complete cessation of bingeing, purging, and other behaviors aimed at weight control
2. Nutritional rehabilitation through adequate caloric intake and, where indicated, weight gain
3. The identification of psychological processes that perpetuate the eating disorder, as well as underlie its genesis

The DHP integrates biological, psychological, and sociocultural interventions. The biological treatment consists of a thorough medical examination, including a physical examination and laboratory investigations aimed at reversing the medical sequelae of starvation, bingeing, and purging. Pharmacotherapy, most commonly antidepressant drugs, is prescribed to approximately half the patients in order to stabilize mood or is prescribed as an anti-bulimic agent to facilitate a cessation of binge eating. Medications are also prescribed to alleviate gastrointestinal symptoms (for example, agents that promote stomach emptying), to reduce anxiety prior to meals, and to relieve the sleep disturbance that often accompanies disordered eating and starvation. Nutritional rehabilitation is achieved through the prescription of a balanced meal plan—between 1,800 and 3,000 calories per day, depending on the need for weight maintenance or weight gain, spread over three meals and two snacks—that incorporates phobic foods and high-calorie binge foods.

**Table 8.1**
**Weekly Schedule for Day Hospital Program**

| Monday | Tuesday | Wednesday | Thursday | Friday |
|---|---|---|---|---|
| 10:00 - 11:30 Leisure & Time Management | 9:30 - 10:30 Food Shopping | 10:00 - 11:00 Weigh Group | | |
| | 10:30 - 12:00 Body Image Group | | | |
| 11:30 - 12:00 Community Meeting | | 11:00 - 12:00 Symptom Strategy Group | 11:30 - 12:00 Cooking | 11:00 - 12:00 Menus |
| 12:00 - 1:00 Lunch 12:00 - 1:15 Lunch Outing | 12:00 - 1:00 Lunch | 12:00 - 1:00 Lunch | 12:00 - 1:00 Lunch | 12:00 - 1:00 Lunch |
| 1:00 - 1:30 Free Time | 1:00 - 1:30 Community Meeting | 1:00 - 1:30 Community Meeting | 1:00 - 1:30 Community Meeting | 1:00 - 2:00 DEBQ Feedback |
| 1:30 - 3:00 Symptom Strategy Group | 1:30 - 1:50 Free Time | 1:40 - 3:00 Family Relations Group | 1:35 - 2:40 Relationship Group | 2:00 - 2:45 Good-Bye Group/ Education Group |
| | 1:50 - 3:00 Gym | | | |
| 3:00 - 3:30 Snack | 3:00 - 3:30 Snack | 3:00 - 3:30 Snack | 3:00 - 3:30 Snack | 2:45 - 3:30 Snack Outing |
| 3:30 - 5:00 Creative Art Group | 3:30 - 4:45 Sexuality Group | 3:30 - 4:30 Assertion Group | 3:30 - 4:00 Free Time | 3:30 - 5:00 Leisure & Time Management |
| | 4:45 - 5:00 Free Time | 4:30 - 5:00 Free Time/ Cooking | 4:00 - 5:00 Nutrition Group | |
| 5:00 - 6:15 Dinner DEBQ Evening Planning | 5:00 - 6:15 Dinner DEBQ Evening Planning | 5:00 - 6:15 Dinner DEBQ Evening Planning | 5:00 - 6:15 Dinner DEBQ Evening Planning | 5:00 - 6:15 Dinner DEBQ Evening Planning |

*NOTE*: DEBQ = Daily Eating Behavior Questionnaire
*SOURCE*: Harper-Giuffre, H., & MacKenzie, K. R. (Eds.). (1992).
*Group psychotherapy for the eating disorders.* Washington, DC:American
Psychiatric Press. Used by permission.

The psychological treatment consists of intensive group psychotherapy that includes psychoeducational, cognitive-behavioral, interpersonal, and psychodynamic paradigms. The group experiences are divided between those that deal directly with disturbed attitudes and behaviors around eating and weight and those that deal with more general areas of psychopathology. The groups that focus on eating and weight-related symptoms include the following:

- Supervised meals, including lunch, afternoon snack, and dinner followed by after-meal discussion (Patients are expected to eat breakfast on their own, as well as an evening snack, which the program provides when patients leave after dinner)
- Supervised meal outings
- Supervised cooking experiences
- Self-monitoring and feedback through the use of a diary, the daily eating behavior questionnaire (the DEBQ)
- Supervised exercise groups
- Weigh Group
- Nutrition Group
- Body Image Group

Groups that focus on non-eating-related areas include the following:

- Relationship Group
- Family Relations Group
- Assertiveness Training Group
- Leisure and Time Management Group
- Sexuality Group
- Community Meetings

All patients attend all groups, and each group is led by two staff. Most groups are semistructured in that they have an educational component, a specific focus, and follow a general outline. In the DHP, no individual therapy is provided, and patients meet with staff outside the therapy group only for family therapy, medical assessments, and psychological testing. The family treatment focuses primarily on the education of parents, siblings, spouses, or significant others in order to facilitate symptoms separation—that is, separating eating symptoms from other aspects of the relationship.

Sociocultural interventions in the DHP include providing vocational counseling, arranging supportive housing, and establishing community supports. We have established a good working relationship with several vocational rehabilitation agencies and one or two group homes, although we continue the struggle to find appropriate housing for our patients.

Over the years, we have established some specific indications and contraindications to treatment in this program. All patients must meet criteria for a *DSM-III-R* (now *DSM-IV*) eating disorder. All patients must have had some previous outpatient treatment that failed to significantly affect their eating behavior. Patients and family members have to be motivated to become involved in an intensive treatment program with the agreed-on expectation of symptomatic change, as opposed to only psychological understanding without behavioral change. The patient has to demonstrate to us some capacity, however limited, to relate in a group setting.

There are relatively few contraindications for involvement in our program. These include the following:

- Acute medical risk that precludes out-of-hospital care (such as severe emaciation or cardiovascular or gastrointestinal complications requiring hospitalization)

- Acute suicide risk

- Severe drug abuse that clearly interferes with normalization of weight, appetite, and eating

# ADVANTAGES AND DISADVANTAGES OF DAY HOSPITAL GROUP TREATMENT

Treating a patient with bulimia nervosa in a program such as ours has clinical as well as financial advantages. The advantages relate to the two unique aspects of the program: (1) the treatment of seriously ill bulimics as outpatients and (2) the treatment of such patients exclusively in groups.

## Clinical Advantages

The clinical advantages of outpatient treatment, compared with inpatient care, are clear. The in-hospital treatment of bulimic as well as anorexic patients is difficult and taxing for both staff and patients. Such patients often have serious underlying character pathology that manifests itself during hospitalization through the development of severe regression, hostile dependency, unstable mood, and impulsive behavior, including self-harm. Such patients often perceive external control as punitive and are compelled to oppose therapeutic maneuvers by splitting staff, superficially complying but continuing to secretly adhere to distorted attitudes and beliefs while engaging in illness-related behaviors. Because of these factors, the inpatient treatment of eating disorders requires a high staff-patient ratio of specially trained professionals who are required to maintain a high level of vigilance. This requirement results in expensive and, at times, inefficient use of highly trained personnel and facilities.

The outpatient aspect of our program addresses several of these difficulties that occur during inpatient treatment. Regression and dependency are minimized as patients have to maintain themselves in a functioning state outside the hospital during intensive outpatient treatment. This approach promotes autonomy and a generalization of newly acquired tools to regulate eating behavior. As a result, it becomes easier for the patients to begin the process of internal integration of external controls. Because patients are not totally externally controlled, there is less need to oppose treatment and a greater likelihood that such treatment will be perceived empathically, rather than punitively. Day hospital treatment is less psychosocially disruptive than inpatient care. In addition, it forces the patient to actively confront disturbed areas of functioning, such as peer and family relationships, while attempting to normalize eating and weight. Such disturbed areas often act as significant perpetuators of the illness and are commonly denied or go unrecognized as playing a role in the eating disorder.

The clinical advantages of group treatment have become clear to us over time and are compelling. Group treatment provides an atmosphere of mutual support while increasing the power of therapeutic intervention through group confrontation and pressure. Regression and dependency are controlled as the intensity of relating is diffused by the presence of group interaction. The sense of isolation that develops as a result of the disturbed eating pattern is alleviated by mutual sharing of what has previously been felt to be humiliating and degrading behaviors. This sharing helps patients "own" their illness, rather than it being denied and dissociated.

## Financial Advantages

Outpatient treatment in a group format has financial benefits. The outpatient component alleviates the need for hospital beds and is cost-effective in that resources are directed at providing treatment, rather than at housing patients. The group format allows greater availability of treatment and flexibility in patient numbers. Many patients can be treated without necessarily requiring more facilities or staff.

At The Toronto Hospital, the cost of a one-night inpatient stay on the Eating Disorder Unit is estimated to be $710.00 for a Canadian resident, compared with $285.00 for one day of day treatment. All health care in Canada is government financed and incurs no direct cost to the patient. Health care costs account, in part, for the higher tax structure in Canada, compared with in the United States; however, the Day Hospital Program is fully financed through a grant from the Community Mental Health Branch of the Ministry of Health of Ontario. At this time, no system in Ontario limits the amount of care that can be provided for any patient or illness, as occurs in the United States, with its managed care systems. The Ontario government has set ceilings on the earnings of physicians, however, and private billing of patients is illegal.

We would now like to illustrate some of the issues mentioned above by describing the case of a patient with bulimia nervosa who successfully completed the Day Hospital Treatment Program.

## THE CASE OF SUE

Sue was initially assessed for the DHP in late winter of 1993. At that time, she was an eighteen-year-old single high school student who lived on her own and supported herself by welfare. She presented with a five-year history of extreme dieting behavior, bingeing and vomiting episodes, and complete preoccupation with weight and shape issues.

Sue began dieting at age thirteen when, encouraged by her mother, she entered a Weight Watchers program. At that time, she weighed 150 pounds at a height of five feet six inches. She lost ten pounds in her first year of dieting and then, following a move to a new high school, began following a more extreme diet in order to feel more popular. She described her dieting by age fifteen as "out of control"; she began bingeing and vomiting soon thereafter. Her weight at the time of assessment was 122 pounds, which represents 94 percent of chart average weight and corresponds to a body mass index of twenty-three (BMI = kilograms/meter$^2$, healthy range twenty to twenty-five). Her heaviest weight had been 150 pounds at age thirteen, when she began menstruating; her lowest weight had been 112 pounds at age fifteen.

Sue reported that, prior to treatment, she was bingeing and vomiting four to six times daily; on some occasions, however, she binged and vomited as often as ten times per day. Bingeing would always be followed by self-induced vomiting, but sometimes she would vomit even after small meals or snacks. A typical binge consisted of ingesting large amounts of high-calorie food rich in carbohydrates and fat and was associated with a feeling of being "out of control" during the binge. She was unclear what triggered her bingeing and felt that the bingeing was a "habit" and "like an addiction." She denied abusing laxatives, diuretics, diet pills, thyroid medication, or ipecac. She exercised twice a week, engaging in two hours of strenuous aerobic activity. When she wasn't bingeing, her eating behavior was characterized by severe caloric restriction and avoidance of a long list of phobic foods. Typically, she would eat no breakfast, have a restricted lunch, and then would begin bingeing in the evening. Sue described feeling completely preoccupied by food and weight issues, stating that her entire life felt "dominated by food."

In the months before her initial evaluation for the program, Sue complained of numerous physical symptoms, including extreme fatigue, dry skin, hair loss, light-headedness, palpitations, abdominal pain, and constipation. At various times, she had been told she was mildly anemic (low hemoglobin) and hypokalemic (low in potassium); she was menstruating at the time she was first seen. Sue also complained of considerable mood lability and experienced periods of depression and irritability. During these times she felt hopeless about her life, discouraged, and often very angry. When she was first seen, there were no neurovegetative symptoms to suggest a comorbid major depression, nor did she display suicidal ideation. She did feel quite isolated and was devoting all of her energy to her schoolwork and to coping with her eating disorder. She also described discrete episodes of depression during her teenage years associated with significant sleep disturbance, and she reported one attempted suicide by overdosing on sleeping medication when she was fifteen.

Sue's past psychiatric treatment for her eating disorder was significant. It included two admissions to specialized eating disorder psychiatric inpatient units, a full year of once-weekly psychotherapy, and a therapeutic trial of Prozac (sixty milligrams for three months)—all of which she found unhelpful in alleviating her symptoms. In addition, she had been hospitalized in a crisis unit at a children's hospital following her overdose.

### History

Sue's medical history is noteworthy and significant. She was born with exstrophy of the bladder. She had needed approximately thirty surgical procedures during her childhood to correct this problem, including plastic surgery necessitating the removal of her navel. She was left with residual medical problems from these operations, including frequent episodes of pyelonephritis and kidney stones. She also had to catheterize herself in order to void and took Septra, an antibiotic, continually. Moreover, she developed significant hearing loss due to intensive antibiotic treatment for kidney infections and wore bilateral hearing aids. These experiences left her with a mistrust of physicians and her own body.

Sue's family psychiatric history included a history of depression in her mother and depression and alcoholism in two uncles, one of whom committed suicide. She believed that her mother suffered from bulimia in the past.

Sue was the older of two children born to a middle-class family in Toronto. Her parents had divorced when she was in her early teens. Her father had since remarried, and Sue had a distant but friendly relationship with her stepmother. Her younger brother attended university at age twenty-four. She was not close to him. Her mother was a forty-five-year-old overweight nurse described by Sue as a chronic dieter who emphasized weight and shape issues in the home.

During Sue's childhood, her mother was chronically depressed and often unable to be nurturing or supportive. Her mother often criticized Sue, calling her "stupid" or commenting negatively on her appearance. She pushed Sue to perform in all areas; she even prodded her daughter into modeling as a young adolescent. On one occasion, the mother attempted suicide after physically assaulting Sue. Sue now characterized their relationship as close but tense; she felt that her mother had "mellowed" somewhat.

Sue's father was a forty-seven-year-old vice president of a major company. He was described as a responsible, intelligent man who was also very controlling and who overemphasized academic achievement. Sue saw him irregularly and characterized her relationship with him as distant. She remembered her parents fighting constantly and saw no evidence of affection between them. Her parents divorced when she was twelve after living separately for several years. Sue remembered feeling saddened by her parents' separation and often thinking her medical problems caused their breakup. During her teens she lived with each parent for a few years but went to live at a group home for one year at age sixteen because of increasing conflict, first with her mother and then with her stepmother. She finally moved out of her father's home and into her own apartment shortly after her seventeenth birthday.

Sue described herself as a shy but fun-loving child. She said that most of her early childhood memories were dominated by memories of medical problems related to her bladder abnormality. Her childhood was marred by frequent hospitalizations, painful operations, and many months away from school. From an early age, she felt betrayed by her body and experienced it as being out of her control. She felt extremely bitter about how she was treated in hospital by medical staff whom she experienced as abusive and uncaring. Following her initial operation, she was left with many physical problems; she had multiple surgical scars over her abdomen, a hearing impairment, and speech difficulties. She had to wear diapers until the age of nine. These physical disabilities left her feeling self-conscious about her body, extremely ashamed, and different from other children. In grade school she was often subjected to teasing from other children and felt very isolated and alone. Despite these problems, she was a good student in school and managed to form a few close relationships.

She described her secondary school years as difficult and stressful. She often felt that she didn't fit in and alternated between wanting to conform and indifference. Following a move to a new school in eighth grade, she began to feel more self-conscious about her body and initiated her dieting behavior in order to feel more attractive. Pressures to diet were also intensified by the modeling career—suggested by her mother—at which she was quite successful over a two-year period. Unfortunately, this experience only made her more self-conscious of her body. She continued to be a good student in high school despite prolonged absences caused by her eating disorder. With the exception of the summer when she was sixteen, during which she drank excessively, she managed to avoid significant alcohol- or drug-related problems.

Sue began dating at age fifteen and became sexually active at age sixteen. During the height of her modeling career, she entered her first serious relationship with an older man who used cocaine regularly. This relationship became physically and sexually abusive, and she described an incident when her boyfriend raped her. In addition, she had distinct memories of her mother's boyfriend, while under the influence of alcohol, fondling her on several occasions when she was nine. She currently found relating physically with men difficult as she felt men were attracted to her initially only because of her pretty face and nice figure but became repulsed when they saw her disfigured abdomen.

Mental status examination revealed an attractive woman wearing a sweatshirt, jeans, and bilateral hearing aids. She had evidence of swollen salivary glands on both sides of her jaw. She told her history clearly and coherently. Her affect was anxious, with some underlying anger. She openly stated her mistrust of doctors. Her thoughts were preoccupied with wanting to recover from her eating disorder, feeling that this problem interfered with everything she wanted to do in her life. She appeared to be intelligent and had some capacity for psychological understanding of her problem.

Diagnostically, Sue clearly had severe bulimia nervosa for four-and-a-half years and had been resistant to previous inpatient, outpatient, and drug therapies. She also had evidence of episodes of major depression in the past. She struggled with difficulties related to issues of control, her sense of identity, body image, regulation of her mood and self-esteem, and her sexuality. She had a family history of depression and substance abuse, was neglected emotionally as a young child, and then became parentified when she was expected to take care of a depressed, ineffectual mother. The combination of multiple surgical assaults on her body, significant childhood and adolescent sexual abuse, and guilt in thinking that her medical problems were responsible for her parents' breakup all contributed to her feeling alienated from and enraged at her body. Being forced into a modeling career only compounded the family's and larger society's preoccupation with weight and shape and contributed further to her viewing her body as a hated object to be controlled.

### Initial Assessment

Despite her significant difficulties, I (Kaplan) was struck at the first interview more by Sue's strength than her difficulties. She came across as very bright and had been successful academically at school. She had managed to negotiate a sense of independence from a neglectful father and demanding mother and had maintained some close, trusting relationships with friends. Despite her stated mistrust of doctors, she was forthright and honest with me in telling her story, and she seemed genuinely motivated to get well.

I (Kaplan) decided that a course of day hospital treatment was preferable to another inpatient stay. Sue had despised the previous inpatient psychiatric treatments as they brought back bad memories of her childhood surgeries, which she saw as medically oriented, cruel, and controlling. She valued her independence and wanted to stay connected to her network of friends. They did not know of her bulimia, however, so I thought group interaction and support would go a long way toward alleviating the sense of isolation she felt with her symptoms. I thought she would find the DHP less threatening because it was less "medically oriented" than her inpatient treatments, with a clear multidisciplinary approach and a focus on group psychotherapy.

Her blood work at the time of the initial assessment revealed normal electrolytes, normal kidney function, and slightly lowered hemoglobin and white blood count. Her electrocardiogram was normal except for a bradycardia of forty-five.

Despite the fact that Sue could have had her preadmission assessment with the day hospital team a few weeks after her initial interview, she wished to finish her school year first and therefore begin treatment in late spring, planning to spend part of the summer in treatment. She therefore was seen for her preadmission assessment late in March, and an admission date was set for the first week of April. At this meeting, the details of the program were explained to her, and she met with all members of the treatment team. She had three concerns about her treatment in the day hospital program. The first related to her meal plan and the amount of calories (two thousand per day) she was expected to eat; she feared that she would gain a great deal of weight on this number of calories. Although she was told that weight gain was not a specific goal of her treatment, she was reminded that she had been significantly heavier prior to the onset of her dieting and that she may have to gain some weight over the course of her treatment. Her second concern related to the bathrooms being locked except half an hour before meals and snacks. She stated that because of her bladder problems, she often had to urinate several times per day and had difficulty holding in her urine for long periods of time. She was reassured when we pointed out that the bathrooms were locked to help people control their urges to purge and to increase the sense of safety on the unit and that she would have at least three opportunities each day to use the washroom. Finally, she had concerns about her family's involvement with the program. Although she was invited to bring either or both parents to the preadmission meeting, she elected not to bring either. It was agreed that separate meetings with her mother and father and stepmother would be set up during her first week of treatment.

In addition, she underwent psychological testing prior to admission. This testing included the Eating Disorders Examination, the Eating Disorder Inventory, the Beck Depression Inventory, the Rosenberg Self Esteem Questionnaire, the Weissman Social Adjustment Scale, and the Structured Clinical Interview for *DSM-III-R* (SCID). She demonstrated the typical areas of disturbance for women with eating disorders. She had no other concurrent comorbid diagnoses on the SCID but met past criteria for major depression.

### Week One

Sue's first week in the program was difficult. She was reluctant to share with the group the nature of her medical problems because she felt embarrassed by them. She did manage, with difficulty, to control her urges to urinate. In group treatment, she maintained a safe distance from most of the other members, although she did participate in the groups that were mostly educational.

Sue found two of the groups particularly disturbing in her first week. The discussion of the Sexuality Group focused on sexually abusive experiences of the members in the group and how these experiences contributed to their eating disorder, as well as practical ways for the women in the group to prevent such experiences from recurring. This discussion brought back memories of Sue having been raped. She found herself experiencing flashbacks in the evenings following the group. In addition, she had a difficult time with the Body Image Group, which focused on images and feelings about her body. Through guided imagery and relaxation techniques, she became more aware of her anger at what had happened to her body and also of some sadness over never having been able to feel normal. This awareness intensified her urges to binge during the program. In her first week, she binged and vomited on three evenings and four times each day on the weekend. She felt guilty for not following the meal plan, for having no regular meals on the weekend, and for skipping her evening snacks on five of her first seven nights.

During the first week, Sue had her first family meeting with her mother and our family therapist. She found this session very stressful and became aware of increasing urges to binge during and after the meeting. The focus of the meeting was the mother's overconcern with Sue's medical problems and her abandonment of Sue's emotional needs.

Sue's goals for the second week were to stick more closely to the meal plan and to begin to verbalize her feelings more clearly to the group.

### Week Two

Sue continued to struggle with her eating during the second week, although she managed to stick more closely to the meal plan, having all of her evening snacks during this week and missing only three meals on the weekend. She reduced her bingeing and vomiting to twice during the week and twice on the weekend. In addition, she was able to connect her bingeing and vomiting on the weekend to contact she had with her mother around mealtimes.

Sue began to feel more comfortable with other members of the group, connecting specifically with two individuals who were her own age and whose parents had also split up during their teenage years. In particular, one of these members she found very supportive. This group member had struggled throughout most of her life with diabetes and had similar feelings to Sue about her illness and the doctors who treated her.

During the Feedback Group, patients submitted their weekly written diaries to staff, who provided feedback to them about their progress that week. Sue was praised in this group for increasing her intake of food and for using strategies such as distraction and delay in order to complete her meals and to tolerate feelings of fullness. It was also noted, however, that she had binged and vomited two times during the week but had written very little in her Daily Eating Behavior Questionnaire (DEBQ) about what had triggered these behaviors.

Sue was unsure what had led to these urges, except to explain that impulses to binge had been mounting during the week and that she thought she "had an addiction to bingeing." This notion led to a general discussion among group members about the common triggers for binge episodes. Several senior group members thought that strong emotions such as anger, sadness, or loneliness might lead them to binge. Sue did remember that one episode of bingeing occurred after speaking with her mother about the DHP. During that conversation, she sensed that her mother was somewhat indifferent to her progress in the treatment; Sue associated this response with early memories of her mother's unavailability during times when she was ill. She was able to say that this left her feeling depressed, angry, and as if her mother had abandoned her. Sue also recalled that she was alone following this phone call and had several hours before going to bed. She was unsure how these feelings had led to her bingeing. A group leader emphasized that Sue could not hope to fully understand her behaviors until she had completely stopped them and that this must be the focus for her in the program. Several group members offered advice about how to better structure her time in the evenings.

### Week Three

During her third week on the program, Sue's eating improved to the point where she had all of her meals and snacks, with some mild restriction over the weekend and with no episodes of bingeing and vomiting. At the Community Meetings all week, however, despite receiving praise for her accomplishments, she appeared withdrawn, preoccupied, and sullen. When concern was expressed by staff about her mood, Sue responded with terse answers or sarcasm. With firmer confrontation, however, she acknowledged that she was feeling "completely out of control" and was experiencing intense mood swings. The staff urged her not to turn away from these feelings but to try to understand them by verbalizing them to the group, who could help her comprehend what was happening now. It was also suggested to her that feeling out of control emotionally was quite common after stopping bingeing and vomiting.

During Body Image Group this third week, Sue talked about her early experiences of feeling out of control when she recounted how betrayed she had felt by her body. She recalled feeling that her body was defective and incomplete. She tearfully remembered an experience when she was in hospital and was given an intravenous needle in front of a group of doctors and medical students. During this experience, most of her body was exposed and she could not cover herself because her hands were tied down. She remembered feeling that her body was "the property of the doctors"—one of many episodes that left her feeling invaded and violated by medical staff. During Sexuality Group, Sue revealed for the first time the sexual abuse by her mother's boyfriend. She got much support for this revelation. In Family Relations Group, she talked about her sense of insecurity caused by her parents' divorce.

Sue began to realize that several childhood events had contributed to her feeling that her personal boundaries and bodily integrity were outside her control. Other members of the group whose parents had split up suggested that her eating disorder was an attempt to adapt to these experiences by rigidly controlling her intake of food and altering her shape and weight. The group leaders then suggested that Sue begin to explore those areas in her life that she could have control over, including career choices and interpersonal relationships. This advice made her feel somewhat more hopeful that she could organize and understand her past experiences and move forward. Most of the time during this third week, however, she remained discouraged and disconsolate, feeling overwhelmed by her anger and sadness.

Despite the fact that she had gained only two pounds in the three weeks, Sue felt increasingly fat and out of control. By the end of the third week, we were concerned about her increasing depression. At the last Community Meeting of the week, she was asked about thoughts related to self-harm; she admitted to having these but denied any specific plans. The two group members she was closest to gave her their phone numbers to call over the weekend and made plans to see her on both Saturday and Sunday. We also reinforced the need for her to go to the hospital emergency room if urges to hurt herself increased.

### Week Four

Immobilized by her depression, Sue had a very difficult weekend. She stayed in her apartment all the time, ate very little, and became increasingly preoccupied with suicidal thoughts. The two members of the group did spend time with her; eventually, they took her to the emergency room on Saturday evening when she began talking about jumping off her balcony. An assessment was done, and staff there felt she was safe to return home. Sue reported on Monday morning that she felt overwhelmed by her depression; she attributed much of the depression to a sense of increasing alienation from her mother and to feelings about her body that had surfaced recently.

We (Spivak and a nurse) met with Sue individually on Monday after Community Meeting and reviewed her mental status. We found her to be significantly depressed, with decreased appetite, increased sleeping, and an increased sense of hopelessness. We proposed starting an antidepressant, and she agreed to take sertraline (fifty milligrams per day) after we reassured her that it would not lead to weight gain. Several other people in the group were taking the same medication, and we encouraged her to speak with them about their experiences taking this medication. We also mentioned that the drug could help control her urges to binge. We told her she might need to take as much as two hundred milligrams to get maximum benefit.

Most of the rest of the fourth week was focused on encouraging Sue to reach out for support from the group while maintaining and consolidating the gains she had made with her bulimic symptoms. Toward the end of the week, some members of the group began to experience frustration around her depression and her somewhat angry stance toward the members of the group when they tried to reach out to her.

After lunch on Friday, Sue impulsively left the unit but returned for supper, stating that she had needed "space for herself" and that she had gone to another washroom in the hospital to vomit. We attempted to help her recognize the effect of leaving the group and of refusing the group member's support: the potential that they would distance themselves from her and leave her alone without support.

Sue also had found the hospitalization that week of a co-member of the group upsetting. This patient had cut her wrists on Wednesday afternoon, following Weigh Group when she found out she had gained over two kilograms during the week. This upset contributed to Sue's leaving the unit to vomit and to her feeling even more hopeless, believing that she, too, would end up in the hospital.

In addition to vomiting on Friday after lunch, Sue binged and vomited twice during the week—once Wednesday night after the co-member had cut her wrists, and another time Tuesday evening in anticipation of a meeting with her mother on Thursday. With the group's help, Sue recognized that the anticipation of the meeting with the mother made her feel extremely anxious because the mother had not understood Sue's recent depression; she had made Sue feel bad for allowing it to happen.

### Week Five

Sue had a noteworthy fifth week. She began Monday morning by stating she had felt unwell throughout most of the weekend and had developed a fever of 40°C (104°F) on Sunday night. She complained of more frequent urges to urinate and had abdominal pain and nausea. She also revealed to me (Spivak) on Monday morning at Community Meeting that she had stopped taking her Septra during the second week of the program for reasons she could not verbalize. Sue was taken to the emergency room immediately after she developed rigors and chills during lunch and was seen there by a resident from internal medicine. After undergoing a complete blood count and urinalysis, the diagnosis of pyelonephritis, a kidney infection, was made, and she was admitted to the medical floor for intravenous antibiotic treatment. Sue remained in hospital for four days, during which she was visited by members of the group and by one of us (Spivak) to monitor her mental status. She was anxious to return to the program and did so on Friday morning. She was pleased to be discharged from the in-hospital treatment. While in the hospital, she realized that she had stopped her antibiotics because she was both angry at doctors and the hospital and fearful of being abandoned by her caregivers should she recover from her eating disorder.

Much of the time spent during Leisure and Time Management Group on Friday afternoon was focused on helping her structure her weekend to minimize the possibility of bingeing and vomiting, to help her follow her meal plan, and to help her take care of her physical health. She planned activities with members of the group for each evening of the weekend and agreed to see her mother only at non-mealtimes. She was also urged to continue taking her antibiotics and her sertraline, which she was tolerating well at two hundred milligrams per day.

## Week Six

During Community Meeting on Monday of week six, Sue reported only one episode of bingeing and vomiting on the weekend. She stated that her mood was somewhat brighter and that the inpatient stay had reminded her of how she had hated being helpless and dependant on doctors. She participated actively in all of the groups and in Sexuality Group began to reveal more details of the abusive experiences she had had with her first boyfriend. Working with the group, she began to realize that starving herself was a continuation of the abuse that her body had previously experienced. She became more determined to follow her meal plan and to not restrict. As she went through this sixth week without restricting, she felt increasingly fat and disgusting. She was struck, however, by the fact that she had actually lost a kilogram during the week. She realized in Weigh Group, with the help of other group members, that feeling fat was for her a way of dealing with all of the negative emotions she had experienced, especially anger and sadness.

She had two family meetings during this week. First, she met with her mother, and it became more obvious to her during this meeting that her mother was simply not able to offer her much emotional support. The mother continued to focus in the meeting on Sue's physical health and could not acknowledge the gains her daughter had made with her eating disorder. In addition, the mother seemed completely preoccupied with her own sadness and the difficulties she was experiencing in a new relationship with a boyfriend. She wanted Sue to arbitrate this relationship. After discussion with the family therapist and the other group members, Sue decided not to have any further meetings with her mother while in the program. The mother asked for a referral for herself for individual treatment, and the family therapist gave her several names of therapists to call.

Sue also met with her stepmother and father. This meeting was helpful in that it allowed both Sue's stepmother and father to verbalize their initial relief but later displeasure at Sue's having moved out of the house to live on her own. The stepmother also said that she often didn't feel that she could express her own opinions but that she had to support what her husband said. She stated that she thought this was changing. Sue, her father, and her stepmother felt that this was a helpful and productive meeting that opened lines of communication between them. They agreed to pursue ongoing family counseling and were given the name and number of our outpatient family therapist to contact after Sue left the program. They all agreed to have one final meeting during Sue's last week in the program.

Sue's mood during the week improved; she continued on sertraline, two hundred milligrams every day. She found herself socializing more with members of the group in the evenings as well.

### Week Seven

Sue had her best week in the program. She ate all of her meals except for a few snacks, and she was binge- and purge-free. She saw some of her friends from school in the evenings, and they commented on how much healthier and happier she looked. She began to think about leaving the program, and she asked the staff to consider a discharge date for her. By the end of the week, it was agreed that she would stay for two more weeks and that, in addition to consolidating the gains she had made with her eating, she would begin looking at what she would do during the remaining time in the summer and preparing herself for school in September. On Friday before leaving for the weekend, Sue met with the occupational therapist from our program, who gave her several ideas about where to look for a job after she left the program.

Sue also discussed aftercare with the staff and group members. She wanted to pursue individual therapy after she finished the day program and thought she could now work with her previous therapist in a more productive fashion. She was encouraged to phone her for an appointment. In addition, Sue was offered follow-up in our outpatient group program. She was encouraged to consider the outpatient group that focused on body image issues or the one that focused on relapse prevention or even both groups. She was given an appointment to discuss this with one of our outpatient group therapists.

Sue began to take a more active role in the groups, especially helping members who had just started the program. She said this was the first time in some while that she felt useful and effective in what she did. Feeling valued, she managed to remain free of symptoms throughout this week.

### Week Eight

Sue experienced one binge-and-vomit episode during the weekend, and the cause was clear to her when she returned on Monday. She stated she had woken up late Sunday morning, skipped her breakfast, and had a late lunch. She had no set plans except to see her mother at some point during the day. Her mother phoned her, and they agreed to meet for coffee in the late afternoon. This meeting upset her because her mother was even more preoccupied about her own problems and made no attempt to acknowledge the progress that Sue had made. After she returned home, she was overwhelmed with her anger around this meeting and found herself shortly thereafter bingeing and then vomiting. After not having done this for several weeks, she was struck by how awful it made her feel. When telling this to the group on Monday, she realized that this "slip" was a necessary reminder of how adversely the bingeing and vomiting affected her. She was able to get back on track for the rest of the week and stayed symptom-free.

Sue focused primarily this week on planning for her discharge. She requested a day off from the program on Friday to do some job hunting and was pleased when the staff and the other members of the group agreed this was a good idea. She continued to be a helpful group member to several patients who were struggling with their eating. They commented to her on how much she would be missed after she left the program. This comment touched her quite deeply, and she began to feel somewhat saddened by the prospect of leaving the group and the program.

In Relationship Group during this eighth week, she dealt more directly with me (Spivak) regarding her feelings about men—specifically, her mistrust of men and yet her desire to have their approval. She had an opportunity to work through some of these feelings in the "here and now" by talking about how she felt when I didn't seem to acknowledge her at Community Meetings; yet she felt very anxious when I sat near her or spoke with her in the Relationship Group. She recognized that these feelings originated, in part, from feelings she had about her father and was able to see how they had affected her relationships with men in the past. She was quite pleased with herself in recognizing these connections and also noticed that when she was through with the Relationship Group, she felt, for the first time in the program, "lighter" and that her feelings of self-disgust and fatness had abated somewhat.

### Week Nine

Sue had a difficult weekend emotionally in the last week of the program. She had an increase in her urges to binge during the weekend but managed to focus on the feelings that were underlying her urges to eat, rather than act on those feelings by bingeing. She reached out to her friends, spending most of Saturday with a group of school friends and Sunday afternoon with two members from the group. She also found that having a structured meal plan helped keep her safe and on track with her eating. She was also able to resist her mother's attempt to involve her in a meal on Sunday and felt good about that.

At Monday's Community Meeting, the two people she had spent time with on Sunday commented on how much they would miss having her around. One of these patients then stated that the feeling of abandonment she felt after leaving Sue on Sunday contributed to her bingeing most of Sunday night. Sue then felt enormously guilty and responsible for what had happened to this member of the group. The other group members, however, helped Sue work through these feelings and clarify the boundaries in her friendship with the members in the group. This experience helped Sue realize that she often had felt responsible for other people's difficulties and that this had led to her maintaining a distance in most of her relationships.

Throughout most of the week, Sue found it difficult to verbalize how she felt about leaving. She was able, however, to state
toward the end of the week that she was excited about the
prospect of getting on with her life but would miss the support
and camaraderie she found with other members in the program.
She stated she had plans to stay in touch with the members of
the group after she left.

Her last family meeting with her stepmother and father continued the pattern of the previous meeting in allowing issues to
be discussed more openly and not be avoided. Sue was able to
say how she had felt abandoned by her father for many years
after he left the family. Her father was able to comment on his
own guilt about having done that. The stepmother clarified her
need to be able to set limits with Sue when these were appropriate. All three of them felt comfortable about pursuing ongoing family therapy.

Sue also told members of the group that she had found a part-
time job for the rest of the summer, working as a tour guide for
a local tourist attraction. She was given a lot of positive feedback
about being able to look after herself in this way. She reported
that her mood and eating continued to be stable during her last
week despite times when she had strong urges to binge. Sue
stated she was sleeping well, felt physically healthier and
stronger, and had, in fact, begun to play tennis during the past
two weeks in the program even though she continued to feel fat
and ugly. In the Weigh Group, she was reminded that she had
gained only two-and-a-half kilograms during her entire nine-
week stay. This fact helped reassure her that her feelings of fatness did not reflect reality, but rather had to do with underlying
emotional issues. She was reassured somewhat when she was told
that feelings of fatness and issues around body image were generally the last symptoms to abate when people recover from an
eating disorder.

On Sue's last day, during her Good-Bye Group, members of
the group exchanged cards with her and enforced how helpful
she had been to them during her stay. After an emotional fare-

well, she left the program, having completed nine weeks of treatment, binge- and purge-free during the final two weeks. Her mood was stable on two hundred milligrams of sertraline and her bladder difficulties were under control with Septra.

Prior to leaving, Sue had met with our psychometrist to repeat some of the psychological tests she had taken at admission. These tests confirmed what Sue reported: she was less depressed, felt more in control of her eating, was less confused about her inner emotions, was less fearful of taking care of herself, was less socially maladjusted, and had increased self-esteem. Not surprisingly, she continued to score high on the body dissatisfaction scale of the Eating Disorder Inventory; the scores reflected her ongoing struggles with negative feelings about her body.

This case illustrates many of the advantages—and difficulties— associated with treating seriously ill bulimic patients exclusively in group therapy in a day hospital setting. This patient had impairment in all spheres of functioning, including physical, psychological, social, and vocational. The comprehensive treatment of patients with eating disorders must use a biopsychosocial model that integrates all of these areas. The treatment program must be flexible enough to allow one of these problem areas to become the major focus of treatment at any given point in time, yet structured enough to provide patients with the necessary containment required for behavior change and to allow the staff to function as a unified treatment team with an agreed-on conceptual model of etiology and intervention.

Sue required medical, psychological, nutritional, occupational, family, and nursing intervention during the course of her stay in the DHP. She benefited from a multidisciplinary treatment team housed in a hospital setting. All of the facilities of the hospital were available to Sue; she required use of the emergency room and the medical inpatient unit, and could have easily also required a crisis intervention on the psychiatric unit. Having ready access to medical and surgical specialists is also a valuable asset and allowed us to maintain Sue as an outpatient despite ongoing problems with her kidneys and bladder. For this patient, who had not found individual therapy helpful in alleviating her symptoms, the group model provided an environment that allowed for a corrective emotional experience that led to symptom alleviation. In this integrative approach using multiple conceptual paradigms, Sue benefited from the cognitive-behavioral interventions as much as the experiential, psychoeducational, interpersonal, and psychodynamic approaches.

The true test of an innovative approach for the treatment of an eating disorder is the staying power of the clinical change induced by such an intervention. Current research suggests that standard treatments for bulimia nervosa are effective in alleviating symptoms in the short term but are associated with high rates of relapse over time. From the two-year outcome studies of bulimics treated in the DHP, the evidence is clear that this approach changes the natural history of previously treatment-resistant patients with bulimia nervosa. From an evaluation of treatment response, the program appears to be an effective intervention, with 80 percent of bulimic patients either completely free of symptoms or symptomatic very occasionally during the last month of treatment. For patients who leave the day hospital symptom-free, over two-thirds will remain that way during the two-year follow-up; only 20 percent will have a relapse of their symptoms, compared with the natural history of bulimia nervosa, in which the relapse rate appears to approach 60 to 70 percent.

Changes to the DHP are underway; they will allow for a more stepped-down model of care, whereby patients will leave the program and enter into a transition program that they can attend initially three, then two, and then one day per week. This stepped-down program will buffer the process for patients who may have difficulty moving from a five-day-a-week intensive program to the usual situation of one hour per week of treatment. Additional refinements to the program are under consideration. Only through the process of careful program evaluation and outcome studies will we begin to approach the ideal treatment for these seriously ill patients, whose pain and suffering are so palpable and disabling.

## NOTES

P. 259, *conceptualized and initiated the Day Hospital Group Therapy Program (DHP) for eating disorders:* Piran, N., & Kaplan, A. S. (Eds.). (1990). *A Day Hospital Group Treatment Program for anorexia nervosa and bulimia nervosa.* New York: Brunner/Mazel.

P. 260, *Pharmacotherapy, most commonly antidepressant drugs:* Garfinkel, P. E., & Garner, D. M. (Eds.). (1987). *The role of drug treatment for eating disorders.* New York: Brunner/Mazel.

P. 264, *Treating a patient with bulimia nervosa in a program such as ours:* Kaplan, A. S., Kerr, A., & Maddocks, S. (1992). Day hospital group treatment for eating disorders. In R. MacKenzie & H. Harper (Eds.), *Group therapies for eating disorders* (pp. 161–181). Washington, DC: American Psychiatric Association Press.

P. 273, *Eating Disorders Examination:* Cooper, P., & Fairburn, C. G. (1987). The Eating Disorders Examination: A semi-structured interview for the assessment of specific psychopathology of the eating disorders. *International Journal of Eating Disorders, 6,* 1–8.

P. 273, *Eating Disorder Inventory:* Garner, D. M., & Olmsted, M. P. (1984). *The Eating Disorder Inventory manual.* Odessa, FL: Psychological Assessment Resources.

P. 273, *Beck Depression Inventory:* Beck, A. T., Ward, C. H., Mendelson, M., Mock, J., & Erbaugh, J. (1961). An inventory for measuring depression. *Archives of General Psychiatry, 4,* 561–571.

P. 273, *Rosenberg Self Esteem Questionnaire:* Rosenberg, M. (1965). *Society and the adolescent self-image.* Princeton, NJ: Princeton University Press.

P. 273, *Weissman Social Adjustment Scale:* Weissman, M. M., Prusoff B. A., Thompson, W. D., Harding, P. S., & Myers, J. K. (1978). Social adjustment of self-report in a community sample and in psychiatric outpatients. *Journal of Nervous and Mental Disorders, 166,* 317–326.

P. 273, *Structured Clinical Interview for DSM-III-R:* Spitzer, R. L., Williams, J.B.W., Gibbon, M., & First, M. B. (1990). *User's guide for the Structured Clinical Interview for DSM-III-R.* Washington, DC: American Psychiatric Press.

P. 286, *Current research suggests that standard treatments for bulimia nervosa:* Keller, M. B., Herzog, D. B., Lavori, P. W., Bradburn, I. S., & Mahoney, E. M. (1992). The naturalistic history of bulimia nervosa: Extraordinarily high rates of chronicity, relapse, recurrence, and psychosocial morbidity. *International Journal of Eating Disorders, 12,* 1–9.

P. 286, *From the two-year outcome studies of bulimics treated in the DHP:* Maddocks, S., Kaplan, A. S., Woodside, D. B., Langdon, L., & Piran, N. (1992). Two-year follow-up of bulimia nervosa: The importance of abstinence as the criterion of outcome. *International Journal of Eating Disorders, 12,* 133–141.

P. 286, *From an evaluation of treatment response:* Maddocks, S., & Kaplan, A. S. (1991). The prediction of positive treatment response in bulimia nervosa: A study of patient variables. *British Journal of Psychiatry, 159,* 846–849.

P. 286, *For patients who leave the day hospital symptom-free:* Olmsted, M. P., Kaplan, A. S., & Rockert, W. (1992). Rate and prediction of relapse in bulimia nervosa. *American Journal of Psychiatry, 151,* 728–743.

# 9

# THE TREATMENT OF A CHILD WITH ANOREXIA NERVOSA

## Rachel Bryant-Waugh and Bryan Lask

The following letter of referral regarding Chloe, age twelve-and-a-half years, was received from her family doctor [in Britain the family doctor is usually known as the general practitioner or GP] and is quoted verbatim:

Dear Dr. Lask,

This letter accompanies this young girl with anorexia nervosa for whom her parents have arranged a second opinion with you. Although Chloe is registered with me as her GP along with her parents, I am afraid to say that to date I have not been involved in her management at all.

This is because she started her anorexic problem while at boarding school, and was therefore registered with the school doctor. However 3 months ago her parents transferred her to a day school. She was referred by the school doctor to an Eating Disorders Unit near her home, where she was admitted for 10 weeks. One month ago she was discharged having regained her lost weight, and has been attending for one day per week, plus for one evening meal.

I understand that although her initial progress after discharge was good overall, her parents feel things have been slipping again and I think this is why her father has arranged this appointment. The consultant looking after her has no objection to this referral and would be delighted to discuss Chloe with you.

Both parents and child are intelligent and articulate, so I am sure they will be able to give you further details of the events to date. I look forward to hearing your expert assessment in due course.

Kind regards.

Such referrals to us are not at all atypical. For the last ten years, we have been responsible for an eating disorders program for children aged seven to fifteen, the only one of its type in the United Kingdom. The service consists of an outpatient clinic, a day program, and an eight-bed inpatient unit. The staffing includes four psychiatrists, of whom two are in training, two postdoctorate psychologists, and an experienced child psychotherapist and social worker. In addition the inpatient unit has nine nurses and two teachers. There is access at all times to pediatricians. We receive between forty and fifty referrals per annum, from throughout the country, and the majority of the children have already been treated elsewhere. All children receive a multidisciplinary assessment, including physical examination and laboratory investigations, and when treatment is offered, this is invariably comprehensive in its orientation.

Before we describe the background to Chloe's disorder, her assessment, and subsequent treatment, we offer a few general remarks about childhood-onset anorexia nervosa.

## CHILDHOOD-ONSET ANOREXIA NERVOSA

Anorexia nervosa arising in childhood bears both similarities to and differences from anorexia nervosa of later onset. The core features that include disturbances in three central areas—behavioral, psychological, and physical—appear to be largely the same. Lack of menstruation in this age-group is usually primary, however, and therefore cessation of menstruation cannot be used as a diagnostic feature. There is no absolutely characteristic form of presentation in this age-group, and the clinical features tend to vary during the course of the illness. This variability, plus the fact that physical symptoms such as abdominal pain or sense of fullness are common presenting symptoms, often leads to additional investigations and delay in diagnosis.

The difference in the distribution of fatty tissue between children, on the one hand, and late adolescents and adults, on the other, leads children to achieve a more severe degree of emaciation than older individuals with a similar degree of weight loss. In consequence children appear to develop the physical effects of severe weight loss more rapidly. These include emaciation; lanugo (fine, downy) hair; pallor; and weakening of heart activity (myocardial decompensation), as manifested by poor peripheral circulation with a slow, weak, and occasionally irregular pulse; cold hands and feet with a bluish color of the skin; and sometimes early skin ulceration.

Fluid deprivation leads to dehydration, with a dry mouth and tongue and loss of skin elasticity, and to electrolyte disturbance, especially when there has been self-induced vomiting.

Emotional and behavioral features, over and above the core features of weight avoidance, distorted body image, and morbid preoccupation with weight and shape, include depressive symptoms, which tend to affect up to 50 percent of these children; obsessive-compulsive behavior, particularly in boys; and poor self-image. Bingeing and laxative abuse tend to occur less commonly than in the older group.

The differential diagnosis of childhood-onset anorexia nervosa includes depression, obsessive-compulsive disorder, and somatoform disorder, as well as the other childhood-onset eating disorders. These include

- *Food-avoidance emotional disorder,* a disorder of the emotions in which food avoidance plays a major part, but there is a failure to meet the full criteria for anorexia nervosa.

- *Selective eating,* in which the child's diet includes a remarkably narrow range of foods. Typically, such children eat only three or four different foods, usually carbohydrate-based. The parents are extremely anxious about this narrow range of foods, but the children almost invariably thrive physically. The main problem is usually one of social functioning.

- *Pervasive refusal syndrome*, which usually presents as anorexia nervosa but soon progresses to a profound and pervasive refusal to eat, drink, talk, walk, or engage in self-care. We consider it to be an extreme version of the avoidance behavior seen in posttraumatic stress disorder.

Because the prognosis in childhood-onset anorexia nervosa is far from satisfactory, with no more than two-thirds making a full recovery, and because of the dangers of serious physical complications, a rapidly initiated, intensive, and comprehensive treatment program is indicated. The essentials of such a program include

- Providing information and education for the parents and other members of the family
- Ensuring that the adults are in charge
- Making a decision about the need for hospitalization
- Calculating a target weight range
- Refeeding
- Providing parental counseling with or without family therapy
- Providing individual therapy
- Considering the need for medication and the child's schooling

## CHLOE'S INITIAL ASSESSMENT

We always see children with eating disorders as quickly as possible because of the very high levels of family anxiety and because of the dangers inherent in the disorder. Consequently, Chloe was seen in our clinic two days after referral and was assessed by three members of our multidisciplinary team: a pediatrician, a psychiatrist, and a child psychotherapist.

Kinderarzt

## Background

The key background features elicited during this assessment were as follows:

1. Chloe was the elder of two siblings, her brother, Tim, being one year younger. Her father, aged forty-two, was an accountant; her mother, aged thirty-nine, described herself as a housewife who makes and sells curtains in her spare time.

2. Prior to the onset of her illness, Chloe had been a happy, outgoing, and popular girl, conscientious and very successful with schoolwork despite a number of changes of school. She also had excelled at sports. Her developmental milestones had been normal, and apart from a febrile convulsion (a seizure due to high body temperature) when aged fifteen months, there had been no previous health problems or concerns about eating or weight.

3. Chloe had experienced a number of school changes in the last three years: the first because the family had moved to a new area; the second when Chloe had reached the age of transfer from primary to secondary school [in the U.K., this occurs in the September after reaching the eleventh birthday]. At this point, Chloe chose to attend a boarding (residential) school but did not like it. Shortly after the start of her second year at that school and four months prior to her referral to us, she transferred to a local day school.

4. The family history revealed only that Chloe's mother had been overweight as a teenager and that one of Chloe's first cousins had had anorexia nervosa in her twenties but was now well.

5. Chloe was first noted to be eating inadequately toward the end of the summer holidays and before she returned to school, seven months prior to referral to us. Early in the school term the nurse at her boarding school became concerned, and the school doctor referred her to a psychiatrist specializing in eating disorders.

Such a rapid referral in children with anorexia nervosa is most unusual. More often than not, the diagnosis is missed, often because many physicians are not aware that anorexia nervosa occurs in children. In this instance the condition was recognized early because Chloe was attending a girls' boarding school. In the United Kingdom, the prevalence of anorexia nervosa is higher in such schools than in any context other than ballet schools.

The psychiatrist to whom Chloe was referred made a diagnosis of anorexia nervosa and admitted her to a private hospital with an eating disorders unit. In the United Kingdom, most people are treated, without payment, through the National Health Service. There is often quite a long wait to see a specialist, except for emergencies, and some prefer to pay for their health care, either directly or through private health insurance. Chloe's parents had opted for the latter and, in consequence, had managed to have her seen by a specialist and admitted to an eating disorder unit within three weeks of the school nurse expressing her concern. We have found, on average, a delay of seven months between onset of childhood anorexia nervosa and the correct diagnosis being made.

6. At the time of admission to the private unit, Chloe was eating and drinking very little and had lost approximately 10 kilograms (22 pounds). Her weight was 31.7 kilograms (about 70 pounds), and height 150 centimeters (four feet, eleven inches). On the Tanner-Whitehouse standards she had a weight for age of 78 percent, a height for age of 100 percent, and a weight for height of 77 percent.

Growth specialists prefer to use the Tanner-Whitehouse standards, which express the weight and height as a percentage of that expected for age. The most crucial measure is the percentage weight for height, with a normal range from 95 percent to 105 percent. A ratio of less than 80 percent indicates wasting. Chloe's weight for height was therefore within the wasting range.

Unfortunately, because all of the other patients at that hospital were several years older than Chloe, there was no treatment program specifically designed or suitable for children. Chloe was treated with a graded refeeding program based on bed rest and increasing activities dependent on weight gain. She also participated in the unit program of group discussions and occasional outings. Her family was seen on a few occasions, but there was no child-oriented treatment program and no schooling.

Chloe gradually gained weight, nonetheless, and, after ten weeks, had reached 41 kilograms (95 percent weight for height) and was deemed well enough for discharge and to attend as a day patient one day per week. Within four weeks she had lost 5.5 kilograms, was eating and drinking very little, and was exercising excessively. It was at this point that she was referred to our clinic.

## Physical Examination

Chloe weighed 36 kilograms (79 pounds) at a height of 150 centimeters (83 percent weight for age, 99 percent height for age, and 85 percent weight for height). Although her weight and weight for height were better than at the time of hospital admission, physical examination revealed a pulse rate of 60 per minute (the norm for her age being around 80) and a sitting blood pressure of 80 / 50, with the norm for her age being 110 / 70. Other signs of circulatory failure included pallor; fine, downy hair on her back and arms; and weak pulses in her feet, which were cold and cyanotic (bluish discoloration). Two sores on her left foot showed early signs of ulceration. Chloe was also dehydrated, with a dry, furred tongue and loss of skin elasticity.

An electrocardiogram confirmed the slow pulse rate, with occasional irregularities, but blood tests were in the normal range, although her potassium level was at the low end of normal. Pelvic ultrasound examination showed marked regression of the size, shape, and content of the uterus and ovaries. These are common findings in childhood-onset anorexia nervosa and are usually reversible, providing there is a return to a healthy weight for height—on average about 97 percent. As is so often the case with children, Chloe's physical state had deteriorated rapidly, with signs of circulatory failure and possible electrolyte imbalance, necessitating urgent hospitalization.

### Mental Status

Chloe was initially seen in the presence of her family and presented as sullen and resentful, seeing no good reason for all the fuss and denying any problem. She said that she did not eat well because she always felt full and that it did not matter because she was overweight anyhow. "I hate being fat, and I'm going to lose weight whatever you say. You're all stupid and a waste of time."

On a ten-point scale—where very thin is one, average is five, and very fat is ten—she rated herself at present as seven and her ideal self as three. She just wanted to be left alone to get on with her own life, without "all these busybodies interfering."

Chloe attributed her history of poor eating to being full. Children rarely present with a clear statement that they are too fat; Chloe was able to admit to weight and shape concerns.

### Individual Assessment

When alone with the child psychotherapist, Chloe was friendlier but still defensive. She described her family as having friendly relationships but then went on to describe frequently losing her temper with both her mother and brother, when she would scream, hit, bite, and kick them. There seemed to be no middle point in her relationships with them. Either life felt absolutely fine, or she was consumed by uncontrollable anger. She did not convey any sense at all of a relationship with her father.

Chloe admitted that she did not eat, but she did not seem to know why. She denied any other problems and insisted that "everything else is fine." When asked to do a drawing of a person, she quickly drew a stick figure, which she described as a girl like her who lived in a very happy family. She related a dream of *jagen, verfolgen*

a monsterlike figure chasing her, and another in which a teacher, with her back to Chloe, was drawing on a blackboard.

This rather mixed presentation is not uncommon in children with anorexia nervosa: denial, especially in front of parents; confusion, fear, and extremes when alone.

## Family Assessment

Chloe's parents appeared to be united in their concern for her and gave a consistent account of the events leading up to the referral. There was a sense of Chloe and her mother in an alliance, with father and Tim on the outside, but not close themselves. Communication was slightly guarded and not direct. The general atmosphere was one of concern and foreboding though tinged with a sense of relief that Chloe was being seen in a specialist center for children.

*small amount of a feeling, emotion*                    *a feeling that smth unpleasant is going to happen*

## Diagnostic Formulation

We made a diagnosis of anorexia nervosa with onset about seven months prior to referral to our clinic. Predisposing factors included a history of anorexia nervosa within the extended family and, given Chloe's mother's history of being overweight as a teenager, possible weight concerns. We also noted that Chloe was a conscientious girl with evidence of high achieving and that she attended for one year a girls' boarding school, where preoccupation with weight and shape is commonplace.

There were some hints of family disharmony, and this would need further exploration. No precipitating factors were obvious, although the onset coincided with the end of the long school holidays and the impending return to a school that Chloe decided to leave within a few weeks. It was not yet clear what factors were maintaining her illness.

We have found, incidentally, that although predisposing, precipitating, and perpetuating factors may, at times, overlap, often the perpetuating factors differ from the predisposing and perpetuating ones. For example, family disharmony may contribute to the development of anorexia nervosa, but sometimes there may be no family difficulties prior to the illness. Once the anorexia nervosa starts, however, the parents may find it hard to work together on the problem in a cohesive and consistent manner.

Chloe's physical state gave us cause for concern, for although her weight for height ratio was not within the wasting range, she had clear signs of poor peripheral circulation, with dehydration and a relatively low potassium level. In addition her fluid intake was minimal and her food intake nil.

## CHLOE'S MANAGEMENT AND ITS RATIONALE

Our initial assessment indicated the need for immediate hospitalization to ensure Chloe's physical safety, followed by the implementation of a comprehensive treatment program. The indications for hospitalization were the dehydration, circulatory failure, and a low potassium level. Other reasons for admitting a child with anorexia nervosa, which Chloe did not manifest, include a weight for height ratio of 70 percent or less, persistent vomiting, or the vomiting of blood.

Unfortunately, we had no vacancies on our unit, and Chloe's parents did not want her to return to the private hospital. Arrangements were made, therefore, for her to be admitted to a local pediatric unit, with intensive psychiatric help being offered in our clinic until we could admit her as an inpatient. This arrangement was far from satisfactory but is commonly imposed by the lack of adequate facilities for children with anorexia nervosa.

Our treatment plan included (1) providing information to Chloe's parents about her illness, (2) ensuring that the adults are in charge, (3) gentle refeeding, (4) setting a target weight range, (5) providing a combination of parental counseling and family therapy, (6) providing individual therapy, (7) serving as liaison with her school, and (8) considering medication.

## Providing Information to Parents

We have found the provision of information to parents one of the most important components of the treatment program. Parents attend our clinic feeling anxious, bewildered, angry, and often guilty. They can't understand why their child won't eat and are devastated by the situation. One mother titled a paper describing her own and other parents' experiences: "Bewildered, Blamed, and Broken-Hearted."

We try to explain what we know about the predisposing, precipitating, and perpetuating factors and to describe the course of the illness and its likely outcome. We do our best to avoid apportioning responsibility, emphasizing instead the genetic, biological, and cultural components of the illness. A further difficulty arises when discussing management, for here parents play a crucial role, and it is easy for them to misconstrue management advice as blame for the illness.

## Putting Adults in Charge

Three important aspects of childhood-onset anorexia nervosa are its life-threatening nature, the child's lack of insight, and the battles around control. The child struggles to retain control and, in so doing, prolongs the illness and imposes more risks. Consequently, it is essential that the adults who are responsible for the child's welfare take charge. It is helpful to make a clear statement to the parents at initial contact, emphasizing the dangers of prolonged starvation and fluid deprivation and the child's inability to judge what is in her interests at this point.

There is no need, however, for the child to relinquish control in areas of her life that are not likely to compromise her health and safety. For example, the decision of whether or not to hospitalize a child is one that the adults must take, notwithstanding the child's resistance. In contrast, what she reads and which television programs she watches are, in general, irrelevant to her health, and to ensure she does have some sense of autonomy, she should be allowed to retain control in such areas.

## Refeeding

Helping a child resume eating when she is terrified of gaining weight is a demanding and time-consuming task that requires patience, sensitivity, and determination. It is hardly surprising that parents, and indeed professionals, find it so difficult. The essential components of the process are

- *The inclusion of the child in the planning.* She is encouraged to state preferences and make choices within the framework of an adequate intake. A dietician's advice here can be invaluable.

- *The support of a sympathetic, understanding, and trusted adult* who can offer guidance and reassurance and sit with the child throughout the meal.

- *A gradual approach to the resumption of eating and drinking—* where possible adopting a pace the child can tolerate. Frequent small meals may be more acceptable than less frequent large ones, and small portions on a large plate are likely to be preferable to large portions on a small plate.

- *Providing structure and tasks.* Mealtimes should have a clear structure: a beginning, a defined task, and an end. The child may need preparation for the meal, with much support and perhaps the use of relaxation techniques. It is often useful to plan tasks for the mealtime; for example, if the child has not eaten for some time, an early task would involve touching cutlery, brushing lips with food, and then taking small portions. The mealtime should be finite, certainly not dragged on endlessly in an atmosphere of negativism and recrimination.

Patience and the ability to gauge a child's potential accurately help the mealtime relationship and let the child know that the staff are prepared to work at her pace. The result is that a child, often for the first time, feels that her real concerns are being acknowledged and that adults understand the link between her not being able to eat and her distress.

If the child's physical health is in immediate jeopardy, then high-calorie or build-up drinks can be used to ensure adequate nutrition in the short term. If the child totally refuses to have adequate nutrition, then nasogastric tube-feeding may be required. This procedure should never be threatened or used as a "punishment," but rather should be presented as a necessary measure to prevent further harm, and should be implemented in a carefully planned manner, with adequate preparation and explanation. It is rare indeed for a child to resist such feeding.

### Setting a Target Weight Range

Most children and their parents find it helpful to know what weight gain is required. Because children with anorexia nervosa are so preoccupied with their weight, there is a temptation to try to distract them from this theme. Such ploys do not work and, if anything, increase anxiety. It seems more sensible to discuss with the child what weight she wants to be, and compare this with what is actually a healthy weight, before commencing the difficult process of helping her gain.

We find it useful to have a target weight range, rather than a target weight. A range is less threatening, allows for some flexibility, and is probably more realistic than the absolute of a specific weight. The weight range is based on a weight-for-height ratio of between 97 percent and 100 percent. The lower end is chosen because it represents the mean at which menstruation commences or resumes in this population.

### Parental Counseling and Family Therapy

Parental counseling and family therapy are the mainstays of psychological approaches to the treatment of childhood-onset anorexia nervosa, and we never exclude them from the treatment of such children. The essence of these treatments is the focus on the interaction between people, rather than on the internal, individual psychological processes. The primary goals are

- The enhancement of parental cohesion, communication, and consistency
- The identification, discussion, and resolution of problems and conflicts
- The promotion of more open and direct family communication patterns
- The expression, acknowledgment, and acceptance of feelings

The techniques that are used to achieve these goals vary among therapists. Our preference is to focus initially on the parental subsystem, helping the couple identify the difficulties they are experiencing in working together on their child's problems. We ask each to outline what approaches he or she wants to use and then to compare the differences. The next step involves each parent suggesting what the other could do to help. In this way the parents are helped to develop a consistent and mutually supportive approach. We then emphasize the importance of consistency not only between each other but also over time. The method they use today must be the same as that they will use tomorrow and the next day.

Integral to this process is the opening up of communication between the parents. Communication needs to be direct and clear, with emphasis on each person speaking for him- or herself, acknowledging each other's viewpoint, and acknowledging and accepting each other's feelings. Feelings may differ or may seem illogical and irrational, but they cannot be wrong, anymore than the color of someone's eyes can be wrong.

Such work can be done in the presence of the children, and in general we prefer to do so because it sets a model for all family members of new and more functional communication styles that can be practiced by everyone. Further, having the children present encourages a natural progression into dealing with wider family issues.

A common phenomenon in such families is the overinvolvement between one parent and child to the exclusion of the other parent and child(ren). Alternatively, a child may be caught up in the conflict between the parents (triangulated) and continuously obliged to take sides or to act as a buffer between them. We take quite an authoritative approach to these issues, pointing them out and suggesting that they are inappropriate and potentially harmful. We use such techniques as altering seating arrangements and reinforcing the parental and sibling alliances. We also encourage the ethos that each family member has age-appropriate autonomy.

In addition to discussing these issues, we make frequent use of toys, games, drawings, and other experiential techniques.

### Providing Individual Therapy

For some children, the severity of the cognitive disturbance or the intensity of the associated psychopathology is so severe that parental counseling and/or family therapy is clearly insufficient. In such cases immediate referral for individual therapy is indicated, generally either cognitive or psychodynamic.

Cognitive techniques are based on the notion that psychological change can be brought about by attention to and attempts to alter the thought processes of the individual. Jeremy Turk recommends that direct efforts to alter eating behaviors are required, as well as management aimed at erroneous assumptions. In severely emaciated children, it is wise to restore physical health to some extent before employing cognitive techniques.

Individual psychodynamic psychotherapy for a child with eating difficulties is designed to help her tolerate emotional experiences, rather than "close her mind" to them. Specifically, the child's emotional immaturity necessitates a wish for control as a defense against relationships. Jeanne Magagna has suggested that the child needs to develop sufficient patience and trust to allow her to experience empathic nurturing and thus feel understood and valued. Then she can develop the capacity for love—

*Unzulänglichkeit*

and tolerance of her parents' shortcomings—and so begin to separate from her parents in a mature way. Successful therapy involves the child forgiving her parents, being concerned about the feelings of others, and taking responsibility for mothering herself.

Individual therapy should be conducted in the context of continuing parental counseling and regular medical evaluations of the child's progress.

## Serving as Liaison with Schools

*to have an effect          make a bad sit worse*

Anorexia nervosa can impinge on healthy intellectual and social functioning at school and can be aggravated by the often high academic expectations such children have of themselves. Schoolwork is often the last activity that such children give up. As part of the multidisciplinary team, teachers can make a significant contribution to assessment and management, providing limitations and professional boundaries are respected. Teachers can also help children express themselves through creative pursuits and can engender feelings of achievement that are not linked to academic success, thus enhancing self-esteem.

Decisions need to be made: is the child well enough to attend school and, if so, how much activity can she pursue? Should meals be supervised and, if so, by whom? With a hospitalized child, similar principles apply, and in addition liaison between the hospital school and the child's school should be implemented and maintained.

## Considering Medication

Only rarely is medication required in childhood-onset anorexia nervosa. Some children are so depressed that the use of antidepressants should be considered, but caution is required, given the possibility of existing circulatory failure and the potentially cardiotoxic effects of antidepressants. Usually, such treatment is reserved for children whose depression persists despite weight gain or who remain both depressed and underweight.

There is little indication for other forms of psychotropic medication. Tranquilizers may be of help rarely to children who experience extreme anxiety. Appetite stimulants have no place in treatment, for hardly ever is there a true loss of appetite. Laxatives should not be used, given that any "constipation" is likely to be due to inadequate food intake and that they may be enlisted as a means of weight control.

## CHLOE'S COURSE OF TREATMENT

Chloe was admitted to the pediatric ward of her local hospital to implement early rehydration and refeeding, while weekly psychiatric treatment was implemented in our clinic. In addition Chloe's name was put on the waiting list for admission to our eating disorder unit.

Because of a misunderstanding—and these frequently arise when care is shared between two hospitals—Chloe was discharged home four days after the admission, having been rehydrated and gaining two kilograms of weight (mostly in the form of fluid). When seen in our clinic three days later, Chloe had not eaten or drunk anything for forty-eight hours and had already lost the two kilograms of weight.

At this point Chloe's parents wanted to keep her at home, at least for the next few days. We consider it important to support parents as much as possible and therefore agreed to this plan, with the proviso that should she deteriorate further, they would arrange for her readmission to the pediatric ward. We advised them along the lines described in the section above on parental counseling, offered daily telephone contact, and arranged to see Chloe and her parents again in one week. We did not think that Chloe required antidepressant or any other form of medication.

By the next attendance Chloe had started eating, albeit relatively small amounts. She had not lost any further weight and was reasonably well hydrated. She seemed more communicative, and her parents marginally more confident. It was agreed to continue the same regimen, with weekly reviews of Chloe's progress and family meetings focusing initially on supporting the parents in Chloe's management.

Four weeks after her first attendance Chloe had gained 0.5 kilogram, and her parents reported that she was trying hard, although her mood and eating were both erratic. She was doing little other than watching television, reading cookery books, and cooking for others. We considered that Chloe was ready to commence individual therapy, and arranged for her to see our individual psychotherapist on a weekly basis; one of us (Lask) continued the parental counseling, without the children present, at bi-weekly intervals.

Despite her initial reluctance to have any individual therapy, in the context of a therapeutic relationship in which her feelings were accepted and understood, Chloe gradually began to explore her concerns about her weight and shape and events that had preceded her illness. In particular she was able to describe some specific difficulties she had experienced. At the boarding school, which she left shortly after the commencement of her illness, she had been teased by some of her peers. They nicknamed her "thunder thighs," and this teasing coincided with her becoming very sensitive about her shape and size.

As Chloe discovered that her therapist could tolerate the intense negative feelings that she expressed both in the transference and toward others, she became able to trust the therapist sufficiently to share with her information that she had previously been unable to tell anyone. The head teacher of the school she attended between the ages of nine and eleven had seemed to have taken a particular interest in her. He would ask her to stay behind after lessons, clearly favored her over other children, made personal comments about her appearance, and put his arm around her. "He seemed to have a crush on me."

After Chloe left that school, he frequently wrote to her and, because he lived in the same village, occasionally visited her home. On at least two occasions, he had kissed Chloe "in the way that a man and woman kiss; I didn't like it, but didn't know how to stop him. I was too embarrassed to tell my parents." The teacher had continued his contact with Chloe during her admission to the private hospital, and eventually she asked her parents to tell him not to visit but could not tell them why. She also asked that he should not telephone, but he continued to write to her.

Chloe told her individual therapist about the teacher at the same time that a major shift was occurring in the focus of the parental counseling: from helping the parents acknowledge their differences of opinion about Chloe's management and work together in a consistent manner to addressing major problems in their marriage.

The teacher was discussed with the parents. Two letters were seen and found to contain inappropriate and highly personal comments about Chloe's appearance and the teacher's feelings for her. The parents decided to intercept any further letters and to tell the teacher not to have any contact with Chloe. All further contact was blocked, and in the individual therapy, Chloe's confusion and concern were explored. Reassurance was offered that she was not responsible in any way for his behavior toward her.

The role of trauma in the origin of childhood-onset anorexia nervosa is yet to be clarified. Our own studies and clinical experience document that up to 20 percent of such children have experienced some form of sexual abuse. Given the secretive nature of such episodes, however, we would not be surprised if the prevalence rate were to prove much higher. In Chloe's case, although there was no genital contact, the inappropriateness and persistence of the teacher's attentions had been sufficient to cause her considerable distress.

Nine weeks after referral, Chloe was described as going from strength to strength. She had gained eight kilograms and had reached her target weight range. Her eating pattern was more regular, and she had regained a wide range of interests. She was generally less sullen and more outgoing. She had moments of extreme anger toward her parents and brother, however, and was generally rude, critical, and spiteful.

We have noted that virtually all children who recover from anorexia nervosa go through a stage of negativism and excessive assertiveness. This behavior appears to be a necessary prelude to a lasting recovery based on the child finding a voice for previously bottled-up and painful feelings. Most children with anorexia nervosa are described as never having been "outspoken" or "difficult." This inability to manage negative feelings may be a necessary predisposing factor for the development of anorexia nervosa. Those children who fail to go through this stage seem either not to recover or to undergo an early relapse.

At this point in her treatment Chloe decided she did not want any more individual therapy. A decision was made, therefore, to terminate the individual sessions and to reconvene the family meetings. As the parents were now more confident in their management of Chloe, it was possible to shift the focus onto the skewed relationships in the family. This shift included reinstating a clearer boundary between Chloe and her mother and a closer relationship between Chloe's brother and his father. Both children showed enthusiasm for these changes and seemed to show relief at the more open acknowledgment of the marital difficulties. The parents asked for a further meeting to discuss these issues and subsequently decided on a trial separation, although Chloe's mother was keener on this than her father.

## Termination

Six months after Chloe's referral, she had maintained a weight for height ratio of 102 percent for three months, was eating satisfactorily, and was behaving in an age-appropriate manner. She remained concerned that she might *become* fat, but she no longer had a distorted body image and perceived her weight and shape as "just about right."

One year after referral, the case was closed. Chloe had maintained the same weight for height ratio and was no longer concerned about weight gain. She was eating normally and was satisfied with her appearance. Physical examination was normal, and pelvic ultrasound scanning showed maturing ovaries and uterus. Chloe's parents had decided on a permanent separation and had adjusted to leading separate lives. The children both seemed to be much happier. A formal complaint had been made jointly by the parents and us to the Education Authority and, following an investigation, the teacher concerned took early retirement.

We received a somewhat unusual follow-up thirty-three months after referral. Out of the blue, Chloe's father telephoned and told us that Chloe was thriving, as was her brother, and that both he and his ex-wife had new partners, both of whom get on well with the children. His own mother had died some weeks previously and had left instructions in her will that he should give a specific amount of money to any cause of his choosing. He wanted our team to be the beneficiaries.

The management of childhood-onset anorexia nervosa is complex and time-consuming and should always be provided by professionals experienced in the assessment and treatment of children and their families. We need to be aware of the differences between children and adults in the presentation and course of the disorder and of the special dangers of dehydration and weight loss in childhood. The involvement of a multidisciplinary team, including a pediatrician, is essential.

## NOTES

P. 290, *appear to be largely the same:* Lask, B., & Bryant-Waugh, R. (1992). *Childhood onset anorexia nervosa and related eating disorders.* Hove, UK: Erlbaum.

P. 291, *Food-avoidance emotional disorder:* Higgs, J., Goodyer, I., & Birch, J. (1989). Anorexia nervosa and food avoidance emotional disorder. *Archives of Disease in Childhood, 64,* 345–351.

P. 291, *Selective eating:* Lask, B., & Bryant-Waugh, R. (1992). *Childhood onset anorexia nervosa and related eating disorders.* Hove, UK: Erlbaum, p. 20.

P. 292, *Pervasive refusal syndrome:* Lask, B., Britten, C., Kroll, L., Magagna, J., & Tranter, M. (1991). Pervasive refusal in children. *Archives of Disease in Childhood, 66,* 866–869.

P. 294, *many physicians are not aware that anorexia nervosa occurs in children:* Bryant-Waugh, R., Lask, B., Shafron, R., & Fosson, A. (1992). Do doctors recognize eating disorders in children? *Archives of Disease in Childhood, 67,* 102–105.

P. 294, *a delay of seven months:* Fosson, A., Knibbs, J., Bryant-Waugh, R., & Lask, B. (1987). Early onset anorexia nervosa. *Archives of Disease in Childhood, 62,* 114–118.

P. 294, *Tanner-Whitehouse standards:* Tanner, J., Whitehouse, R., & Takaishi, M. (1966). Standards from birth to maturity for height, weight, height velocity, and weight velocity: British children. *Archives of Disease in Childhood, 48,* 454–471, 613–615 (1965 Parts 1 and 2).

P. 296, *on average about 97 percent:* Lai, K., De Bruyn, R., Lask, B., Bryant-Waugh, R., & Hankins, M. (1994). Use of pelvic ultrasound to monitor ovarian and uterine maturity in childhood onset anorexia nervosa. *Archives of Disease in Childhood, 71,* 228–231.

P. 299, *"Bewildered, Blamed, and Broken-Hearted":* MacDonald, M. (1992). Bewildered, blamed, and broken-hearted: Parents' views of anorexia nervosa. In B. Lask & R. Bryant-Waugh (Eds.), *Childhood onset anorexia nervosa and related eating disorders* (pp. 1–16). Hove, UK: Erlbaum.

P. 300, *Patience and the ability:* Glendinning, L., & Phillips, M. (1992). Nursing management. In B. Lask & R. Bryant-Waugh (Eds.), *Childhood onset anorexia nervosa and related eating disorders* (pp. 137–156). Hove, UK: Erlbaum.

P. 301, *The lower end is chosen:* Lai, K., De Bruyn, R., Lask, B., Bryant-Waugh, R., & Hankins, M. (1994). Use of pelvic ultrasound to monitor ovarian and uterine maturity in childhood onset anorexia nervosa. *Archives of Disease in Childhood, 71,* 228–231.

P. 302, *The techniques that are used:* Lask, B., & Bryant-Waugh, R. (1992). *Childhood onset anorexia nervosa and related eating disorders.* Hove, UK: Erlbaum, pp. 11–19; Van der Linden, J., & Van der Eycken, W. (1993). Guidelines for the family therapeutic approach to eating disorders. *Psychotherapy and Psychosomatics, 56,* 36–42.

P. 303, *toys, games, drawings, and other experiential techniques:* Lask, B., & Bryant-Waugh, R. (1992). *Childhood onset anorexia nervosa and related eating disorders.* Hove, UK: Erlbaum, pp. 11–19.

P. 303, *Jeremy Turk:* Turk, J. (1992). Cognitive approaches. In B. Lask & R. Bryant-Waugh (Eds.), *Childhood onset anorexia nervosa and related eating disorders* (pp. 177–190). Hove, UK: Erlbaum.

P. 303, *Jeanne Magagna:* Magagna, J. (1992). Individual psychodynamic psychotherapy. In B. Lask & R. Bryant-Waugh (Eds.), *Childhood onset anorexia nervosa and related eating disorders* (pp. 191–210). Hove, UK: Erlbaum.

P. 304, *liaison between the hospital school and the child's school:* Tate, A. (1992). Schooling. In B. Lask & R. Bryant-Waugh (Eds.), *Childhood onset anorexia nervosa and related eating disorders* (pp. 233–248). Hove, UK: Erlbaum.

P. 307, *negativism and excessive assertiveness:* Lask, B., & Bryant-Waugh, R. (1992). *Childhood onset anorexia nervosa and related eating disorders.* Hove, UK: Erlbaum, pp. 134–135.

P. 308, *inability to manage negative feelings:* Magagna, J. (1992). Individual psychodynamic psychotherapy. In B. Lask & R. Bryant-Waugh (Eds.), *Childhood onset anorexia nervosa and related eating disorders* (pp. 191–210). Hove, UK: Erlbaum.

# MULTIMODAL THERAPIES FOR ANOREXIA NERVOSA

## Paul E. Garfinkel

Detailed clinical studies over the past two decades have taught us much about the nature and course of anorexia nervosa. Opinions have varied considerably about the outcome of this disorder because, in fact, it can be extremely variable, ranging from a mild single illness in adolescence to a lifelong recurrent or persistent disorder with a significant mortality.

For the most part, however, anorexia nervosa is a chronic disorder. The Toronto Outcome Study followed patients from five to fourteen years after diagnosis of anorexia nervosa, and it is fairly representative of work in this area. Findings here indicated that while roughly 38 percent of the sample had fully recovered and a further 27 percent were significantly improved, 27 percent still struggled with the illness and 8 percent were deceased. Theander has provided long-term follow-up data of women seen in Sweden over a thirty-year period, which revealed the gradual nature of the recovery process: while only half of the anorexic subjects were recovered after six years, a further 20 percent were recovered after twelve years. Thus, the recovery process from the eating disorder is a gradual one. As clinicians, we must keep this in mind. Furthermore, after recovery the individual may be vulnerable to other psychiatric disorders, such as anxiety and depression. These factors are highlighted in the case example that follows.

In addition to knowledge about the course of anorexia nervosa, the past two decades have provided a more comprehensive understanding of the nature of this disorder as a final common pathway, the product of a variety of forces operating within any given individual.

As a result of this information, our treatments have become more flexible. Ideally, these will be tailored to the individual's particular needs at any given point in time. Treatments should begin with the least intrusive, least costly, but most effective form. We should move to more intensive treatments only as warranted by the clinical situation. For such tailored treatments to be properly delivered, we need to know a great deal about the natural history of anorexia nervosa and to have available results of comparative treatment trials that have identified predictors to specific treatments.

Unlike the situation for depression or bulimia nervosa, scant data are available from controlled trials in anorexia nervosa at the present time. As a result, flexible treatments are often provided according to what is deemed to be the clinician's best judgment, rather than according to empirical evidence. Consequently, a variety of treatments cover the entire range of physiological difficulties that people with anorexia nervosa may experience. Individual, marital, and group psychotherapies may be needed for the patient, and as we see in the following case, treatment may be required for the children because of their heightened risk to psychiatric disturbance.

## THE STORY OF MRS. L. R.

Here is an example of the application of multimodal therapy in treating a case of anorexia nervosa.

Mrs. L. R. was a thirty-three-year-old married nurse, five feet five inches tall, and ninety-five pounds. She had been referred by an endocrinologist from a nearby teaching hospital because of persistent amenorrhea (failure to menstruate) following the birth of a child three years earlier. She and her husband had wanted a second pregnancy and had consulted the endocrinologist regarding amenorrhea and the inability to conceive. The physician recognized features of the eating disorder and referred her for treatment.

Mrs. L. R., when seen, weighed herself daily to be absolutely certain her weight remained below one hundred pounds, which to her had become "a magical number" that must never be exceeded. She had no previous history of obesity. She weighed eight pounds at birth and as a child was thin. In her teens, she developed what she described as a "bouncy figure." She became a cheerleader and then a beauty queen at university. At that time she weighed her maximum, 120 pounds. At age nineteen she became diet conscious after she joined a modeling school and was told to lose "inches." Her weight fell from 119 pounds to 85 pounds over the next ten months.

In the following year, 1961, Mrs. L. R. was admitted by a psychiatrist to a community hospital for treatment of the severe weight loss. She was given medications, including chlorpromazine, was restricted to bed rest, and was encouraged to eat. She resisted this program and gradually became very depressed. She was then given a series of ten electroconvulsive therapies (ECT), and her mood was noted to be improved. Her weight increased gradually to 110 pounds, and she was discharged with little attention to aftercare. She seemed to function well in her professional studies and her relationships and she maintained her weight over the following decade. In 1971, at the time of her pregnancy, she was 106 pounds. She enjoyed the pregnancy and was able to gain 16 pounds. She felt well during the normal delivery and during the nine-month period of nursing her baby daughter.

Mrs. L. R. consistently weighed between 110 to 112 pounds during this period. Five months after the delivery, she returned to her position in pediatric nursing, and her food and weight preoccupations began to recur about that time. Over the subsequent year, her weight fell gradually; then for the year prior to her assessment, she stayed at her presenting weight of 95 pounds. She had stopped working several months prior to the consultation.

Mrs. L. R. was extremely conscious of her appearance and what others might think of her. She worried excessively about her complexion; even the slightest blemish or the idea of a hair being out of place bothered her, but her greatest fear was of her stomach protruding, which she imagined was noticeable with any weight gain. She was able to relate this fear to concerns about her mother's appearance. Her mother, who had also valued her appearance and had been considered beautiful, had developed "a pot" after the delivery of her children. Mrs. L. R. was aware that her self-esteem was tied to her appearance as reflected in a mirror. She regularly checked herself sideways in the mirror, and if her stomach appeared flat, she was pleased with herself for that day. She was well aware of her terror of becoming obese and yet knew this was strange because she had never been that way. She felt guilty if she ate anything more than her daily allotment, and she jogged daily at least five miles and up to eight. She could not miss one day of exercise, even if unwell.

At the time of the initial assessment, Mrs. L. R. had developed a rigid pattern of eating: a muffin and some cheese and coffee for breakfast; no lunch; and a small amount of meat and vegetables for supper. She tried to omit starches. She rarely allowed herself snacks or dessert, and then only when her husband or someone else was present. She had no objective binge episodes. She did feel out of control, however, if she ever ate more than her allotment. Two cookies in the evening could trigger intense anxiety and endless scrutiny in the mirror. She had no history of misuse of diuretics or diet pills. At age nineteen, she did induce vomiting following evening meals, but this behavior had not returned during the current episode. For the last year, however, she had been using Ex-Lax—up to six tablets at a time, twice weekly—to induce diarrhea, which would prevent the absorption of calories.

When seen, Mrs. L. R. was not subjectively depressed. She was anxious—about her weight and about a second pregnancy. Her sleep had been disturbed for several years and was characterized by a fragmented pattern, with early morning awakening. Her concentration and interests were maintained.

Mrs. L. R. was born and grew up in Toronto. She was the product of a normal pregnancy and delivery, and her developmental milestones were normal. She recalled being very nervous as a child and was often sent home from school because of this. She worked hard and excelled scholastically. She was often the teacher's favorite in junior high school. In high school she participated widely in music, dance, and cheerleading. After high school she entered a nursing course and began working in pediatric nursing, where she excelled and received several commendations for her achievements.

Mrs. L. R. described a rather chaotic early life. Both of her parents were alcoholics. Her mother had cirrhosis of the liver and died at age forty-seven in 1968. At the time of the initial assessment, she characterized her mother in ambivalent terms. When mother was sober, she and daughter were best friends and exceptionally close. When she went on drinking binges, however, mother was oblivious to the family for lengthy periods, and often Mrs. L. R. had to assume responsibility for caring for the household. Mrs. L. R.'s mother had conducted a lengthy, somewhat public affair with her employer—a source both of some shame and also of intimacy and love. She had confided in her daughter about this regularly.

At the time of assessment, Mrs. L. R.'s father was sixty-one years old and working in insurance. He was described as youthful-looking and attractive, and although he too had had a drinking problem and could be violent during drinking episodes, he had by now remarried and had stopped drinking. He was leading a rather private life and had removed himself from his children's activities. He had a somewhat paranoid, mistrustful stance to any outside influence in the family life. Friends were always discouraged from visiting. Both parents, but especially the father, had set exceptionally high goals for Mrs. L. R. She felt she was never able to meet these but did not rebel against them; she merely tried harder and became more self-critical.

Mrs. L. R. was the middle of three siblings. An older brother was a chronic alcoholic. He was single, with no friends, and had never been able to hold down a job. A younger brother worked in teaching and lived with the father. He was also described as being a rather isolated man.

Mrs. L. R.'s husband, age thirty-one at the initial assessment, was a general physician. At the time of the consultation, Mrs. L. R. described their marriage as being stable and well grounded. She felt that he pressured her to live up to great expectations, however, and that she had surrendered autonomy within the marriage. Over time, he had gradually assumed responsibility for more and more. Because of her lack of interest, their sexual life had all but ceased since the birth of their daughter three years earlier. Mrs. L. R. described herself as a very caring mother. Her husband, however, thought she was overconcerned about responding to their child's every need.

## Making the Diagnosis

Mrs. L. R. presented with a number of features typical of anorexia nervosa. In late adolescence, in response to strong pressures to measure up to external standards, she began a restrictive diet. She developed an exaggerated desire for thinness and an intense fear of being fat. She believed her body size to be too large and had to keep below a magical weight—in this case, one hundred pounds. Her self-esteem was extraordinarily governed by the readings on the scale and the image in the mirror.

Associated with the intense drive for thinness was a repertoire of unusual eating behaviors, including a rigidly adhered-to diet, slow eating, and toying with food. Although binges were not present, laxative abuse to prevent absorption of calories was a feature. Diminishing consumption was paralleled by an increasing preoccupation with food. Mrs. L. R. became a gourmet cook and loved feeding others. This behavior intensified the fear of yielding to the impulse to eat and further heightened her prohibitions against it.

Characteristic thinking styles were present, including a black-and-white pattern termed *dichotomous thinking*. In this type of thinking, a pound gained is perceived as an inevitable trajectory toward obesity. Coupled with this distortion was a relative inability to recognize feeling states, whether biological signals of hunger and satiety or more purely emotional states.

Mrs. L. R. also exhibited some of the fundamental psychodynamics of anorexia nervosa. Frequently, this relates to the individual's intense need to maintain her sense of self-worth through undue control in the area of weight. This fear of loss of personal control has been linked to underlying feelings of helplessness and to a sense of personal mistrust. Mrs. L. R. had a sense of helplessness in response to attempts, as a child, to please her parents and to live up to their heightened expectations and in relation to the sudden loss of her mother from complications of alcohol misuse. Rather than experience pleasure from her body, she saw her body from adolescence on as something that had to be artificially controlled. Her view was partly a response to external pressures, as a cheerleader, as a model, and as a beauty queen. But it was also related to her view of a female body that can be out of control and lead to problems, including sexual ones.

Because of these feelings of helplessness and pressures to perform, Mrs. L. R. had feared the demands of maturity and increased independence. After weight restoration and treatment for depression, however, she was able to assume a more normal lifestyle, marry, and begin her family and career. Now, with increasing pressures to perform from her husband, a sense of lost autonomy, and a need to be responsive to her child's every need, her syndrome had recurred.

As commonly occurs in this syndrome, both parents had exhibited misuse of alcohol, as did one of the siblings. It was not clear whether the family also had a history of affective disorder. Whether the alcohol abuse produced a risk for illness for genetic or for experiential reasons was not clear. It was readily apparent how helpless and angry Mrs. L. R. felt in adolescence when she came home from school to find her parents drunk and abusive to each other. As a result, she avoided all alcohol.

Initially, I saw Mrs. L. R. as an individual whose self-esteem was highly bound to external standards; how her parents, teachers, peers, and husband felt about her determined how she felt about herself to an inordinate degree. She was extremely eager to conform to external standards and had a dichotomous thinking style so that a particular cultural look or an image could be carried to a pathological extreme.

### Course of Early Treatment

When I first saw her, I presented the above formulation to Mrs. L. R. She was encouraged to return with her husband for an assessment of the marriage and for a nutritional consultation to help plan a program of nutritional rehabilitation. In addition it was suggested that a relationship form of psychotherapy—which would highlight some of her cognitive distortions, help clarify affective states, and help free up her self-esteem from the tyranny of the scales—would be the preferred method of treatment. Mrs. L. R. voiced ready agreement with these plans. She was frightened of being admitted to hospital or being given ECT.

One week later the patient and her husband were seen together. The assessment revealed him to be a well-meaning and caring man who was frightened by his wife's clinical state. He described elements of his parents' marriage: their incessant arguing and his mother's continually putting his father down. Dr. R. was also very controlling of his wife's behavior, and there was an element of competitiveness regarding her successful career in nursing. This competition spilled over into their home life—in their endeavors to be gourmet cooks, for example. During the past year, Dr. R would jog with his wife and try to run beyond her five to eight miles.

The patient agreed that she would eat three regular meals per day until the nutritional consultation the following week. She would also stop weighing herself but be weighed only by the nutritionist or in my office. She would keep a dietary record of her intake for the coming week for review with the nutritional consultant. She was urged to recognize feeling states that might precede laxative misuse and to develop alternative and more appropriate ways of dealing with such feelings.

We agreed that in the following week I would see both husband and wife together and the wife alone for the start of her individual psychotherapy.

The referring physician had noted in a conversation with me that Mrs. L. R.'s physical state was good, but that her potassium level was in the borderline low range (3.2 milliequivalents per liter). I thought that monitoring the potassium level was warranted until Mrs. L. R. gave up the use of laxatives, and that, at least for the next four weeks, potassium levels should be obtained weekly. Because they lived so far from the hospital, Dr. R. suggested that he perform venipuncture on his wife and take the blood to the lab in the hospital where he worked.

The following week, hours after the first venipuncture, Mrs. L. R. presented in the emergency department of the hospital with a paralysis of her left arm, from which the blood had been obtained. Dr. R. was frantic, full of self-blame, and also very angry with his wife.

I felt angry with myself at having agreed to such a plan and also embarrassed at how visible this failed treatment approach had become. Mrs. L. R. was weepy and regretful at all the fuss this new symptom had caused.

In the emergency room, sodium amytal was given, with no effect. It was decided to admit Mrs. L. R. to hospital and to provide alternative care for her child through her mother-in-law. She was admitted that night and given fifty milligrams of chlorpromazine at bedtime. Her weight on admission had fallen to eighty-nine pounds. On awakening the following morning after a long and restful sleep, Mrs. L. R. had full use of both arms. After further discussion, it was decided to have her remain in hospital and plan a more detailed program of nutritional and psychosocial rehabilitation.

## What Went Wrong?

My initial intent had been to try to help Mrs. L. R. through marital and individual psychotherapy. The therapy would be geared to encourage autonomy, to heighten sensitivity to affective states, and to clarify conceptual confusion. This treatment approach was readily thwarted, however, by a plan that, in retrospect, was faulty.

This situation in which through the venipuncture the spouse became directly involved in providing his wife's care, despite our attention to issues of autonomy, control, and competitiveness, could only backfire; and so it did. The treatment goals quickly altered when Mrs. L. R. presented with a conversion disorder.

Furthermore, during the course of the first two weeks of assessment and initiation of treatment, Mrs. L. R. had lost six pounds, more than she had lost in the previous year. Why this initial weight loss occurred was not clear. Sometimes, removing the "guideposts" of the weighing scales makes people initially overly cautious. At other times, such a precipitous loss can be seen as a cry for help: people who are feeling completely imprisoned by their illness may lose weight to call out for someone else to assume responsibility for their care.

Although today most people with an eating disorder can be managed out of hospital, a significant minority require hospital admission because of the severity of the weight loss, a lack of control over weight, or the emergence of complications. In this instance, the sudden severe weight loss, together with the development of an acute conversion disorder, precipitated hospital admission.

## Course in Hospital

When admitted to hospital, Mrs. L. R. underwent a one-week period of observation, as was the custom for all admissions to this unit in the mid-1970s. We eventually stopped this procedure because we found it difficult to obtain a patient's cooperation with bed rest or other treatments after being given ward privileges for one week. In Mrs. L. R.'s circumstance, however, this one-week period was useful in that it verified her rigid eating habits, her very slow consumption, her refusal to eat high-fat and carbohydrate foods, and her strong drive to exercise after meals. After one week in which she was eating about seven hundred to nine hundred calories per day and engaging in exercise, Mrs. L. R. was put on bed rest with contingencies for weight gain.

The in-hospital treatment of anorexia nervosa during the 1970s in Toronto went through three phases. In the first, from 1970 to 1973, we followed Hilde Bruch's creative approach to understanding core psychological features in patients with anorexia nervosa. On the basis of her clinical experiences and the theoretical underpinnings of Harry Stack Sullivan, Bruch had become very critical of traditional psychoanalysis in the treatment of people with eating disorders. She thought that when such a patient received interpretations in a traditional setting, this might represent a painful reexperiencing of being told what to feel and what to think. Such interpretations would confirm her sense of inadequacy and interfere with the development of self-awareness and trust in her own psychological abilities. Bruch therefore set out to treat these patients in a way that encouraged the anorexic's autonomy and self-directed identity. What the patient said was listened to and made the object of repeated exploration. At that time, we were very impressed with Bruch's description of the psychological states of these patients, and we began to develop this type of psychotherapy on an inpatient unit. We were quickly frustrated, however, in this endeavor by our patients' resistance to gain weight.

A number of articles began to appear on the value of operant conditioning in anorexia nervosa. To us, this method seemed to address the problem we were facing: our patients were in hospital for long periods and made what appeared to be psychological progress and yet remained physically emaciated. So we began to provide reinforcements for weight gain. These were individualized for each person but typically involved time out of bed, access to telephone or television, and eventually full ward activities.

These behavioral techniques offered a number of advantages. Staff became unified in their understanding of one approach to treatment. As a result, patients did gain weight. At times, the patient felt actively involved with the weight restoration, and the team did not have to resort to more extreme restrictions (for example, placing the patient in a barren environment, stripped of all possible reinforcers). We were also struck, however, by how easily the details of the operant program could become the entire focus of treatment, rather than just one component of it and how, at times, the operant program could be applied without sensitivity to a particular patient's pathology. For these reasons, by 1977, we began to follow the British method advocated by Russell and Crisp. This method involved bed rest, intensive nursing care, and the addition of psychological treatments as the person gained weight. We continue to follow this approach, which may result in hospital admissions of six to ten weeks and prepares people for outpatient psychotherapy.

On admission, Mrs. L. R. was a moderately emaciated woman looking much older than her stated age. She had lanugo (fine, downy) hair over the back of her neck. There was some hair loss from her scalp and a loss of fatty tissue throughout her body. Blood pressure was 90 / 60 sitting. She had significant orthostatic hypotension; her heart rate was forty-four. Her potassium level on admission was 2.8. She was placed on a potassium supplement; no other medication was prescribed at this time.

Shortly after admission, Mrs. L. R. was seen in nutritional consultation. Her food diaries were reviewed. These revealed a diet of seven hundred to eight hundred calories per day, of foods especially low in fat and carbohydrate, and confirmed the rigidity and repetitive quality of her daily intake. She completely avoided any sweet desserts, breads, potatoes, and pastas. She exercised a specific amount, depending on how many calories she perceived herself to have eaten. She had also lost a sense of normal portions of foods. She was given a 1,500-calorie diet, low in fat but otherwise balanced. She was repeatedly shown models of normal-sized portions of foods. She was encouraged to complete all meals; and if unable to do so, she received a high-calorie liquid supplement to complete her caloric allotment for the day. Food intake was increased in three-hundred-calorie increments when she met specific weight targets. Privileges from bed rest, including periods of time out of bed, were clearly defined. Forbidden foods were gradually introduced. She was weighed each morning in a hospital gown, after voiding (later in the unit's evolution, the frequency of weigh-ins was reduced).

A clear nursing plan was developed. Nursing staff provided Mrs. L. R. with considerable support and encouragement to complete meals and spent at least one hour with her after meals to help her learn to discuss her feelings regarding eating and feeling fat. In addition, the nursing staff encouraged Mrs. L. R. to deal with the bloating that followed withdrawal of the laxatives (these feelings reached a peak about three weeks after stopping all laxatives). Staff also helped her examine her cognitive distortions as they occurred, particularly the black-and-white thinking that was so problematic. Most nursing staff were women of approximately Mrs. L. R.'s age and profession. Some identified with her as a nurse; others became very angry with her. How could she do this to herself when she had a child who needed her? They blamed her as if she could control her symptoms and just make them disappear. There was considerable need for staff and team meetings to clarify the approach and feelings to this particular patient.

After several weeks in hospital, Mrs. L. R. was able to complete her meals and had gained about eight pounds. She began regular meetings with her husband. The marital relationship seemed to be based on a genuine caring and concern for each other and for their child. It also became clear, however, that Dr. R. had significant difficulty with Mrs. L. R.'s considerable achievements and success at work—and with an earlier steady boyfriend of hers who had achieved notable professional success in Dr. R.'s field. Not only was Dr. R. anxious and self-blaming, he began, as well, to disparage the treatment and the treatment team. Effort had to go into preventing him from signing her out against medical advice halfway through the hospital stay. After four weekly marital sessions, Dr. R. was referred for individual psychotherapy, with a recommendation that the marital therapy resume after discharge.

Mrs. L. R. was in hospital for nine weeks. At the time of discharge, she was 108 pounds and had been at this weight for almost two weeks on a diet of 2,200 calories per day. She had not used laxatives for six weeks. (Staff had found some Ex-Lax in tissue boxes in the third week of her hospital stay and had confronted her. No further misuse of laxatives was noted, and her potassium level was subsequently consistently normal.) Mrs. L. R. was now eating a good variety of foods; she still felt fat, particularly in her stomach, and was terrified of losing control. She avoided all exercise and voiced concern that if she resumed running at all, she would likely get drawn back into the full syndrome. She was encouraged to stay on the potassium supplement, but this medication was stopped about six weeks after discharge.

### Individual Psychotherapy After Discharge

After leaving hospital, Mrs. L. R. was seen in individual psychotherapy once per week for the following two and a half years. During the first four months, she and her husband were seen in marital therapy by a colleague in social work in marital therapy, and her husband continued his own individual therapy on a weekly basis for one year.

Mrs. L. R. had had no outpatient follow-up after her first hospital admission at age nineteen. At the time of this discharge, she was very motivated for a psychotherapeutic approach. She was terrified of a recurrence of her illness, which she saw as quite possible if she began dieting or exercising again.

Major themes of the therapy involved:

1. Examination of factors related to her thrill for thinness.

2. Clarification of the cognitive distortions, particularly of the dichotomous (all-or-nothing) thinking and of her personalizing a variety of situations. In the latter she misinterpreted events in a personal and critical way—walking into a room, for example, and feeling that others were judging her harshly for having gained a few pounds. The former, also called *black-and-white thinking*, reflects an extremism—there are no "in betweens." This extremism is obvious in how anorexics see food and weight. What is less apparent is that it permeates all of their thinking: "If I don't excel at scholastics or athletics, then I'm terrible." Also, other people are idealized or vilified. And anorexics view themselves as well in all good or all bad terms, often in response to how they measure up to external goals.

3. Recognition of different affective states and development of an ability to respond appropriately to such affects. Mrs. L. R. became more comfortable with being angry; she no longer felt totally dependent on having everyone like her.

4. Encouragement that she see her body as a source of comfort, rather than as an object only needing to be controlled. She started yoga and painting, began to experience more pleasure in her body, and after a number of months developed an interest in sex.

5. Help to mourn the loss of her mother and to understand its meaning in her world. She was able, as well, to reflect on her mother's affair not only for the shame it brought but also for the comfort her mother must have derived when in such a loveless marriage. She began to feel resentful for having to give up her own adolescence to care for her parents and for having to achieve, to overcome what she felt was the family's status as outsiders. And she mourned the loss of her father, who had emotionally deserted her, gradually becoming closer to her younger brother.

6. Recognition of how her self-esteem had been so dependent on what others thought or wished for her. She began to exert more personal choices, was less passive with her husband, and gave up her nursing career to pursue an interest in music. Her creative side flourished.

7. Recognition, with some difficulty, that her wish to satisfy her daughter's every need was an extension of her wish to control her daughter.

After two and a half years of individual therapy, Mrs. L. R. maintained a weight of 115 to 120 pounds (although she never weighed herself and refused to be weighed by a physician). She ate a good variety of foods, whether alone or with others present. She denied a preoccupation with food and avoided exercise. She was much happier in her marriage, as was her husband. She had a second child and began to pursue a music career seriously. A third child was born three years later when Mrs. L. R. was forty-one. During each of the latter two pregnancies, she gained more than twenty-five pounds without experiencing anxiety, nor did she have difficulty in losing the weight after the deliveries.

## Course After Psychotherapy

About one year after the birth of her youngest child, Mrs. L. R. was seen for major depression. She had been agitated for several months, was sad and weepy and at times hopeless. No suicidal ideation was present; she was preoccupied, however, about her own health and she had begun seeing many doctors for physical examinations and elaborate medical workups. Often, her concerns related to a fear of malignancy involving the liver. She was also preoccupied with the welfare of her children and feared not being there to look after them. She showed vegetative features of a depressed state, including sleep disturbance, poor concentration, and loss of interest. She weaned her youngest child and was then treated with a tricyclic antidepressant in the standard doses. She made an excellent response and was maintained on desipramine for one year.

For the seven years since then, Mrs. L. R. has been seen infrequently and has done very well. She continues to have intermittent anxiety regarding her physical well-being and at times becomes preoccupied with a feature of her body—for example, a mole, a lump, or headaches that could be the presentation of malignancies—and is aware that these worries usually reflect a period of increased stress in her life and require some psychotherapeutic support. She has become aware of circumstances that are liable to produce these anxieties: often, feelings of competition with another woman or pressures to perform in her music career. Although aware of these circumstances, she is unable to stop focusing her anxiety on a particular body part and the risk of illness. It is interesting that Mrs. L. R., who previously displayed a mistrust of her body through undue weight control, now demonstrated such mistrust in fears of terminal illness.

She is very aware of the potential of losing her happy family and of risking her daughters to the type of adolescence she herself experienced. She did see her middle child develop a school phobia and multiple anxieties at age nine—problems that required attention from a child psychiatrist prior to the resumption of normal schooling. At the present time, the children range in ages from fifteen to seven and all are in good health. Mrs. L. R. and her husband describe a good marital relationship, and aside from the periodic anxieties regarding her own physical health or that of her children, she remains well and active with a new musical career.

## PRINCIPLES OF A MULTIMODAL TREATMENT

While every patient is unique, this case description of an individual seen over a twenty-year period highlights several important points that apply to treating anorexia nervosa in general:

1. *We must have respect for the psychological state of the individual and recognition of factors operating at any given time.* In the syndrome of anorexia nervosa, features that were important to this married mother will be very different from those that may operate in a young adolescent who may be trying to separate from her family. It is important for treatment guidelines to be just that— guidelines, that must be interpreted according to an individual's requirements and must be informed by a detailed understanding of the individual and her world. Recognition of this point would have prevented the disastrous involvement of Mrs. L. R.'s husband for venipuncture.

2. *Although there must be respect for the individual, we may still have to intervene directly, at times with lifesaving measures.* It must be emphasized that people with anorexia nervosa have a defect in judgment in a focal area—regarding their well-being and physical health. So the clinician may have to stress firmly the necessity of nutritional restoration, hospital care, and, even, on infrequent occasions, involuntary detention and refeeding.

3. *A multidisciplinary team with expertise in a variety of domains should be called on for advice and management.* Nutritional, metabolic, and pharmacological care must be interwoven with an empathic but firm nursing approach and an understanding of intrapsychic and interpersonal dynamics. Because staff bring different views and attitudes to people with anorexia nervosa, careful attention must be directed to the provision of a unified effort. It is easy for some staff to infantilize such small patients, others to be angry at their resistance, and still others to focus only on the physiology and nutritional chaos. A clear and unified conceptual frame is necessary at all times. Such a framework reduces staff anxiety and enables members of the treatment team to work together, to make predictions about specific interventions.

4. *Although the eating disorder affects one individual in a family, it has not arisen in a vacuum; cultural and familial factors are also of importance in the genesis and perpetuation of the disorder.* And, for many adult patients, the family is both the family of origin and

the family developed with one's partner. In this case, the patient's parents had a clear impact on her difficulties in late adolescence and on her choice of a spouse, and the spouse's behavior had a definite effect on the patient's symptoms. This patient, years later, felt that her husband's psychotherapy was a critical factor in enabling her own growth. In addition, it was my impression that the husband, though contributing to some of the difficulties, also provided a great deal of support and a form of "holding environment"; at no time did he threaten to leave or to end the marriage. The importance of the spouse as a source of support during the difficult period of acute symptoms warrants research to aid in future understanding of the process of improvement from anorexia nervosa.

5. *The treatments applied in this case varied from pharmacological to individual and couples therapy, to treatment for the patient's daughter.* This variety demonstrates the need for flexibility of the clinician in adapting to the patient's state. Multimodal therapy can be misunderstood, however, to mean that anything goes. This is far from the case. Standards count and must be continuously applied. While we can advocate a multimodal psychotherapy, the clinician has to have a fundamental grounding in a clear understanding of the doctor-patient relationship; otherwise, it is easy for boundaries to be eroded. There must be self-scrutiny at every step of the treatment. A second opinion is often of value (one was obtained on three occasions in this case over the twenty years).

6. *This case also demonstrates the presence of other psychiatric disorders after recovery from anorexia nervosa.* This individual experienced one clear depressive episode and a prolonged period of anxiety regarding her body. The Toronto Follow-Up Study of anorexia nervosa revealed the high rate of such symptoms over time: 60 percent of the anorexics experienced a major depression, independent of whether they had recovered; and over 50 percent had some form of anxiety disorder. Although the mechanisms for the later development of these disorders is not understood, knowledge of the likelihood of the co-occurrence should be borne in mind.

7. *Women with anorexia nervosa can regain normal fertility and may have normal pregnancies if they are well at the time of conception.* The patient described in this report had three normal pregnancies, with reasonable weight gain and healthy babies. Those actively ill may not conceive, or if they do, often gain little weight and have tiny and sickly babies. Not much is known about the offspring of women with anorexia nervosa. Anecdotal reports suggest that many are very caring mothers; some may be oversolicitous. This case example shows, however, an episode of anxiety disturbance in one of the patient's daughters.

8. *Delivery of health care cannot be removed from economic considerations, and some may view the rather lengthy psychotherapy with this patient with skepticism.* The cost of this process, however, about $12,000 (Canadian) and the husband's psychotherapy ($5,000) and couples therapy ($1,200) must be weighed against the cost of the patient's in-hospital stay (almost $20,000) and repeated and costly medical investigations (over $12,000). With all of the emphasis on managed care and accountability for care provided, it is important to maintain a full array of clinical services and to see that they are provided when the clinical need dictates. Saving money by reducing service in the short term is false economy; it often leads to greater spending in later years.

In this chapter, I have tried to highlight how multimodal treatment may be applied to an individual with restricting anorexia nervosa. Such treatments require vigilance and flexibility on the part of the clinician, but when applied with sensitivity to the individual patient, may produce excellent results.

## NOTES

P. 313, *Findings here indicated:* Toner, B., Garfinkel, P. E., & Garner, D. M. (1986). Long-term follow-up of anorexia nervosa. *Psychosomatic Medicine, 48,* 520–529.

P. 313, *Theander has provided long-term follow-up data:* Theander, S. (1985). The outcome of anorexia nervosa. *Journal of Psychiatric Research, 19,* 493–508.

P. 314, *Unlike the situation for depression or bulimia nervosa:* Agras, W. S., Rossiter, E. M., Arnow, B., et al. (1992). Pharmacologic and cognitive-behavioral treatment for bulimia nervosa: A controlled comparison. *American Journal of Psychiatry, 149,* 82–87.

P. 319, *Characteristic thinking styles were present:* Garner, D. M., Garfinkel, P. E., & Bemis, K. (1982). A multidimensional psychotherapy for anorexia nervosa. *International Journal of Eating Disorders, 1,* pp. 3–46.

P. 321, *potassium level was in the borderline low range:* Kaplan, A. S., & Garfinkel, P. E. (1993). *Medical issues and the eating disorders.* New York: Brunner/Mazel.

P. 322, *most people with an eating disorder can be managed out of hospital:* Piran, N., Kaplan, A. S., Kerr, A., Shekter-Wolfson, L., Winokur, J., & Garfinkel, P. E. (1989). A day hospital group therapy program for patients with serious eating disorders. *International Journal of Eating Disorders, 8,* 511–521.

P. 323, *The in-hospital treatment:* Kennedy, S. H., & Garfinkel, P. E. (1992). Advances in the diagnosis and treatment of anorexia nervosa and bulimia nervosa. *Canadian Journal of Psychiatry, 37,* 309–315.

P. 323, *Hilde Bruch's creative approach:* Bruch, H. (1973). *Eating disorders.* New York: Basic Books.

P. 326, *Major themes of the therapy:* Garfinkel, P. E., & Goldbloom, D. S. (1993). Bulimia nervosa: A review of therapy research. *Journal of Psychotherapy Practice and Research, 2,* 38–50.

P. 329, *every patient is unique:* Garfinkel, P. E., & Garner, D. M. (1982). *Anorexia nervosa: A multidimensional perspective.* New York: Brunner/Mazel.

P. 331, *The treatments applied in this case:* Goldbloom, D. S., & Garfinkel, P. E. (1990). The serotonin hypothesis of bulimia nervosa: Theory and evidence. *Canadian Journal of Psychiatry, 35,* 741–744.

# II

# EXTENDING THE FRAME
## Working with Managed Care to Support Treatment for a Refractory Patient

### Kathryn J. Zerbe

As clinicians treating eating-disordered patients, we encounter many paradoxes and challenges in our work. Some patients appear to have all of the psychological resources to get well but resist doing so; others improve with more limited support or motivation for change. As this book clearly attests, contemporary psychiatry offers patients a variety of treatments that are proving effective over the long run for a substantial number of individuals afflicted with anorexia nervosa or bulimia nervosa.

As clinicians have more options available, however, financial resources to support treatment are growing more limited. More and more patients are finding support for mental health services challenged by third-party payers. While clinicians work to provide state-of-the-art care—medications, group and individual therapies, hospitalization, or highly structured outpatient protocols when indicated—our patients are often forced to accept what we consider less than ideal recommendations. Third parties—in particular, case managers employed by insurance companies—have more to say about parceling out treatment resources than either the patient herself or her primary clinicians.

All individuals involved in the care of the patient are in an insoluble bind. The patient, whose very identity is embedded in her eating disorder, naturally resists giving it up even though she realizes it ravages her body and spirit. Many patients even speak of their diagnosis of anorexia or bulimia as a friend or ally, as if the pathology itself helps them heroically in the struggle to survive.

Therapists must challenge this notion and reassert that a healthier, fuller sense of self will be found as the eating difficulties are arrested. Despite long-standing and what appear to be intractable problems, through the variety of contemporary treatment approaches the patient must form a new identity other than her eating disorder. She must mourn the eating disorder as a beloved, albeit ambivalent, source of psychic survival in order to thrive and grow in new ways. In a process akin to the development from childhood to maturity, she must build a sense of self—a new identity.

The problem, of course, is that this maturation will take time, and in the current age, time is our most precious commodity. Intuitively, even those least friendly to psychology or knowledgeable about our therapeutic tools realize that no individual develops a sense of who one is overnight. In a managed-care environment, however, this appears to be exactly what our patients are often required to do. Sparse mental health benefits give the implicit message that emotional symptoms are as easy to reverse as the common cold. Yet, when the individual must build a new identity, we might more aptly employ a simile from rehabilitation medicine. The eating disorder would then be likened to a severe accident that leaves the individual crippled or incapacitated in her attempt to negotiate life's entangled pathway. The individual must overcome the severe trauma to be able to function in the multiplicity of roles and circumstances our lives demand.

Thus, while psychotropic medication relieves symptoms, brief individual or group psychotherapy provides containment and insight, and cognitively based, patient-centered educational processes teach new skills, such tools will rarely, if ever, provide all of the psychological nutrients that patients require. To reverse egosyntonic but physically and emotionally incapacitating eating disorders, patients need all of these rehabilitative efforts over a long period of time to grow and to thrive. In the face of such seemingly insurmountable problems, we maintain a sense of hopefulness that the patient can and will get well.

Most clinicians are painfully aware of these facts: although a minority of individual patients will recover with brief, symptom-focused interventions, long-term follow-up studies of eating-disordered patients are sobering. Mortality and morbidity for these illnesses are high. The symptoms themselves tend to recur, if not persist, at a lower virulence.

More disconcerting, when one looks beneath the facade of their typically engaging, energetic visages, is the quality of life that patients maintain. What patients report in follow-up interviews shows lives replete with hidden, stultifying misery. Failed interpersonal relationships, including marriages and friendships, are the norm. Work may go well superficially but be devoid of meaning and purpose. A sense of joy and pleasure in life's big and little blessings is lacking. In short, those experiences and relationships that define a life well lived are missing.

Knowing these austere facts changes the role of mental health professionals working with eating-disordered patients. No longer can we simply be advocates for our patients in the hours we formally meet with them. Now we must champion their need for care and development to a wider audience—the managed care industry, insurance companies, businesses, and even local, state, and federal governments. We must help others who have not been traditionally friendly to mental health services to become much more conversant with our methods, our tools, and our goals. In essence, our formidable task is to make those whose interest is primarily to save money by restricting access to become much more supportive of treatment.

Clinicians must ally themselves with managed care providers to provide the most cost-effective treatment modalities. Simultaneously, we must help third parties realize that treatment "on the front end" is actually cheaper in the long run for the insurance company. Emerging cost-offset studies in psychiatry can help clinicians justify treatment protocols by underscoring the sound economics of early intervention. Definitive mental health care avoids later expensive acute hospitalizations, long-term incapacitation in the work arena, and a huge expenditure of medical and psychiatric benefits to treat the chronic eating disorder.

Sophisticated outcome research will help us demonstrate as a profession that human suffering is assuaged by specific mental health interventions; we must use those studies to underscore to a society burdened with rising health care costs that treatment of emotional problems is not only a humanitarian goal but also a solid financial investment. In this redoubtable struggle rests not only the future of the profession but also the very lives of our patients.

## A Case in Point

The case I present describes how I worked with a case manager over a prolonged period of time to treat a woman who suffered from severe refractory anorexia nervosa. The case highlights many aspects of treatment and pays particular attention to issues raised when one encounters the scrutiny of the case management process. In particular, concerns about confidentiality of the patient, the challenge of describing psychological work to another professional from a different world, and the personal toll extracted by the time and energies invested are reviewed.

It is my belief that only as the practice of psychotherapy becomes less mysterious and scary to laypersons will it be sanctioned by our society on equal parity with other lifesaving medical procedures. Only then will the mentally ill be able to seek treatment without the shamefully felt stigma they now encounter. For the foreseeable future psychotherapists will need to extend the frame of our work to protect the treatment needs of our patients. We must advocate our contemporary treatment methods to a largely hostile audience on a case-by-case basis.

Some practitioners will likely experience this endeavor as masochistic. Third-party payers have not been receptive to modalities that are expensive and time-consuming and that appear unfocused or obscure. Moreover, the mentally ill have never been an influential lobbying force.

Potential benefits for engaging in the struggle, however, are enormous. Consider the quotation from the Talmud used in the film *Schindler's List:* "To save one life is to save an entire world." Whenever mental health professionals describe, discuss, debate, and thereby champion the need for effective treatment strategies, the lay public and third-party payers become more conversant with our methods. We thus have the potential of transforming their antiquated ideas about mental illness by sharing what contemporary practice offers. We hold the power to reshape how broader audiences think about what we do, even as we reshape the identity of our profession by extending the frame of our efforts. In the process, some patients will receive the services they need in order to grow and thrive as the human beings they are.

In the case that follows, I outline how I have worked with a patient, her family, and a case manager to secure benefits for her extended treatment. Embedded in the description are principles I have found useful in working with patients, regardless of the third-party issues that one must contend with in the current climate. My hope is to explicate some of those principles while examining some new ways they can be integrated into our work with case managers and third parties. I also want to show that, by extending the frame of our work to include third parties, we may sometimes also enhance the psychological work with the patient; by taking on the new functions as their advocates to the world outside the particular therapeutic arena, we serendipitously model the tenacity and vitality required of life. Such a view poses many challenges and potential pitfalls, but at least for the foreseeable future, we must learn to work in the context of a rapidly changing, highly resistant managed care environment.

# A Challenging Patient

When Erin was referred to me for consultation, she was a twenty-year-old college junior who had suffered for eleven years from long periods of self-starvation punctuated with episodic purges (vomiting; laxative, diet pill, and diuretic abuse). Already hospitalized on six occasions for her eating disorder, she and her parents now presented with palpable despair about her condition. Her double major in nutritional science and sociology spoke to her intellectual acumen and psychological mindedness; her preoccupation with having a thin body, eating minuscule amounts, and remaining slender at all costs appeared to stave off depression. As she put it, "My eating disorder is my savior. Why should I give it up?"

Indeed, she had already triumphantly defeated two renowned psychopharmacologists who had first employed generally accepted antidepressants and then moved to trials of newer agents. When medication and other treatments such as individual therapy, cognitive-behavioral interventions, and group modalities failed, Erin and her parents turned to other measures. They debated about the use of acupuncture and other nontraditional healing methods, feeling that some procedure must be found to disrupt her self-destructive pattern.

Erin's parents sadly told me they were at their wits' ends with their daughter. To be balanced and realistic without giving false hope, I replied that the discouragement felt by all members of the family was understandable, given what each had been through to put Erin's life on a better track. I also commented that it must be quite confusing that Erin could do so well in some areas of her life, like college, only to have her dreams spoiled by her persistent eating disorder. I told the patient and her parents that I believed that part of her wanted to get well or else she would not be sitting in my office; we needed to pay attention to that part of her even as we listened closely to other aspects of her "real self" that did not want to get well.

Although Erin did not have a formal diagnosis of dissociative disorder, pointing out the two parts of her soul that seemed to be warring with each other resonated with her. To my surprise, she asked to see me alone the following day, at which time she agreed to again consider psychiatric hospitalization. I had offered this to her and her family as a way of not only stabilizing her eating disorder but also getting a better understanding of the roots of her problem and the medical consequences of her physical debilitation. At this point, she was abusing diuretics and diet pills daily, weighed ninety-five pounds at five feet four inches in height, and looked emaciated, although her laboratory values were still within normal limits.

Her parents told me that they would be supportive of a trial of intensive work but worried that it would not be supported by their insurance carrier. After all, treatment had already failed despite repeated efforts, significant resources had already been used, and at least one case manager who had worked with the family believed Erin to be "suffering from a terminal eating disorder." Although insurance benefits had been generous up to this point, the family anticipated that just as they were impatient and frustrated, so those responsible for allocating the treatment benefits would wonder whether they were "throwing good money after bad."

The family gave me the name of a case manager who worked directly with the principal insurance company. The patient's father told me I would need to speak with this individual on the phone to discuss Erin's clinical needs and to determine benefits. Therefore, prior to seeing Erin for the next hour of consultation, I spoke with the case manager to review significant laboratory data, the long-term history, and the present difficulties and to recommend that Erin be admitted to residential psychiatric care.

In many cases even life-threatening eating disorders can no longer be treated in an inpatient facility. Third-party payers do not see these illnesses as imminently lethal and, therefore, do not consider them medically necessary. Fortunately, in Erin's case, the case manager had a very good understanding of the insidious nature of eating disorders. He was familiar with the fact that individuals can look fairly healthy and have normal laboratory studies (for example, electrolytes, other blood chemistries, electrocardiogram) yet be in dire physical danger.

I reviewed that, despite the apparently pessimistic treatment history of the patient, she had a number of good prognostic factors, including her intelligence, sense of humor, psychological mindedness, and desire to change her life. I also pointed out the investment that both parents had in helping their daughter, particularly their willingness to stay involved in her care. They had already agreed to a treatment contract that committed them to come for regular family therapy meetings despite living more than eight hundred miles from the treatment facility. Pointing out the realistic strengths and weaknesses of the patient and her family, while also sharing that no promises for recovery could be made, led the case manager to approve seven to fourteen days of hospitalization to stabilize the eating disorder, more fully understand the depth of Erin's difficulties, and formulate why she had remained ill for so long.

### Education as a Means of Establishing Rapport

I have found it crucial that clinicians share from the outset as many details as possible with the case manager so that the treatment relationship can be supported. I also listen to the case manager's concerns and suggestions. As in working with patients and families, openness builds support and the alliance.

Although at this juncture the case manager was understanding and supportive of hospitalization and psychotherapy, I also discussed the long-term mortality rates of anorexia nervosa. It's necessary to point out that research has not yet provided a definitive prognostic picture for bulimia nervosa; it has been considered a bona fide illness for only a few years. On occasion, I send articles documenting statistics and research trends.

As cost-offset data and outcome research become more available, these should also be added to the package. Documenting psychiatry's efficacy, compared with other specialties, will augment our impact. To answer all of the questions that arise at each stage of the treatment and to provide pertinent, succinct reading material takes significant time, but this expenditure of time is often a critical, first step in educating reviewers about the ramifications of the illness and what can be done to alleviate it. Facts and figures that clinicians consider common knowledge are often news to those not immersed in the subspecialty literature. For example, third-party payers are quite struck with the myriad medical complications, high mortality and suicide rates, and associated comorbid conditions that routinely accompany eating disorders.

Workups and treatment for these life-threatening symptoms are expensive but prevent the even greater outlay if the patient develops a chronic condition. Definitive intervention not only serves to interrupt the life-threatening medical symptoms (for example, electrolyte abnormalities, cardiac arrhythmias) but saves costly medical services over the years. Comprehensive treatment requires an initial investment that ultimately pays off in cost-saving benefits. Periodontal reconstruction, extensive cardiovascular tests, weekly and biweekly measurements of blood chemistries, and diagnostic gastrointestinal procedures are just some of the medical costs avoided when the eating disorder is brought under control. Overall, precious health care resources are ultimately conserved by decisive psychiatric intervention.

## A Conflict over Pharmacotherapy

Erin was always reluctant to take psychotropic medication. Two previous psychiatrists addressed her opposition successfully, however, and were able to try a variety of medications commonly used in the treatment of anorexia nervosa and bulimia. Over the protracted treatment course before she became my patient, she had already been given trials of three tricyclic antidepressants, a

monoamine oxidase inhibitor, lithium carbonate, sodium val-
proate, and two antipsychotic medications. Although her dysphoria and emotional lability made plausible the rational use of
antidepressants and mood stabilizers, her ego was never so fragmented that a thought disorder or psychotic process was in question. I understood the use of antipsychotic medication as a
desperate attempt on the part of her physicians to bring her
emotional turmoil under a modicum of symptomatic control.

Because psychotropic medication had not been helpful in the
past, and because Erin needed to exert control over what she
believed "should and should not go into my body," she refused
any additional trials of medication. My typical stance is to work
with and integrate this veiled attempt to maintain autonomy.
When appropriate, I suggest pertinent publications about medications, written for patients and family members, that contain
the details these bright and involved individuals desire to know.
Usually, this approach helps reassure patients that medication
will not be employed as a kind of thought or mind control and
that medication will not rob them of their autonomy or make
them feel like automatons. I also discuss other fantasies the
patient may have about medication and point out its legitimate
benefits while underscoring that it is not a panacea for the existential and identity issues the patient brings to treatment. This
discussion frequently moves the patient to work with the pre-
scriber, who can be a psychiatrist, nurse clinician, or primary care
physician with expertise in the pharmacotherapy of eating disorders—a challenging arena in the best of circumstances.

Erin's case manager was dissatisfied with my approach. His
own physician consultants were placing pressure on him to insist
that fluoxetine, a selective serotonin reuptake inhibitor, be prescribed immediately. They argued that titrating this medication
to an effective dose might lessen the manifest anorexic and
bulimic symptomatology. They resorted to my technique of
sending articles, faxing me the latest offprints or pharmacological methods in treating eating disorders! When Erin was recalcitrant, the case manager insisted all the more that she try

medication again. After all, "Was she interested in helping herself or merely using her benefits to stay sick?" he asked.

Because psychotropic medication has been shown to be effective in a large number of cases, I could understand the case manager's rationale. To attempt to force the patient to take medication, however, seemed unethical and undermining. I attempted to assuage the case manager temporarily by describing my approach of waiting and working with the resistances. As weeks and months passed with no change in Erin's position, I felt more and more trapped in discussions with the case manager. Finally, we received an ultimatum. Erin would either take medication or her benefits would immediately cease.

This stalemate between patient and case manager is more typically played out in other arenas of treatment as the patient takes a firm stance against her primary therapist, members of her treatment team, her parents, or her significant other. The meaning behind these self-defeating patterns can usually be elucidated over time as the patient finds life domains in which to exert her independence.

In this situation, the third party had already been more than generous by contemporary standards in allotting additional time to work with the underlying personal issues. From the insurer's perspective, it was time for Erin to fish or cut bait, to show whether she was truly interested in helping herself or remaining self-destructively tied to her manifest symptomatology.

Although many patients do derive a great deal of unconscious satisfaction in undermining the therapy, I did not sense this was the case with Erin. The dispute over medication made me wonder whether she refused out of a sense of shame that prior trials had not been successful. Perhaps she felt different from others— as if she inhabited an odd, monstrous body. In effect, she would rather stop treatment than be subjected to another medication that did not work and that would leave her feeling all the more disparaging and ridiculing of herself.

As a general matter, of course, the primary therapist must deal straightforwardly with both parties and supply as much psychological detail as warranted to support the treatment. Therefore, I discussed this tentative formulation first with the patient and, after permission was granted, with the case manager. Eventually, Erin was able to accept the medication trial, and fluoxetine did prove useful in moderately alleviating her bulimic symptoms, as well as her dysphoria. As in most other cases, it played only an adjunctive role, neither being the panacea the insurance company had hoped for nor the malevolent usurper of personal power the patient had anticipated. The tightrope we must walk demands attention to both points of view.

Explaining any psychological difficulties the patient has in accepting medication may also be valuable for building the alliance among patient, the treatment team, and the managed care personnel. This dialogue is as workable as any other, more overtly psychological concern.

### The Case Manager as Customer

In recent years, hospitals and clinics have assumed a more customer-focused relationship to patients. As in any business, this relationship entails treating the patient and her family first and foremost as consumers. Instead of arbitrarily assigning the patient to particular ways of treatment, treatment is formulated on an individual basis to meet the needs of the patient. Psychotherapy then becomes "customer driven," meaning that one simply does not confront or interpret the patient's modes of interacting pejoratively, but rather is always thinking first about how to engage the patient for the most desirable outcome. Implicit is the view that the consumer desires the most positive outcome for the least cost. All customers, regardless of the product for which they shop, demand the biggest "bang for their buck."

Because representatives of managed care have traditionally been considered adversaries in the treatment process, they have not been treated with a customer-oriented approach. But in working with these individuals, it is crucial for us to maintain an attitude of respect, understanding, and flexibility, sometimes under the duress of having one's formulated treatment plan openly challenged. For example, the initial relationship with Erin's case manager was forged by listening to his perspective on the case and only then pointing out some new directions that needed to be tried.

Additional tactics involved asking the case manager to travel to Topeka to meet with me about the treatment and assuring him that he would be able to consult with other team members about their perspectives. Finally, assurance that additional consultation would be sought and the treatment reviewed at pivotal points convinced him that treatment monies would not simply be drained without periodic and critical reevaluation. The hope was to enlist him as an ally in the care by openly incorporating his suggestions and ideas as much as possible while demonstrating what we believed we had to offer this troubled patient.

This tack evolved from the philosophy that the more case managers know about what clinicians do and why we do it, the more they will feel both knowledgeable about the field and able to dispense benefits at the behest of the patient. Unlike other representatives, Erin's case manager did not visit, but rather learned about the treatment at a distance. Assuming a truly collegial, nondefensive demeanor avoided the diatribes that have sometimes accompanied other treatment reviews.

### Issues of Confidentiality

Confidentiality is clearly a cornerstone of our work as therapists. Patients will not confide their secret fears and longings unless they believe their words are held sacrosanct. The case management process is felt to be undermining of psychotherapy because clinicians are implored to share so many details with the reviewer or third party.

Like all patients, Erin was told about the dilemma in which the case management process placed us both. We negotiated that the psychological issues she was dealing with would only be discussed in the most general terms and that, after each discussion with the case manager, I would report back to her on the content and tone of the meeting. This approach was taken to help Erin feel more empowered in the relationship with me and in her life. I openly explained as best I could that there was no way she could feel the same level of privacy about her treatment as in earlier times when case management did not intrude into the work. I underscored with her and her family that, in the current age, clinicians must work with the case management process until a better, more direct way is found to adjudicate claims.

I further underscored that eating disorders thrive in an environment of secret-keeping. It was unlikely that Erin could get better if I was not open with her about all of the risks and benefits to her treatment, including the case management process. Although her case manager was supportive of her work, I realized that his involvement would be experienced as an intrusion into her privacy and that it would need to be a focus of our work together. Here I attempted to transform one of the most negative aspects of case management into a more positive one. Eating-disordered patients harbor a "secret self" that encompasses the eating disorder and many other personal facts about their lives. Consequently, it is crucial for the therapist to be scrupulously straightforward and honest with them. This enables the patients to throw light on what they consider to be the darker, malevolent aspects of their beings.

I underscored to both the case manager and Erin that I would only share a broad outline of the issues she was struggling with in treatment. Still, I acknowledged to myself that this compromise position felt distasteful and possibly countertherapeutic. It seemed that so many competing masters had to be served. How could I possibly provide information about the depth of the treatment relationship and what was going on to ensure benefits while maintaining Erin's trust that her ideas, troubles, yearnings, and despair were safely contained within our relationship? I decided to turn this dilemma that was residing in me onto the patient to help her develop her autonomy and become her own best advocate for care.

To empower the patient to take more control of her life and develop her sense of personal responsibility, I also suggested that she correspond with the case manager. This intervention became particularly important at those times when it seemed likely that treatment would be interrupted. No clinician expects the long-term treatment of a severe eating disorder to proceed without regressions and resistances. Indeed, it is the tenacious working through these difficult periods that is often most helpful in helping the patient consolidate a new sense of self and establish a feeling of greater alliance with the clinician. Those clinicians without experience in working with difficult, refractory patients may feel most pessimistic at these points. Erin herself wondered whether she could really ever get better but wanted to continue to try.

When Erin wrote to the case manager, she found novel ways to communicate her needs that helped establish her identity. With typical veracity, she described how many of the early months of her work with me had been spent in a "lost and mixed zone." She said that although it appeared that she was losing her footing now in treatment, for the first time in her life she was alive. She believed that only through understanding herself better and finding out who she really was could she take hold of her life. She pleaded for the chance. She wrote that it would not be easy for her to do so but that continued treatment seemed like a lifeline.

I suspect her direct plea was, for the case manager, a unique window on a prolonged and convoluted treatment course. Most patients cannot articulate their plight so intelligently and movingly. Erin was able, despite her emotional pain, to be her own advocate at this point. In so doing, she also demonstrated that she was moving forward with her life and proved to herself that she was building a sense of her own desires, beliefs, and purposefulness. When patients can defend their own treatment needs, they are well along the path to becoming their own best advocates.

### Enlisting Parental Support

Just as case managers must now be counseled in a sophisticated way about the theoretical underpinnings, medical concerns, and treatment goals of patients, so must clinicians strive to educate family members about these same issues and about the arduous road to wellness. This approach supplements, but does not obviate, the need for individual family therapy. Just as I "prescribed" reading to Erin and her case manager, so I established an alliance with this family by giving them brochures, pamphlets, and copies of professional articles, as well as providing them with a written outline of the course of treatment.

I then spoke directly about their necessary involvement with the case manager, their insurance company, and advocacy groups for patients and families (for example, NAMI—The National Alliance for the Mentally Ill; ANAD—the National Association for Anorexia Nervosa and Associated Disorders). I told them they could not afford to take a back seat in these areas of Erin's treatment. This was not a time for the faint of heart; they needed to divert their investment in knowing about Erin's daily life to more goal-directed advocacy of maintaining treatment benefits. Their concern for their daughter was thus reframed and rechanneled; they had to "stick like glue" to the fiscal issues at hand and pry themselves from intrusions into their daughter's personal thoughts and feelings. Erin's autonomy was thereby also promoted. In the present age families must ally themselves as much with the case management procedures as they do the more intricate, technical family therapy meetings; this can, as we have seen, also promote the overall treatment goals.

I explained to the family that I would need their help in many ways during the treatment, including working with the insurance company. Attempting to model a sense of open dialogue about meaningful life issues, I met with Erin and her parents to explain the rugged contemporary terrain of insurance coverage. Because Erin's parents were different from many other families who covertly undermine treatment, they immediately sensed the need to become involved with the insurance issues. Perhaps they capitalized on an unconscious sense of guilt they harbored with respect to Erin's illness. Perhaps their involvement also can be understood as a solution to their conflict between desiring to maintain parental control over Erin's treatment while also exhibiting deep caring about how that treatment could be funded. They were not wealthy people, and so maintaining benefits was necessary to sustain the treatment and help Erin break the ties that had bound her to her eating disorder.

After some preliminary meetings and phone calls between the patient and her family, the parents eagerly involved themselves in maintaining contact and developing a relationship with the insurance company personnel who handled their policy. The insurance, a benefit of the small company for which the father worked, had a catastrophic illness clause. Erin's father "went to work" to ensure that his daughter could use it after basic benefits were exhausted. His company's senior management believed that his own job performance had significantly improved when Erin's condition had finally temporized. Erin's parents' concerted work directly with the insurance company and indirectly with representatives at the job site helped secure substantial additional benefits for the life of the treatment.

## THE FUTURE OF MANAGED CARE

In today's climate the case management process is typically regarded as a necessary evil in psychiatric treatment. Particularly for patients like Erin, who have been refractory to myriad interventions, benefits for further treatment are often denied. When clinicians request any more support than the briefest, most focused interventions, we are increasingly having to wage extended battles with third parties to secure any benefits. Until health care reform has addressed the needs of the mentally ill, particularly the long-term refractory patient, clinicians will have to present our case for treatment to managed care providers on an individual basis. We have little choice but to adapt to the managed care contingency because often life hangs in the balance if treatment is denied.

## *Capitation*

As medical care in general and mental health in particular move toward regional integrated systems of care where capitation is the norm, a set amount of money will be allowed per covered patient. The clinician will then bear a large part of the responsibility for budgeting and distributing how health care dollars will be spent for a given patient's individual care. On the surface, this approach appears to put both patient and clinician "in the driver's seat" and to enable them to form the most comprehensive treatment plan based on one total annual payment. Notably, the clinician will assume the risk as fewer case managers will be needed to allocate benefits.

Superficially, this seems like a more reasonable, responsible position for the clinician. Unfortunately, patients like Erin will likely have even greater difficulty accessing subspecialty care in a capitated system. Clinicians will likely be motivated to keep costs as low as possible and to reduce their financial risk. Clinicians who treat patients like Erin or work in tertiary settings may easily be driven out of the market because severe cases will always demand a significant quantum of services, at least for a period of time. These services are costly. Those providers who are deemed to be too expensive because of the services they recommend or provide will not be retained by many health care plans. In a capitated system, the clinician who chooses to work with patients who have severe eating disorders may see fewer and fewer patients like Erin for still other reasons. Although the need will remain, there will be a financial disincentive for primary care providers to refer to specialists. In a profit-driven industry, it may simply be too expensive to meet the needs of the severely ill.

As market reforms drive the allocation of mental health benefits, individual like Erin are less and less likely to get the care they need. More than ever, mental health professionals must argue in a public forum to face down stigma and to make the tools of our profession known. Only by taking our case to patients, their families, and governmental representatives can we be assured that mental health services will not be given the short shrift they have traditionally received in comparison with other medical and surgical specialties. In the meantime, we must work with managed care providers to help them see that, for some patients, a low level of care and cost is not necessarily in the best long-term interest of either fiscal effectiveness or the individual patient's mental health.

### What We Can Do

Erin's vignette describes one way of moving forward with this process. Just as we, as individuals, are faced with making the best resolution of unpalatable situations and difficult dilemmas, so Erin's treatment demonstrates how patients and therapists must wrestle with making the best out of the realities of the current health care environment. Although third parties are criticized for their often arbitrary and noxious control over treatment interventions and strategies, in this case, regular reviews, focused readings, involvement on the part of the patient and her parents, and an openness to discussing all facets of the treatment led the insurance company to support extended multimodal treatment. The aphorism "When life gives you scraps, make a quilt" took on new meaning as those involved in Erin's case stitched together a patchwork of interventions to repair a shattered self.

After two and a half additional years of benefits, a most unusual scenario in the mid 1990s, Erin moved through the phases of treatment characteristic of hospital work half a generation ago; she partook of nine months of acute hospitalization and eventually moved to partial hospitalization structure. Thrice weekly individual psychotherapy, adjunctive group therapies and patient education modalities, and judicious psychotropic medication all became integrated into her total treatment package. Helping provide a third party with an accurate understanding of Erin's desire to use treatment as well as her innate potential to do so helped secure these benefits.

Erin's own capacity to argue her case and to use the treatment opportunities as a "laboratory" for developing her sense of self augmented my appeals. Obviously, encouraging this family to shift their need for dominance over Erin to control of an external source—the insurance company—furthered our goals. Pressure that the family members had formally exerted on Erin was now diverted to engage the insurance company and thus buttressed my arguments for continued benefits.

Without the support of compassionate, sophisticated case management, however, none of these strategies would have borne fruit. In retrospect, it now seems that this individual case manager was the hero in Erin's treatment. From the first, he sensed that she could not get better quickly. He also appreciated her strengths. Despite the refractory nature of her illness, her ability to engage with others, to verbalize concerns and conflicts, and to allow herself to experience affect profoundly were all positive prognostic factors. He approved additional benefits early on and later argued her case to the "catastrophic illness committee" of his company when it came time to procure this additional benefit.

In some fortuitous circumstances, case managers can thus be nudged to become allies in the long-term treatment process. By extending the traditional treatment frame of our work, mental health professionals also move the profession forward by reaching out to other disciplines and groups that have not traditionally supported our efforts. By helping case managers hear and understand the silent misery and secret yearnings of even one patient, we demystify the process of psychotherapy and psychiatric treatment. This endeavor is arduous and anxiety provoking. Enormous energy must be expended as each treater finds creative new solutions to making our collective voice heard. In some fortuitous circumstances, patients will take advantage of these hard-won resources to find their voice and to live creatively. It is my belief that these vigorous efforts will not be in vain.

# NOTES

P. 335, *identity is embedded in her eating disorder:* For a deeper understanding of these identity issues and other medical and psychological consequences for an eating disorder, see Zerbe, K. (1993). *The body betrayed: Women, eating disorders, and treatment.* Washington, DC: American Psychiatric Press; also published in paperback as *The body betrayed: A deeper understanding of women, eating disorders, and treatment* (1995, Gurze Books).

P. 337, *symptom-focused interventions:* For a thorough look at the physical and psychological profile of eating-disordered patients over time, see Theander, S. (1970). Anorexia nervosa: A psychiatric investigation of 94 female patients. *Acta Psychiatrica Scandinavica* (Suppl. 214); and Theander, S. (1985). Outcome and prognosis in anorexia nervosa and bulimia: Some results of previous investigations compared with those of a Swedish long-term study. *Journal of Psychiatric Research, 19,* 493–508. In addition to this classic, see the recent updates on follow-up in Andersen, A. (1992). Analysis of treatment experience and outcome from the Johns Hopkins Eating Disorders Program: 1975–1990. In K. A. Halmi (Ed.), *Psychobiology and treatment of anorexia nervosa and bulimia nervosa* (Chap. 6, pp. 93–124). Washington, DC: American Psychiatric Press; and Hsu, L. (1992). Critique of follow-up studies. In K. A. Halmi (Ed.), *Psychobiology and treatment of anorexia nervosa and bulimia nervosa* (Chap. 7, pp. 125–147). Washington, DC: American Psychiatric Press.

P. 339, *Third-party payers have not been receptive:* For a brilliant critique of how managed care is eroding the practice of mental health, see Wooley, S. (1993). Managed care and mental health: The silencing of a profession. *International Journal of Eating Disorders, 14*(4), 387–401.

P. 342, *be in dire physical danger:* See Mehler, P., & Weiner, K. (1994). Frequently asked medical questions about eating disorder patients. *Eating Disorders: The Journal of Treatment and Prevention, 2*(1), 22–30.

P. 344, *titrating this medication to an effective dose:* With respect to the limits of fluoxetine in particular and medications in general in the treatment of eating disorders, this review by an internist and director of the Wilkins Center for Eating Disorders is superb: Mickley, D. (1994). The Prozac hype. *Eating Disorders: The Journal of Treatment and Prevention, 2*(2), 188–192.

P. 346, *customer-focused relationship to patients:* A review of how a customer-oriented approach is influencing the rendering of health care can be found in Gaucher, E., & Coffey, R. (1993). *Total quality in health care: From theory to practice.* San Francisco: Jossey-Bass.

P. 348, *Eating-disordered patients harbor a "secret self":* Sands, S. (1991). Bulimia, dissociation, and empathy: A self-psychological view. In C. L. Johnson (Ed.), *Psychodynamic treatment of anorexia nervosa and bulimia* (pp. 34–50). New York: Guilford Press.

P. 349, *To empower the patient to take more control:* Bloom, C., Gitter, A., Gutwill, S., Kogel, L., & Zaphiropoulos, L. (1994). *Eating problems: Feminist psychoanalytic treatment model.* New York: Basic Books; Fallon, P., Katzman, M., & Wooley, S. (1994). *Feminist perspectives on eating disorders.* New York: Guilford Press.

P. 352, *Those providers who are deemed to be too expensive:* For a brief but pointed critique of the capitated system and its impact on mental health care services, see Stone, A. A. (1995). Psychotherapy and managed care: The bigger picture. *Harvard Mental Health Letter, 2*(8), 5–7; also see Zerbe, K. (1994). The last word. *Eating Disorders: The Journal of Treatment and Prevention, 2*(3), 284–286.

# ABOUT THE AUTHORS

*Bruce Arnow, Ph.D.*, is assistant professor of psychiatry and chief of the psychology service at the Stanford University School of Medicine. He is also director of the behavioral medicine clinic, in which the eating disorders, obesity, and anxiety disorders programs for the Department of Psychiatry are located. He is coauthor (with C. Barr Taylor) of the book *The Nature and Treatment of Anxiety Disorders* and numerous journal articles, including studies examining outcome of different treatments for bulimia nervosa and binge-eating disorder, and studies investigating the causes, consequences of, and assessment of emotional eating among the obese.

*Judith Brisman, Ph.D.*, a graduate of the William Alanson White Institute of Psychoanalysis, is director and co-founder of the Eating Disorder Resource Center, a privately run outpatient center in New York City for the treatment of bulimia, compulsive eating, and anorexia. She is coauthor of *Surviving an Eating Disorder: Strategies for Family and Friends* (1988) and is on the editorial board of *Eating Disorders: The Journal of Treatment and Prevention*. She has written and lectured extensively in the area of eating disorders and women's issues and maintains a private practice in Manhattan.

*Rachel Bryant-Waugh, MSc, DPhil, CPsychol (Clin)*, is consultant psychologist at Great Ormond Street Hospital for Children in London, U.K. She is responsible for the eating disorders research program, directing an active research team investigating various aspects of childhood-onset eating disorders. More than ten years of work in this area have led to her becoming widely known, together with Dr. Bryan Lask, as an authority on the subject of eating disorders in children. She is also clinical director of an adolescent eating disorders service at Huntercombe Manor Hospital in Maidenhead, U.K., where she oversees a comprehensive hospital-based service for young people with eating disorders and their families. She has published many papers and chapters and has coedited (with Bryan Lask) *Childhood Onset Anorexia Nervosa and Related Eating Disorders*.

*Arthur H. Crisp, M.D., DSc, FRCP, FRCPsych.*, is professor of psychiatry in the University of London, U.K., and chairman of the Department of Mental Health Sciences, St. George's Hospital Medical School, London SW17ORE. He has produced more than 300 publications, including about 150 on anorexia nervosa, and several books. He was for some years dean of the faculty of medicine in the University of London.

*Ivan Eisler, Ph.D.*, is senior lecturer in the section of psychotherapy at the Institute of Psychiatry and an honorary consultant clinical psychologist at the Bethlem Royal and Maudsley Hospital in London, U.K. Since 1982 he has been part of a clinical research team investigating psychotherapies for anorexia and bulimia nervosa and has published extensively on this subject. He is the course director of the Msc in family therapy at the Institute of Psychiatry and is also in charge of the masters family therapy training program at the Institute of Family Therapy in London. His other special interests include the link between research and clinical practice in the field of family therapy and the role of family therapy in the context of medical institutions.

*H. Charles Fishman, M.D.*, received his medical training at the Medical College of Wisconsin, served his psychiatric residency at the University of Pennsylvania School of Medicine, and received his child psychiatry training at the Philadelphia Child Guidance Center, where he later served as director of training. He has authored four books: *Intensive Structural Therapy, Treating Troubled Adolescents, Family Therapy Techniques* (with Salvador Minuchin), and *Evolving Models for Family Change: A Festschrift in Honor of Salvador Minuchin* (with Bernice Rosman). He is a 1995 fellow at the Annie E. Casey Foundation in Baltimore and resides in Philadelphia with his wife and two children.

*Paul E. Garfinkel, M.D., F.R.C.P.(C)*, is professor and chair, Department of Psychiatry, University of Toronto, and director and psychiatrist-in-chief of the Clarke Institute of Psychiatry. Since the early 1970s, he has pursued an interest in the eating disorders. He has developed a multifaceted treatment program at the Toronto General Hospital and has published research on and treatment of these disorders. He has coauthored several books on eating disorders and has published numerous original papers, articles, and chapters in scholarly, scientific, and medical journals. He is an authority on the multidimensional model as the basis for the contemporary understanding and treatment of eating disorders. He also serves on the editorial board for the *International Journal of Eating Disorders, Appetite and Eating Disorders Review*. Professional awards received include the ANAD Award (Anorexia Nervosa and Associated Disorders–Chicago); BASH Award (Bulimia, Anorexia, Self-Help–St. Louis); Canadian Psychiatric Research Foundation Award; and John Dewan Award, Ontario Mental Health Foundation.

*Paul Hamburg, M.D.*, is assistant professor of psychiatry at Harvard Medical School and associate psychiatrist at the Massachusetts General Hospital (MGH), where he coordinates the clinical team in the outpatient Eating Disorders Unit. Following ten years as a primary care physician in rural Vermont, he pursued psychiatric training in Boston and currently combines the full-time practice of psychoanalytic psychotherapy with extensive teaching in the MGH psychiatry and psychology programs. Publications include theoretical and clinical papers about eating disorders and studies regarding the application of postmodern theory to psychotherapy.

*Allan S. Kaplan, M.D., MSc., FRCP(C)*, is head of the eating disorders program, the Toronto Hospital/General Division; and director of training in postgraduate education and associate professor of psychiatry, Department of Psychiatry, University of Toronto. The eating disorder program was awarded the Gold Achievement Award by the American Psychiatric Association

Hospital and Community Psychiatry Division in 1990. His publications include two edited books: *A Day Hospital Group Treatment Program for Anorexia Nervosa and Bulimia Nervosa* (edited by N. Piran and A. S. Kaplan, 1990) and *Medical Issues and the Eating Disorders: The Interface* (edited by A. S. Kaplan and P. E. Garfinkel, 1993). In addition, he has published papers on the course and outcome of bulimia nervosa, including articles on the rate and prediction of relapse in bulimia nervosa; the prediction of treatment of response in bulimia nervosa; and a study on the two-year follow-up of bulimia patients. Additionally, he has published work on the relationship between eating disorders and mood.

*Bryan Lask, MB, BS, MPhil, FRCPsych*, is consultant psychiatrist at Great Ormond Street Hospital for Children, London, U.K., where he is head of the Department of Psychological Medicine and director of the eating disorder program. He also is medical adviser to the eating disorders program at Huntercombe Manor Hospital, Maidenhead, U.K. With Rachel Bryant-Waugh, he has been involved in many years of research into childhood-onset eating disorders and has published widely and taught around the world. He is coeditor (with Rachel Bryant-Waugh) of *Childhood Onset Anorexia Nervosa and Related Eating Disorders* (1993).

*James E. Mitchell, M.D.*, is professor of psychiatry, University of Minnesota, where he is the co-director of the eating disorders program. He earned his M.D. from Northwestern University, conducted his internship in internal medicine at the Indiana University Hospital, and served his residency in psychiatry at the University of Minnesota. He has been active in teaching, research, and clinical work in the area of eating disorders since 1979. In addition, he has served on several grant review committees and editorial boards, including the *International Journal of Eating Disorders*. He has published more than two hundred articles and chapters and is the author of *Bulimia Nervosa* (1990) and the editor of *Anorexia Nervosa and Bulimia: Diagnosis and Treatment* (1985).

*Carol B. Peterson, Ph.D.*, is a postdoctoral fellow in the eating disorders program in the Department of Psychiatry, University of Minnesota. She received her B.A. from Yale University in 1986, where she was awarded the Albert E. Angier Prize for Outstanding Research in Psychology. She did her predoctoral psychology internship in 1991–1992 at the Yale University Department of Psychiatry and received her Ph.D. in clinical psychology from the University of Minnesota in 1993. She is a member of Phi Beta Kappa, Sigma Xi, and Phi Kappa Phi. She has published in the areas of taste perception, body image, and the treatment of eating disorders.

*Harold I. Spivak, M.D., FRCP(C)*, is psychiatric consultant to the eating disorders program and an assistant professor of psychiatry, Department of Psychiatry, University of Toronto. He has previously published on the psychology of factitious disorders.

*Joellen Werne, M.D.*, is clinical associate professor of psychiatry at the Stanford University School of Medicine, where she supervises residents in the Department of Psychiatry and Behavioral Sciences and teaches in the behavioral medicine clinic and at the university's counseling and psychotherapy service. She is a graduate of the Yale University School of Medicine and received her psychiatric training at Yale and Stanford. Between 1975 and 1980, she was clinical director of Stanford's first multimodal inpatient treatment program for anorexia nervosa. For the past 20 years, she has had a private practice of psychotherapy with a special interest in treating eating disorders. She lives in Menlo Park, California, with her husband and two children.

*Kathryn J. Zerbe, M.D.*, is vice president for education and research and the Helen Maslin Palley Professor of Psychiatry at the Menninger Clinic. A staff psychiatrist and psychoanalyst, her previous clinical appointments have included directing the eating disorders unit of the C. F. Menninger Memorial Hospital for five years and serving as director of the adult outpatient department and as medical director of the women's program of the

Menninger Clinic. She has published numerous professional articles on eating disorders, women's issues, psychotherapy, and the integration of feminist thought with psychodynamic theory. Her book *The Body Betrayed: Women, Eating Disorders, and Treatment* (1993) is considered a landmark publication in the field. Professional awards received include the William C. Menninger Teacher of the Year Award; the Women Helping Women Award (ANAD—Anorexia Nervosa and Associated Disorders); and the Hilde Bruch Lectureship (NEDO—National Eating Disorders Organization). She serves on the editorial boards of the *Bulletin of the Menninger Clinic* and *Eating Disorders: The Journal of Treatment and Prevention*. She is a fellow of the American Psychiatric Association.

# INDEX